SOFT SKILLS FOR THE EFFECTIVE LAWYER

In this groundbreaking book, Randall Kiser presents a multidisciplinary, practice-based introduction to the major soft skills for lawyers: self-awareness, self-development, social proficiency, wisdom, leadership, and professionalism. The work serves as both a map and a vehicle for developing the skills essential to self-knowledge and fulfillment, organizational respect and accomplishment, client satisfaction and appreciation, and professional improvement and distinction. It identifies the most important soft skills for attorneys, describes and applies hundreds of studies regarding psychology, law, and soft skills, and provides concrete steps and methods to improve soft skills. The book should be read by law students, attorneys, and anyone else interested in how lawyers should practice law.

Randall Kiser is an internationally recognized authority on attorney performance. He is the author of three books on effective advocacy and durable attorney–client relationships, and he has taught at the University of Washington School of Law, Pepperdine University School of Law, University of Nevada School of Law, and Indiana University School of Law. Kiser is a principal analyst at DecisionSet® in Palo Alto, California, and his work has been featured in popular and scholarly publications, ranging from *The New York Times* to the *Harvard Negotiation Law Review*. His writing integrates both academic and practical perspectives derived from twenty years' experience as a litigation attorney and thirteen years as a researcher, consultant, and educator. Kiser received his law degree in 1978 from the University of California at Berkeley.

Soft Skills for the Effective Lawyer

RANDALL KISER
DecisionSet®

CAMBRIDGE
UNIVERSITY PRESS

University Printing House, Cambridge CB2 8BS, United Kingdom

One Liberty Plaza, 20th Floor, New York, NY 10006, USA

477 Williamstown Road, Port Melbourne, VIC 3207, Australia

4843/24, 2nd Floor, Ansari Road, Daryaganj, Delhi – 110002, India

79 Anson Road, #06–04/06, Singapore 079906

Cambridge University Press is part of the University of Cambridge.

It furthers the University's mission by disseminating knowledge in the pursuit of education, learning, and research at the highest international levels of excellence.

www.cambridge.org
Information on this title: www.cambridge.org/9781108416443
DOI: 10.1017/9781108238816

First published 2017

Printed in the United States of America by Sheridan Books, Inc.

A catalogue record for this publication is available from the British Library.

ISBN 978-1-108-41644-3 Hardback
ISBN 978-1-108-40350-4 Paperback

Cambridge University Press has no responsibility for the persistence or accuracy of URLs for external or third-party internet websites referred to in this publication and does not guarantee that any content on such websites is, or will remain, accurate or appropriate.

This book was written for information and educational purposes and should not be considered as any form of legal or medical advice, counseling or treatment. This book does not contain and is not intended to be a substitute for professional advice.

Contents

Tables

Acknowledgments

The idea of writing a book on attorneys' soft skills crystallized after I interviewed 78 exceptional attorneys for the 2011 book, *How Leading Lawyers Think: Expert Insights into Judgment and Advocacy*. Those attorneys consistently stated that their adversaries were quite knowledgeable about the law but lacked an understanding of human emotions and behavior. As one attorney commented, "They know what they're doing as lawyers, but not as trial attorneys and trial evaluators. They get lost in the maelstrom." I thank each of the 78 attorneys interviewed for that study. Their remarks about attorneys' shortcomings in soft skills piqued my interest in the subject, and their opinions turned out to be substantiated by the extensive research summarized in this book.

Jean Sternlight, director of the Saltman Center for Conflict Resolution at the University of Nevada and coauthor of *Psychology for Lawyers*, encouraged my initial academic probe into attorneys' soft skills. Her review in 2013 of my article, "The Emotionally Attentive Lawyer: Balancing the Rule of Law with the Realities of Human Behavior," led to its acceptance for presentation at the "Psychology and Lawyering: Coalescing the Field" conference in 2014 and subsequent publication in a symposium edition of the *Nevada Law Journal*. That article demonstrated that soft skills are critical for effective attorney–client relationships and that the legal profession is years behind the medical profession in identifying, teaching, and evaluating soft skills. I thank Professor Sternlight for encouraging that initial research.

During the years spent conducting research and drafting book chapters, I have benefitted greatly from interactions with law students in my courses taught at the University of Washington School of Law, Pepperdine University School of Law, University of Nevada School of Law, and Indiana University School of Law. I thank those students for their ideas, imagination, enthusiasm, and candor.

I also thank William Henderson, Donna Shestowsky, Peter Zeughauser, Tom Stipanowch, Peter Huang, and Deborah Maranville for their many insights that influenced the purpose, scope, and content of this book. I am particularly appreciative of the information provided by Alli Gerkman, director of the Educating Tomorrow's Lawyers project, in advance of the Institute for the Advancement of the American Legal System's publication of *Foundations for Practice: The Whole Lawyer and the Character Quotient*.

Three anonymous reviewers also evaluated and provided their opinions regarding the objectives, topics, organization, and overall soundness of this book. I am grateful for their recommendations, and I hope the book reflects their high standards and valuable contributions.

In preparing the manuscript and facilitating its publication, I have benefitted greatly from the remarkable efforts of Matt Gallaway, my editor at Cambridge University Press. Mr. Gallaway's organizational skills, efficiency, responsiveness, and expertise are without parallel. I also thank Samantha Cassetta for her skill and dedication in continuing to serve as an editor for my books. Lastly, and most importantly, I express my appreciation for my wife, Denise, who steadfastly provided the encouragement, discernment, and advice essential to planning and writing this book.

1

Introduction

Anthony Sonnett, Ford Motor Company's trial attorney, had nearly completed his cross-examination of Barry Wilson. After listening to Mr. Wilson describe how he showers, catheterizes, and frequently repositions his paralyzed wife, following an accident in which her Ford Explorer rolled over and fractured her spine, Mr. Sonnett posed his final question to Mr. Wilson: "The silver lining, to the extent that there could be one, it has brought you and Benetta [Mrs. Wilson] and the family closer together?" Mr. Wilson responded: "I think where we were together before, we are together after. I don't think it's done more for us. I think it's – I don't think it's a benefit or a plus in any way. I am sorry, I don't think I can see it that way."[1]

The jury returned a verdict against Ford for $4.6 million in economic losses, $105 million in noneconomic losses, and $246 million in punitive damages. Reviewing the verdict on appeal, the California Court of Appeal honed in on Mr. Sonnett's "silver lining question" and noted, "This question implied that the family should find a silver lining in what befell Mrs. Wilson. It may very well have been viewed as callous by the jury and might explain, in some manner, the actions of the jury in rendering a verdict so out of line with the amounts requested by the Wilsons' own counsel." The question, the court stated, "might well have inflamed the passions of the jury." Concluding that the award against Ford was excessive, the court reduced the noneconomic damages award to $18 million and lowered the punitive damages award to $55 million.

---

[1] *Benetta Buell–Wilson, et al., Plaintiffs and Respondents v. Ford Motor Company et al., Defendants and Appellants.* Nos. D045154, D045579. Court of Appeal, Fourth District (San Diego), Division 1, California. March 10, 2008. As Modified on Denial of Rehearing April 10, 2008. Review Granted July 9, 2008. Review Dismissed, Cause Remanded April 22, 2009. Liptak, Adam. (2007, February 19). When lawyers and juries mete out punishment. *The New York Times.*

The silver lining question, according to Adam Liptak, the Supreme Court correspondent of *The New York Times*, "was a legal classic that has echoed through the appeal of the case." "The Wilsons' case," he opines, "suggests that a lot can turn on little things, including flat-footed lawyers and stupid questions."[2]

Attorneys can argue endlessly about the appropriateness and impact of the silver lining question. That argument obscures the fact that judgment calls like the silver lining question permeate a lawyer's daily existence and are not resolvable by statutes, rules, regulations, appellate court opinions, or practice guides. These judgment calls are invariably subjective and inherently danger-ous; they tend to be more personal than rule-based, more intuitive than empirical. They require a broader set of skills than technical legal knowledge and analysis and necessarily implicate "soft skills" like sensitivity, discernment, empathy, perspective-taking, and foresight.

In making these judgment calls, whether cross-examining a witness or negotiating contract terms, attorneys rely heavily on their personal experiences and their sense for people. They ask themselves imponderable questions: How am I coming across to everyone else in this room? Do they trust me? What do they expect of me? Have I realistically assessed this challenge? Am I ade-quately prepared? Is my sense of what is happening here affected by how I feel about something else today? What will I do if I fail here? This book is about these types of questions – how we pick the questions to ask ourselves about ourselves, how accurately we answer them, and how we can improve the soft skills that are ignored in educational testing but turn out to be dispositive in life.

Attorneys' careers pivot on their soft skills. These seemingly intangible qualities enable us to understand, motivate, and direct ourselves and recog-nize, respect, accommodate, and adapt to the needs, values, and feelings of other people. Attorneys who progress to leadership positions rely on soft skills to perceive, assess, and replicate the circumstances in which people feel safe and inspired to collaborate with colleagues, experiment with potentially better methods and techniques to complete their assignments, express and realize evolving aspirations, and assume new responsibilities. Although legal education emphasizes technical skills like research, writing, analysis, advo-cacy, and substantive legal knowledge, it is the soft skills that most frequently distinguish an exceptional attorney from an ordinary attorney. As Lynne Hermle, a leading employment law attorney and partner at Orrick, Herrington & Sutcliffe, explains, "How you connect with people, win people

---

[2] Liptak, *supra* note 1.

over, despite their suspicions about you, how clients learn to like and trust you, all of those things are much more important than law school will ever tell."[3]

Despite the evidence consistently demonstrating that soft skills predominate over technical skills, many attorneys disparage and neglect soft skills. Surveys of clients and their attorneys and large-scale assessments of attorney personality indicate that the very concept of attorney soft skills strikes some as oxymoronic, like putting obligate carnivores on a vegetarian diet. Consequently, and much to the chagrin of people who work or live with attorneys, attorney soft skills are often ignored or underdeveloped. As law professor Deborah Rhode observes, "Lawyers lacking in 'soft skills' tend to devalue their importance rather than address their absence."[4]

The purpose of this book is to correct attorneys' deficiencies in soft skills. It aims to enhance attorney performance through the key soft skills of self-awareness, self-development, social proficiency, leadership, wisdom, and professionalism.[5] By emphasizing those soft skills, the book provides both a map and a vehicle for developing the skills essential to self-knowledge and fulfillment, organizational respect and accomplishment, client satisfaction and appreciation, and professional improvement and distinction.

This first chapter introduces many general concepts that facilitate the development of soft skills, and it answers five threshold questions:

1. What are soft skills?
2. What is the difference between soft skills and "emotional intelligence?"
3. Are soft skills important?
4. Do highly intelligent people need soft skills?
5. Can soft skills be learned?

The chapter concludes by describing the organization and previewing the themes of this book.

---

3 Broderick, Pat. (2011, May 11). Lynne Hermle. *San Francisco Daily Journal* [Special Edition, Daily Journal Supplement, Top Women Litigators], p. 7.
4 Rhode, Deborah. (2013). *Lawyers as leaders* (p. 5). New York: Oxford University Press.
5 The chapter sequence is generally consistent with, but not intended to replicate, Hogan and Warrenfeltz's "domain model" with four categories of skills that, at least conceptually, build upon each other: intrapersonal skills (self-awareness, self-esteem, resiliency, and self-control); interpersonal skills (perspective-taking, empathy, and anticipating others' actions); leadership skills (recruiting, retaining, and motivating a team, persistence and promoting a vision); and work skills (planning, organizing, coordinating, innovating, compiling, and selecting). Hogan, R., & Warrenfeltz, W. (2003). Educating the modern manager. *Academy of Management Learning and Education*, 2, 74–84.

WHAT ARE SOFT SKILLS?

In a general sense, soft skills are to hard skills as software is to hardware. Software is an intangible product that enables us to accomplish a specific task, while hardware is a tangible device that enables the software to operate. Software and hardware are interdependent; software is virtually useless without hardware, and hardware can only perform basic functions without software.

Soft skills and hard skills, like software and hardware, are interdependent and often viewed as intangible and tangible. Soft skills include subjective abilities, traits, and habits like empathy, communication, resilience, leadership, and self-development, while hard skills include more fact-based capabilities like technical proficiency, accounting, subject matter knowledge, and quantitative assessment.[6]

Exceptional performers in most organizations recognize the necessity of developing both soft and hard skills. They deftly integrate these dual capabilities in providing products and services to clients, embodying the values, standards, and principles of their disciplines, and leading their organizations by example, ideals, and determination. Exceptional performers tend to be "bimodal," toggling easily and rapidly between areas of the brain associated with planning and logical reasoning and areas involved in social and emotional thinking.[7] "While being technically proficient at one's craft is essential for both professionals and organizations," explains Christina Martini, Chair of the Chicago Intellectual Property Practice Group at DLA Piper, "it is no longer enough."[8]

In the legal profession, the characteristics commonly associated with soft skills include "intrapersonal and interpersonal competencies such as practical problem solving, stress management, self-confidence, initiative, optimism, interpersonal communication, the ability to convey empathy to another, the ability to see a situation from another's perspective, teamwork, collaboration, client relations,

---

[6] The difference between soft skills and hard skills, notes Nassim Nicholas Taleb, can be viewed as the difference between "know-how" and "know-what" or "techne" (craft) and "episteme" (knowledge, science). Know-what, he notes, is "more prone to nerdification." Another distinction is made between tacit and formal knowledge. Taleb states that "thinkers of the Austrian school, to which [Friedrich] Hayek belonged, used the designations *tacit* or *implicit* precisely for that part of knowledge that cannot be written down, but that we should avoid repressing." Taleb, Nassim Nicholas. (2006). *The black swan* (p. 182). New York: Random House.

[7] Blackman, Andrew. (2014, April 27). The inner workings of the executive brain. *The Wall Street Journal.*

[8] Martini, Christina. (2011, March 22). Emotional intelligence: Driving success in today's business environment. *Intellectual Property and Technology News.* Retrieved from www.dlapiper .com/en/us/insights/publications/2011/03/emotional-intelligence-driving-success-in-todays__/.

business development, and the like."[9] Hard skills, in contradistinction, tend to be associated with traditional proficiencies emphasized in law school: "legal research and writing, legal analysis, oral and written advocacy, knowledge of substantive law and doctrine, as well as the ability to marshal and summarize facts, apply rules of law to facts, reach and articulate legal conclusions, brief cases, and distinguish cases."[10] Again, we see that soft skills and hard skills are interdependent. An attorney's soft skills in communication and problem solving are virtually useless without the substantive legal knowledge necessary to competently provide legal services; and an attorney's hard skills in knowing the governing statutes and regulations are nearly worthless without the ability to communicate that knowledge to a client and use that knowledge for effective problem solving.

It is often difficult to distinguish soft skills from hard skills because both terms are imprecise and no consensus exists regarding their categorization.[11] Reflecting the widespread frustration with the imprecision of "soft skills," education writer Anya Kamenetz finds that employers "commonly use 'soft skills' to include anything from being able to write a letter, to showing up on time and having a firm handshake."[12] To develop a clearer conceptual sense of soft skills and hard skills, we may benefit from visualizing them on a spectrum of traits and capabilities rather than struggling to fit them into discrete categories. Table 1.1 shows how we would place soft skills on six spectrums for different types of intelligence, knowledge, and abilities. These six spectrums are practical intelligence–analytical intelligence; procedural knowledge–declarative knowledge; tacit knowledge–explicit knowledge;

9   Daicoff, Susan. (2015). Teaching relational skills: The evidence. In Maranville, Deborah, Bliss, Lisa Radtke, Kaas, Carolyn Wilkes, & Lopez, Antoinette Sedillo (Eds.). *Building on best practices: Transforming legal education in a changing world* (p. 316). New Providence, New Jersey: LexisNexis.
10 Ibid.
11 Heckman, James J., & Rubinstein, Yona. (2001). The importance of noncognitive skills: Lessons from the GED testing program. *The American Economic Review*, 91(2), 145–149. Heckman, James, Stixrud, Jora, & Urzua, Sergio. (2006). The effects of cognitive and noncognitive abilities on labor market outcomes and social behavior. *Journal of Labor Economics*, 24(3), 411–482. See Garcia, Emma. (2014, December 2). *The need to address noncognitive skills in the education policy agenda* [Briefing paper #386]. Washington, DC: Economic Policy Institute. ("To our knowledge, however, such a list does not yet exist, and indeed, this can represent one major challenge to moving this field forward. The lack of such a classification delays the development of metrics to measure and assess skills, and the design of strategies to nurture them. Additionally, crafting such a list likely engenders controversy, in terms of which skills belong on the list, and how we can know this in the absence of proper metrics.")
12 Kamenetz, Anya. (2015, May 28). Nonacademic skills are key to success: But what should we call them? *NPR Higher Ed.* Retrieved from www.npr.org/sections/ed/2015/05/28/404684712/non-academic-skills-are-key-to-success-but-what-should-we-call-them.

TABLE 1.1. *Soft skills, hard skills, and their relation to types of intelligence, knowledge, abilities, and competencies*

Soft Skills		Hard Skills
Practical Intelligence	–	Analytical Intelligence
Ability to apply knowledge to "real-world" problems		*Ability to solve test problems*
Procedural Knowledge	–	Declarative Knowledge
Knowledge of procedures and strategies; knowing "how"		*Knowledge of facts, principles, and laws; knowing "that"*
Tacit Knowledge	–	Explicit Knowledge
Ability to accomplish tasks		*Knowing facts and rules*
Fluid Intelligence	–	Crystallized Intelligence
Ability to reason, solve problems, manipulate concepts, theories, and abstractions		*Knowledge of facts, memory, and retrieval of data and events*
Noncognitive Abilities	–	Cognitive Abilities
Critical thinking, problem-solving skills		*Arithmetic reasoning, paragraph comprehension, mathematical knowledge*
Behavioral Competencies	–	Technical Competencies
Leadership, teamwork, and communication-related competencies		*Occupation or industry-specific behaviors, skills, and knowledge*

fluid intelligence–crystallized intelligence; noncognitive abilities –cognitive abilities; and behavioral competencies–technical competences.[13]

Psychologist Robert Sternberg illuminates the extreme points on these spectrums as he describes the differences between analytical intelligence (hard skills alignment) and practical intelligence (soft skills alignment). "Analytical intelligence," he states, "can loosely be translated as IQ; it emphasizes the ability to solve test problems." Practical intelligence, on the other

[13] Sternberg, Robert. (2003). *Wisdom, intelligence, and creativity synthesized.* New York: Cambridge University Press. Heilman, Kenneth. *Creativity and the brain.* Hove, United Kingdom: Psychology Press. Simonton, Dean. (2009). *Genius 101.* New York City: Springer Publishing Company. Ericsson, K. Anders, & Charnes, Neil. (2006). *Cambridge handbook of expertise and expert performance.* New York: Cambridge University Press. Page, Scott. (2008). *The difference.* Princeton, New Jersey: Princeton University Press. Klein, Gary. (2009). *Streetlights and shadows.* Cambridge, Massachusetts: MIT Press. Heckman, & Rubinstein, *supra* note 11. Heckman, Stixrud, & Urzua, *supra* note 11. Berman, Lori, & Bock, Heather. (2012). Developing attorneys for the future: What can we learn from the fast trackers? *Santa Clara Law Review* 52, 875. Baumeister Roy F., Schmeichel, Brandon J., & Vohs, Kathleen D. (2007). Self-regulation and the executive function: The self as controlling agent. In Kruglanski, A. W., & Higgins, E.T. *Social psychology: Handbook of basic principles* (2nd ed.) (pp. 516–539). New York: Guilford.

hand, "captures a person's ability to apply scholarly knowledge to real-world situations." As an example,

> a person of high practical intelligence can apply her tools when confronted with how much wood to buy to build a deck, but may perform poorly on a math problem. A person with low practical intelligence may be able to solve calculus problems for the area under a graph and then buy five times as much paint as needed when redecorating a room. These two people may marry. If so, all will be fine.[14]

Although we would like to think of ourselves as possessing both soft skills and hard skills, research indicates that this cognitive dream team is less common than we may assume. A negative correlation exists between tacit knowledge and crystallized intelligence, for instance,[15] and "general intelligence and practical intelligence are orthogonal: the presence of one doesn't imply the presence of the other."[16] As Malcolm Gladwell, the author of the best-selling book *Outliers*, notes, "You can have lots of analytical intelligence and very little practical intelligence or lots of practical intelligence and not much analytical intelligence."[17]

WHAT IS THE DIFFERENCE BETWEEN SOFT SKILLS AND "EMOTIONAL INTELLIGENCE"?

In everyday conversations, we often use the terms "soft skills" and "emotional intelligence" interchangeably. This mashing of the two concepts, however, obscures their distinct meanings, functions, and applications. Since this book emphasizes both emotional intelligence and soft skills, let's make sure we understand how emotional intelligence is defined and how it differs from the broader category of soft skills.

Daniel Goleman popularized the term "emotional intelligence" in his book of the same name, published in 1995. In that book, Goleman asserts that personal success is more strongly determined by emotional intelligence than IQ.[18] He defines emotional intelligence as consisting of five basic emotional and social competencies: (1) self-awareness (recognizing moods, emotions, and drives; using emotions to guide decision making; and realistically assessing abilities and confidence levels); (2) self-regulation (handling emotions to facilitate task performance; delaying gratification and redirecting impulses to achieve goals; being conscientious; and recovering from

---

[14] Page, *supra* note 13.   [15] Sternberg, *supra* note 13 at 58.
[16] Gladwell, Malcolm. (2008). *Outliers* (p. 101). Boston, Massachusetts: Little, Brown & Company.
[17] Ibid.
[18] Goleman, Daniel. (1995). *Emotional intelligence* (pp. 35–36). New York: Bantam Books.

emotional distress); (3) motivation (taking initiative; striving to improve; persevering through setbacks; and understanding preferences to move toward goals); (4) empathy (sensing other people's feelings; understanding others' perspectives; and establishing rapport with people); and (5) social skills (accurately reading social situations; interacting smoothly with other people; handling emotions in relationships; and using social skills to persuade, lead, negotiate, and resolve conflict).[19]

Psychologists John Mayer and Peter Salovey, whose research deeply influenced Goleman, present a roughly similar definition of emotional intelligence: "Emotional intelligence is the ability to perceive emotions, to access and generate emotions so as to assist thought, to understand emotions and emotional knowledge, and to reflectively regulate emotions so as to promote emotional and intellectual growth."[20] Mayer and Salovey regard emotional intelligence as a component of social intelligence, enabling us to "monitor one's own and other's feelings and emotions, to discriminate among them, and to use this information to guide one's thinking and actions."[21]

Emotional intelligence, not surprisingly, is centered on emotions and does not encompass the broader set of capabilities that we call soft skills. Emotional intelligence may be regarded as a subset of soft skills, but it is not a surrogate for them. Soft skills, as we saw earlier, include self-development, initiative, decision making, project management, professionalism, and other traits and habits that may be enhanced but are not circumscribed by emotional intelligence. Many of the critical soft skills and competencies discussed in this book lie outside the ambit of emotional intelligence: creativity, foresight, expertise, accountability, open-mindedness, problem solving, professionalism, innovation, strategic planning, and courage, to name just a few.

ARE SOFT SKILLS IMPORTANT?

In 1992, "technical mastery" was identified as the most important competency in a survey of business, government, education, and nonprofit leaders.[22] Twenty

[19]   Ibid. at 43. Goleman, Daniel. (1998). *Working with emotional intelligence* (p. 318). New York: Bantam Dell. Goleman, Daniel. (2004, January). What makes a leader. *Harvard Business Review*.

[20]   Mayer, J. D., & Salovey, P. (1997). What is emotional intelligence? In Salovey, P., & Sluyter, D. J. (Eds.). *Emotional development and emotional intelligence: Educational implications* (p. 5). New York: Harper Collins.

[21]   Salovey, P., & Mayer, J.D. (1990). Emotional intelligence. *Imagination, Cognition and Personality*, 9, 185, 189.

[22]   Van Velsor, Ellen, & Wright, Joel. (2012, October). *Expanding the leadership equation: Developing next generation leaders* (p. 4). Greensboro, North Carolina: Center for Creative Leadership.

years later, when the survey was administered again in 2012, technical mastery was no longer among the five most important competencies, having been displaced by these soft skills: self-motivation/discipline, effective communication, learning ability, self-awareness, and adaptability/versatility.[23] When asked to identify the competencies that will be most important "ten years from now," the leaders again identified soft skills: adaptability/ versatility, effective communication, learning agility, multicultural awareness, self-motivation/discipline, and collaboration.[24]

The priority currently placed on soft skills is supported by extensive research demonstrating that soft skills may be more important than hard skills in achieving professional success.[25] Daniel Goleman, in his comprehensive analysis of the relative importance of intelligence, technical skills, and emotional intelligence, found that "emotional intelligence proved to be twice as important as the others for jobs at all levels."[26] Emotional intelligence, moreover, "played an increasingly important role at the highest levels of the company."[27] As individuals assumed greater responsibilities within a company, the importance of soft skills increased, as Goleman explains: "When I compared star performers with average ones in senior leadership positions, nearly 90% of the difference in their profiles was attributable to emotional intelligence factors rather than cognitive abilities."[28]

Other studies suggest that emotional intelligence may play a significant but smaller role than Goleman found, accounting for 30–60 percent of occupational performance.[29] But, consistent with Goleman's research, the other

---

[23] Ibid.　[24] Ibid.

[25] See McClelland, David C. (1973, January). Testing for competence rather than for intelligence. *American Psychologist*, 28, 1. McClelland, David C. (1998, September). Identifying competencies with behavioral-event interviews. *Psychological Science*, 9(5), 331. Bradberry, Travis, & Greaves, Jean. (2009). *Emotional intelligence 2.0*. San Diego, California: TalentSmart. Gladwell, Malcolm. (2002, July 22). The talent myth. *The New Yorker*. Goleman, Daniel. (2013, December). The focused leader. *Harvard Business Review*. Goleman (1998), *supra* note 19.

[26] Goleman (2004), *supra* note 19.　[27] Ibid.　[28] Ibid.

[29] O'Boyle, Ernest, Humphrey, Ronald, Pollack, Jeffrey, Hawver, Thomas, & Story, Paul. (2011). The relation between emotional intelligence and job performance: A meta-analysis. *Journal of Organizational Behavior*, 32, 788–818. Bharwaney, G., Bar-On, R., & MacKinlay, A. (2007). *EQ and the bottom line: Emotional intelligence increases individual occupational performance, leadership and organizational productivity*. Bedfordshire, United Kingdom: Ei World Ltd. Bradberry & Greaves, *supra* note 25. Neels, Gretchen. (2009). The EQ difference. *Legal Management*, 28(2), 44, 46. Murphy, Mark. 2011. *Hiring for attitude*. New York: McGraw-Hill Education. Lynn, Adele B. (2008). *The EQ interview: Finding employees with high emotional intelligence*. New York: AMACOM.

studies also document a major increase in the effect of emotional intelligence when leadership abilities are evaluated separately from general occupational performance. In these other studies, emotional intelligence appears to account, on average, for 67 percent of leadership performance, somewhat less than Goleman's attribution of 90 percent.[30]

Concordant with this research regarding the relative importance of emotional intelligence, numerous studies find that soft skills like character, grit, perseverance, drive, and energy exert a remarkably powerful effect on personal achievement and financial performance.[31] Summarizing her extensive studies and related studies of grit and correlated character strengths like self-control and optimism, psychology professor Angela Duckworth states that "in every field grit may be as essential as talent to high accomplishment."[32] Her research corroborates earlier research demonstrating that "drive and energy in childhood are more predictive of success, if not creativity, than is IQ or some other more domain-specific ability."[33] Applying these concepts in a practical, business context, Gary Smith, president and chief executive officer of Ciena, an international broadband and telecommunications company, comments, "I think a lot of people pay attention to the technical stuff and the hard stuff about whatever discipline they're in. But it's the softer side that will get you every time if you're not paying attention to it. It's probably the biggest determinant of whether you're going to be successful."[34]

Soft skills are no longer regarded as incidental attributes of successful people; soft skills have been proven to be essential for nearly all successful executives and professionals. Studies demonstrate that people who score high in assessments of their soft skills earn more income and generate more profits

[30] Bharwaney, Bar-On, & MacKinlay, *supra* note 29.
[31] Kaplan, Steven N., Klebanov, Mark M., & Sorensen, Morten. (2012, June). Which CEO characteristics, and abilities matter? *The Journal Of Finance*, 67(3), 973–1007. Hogan, Joyce, Hogan, Robert, & Kaiser, Robert B. (2011). Management derailment: Personality assessment and mitigation. In Zedeck, Sheldon (Ed.). APA *handbook of industrial and organizational psychology* (Vol. III) (pp. 555–575). Washington, DC: American Psychological Association. Deming, David. (2015). *The growing importance of social skills in the labor market* [NBER Working Paper No. 21473]. National Bureau of Economic Research. Chamorro-Premuzic, T., & Furnham, A. (2003). Personality traits and academic exam performance. *European Journal of Personality*, 17, 237–250.
[32] Duckworth. Angela L. (2007). Grit: Perseverance and passion for long-term goals. *Journal of Personality and Social Psychology*, 92(6), 1100. See Duckworth, Angela L. (2016). *Grit.* New York: Scribner.
[33] Winner, Ellen. (1997). *Gifted children: Myths and realities* (p. 293). New York: Basic Books.
[34] Bryant, Adam. (2015, October 3). Gary Smith of Ciena: Build a culture on trust and respect. *The New York Times.*

for their employers;[35] exhibit superior leadership, decision-making, and pre-diction skills;[36] experience fewer malpractice and disciplinary claims;[37] and enjoy greater employment security.[38] Conversely, "emotionally ignorant lea-ders ranked among the bottom fifteen percent in decision-making skills. Those who fail to handle conflict effectively and remain unaware of their own fear, anger or excitement are dreadfully inept at making decisions."[39]

To determine whether companies actually derive a superior financial return from an executive's "character," Fred Kiel, a leadership consultant, recently surveyed 8,600 employees at 84 companies. The employees evaluated their companies' CEOs based on four soft skills that, Kiel determined, best

[35] Boyatzis, Richard E. (2006). Using tipping points of emotional intelligence and cognitive competencies to predict financial performance of leaders. *Psicothema*, 18, 124–131. Goleman (2013), *supra* note 25. Mayer, John, Roberts, Richard, & Barsade, Sigal. (2008). Human abilities: Emotional intelligence. *Annual Review of Psychology*, 59, 507.

[36] McClelland (1998), *supra* note 25. Seo, Myeong-Gu, & Barrett, Lisa Feldman. (2007). Being emotional during decision making, good or bad? An empirical investigation. *Academy of Management Journal*, 50(4), 923–940. Gilkey, Roderick, Caceda, Ricardo, & Kilts, Clinton. (2010, September). When emotional reasoning trumps IQ. *Harvard Business Review*. Hogan, Hogan, & Kaiser (2010), *supra* note 31. O'Boyle, *supra* note 29 788–818. Tasler, Nick. (2009). *The impulse factor* (pp. 158–159). Rosete, D. & Ciarrochi, J. (2005). EI and its relationship to workplace performance outcomes of leadership effectiveness. *Leadership & Organization Development Journal*, 26(5), 388–399. Goleman (2004), *supra* note 19. Guillen, L., & Florent-Treacy, E. (2011). *Emotional intelligence and leadership effectiveness: The mediating influence of collaborative behaviors* [INSEAD Faculty & Research Working Paper]. Pham, Michel Tuan, Lee, Leonard, & Stephen, Andrew T. (2012, October). Feeling the future: The emotional oracle effect. *Journal of Consumer Research*, 39(3) 461–477. Prati, L. Melita, Douglas, Ceasar, Ferris, Gerald, Ammeter, Anthony, & Buckley, Ronald. (2003). Emotional intelligence, leadership effectiveness, and team outcomes. *The International Journal of Organizational Analysis*, 11(3), 21.

[37] Filisko, G.M. (2011, October). Give om a chance. *ABA Journal*, pp. 24–25. American Bar Association Standing Committee on Lawyers' Professional Liability. (2012). *Profile of legal malpractice claims: 2008–2011*. Chicago: American Bar Association. MacKillop, Kara, & Vidmar, Neil. (2006, June 29). Legal malpractice: A preliminary inquiry. Unpublished manu-script. Retrieved from http://ssrn.com/abstract=912963. Hamilton, Neil, & Monson, Verna. (2011). The positive empirical relationship of professionalism to effectiveness in the practice of law. *Georgetown Journal of Legal Ethics*, 24,137. Silver, Marjorie A. (2000). Love, hate, and other emotional interference in the lawyer/client relationship. In Stolle, Dennis P., Wexler, David B., & Winick, Bruce J. (Eds.). *Practicing therapeutic jurisprudence: Law as a helping profession* (pp. 357–418). Durham, North Carolina: Carolina Academic Press. Landro, Laura. (2013, April 8). The talking cure for health care. *The Wall Street Journal*.

[38] Deming, *supra* note 31. Zatzick, C. D., Deery, S. J. & Iverson, R. D. (2015). Understanding the determinants of who gets laid off: Does affective organizational commitment matter? *Human Resource Management*, 54(6), 877–891. Pink, Daniel H. (2011). *Drive: The surprising truth about what motivates us* (p. 28). New York: Riverhead Press. Wu, Lynn. (2013). Social network effects on productivity and job security: Evidence from the adoption of a social networking tool. *Information Systems Research*, 24, 30–51.

[39] Tasler, *supra* note 36 at 158–159.

describe character: integrity, responsibility, forgiveness, and compassion. Kiel had expected to find a small relationship between character and financial results and says he was "unprepared to discover how robust the connection really is."[40] The CEOs who received high scores for character led companies with an average 9.35 percent return on assets over a two-year period, while the CEOs who received lower character scores oversaw companies with an average 1.93 percent return on assets over the same two-year period.[41]

Ironically, the CEOs who received the highest scores from employees had given themselves lower scores, while the CEOs with the lowest employee ratings had given themselves higher ratings than their employees did. Just as strong soft skills were dispositive in the success of the highest scoring CEOs, weak soft skills were determinative in the failures of the lowest rated CEOs. The underperforming CEOs were depicted by employees as being woefully deficient in soft skills – incapable of being trusted, frequently passing off blame to others, telling the truth "slightly more than half the time," and being "especially bad at caring for people."[42]

The soft skills revolution has been missed, thwarted, or suppressed by many lawyers and law firms. Although lawyers have been quick to argue that the legal profession is "different" and the skills essential to success in other fields are not applicable to the more rarefied practice of law, soft skills are just as important in the legal profession as they are in other companies and organizations. The most recent study of the essential skills for lawyers, based on 24,137 responses from attorneys who hire, supervise, and work with other attorneys in private practice, corporate legal departments, governmental entities, and nonprofit organizations, reveals that soft skills predominate over hard skills. The ten skills and traits selected as "necessary in the short term" are as follows: (1) keep information confidential; (2) arrive on time for meetings, appointments, and hearings; (3) honor commitments; (4) integrity and trustworthiness; (5) treat others with courtesy and respect; (6) listen attentively and respectfully; (7) promptly respond to inquiries and requests; (8) diligence; (9) have a strong work ethic and put forth best effort; and (10) attention to detail. The skill "research the law" was not in the "top ten" list and was ranked below conscientiousness, common sense, and attention to detail.[43]

[40] Measuring the return on character. (2015, April). *Harvard Business Review*, pp. 20–21.
[41] Kiel, Fred. (2015). *The return on character.* Watertown, Massachusetts: Harvard Business Review Press.
[42] Measuring the return on character, *supra* note 40.
[43] Gerkman, Alli, & Cornett, Logan. (2016, July). *Foundations for practice: The whole lawyer and the character quotient.* Denver, Colorado: Institute for the Advancement of the American Legal System.

Consistent with the high priority placed on soft skills, law review and journal experience were ranked as the least helpful hiring criteria, while experiential education, life experience between college and law school, legal externship, legal employment, and recommendations from practitioners or judges were the most useful factors. "Participation in law school clinic" was ranked above "class rank," and federal and state court clerkships were ranked above "law school attended."[44]

In another recent study regarding lawyers, three professors conducted formal focus groups consisting of six or eight legal employers. The focus group moderators posed questions like, "How would you describe the ideal recent law school graduate?" and "What strengths do you see in your recent hires?" The professors described their "most surprising outcome" as discovering that employers place primary importance on the "'intra – and interpersonal (socio-emotional)' – soft skills – needed for workplace success." The priority placed on soft skills, the professors acknowledge, "caught us by surprise in part because we were seeking (and expecting) comments related to the basic practice skills, i.e., writing, analysis, and research. But more than that, we also did not anticipate that beyond being mentioned, they would threaten to dominate the discussion."[45] Among the critical soft skills identified by the legal employers were willingness to take initiative, strong work ethic, dedication, enthusiasm, drive, ability to collaborate well with colleagues and clients, goal orientation, sense of perspective, knowing how to interact in a professional setting, and stepping up to "own the case."[46]

Aric Press, reflecting on his 16 years as editor of *The American Lawyer*, describes the increasing importance of soft skills for lawyers and alludes to the undercurrent of skepticism about soft skills:

> Soft skills matter. Clients have so many good law firms to choose among that they don't have to hire jerks anymore. When high-performance skill is a given, other factors loom larger: trust, comfort, dedication and empathy. These once were dismissed as "soft" or emotional traits. It turns out they're only soft for hard people.[47]

In a similar vein, law school professor Neil Hamilton comments, "In a globalized economy, lawyers who focus just on a technical professionalism

44 Ibid. at 39. See also Gerkman, Alli. (2015). "Foundations for Practice" PowerPoint presentation, on file with author.
45 Wawrose, Susan C. (2013). What do legal employers want to see in new graduates?: Using focus groups to find out. *Ohio Northern University Law Review*, 39, 505, 522.
46 Ibid. at 525–526.
47 Press, Aric. (2015, January). Big Law and me. *The American Lawyer*, p. 69.

are increasingly like a commoditized service that can be secured from suppliers world-wide at lower prices." Lawyers with soft skills, he states, exhibit a competitive advantage and can escape the strictures of commoditized practices: "In contrast, a lawyer who internalizes a moral core of professional formation over a career will benefit from excellent trustworthiness, relationship skills, teamwork skills and persuasive communication that flow from a deep understanding of others."[48]

DO HIGHLY INTELLIGENT PEOPLE NEED SOFT SKILLS?

Soft skills may seem like useful additions to the skill sets of ordinary people, but if you're really smart, like most attorneys and law students, do you need them? The unsettling answer is that smart people often have enormous performance gaps that cannot be mitigated – and sometimes are exacerbated – by their high intelligence. But the idea that high intelligence, as measured by grades and aptitude tests, may not be the answer to all that ails the legal profession is unorthodox if not heretical; it has been effectively squelched for decades despite evidence demonstrating that professional performance has little or no empirical relation to IQ, test results, and academic achievement.[49] As Geoff Colvin, *Fortune* magazine editor and author of *Talent Is Overrated*, writes, "It seems our view that intelligence necessarily produces better performance is so deep that it may occasionally even blind us to reality."[50]

Although lawyers may regard soft skills as cerebral dicta, adding no substantive content to an otherwise complete mind, research informs us that high intelligence is a weak foundation for a professional career and an unreliable basis for professional judgment. A meta-analysis of IQ effects, for instance, shows that IQ "predicts only about 4 percent of variance in job performance," while other studies "conclude that at best I.Q. constitutes about 20 percent to

[48] Hamilton, Neil. (2013). The qualities of the professional lawyer. In Haskins, Paul (Ed.). *Essential qualities of the professional lawyer* (pp. 1–18). Chicago: ABA Publishing.
[49] Tough, Paul. (2013). *How children succeed* (p. 153). New York: Mariner Books. Gladwell (2002), *supra* note 25. Groysberg, Boris. (2010). *Chasing stars* (pp. 23–24, 34). Princeton, New Jersey: Princeton University Press. Wenke, Dorit, & Frensch, Peter A. (2003). Is success or failure at solving complex problems related to intellectual ability? In Davidson, Janet E., & Sternberg, Robert J., (Eds.). *The psychology of problem solving* (pp. 88, 94). Cambridge, United Kingdom: The Cambridge University Press. Hogarth, Robin M. (2001). *Educating intuition* (p. 164). Chicago, Illinois: The University of Chicago Press. Ericsson, K. Anders, Prietula, Michael J., & Cokely, Edward T. (2007, July–August). The making of an expert. *Harvard Business Review*, pp. 114–121.
[50] Colvin, Geoff. (2008). *Talent is overrated* (p. 43). New York: Portfolio.

life success."[51] The correlation between grades and the Law School Admission Test (LSAT), on one hand, and lawyer effectiveness and career success, on the other, ranges from slight to negative.[52]

High intelligence actually appears to be detrimental under some circumstances. At least four prominent psychologists have observed and described specific deficiencies in problem solving that are correlated with high intelligence, suggesting that, unperturbed by soft skills, high intelligence may be hazardous to clients. Edward de Bono, a psychologist, physician, and former faculty member at Harvard University, University of Oxford, and University of Cambridge, finds that we tend to mistake verbal fluency for thinking, and, as a result, fail to recognize that highly intelligent people are not necessarily effective thinkers. In his studies of highly intelligent people, Professor de Bono has discovered that they often suffer from an "intelligence trap" – they place a higher value on cleverness than wisdom, spend more time proving someone else wrong than constructively using their own intelligence, prefer reactive thinking, and tend to jump to conclusions.[53] Highly intelligent people, Professor de Bono concludes, "may need as much, or more, training in thinking skills than other people."[54]

A similar concern about highly intelligent people was voiced by Chris Argyris, Professor Emeritus at Harvard Business School. He notes that the success experienced by intelligent people with impressive academic backgrounds "can reduce their willingness to examine their own assumptions."

[51] Brooks, David. (2011). *The social animal* (p. 165). New York: Random House.

[52] Shultz, Marjorie, & Zedeck, Sheldon. (2009, January 30). *Final report – Identification, development and validation of predictors for successful lawyering.* Retrieved from http://ssrn .com/abstract=1353554. Lempert, R. O., Chambers, D. L. & Adams, T. K. (2000). Michigan's minority graduates in practice: The river runs through law school. *Law & Social Inquiry, 25,* 395–505. Henderson, William D., & Zahorsky, Rachel M. (2012, July 1). The pedigree problem: Are law school ties choking the profession? *ABA Journal.* Shultz, Marjorie. (2011). Predicting professional effectiveness. *Law & Social Inquiry, 36,* 620. Weiss, Debra Cassens. (2008, October 16). School rank and GPA aren't the best predictors of BigLaw success. *ABA Journal Law News Now.* Gerkman, Alli, & Harman, Elena. (2015, January). *Ahead of the curve: Turning law students into lawyers* (p. 21). Denver, Colorado: Institute for the Advancement of the American Legal System. Gibson, Steve, Henderson, William, Stacy, Caren Ulrich, & Zorn, Chris. (2011, October 10). Moneyball for law firms. *The AmLaw Daily.* Retrieved from http://amlawdaily.typepad.com/amlawdaily/2011/10/moneyball-for-law-firms.html. Cf. Morriss, Andrew P., & Henderson, William D. (2008). Measuring outcomes: Post-graduation measures of success in the U.S. News & World Report law school rankings. *Indiana Law Journal, 83*(3), 791.

[53] Cooley, John W. (2005). *Creative problem solver's handbook for negotiators and mediators,* (Vol. 1) (p. 18). Chicago: American Bar Association.

[54] Ibid.

As a result, they engage only in "single-loop learning, or learning that tends to confirm what they already know or think that they know."[55]

Robert Sternberg, a professor of psychology at Cornell University and former professor at Yale University and Tufts University, has studied the unique characteristics of highly intelligent people. He finds that, because they have been rewarded very well for their intelligence, they often lose sight of "what they do not know" and "their own limitations."[56] He identifies and describes four specific fallacies that afflict people rated high in conventional intelligence:

- *Stable-trait fallacy* – the belief that "once smart, always smart." As a result many smart people stop learning and "lose their edge."
- *General-ability fallacy* – the belief that people smart in one thing are smart in everything. They "often think that their high levels of performance in these domains mean they will be expert in any domain. Typically they are wrong."
- *Life-success fallacy* – the belief that success on tests means "the rest is guaranteed." Some smart people never learn that conventional intelligence "may be necessary for success in life but is far from sufficient."
- *Moral-equivalence fallacy* – the belief that "to be smart is to be good." They are unaware that many smart people are not good, and many good people are not smart.[57]

Succumbing to these four fallacies and displaying a sense of omniscience, smart people "are at times especially susceptible to foolishness."[58]

To complete our understanding of the possible limitations affecting smart people, let's turn lastly to the research undertaken by psychologist Sian Beilock at the University of Chicago. She finds that people who "wield too much brainpower" are not particularly adept at problem solving and display a peculiar inability to find simpler solutions: "High powered folks often opt for the most difficult way to get through tasks and, even when they do come up with the correct answer in the end, they waste a lot of time and energy doing so."[59] Ironically, people with more working memory overlook economical approaches to solving problems and are less capable of discerning alternative solutions. "Those who rely too heavily on their prefrontal cortex," she observes, "may miss unexpected events precisely because they are not getting as much benefit from the brain areas best equipped to process the outside world."[60]

---

[55] Hogarth, *supra* note 49 at 225.   [56] Sternberg, *supra* note at 160.   [57] Ibid. at 46.
[58] Ibid. at 160.   [59] Beilock, Sian. (2010). *Choke* (p. 69). New York: Free Press.
[60] Ibid. at 72.

This brief overview of the research conducted by professors De Bono, Argyris, Sternberg, and Beilock hopefully illuminates some of the problems that may arise when attorneys rely exclusively on the high intelligence that facilitated their law school admission and supports their legal careers. The research regarding conventionally smart people suggests that soft skills are not merely desirable but may be essential to offset the occasionally perverse effects of high intelligence.

CAN SOFT SKILLS BE LEARNED?

Even if we acknowledge, however begrudgingly, that soft skills are essential, many of us assume that they cannot be learned. We adopt a "you either have it or you don't" attitude, or as one law student enrolled in an emotional intelligence course said, "You've either got this EI thing or you don't by this stage of life."[61] The idea that soft skills are a fixed part of our personality and cannot be learned may be cast firmly in our minds, but it has been debunked by research and disproven in actual practice.[62] The good news is that soft skills, including emotional intelligence, can be learned; the bad news is that, as we near the end of this introductory chapter, we are rapidly depleting excuses for not assessing and developing our own soft skills.

Soft skills have been taught successfully in elementary, intermediate and secondary schools, colleges, universities, graduate schools, public entities, and large corporations.[63] Studies indicate that relatively brief programs – some

---

[61] Cain, Paul J. (2004, March). A first step toward introducing emotional intelligence into the law school curriculum: The "emotional intelligence and the clinic student" class. (Unedited version). *Legal Education Review*, 14(1), 1.

[62] Reuben, Ernesto, Sapienza, Paola, & Zingales, Luigi. (2009, October). Can we teach emotional intelligence? Columbia Business School Research Paper Series. Nelis, Delphine, Kotsou, Ilios, Quoidbach, Jordi, Hansenne, Michel, Weytens, Fanny, Dupuis, Pauline, & Mikolajczak, Moira. (2011, April). Increasing emotional competence improves psychological and physical well-being, social relationships, and employability. *Emotion*, 11(2), 354–366. Bharwaney, Bar-On, & MacKinlay, *supra* note 29. Slaski, M., & Cartwright, S. (2002). Health, performance and emotional intelligence: An exploratory study of retail managers. *Stress and Health*, 18, 63–68. Slaski, M., & Cartwright, S. (2003). Emotional intelligence training and its implications for stress, health and performance. *Stress and Health*, 19, 233–239. Jordan, Peter, Ashkanasy, Neal, Hartel, Charmine, & Hooper, Gregory. (2002). Workgroup emotional intelligence: Scale development and relationship to team process effectiveness and goal focus. *Human Resource Management Review*, 12(2), 195–214. See Marks, Alexia Brunet, & Moss, Scott A. (2016). What predicts law student success? A longitudinal study correlating law student applicant data and law school outcomes. *Journal of Empirical Legal Studies*, 13(2), 205, 217.

[63] See Kahn, Jennifer. (2013, September 11). Can emotional intelligence be taught? *The New York Times*. Miller, Claire Cain. (2015, October 16). Why what you learned in preschool is

lasting as few as 16 hours – result in large, statistically significant improvements in resilience, interpersonal relationships, stress tolerance, empathy, self-awareness, and general mood.[64] In some studies, soft skills programs also result in increased employability, productivity, and profitability. Summarizing the results of multiple studies, psychology professor Moïra Mikolajczak and her colleagues find that these programs significantly enhance emotional competence and provide "durable benefits in terms of well being, health, social relationships, and work success."[65] Specific improvements in emotional competencies include increased self-awareness (sensing and understanding emotions); emotional acceptance (perceiving and managing distressing emotions to decrease emotional avoidance); self-efficacy (feeling confident about the ability to change); emotional flexibility (learning new ways to react in emotional situations and avoiding rigidity); and care of oneself (using emotions to monitor needs and improve life satisfaction).[66]

Both business schools and medical schools have integrated soft skills training into their admissions process and curriculum. The Yale School of Management, for example, requires full-time MBA students in its leadership programs to take standardized emotional intelligence tests and is integrating those tests into its admissions process.[67] Columbia Business School, recognizing that "what seems to differentiate the star manager from the average one is the set of both interpersonal skills and intrapersonal skills that comprise emotional intelligence," established the Program on Social Intelligence.[68]

crucial at work. *The New York Times*. Ubel, Peter. (2012). *Critical decisions* (p. 319). San Francisco: HarperOne. Stein, Steven, Book, Howard, & Kanoy, Korrel. (2013). *The student EQ edge*. San Francisco: Jossey-Bass. Bellizzi, Frank. (2008). Teaching emotional intelligence in the business school curriculum. *American Journal of Business Education*, 1(1), 37. Murray, J. P., Jordan, P. J., & Ashkanasy, N.M. (2006). *Training to improve emotional intelligence and performance: What interventions work?* Paper presented at the 20th Annual Conference of the Annual Meeting of Australian and New Zealand Academy of Management, Rockhampton, Australia.

[64] Reuben, Sapienza, & Zingales, *supra* note 62. Mikolajczak, Moira, Kotsou, Ilios & Nelis, Delphine. (2013). Efficient programs to improve trait and ability EI in adults: Lessons learned from the Louvain emotional competence training. In Pérez-González, J.C., Mavroveli, S. & Anaya, D. *Assessment and education of emotional intelligence*. Nelis (2011), *supra* note 62.

[65] Mikolajczak, Kotsou & Nelis, *supra* note 64.   [66] Ibid.

[67] DiMeglio, Francesca. (2013, May 15). Want an MBA from Yale? You're going to need emotional intelligence. Retrieved from www.bloomberg.com/news/articles/2013–05-15/want-an-mba-from-yale-youre-going-to-need-emotional-intelligence.

[68] EQ focus: Three programs to improve your social/emotional intelligence. (2008, August 15). Jerome A. Chazen Institute for Global Business, Columbia Business School. Retrieved from www8.gsb.columbia.edu/chazen/publication/388/eq-focus-three-programs-to-improve-your-social-emotional-intelligence. For courses, see www8.gsb.columbia.edu/courses/centers-and-programs/program-social-intelligence.

Topics addressed in that program's courses include leadership, networking, storytelling, public speaking, running meetings, coaching, and career management. Other business schools like Dartmouth's Tuck School of Business, Notre Dame's Mendoza School of Business, and Case Western Reserve University's Weatherhead School of Management also have incorporated soft skills assessments and courses into the curriculum.[69]

Since 2015, the Medical College Admissions Test (MCAT) includes a new section, "Psychological, Social and Biological Foundations of Behavior."[70] This new section assesses knowledge of psychological factors such as motivation, emotion, stress, intuition, bias, status, attitudes, identity, and socialization.[71] These psychological factors, traditionally overlooked or underemphasized in medical school education, have proven to be strongly determinative of patient satisfaction and outcomes.[72]

In addition to changing the MCAT to assess knowledge of psychology, medical schools are measuring and developing students' soft skills through 360-degree evaluations by nurses, professors, faculty advisors, and residents; workshops on communication and empathy; self-report tests like the Bar-On Emotional Quotient Inventory ("EQ-I") and the Self-Report Emotional Intelligence Test ("SREIT"); ability-based tests like the Mayer–Salovey–Caruso Emotional Intelligence Test ("MSCEIT"); physician-specific assessments like the Jefferson Physician Empathy Scale; and videotaped discussions between patients and students during which the patients' galvanic skin responses (moisture level fluctuations signaling periods of emotional arousal) are simultaneously displayed.[73] These comprehensive, intensive efforts to

[69] Nagar, Minakshi. (2012, May–August). Incorporation of emotional intelligence (EI) into the business curriculum: Redefining the success mantra at workplace. *International Journal of Management*, 3(2), 213–221. DiMeglio, Francesca, *supra* note 67.

[70] For an extended discussion of MCAT changes and medical school training, see Kiser, Randall. (2015). The emotionally attentive lawyer: Balancing the rule of law with the realities of human behavior. *Nevada Law Journal*, 15(2), 442. Retrieved from http://scholars.law.unlv .edu/nlj/vol15/iss2/3. This paragraph contains excerpts from that article.

[71] Association of American Medical Colleges. (2012). *Preview guide for the MCAT 2015 exam* (2d ed.), 94–98, 101–108, 113. Association of American Medical Colleges. What's on the MCAT 2015 exam? Psychological, social, and biological foundations of behavior. Retrieved from www.aamc.org/students/download/374014/data/mcat2015-psbb.pdf.

[72] Mann, Sarah. (2012, March). AAMC approves new MCAT exam with increased focus on social, behavioral sciences. AAMC *Reporter*. Retrieved from www.aamc.org/newsroom/reporter/march 2012/276588/mcat2015.html. Lewis, Richard. (2013, April). MCAT revision anticipates psychological science. APS *Observer*. Retrieved from www.psychologicalscience.org/index.php/publica tions/observer/2013/april-13/mcat-revision-anticipates-psychological-science.html.

[73] See, e.g., Austin, Elizabeth J., Evans, Phillip, Goldwater, Ruth, & Potter, Victoria. (2005). A preliminary study of emotional intelligence, empathy and exam performance in first year medical students. *Personality & Individual Differences*, 39(8), 1395, 1399. Carrothers, Robert

enhance physicians' soft skills stem from the recognition that, as Baylor College of Medicine Provost Alicia Monroe explains, "We teach students the technical and academic side of medicine, but we don't necessarily help them cultivate mindfulness, self-awareness, empathy, and other personality traits equally critical to their success as physicians."[74]

Law schools, often contrarians in academia, have distinguished themselves by their lonesome resistance to teaching soft skills. This resistance is captured in one law student's sigh, "If I'd wanted to learn about feelings, I wouldn't have gone to law school,"[75] and a law professor's counterpart, "If I wanted to teach about feelings, I wouldn't have become a law professor."[76] A notable exception to this resistance is the University of Chicago Law School's Keystone Professionalism and Leadership Program. Since its inception in 2011, the Keystone Program has enlisted about 400 students and has sponsored about 280 programs. To satisfy Keystone requirements, students must earn 400 points from attendance at programs typically offering ten points per event. The programs are grouped into five categories of soft skills:[77]

- *Emotional Intelligence and Diversity in the Profession* – understanding and embracing diversity and "using, understanding, and managing emotions, social bias, and stereotypes in positive ways to relieve stress, communicate effectively, empathize with others, overcome challenges, create solutions, and defuse conflict."
- *Professional Judgment and Ethics* – developing and strengthening professional judgment while "meeting billing requirements, establishing a good reputation with other attorneys, and building relationships with clients."

M., Gregory, Jr., Stanford W., & Gallagher, Timothy J. (2000). Measuring emotional intelligence of medical school applicants, *Academic Medicine*, 75, 456. Grewal, Daisy, & Davidson, Heather A. (2008). Emotional intelligence and graduate medical education. *Journal of the American Medical Association*, 300(10), 1200, 1201.

[74]   Martin, Mike. (2011, December). New medical education program selects students for "emotional intelligence." *AAMC Reporter.* Retrieved from www.aamc.org/newsroom/reporter/december2011/268876/emotional-intelligence.html.

[75]   Nelken, Melissa L. (1996). Negotiation and psychoanalysis: If I'd wanted to learn about feelings, I wouldn't have gone to law school. *Journal of Legal Education*, 46, 420, 422.

[76]   Nelken, Melissa L., Schneider, Andrea Kupfer & Mahuad, Jamil. (2010). If I'd wanted to teach about feelings, I wouldn't have become a law professor. In Honeyman, Christopher, Coben, James, & DePalo, Giuseppe (Eds.). *Venturing beyond the classroom* (p. 357). Saint Paul, Minnesota: DRI Press. Marquette Law School Legal Studies Paper No. 10–41. Available at SSRN: http://ssrn.com/abstract=1691274

[77]   Dean of Students. Keystone professionalism & leadership program, 2015–2016 Keystone Program. University of Chicago. Retrieved from www.law.uchicago.edu/2015keystone.

- *Practical Skills* – introducing "basic survival skills," including oral communication, negotiations, depositions, mediations, contract review, and orientation to the court systems in Chicago.
- *Managing and Building Your Career* – learning from leaders to develop skills like "networking, marketing yourself, and mentoring."
- *Legal Community Citizenship* – creating a personal legacy, promoting justice, making justice accessible to all people, giving back through legal and non-legal services, and contributing to society.

Completion of the Keystone Program is shown on students' transcripts and may be listed on their resumes. Evincing the importance of soft skills and the weight that law firms assign to this unique program, a law firm made ten offers to the law school's graduates, eight of whom had completed the Keystone Program. As Dean of Students Amy Gardner comments, "I think it's a signal that you appreciate the importance of professionalism and leadership."[78]

ORGANIZATION OF THIS BOOK

This first chapter has introduced the concept of soft skills, defined and explained their importance, distinguished soft skills from emotional intelligence, discussed the limitations of high intelligence and the attendant need to develop soft skills, and summarized studies and described programs indicating that soft skills can be learned. The remainder of this chapter outlines the organization and crystallizes the themes of this book.

The purpose of this book is to enhance attorney performance through self-awareness, self-development, social proficiency, wisdom, leadership, and professionalism.[79] These traits, abilities, and skills are addressed sequentially in Chapters 3–8 of this book, following a chapter that pinpoints the most important soft skills for attorneys and assesses the present quality of attorneys' soft skills.

The chapter on self-awareness (Chapter 3) answers threshold questions about how well we understand ourselves, how accurately we evaluate our own performance, and what biases distort our self-perception. That chapter

---

[78] Heagney, Meredith. (2013, Fall). The impact of "soft skills." University of Chicago. Retrieved from www.law.uchicago.edu/alumni/magazine/fall13/keystone.

[79] As explained in footnote 5, the structure is roughly consistent with Hogan and Warrenfeltz's "domain model" with four categories of skills that are designed to build upon each other: intrapersonal skills (self-awareness and self-development), interpersonal skills (social proficiency), leadership skills, and work skills. The chapters on essential skills (Chapter 2), wisdom (Chapter 6), and professionalism (Chapter 8) do not track the domain model, although they share some conceptual similarities. Hogan & Warrenfeltz, *supra* note 5 at 74–84.

also analyzes motivation and discusses how different types and sources of motivation affect our professional performance. Chapter 4 emphasizes self-development, explaining how we unknowingly impede our own development, identifying characteristics and habits that can facilitate self-development, and describing how professionals develop expertise.

The chapters on self-awareness and self-development focus on soft skills deployed at a personal level. In the ensuing chapter on social proficiency (Chapter 5), the book shifts from a personal context to a social context, evaluating our skills in understanding and communicating with other people, discussing the importance of building trust and instilling confidence, and describing methods to enable groups to function as exceptional problem solvers.

The next three chapters center on the soft skills of wisdom, leadership, and professionalism. The chapter on wisdom (Chapter 6) examines what it means to be wise and how people acquire wisdom. It analyzes the key elements of wisdom – perceptiveness, foresight, creativity, fairness, judgment, self-renewal, and courage – and describes how these qualities can bring us closer to attaining wisdom. Turning our attention next to leadership, Chapter 7 shows how nearly all attorneys assume leadership roles in direct or indirect leadership and how leadership skills can be applied to enhance our capabilities in planning, leading teams and law firms, managing cases and projects, promoting moral leadership, and handling crises. Following this grounding in wisdom and leadership, the chapter on professionalism (Chapter 8) considers the difficult challenges imposed upon conscientious, thoughtful attorneys and delineates what attorneys owe to themselves, clients, judges, other attorneys, the legal system, and the general society. As that chapter describes the meaning and clarifies the responsibilities of professionalism, it becomes evident that professionalism is as much an inspiration as it is a duty, as much a privilege as it is a commitment.

2

Essential Soft Skills

Abraham Verghese, an eminent physician, author, and medical school professor, describes the interaction between a physician and a patient as a ritual that starts with trust. When the patient seeks help and confides in the physician "and then incredibly, disrobes and allows touch, that has all the trappings of a ritual – it is not a mere cognitive exercise. Instead it is a ritual that is fundamental to the doctor-patient relationship and one, particularly in chronic disease or in terminal illness, that conveys to the patient a sense of the physician's commitment to being there, to never abandoning the patient."[1]

Although the attorney–client relationship lacks this physical intimacy, it compels an even deeper level of human intimacy and commitment as clients reveal nearly every other dimension of themselves – their personalities, histories, families, friends, colleagues, interests, and finances and the potentially embarrassing emotions, values, ambitions, prejudices, priorities, and idiosyncrasies that define their lives. Because clients, like patients, share the most intimate confidences and need the strongest assurance of a professional commitment, the interaction between clients and attorneys is profoundly personal, "not a mere cognitive exercise." The personal nature of that interaction requires attorneys to recognize that, despite their preoccupation with technical legal knowledge, the attorney–client relationship is ultimately a person-to-person, private bond. As California Superior Court Judge Michael Washington reflects on his years in private practice before appointment to the bench, "Because I was willing to be emotionally engaged with my clients, they were more willing to be trusting with me. It wasn't that I just wanted to resolve the case. I wanted to help put them on a path after the case was over."[2]

---

[1] Verghese, Abraham. (2011, October 2). Doctors, listen to your patients. [Special to CNN]. Retrieved from www.cnn.com/2011/10/02/opinion/verghese-doctors-touch/.

[2] Broderick, Pat. (2014, October 14). Eagerly engaged. *San Francisco Daily Journal*, p. 2.

Recognizing that the practice of law, like the practice of medicine, is more than the transfer of information and advice and that confidence, care, and trust are integral elements of sound professional relationships, we may logically question whether attorneys are presently meeting the challenges and discharging the responsibilities of client service. To answer that question in this chapter, we determine (1) which soft skills are most important for attorneys, as specified by clients and other attorneys; and (2) whether a gap exists between the most important soft skills and attorneys' current capabilities.

MOST IMPORTANT SOFT SKILLS

Considering that about 120,000 students are currently enrolled in law schools and about 1.3 million attorneys are licensed to practice law in the United States, it is remarkable how little research has been conducted to identify essential lawyering skills.[3] Like instructors at a driving school without cars, educators make a lot of assumptions about the hazards to be encountered in actual practice and the skills that should be developed to handle those hazards. Very little information about the skills required to excel in law practice has been obtained, and to the extent information has been compiled, it has little effect on law school curricula and continuing education programs.

As a result of the chronic inattention to identifying essential lawyering skills, we are left with few empirical studies and little guidance into how their findings can be incorporated into attorney development programs. Nevertheless, the extant studies indicate that clients and practitioners place a higher priority on soft skills than hard skills, and certain soft skills are consistently rated as being more important than others. "There is a paucity of high quality empirical research on the factors that contribute to lawyer effectiveness," states William Henderson, a law professor at the Maurer School of Law at Indiana University Bloomington. "But what little evidence there is," he notes, "suggests that academic indicators are less important than what some of us law professors might believe."[4]

---

[3] Hansen, Mark. (2015, March). Count off: Law school enrollment continues to drop, and experts disagree on whether the bottom is in sight. *ABA Journal*. American Bar Association. (2015). *Lawyer Demographics, Year 2015*. Retrieved from www.americanbar.org/content/dam/aba/administrative/market_research/lawyer-demographics-tables-2015.authcheckdam.pdf.

[4] Henderson, William. (2013). A blueprint for change. *Pepperdine Law Review*, 40(2), 461, 498.

About 30 empirical studies, conducted during the last 35 years, have attempted to identify the most important skills for lawyers.[5] Although these studies adopt different methodologies, their findings "are very consistent with

[5] Berman, Lori, & Bock, Heather. (2012). Developing attorneys for the future: What can we learn from the fast trackers? *Santa Clara Law Review*, 52(3), 875. Boccaccini, Marcus, Boothby, Jennifer, & Brodsky, Stanley. (2002, Spring). Client-relations skills in effective lawyering: Attitudes of criminal defense attorneys and experienced clients. *Law & Psychology Review*, 26, 97. Boccaccini, Marcus, & Brodsky, Stanley. (2001, Spring). Characteristics of the ideal criminal defense attorney from the client's perspective: Empirical findings and implications for legal practice. *Law and Psychology Review*, 25, 81. BTI Consulting Group. (2007). The 2008 BTI client service all stars, executive summary. Chitwood, Stephen, Gottlieb, Anita, & Mara, Evelyn Gaye (2005). *A business skills curriculum for law firm associates*. Chicago: Association of Legal Administrators. Coates, John C., Fried, Jesse M., & Spier, Kathryn E. (2015, February). What courses should law students take? Lessons from Harvard's Big Law survey. *Journal of Legal Education*, 64(3), 443. Doyel, R. (1986). National College-Mercer criminal defense survey: Some preliminary observations about interviewing, counseling and plea negotiations. *Mercer Law Review*, 37(3), 1019. Garth, Bryant G., & Martin, Joanne. (1993). Law schools and the construction of competence. *Journal of Legal Education*, 43, 469. Gerdy, Kristin. (2008). Clients, empathy, and compassion: Introducing first-year students to the "heart" of lawyering. *Nebraska Law Review*, 87, 1. Gerkman, Alli, & Cornett, Logan. (2016, July). *Foundations for practice: The whole lawyer and the character quotient*. Denver, Colorado: Institute for the Advancement of the American Legal System. Gerst, Stephen, & Hess, Gerald. (2009). Professional skills and values in legal education: The GPS model. *Valparaiso University Law Review*, 43(2), 513, 523–525, 548. Hamilton, Neil. (2014). Changing markets create opportunities: Emphasizing the competencies legal employers use in hiring new lawyers (including professional formation). *South Carolina Law Review*, 65, 567. Hamilton, Neil. (2013). Law firm competency models and student professional success: Building on a foundation of professional formation/professionalism. *University of St. Thomas Law Journal*, 11(1), 6. Kiser, Randall. (2011). *How leading lawyers think*. Berlin, Heidelberg: Springer. LexisNexis. (2015). The age of the client. *LexisNexis Bellwether Report*, 3, 19–21. Mudd, John O., & LaTrielle, John W. (1988). Professional competence: A study of new lawyers. *Montana Law Review*, 49, 11. NYSE Governance Services, & Barker Gilmore. (2016). *The rise of the GC: From legal adviser to strategic adviser* (p. 5). Retrieved from www.barkergilmore.com/hubfs/The_Rise_of_the_GC_-_From_Legal_Adviser_to_Strategic_Adviser.pdf?t=1461255829126. Shultz, Marjorie M., & Zedeck, Sheldon. (2009, January 30). Final report: Identification, development, and validation of predictors for successful lawyering. Retrieved from http://papers.ssrn.com/sol3/papers.cfm?abstract_id=1353554. Shultz, Marjorie M., & Zedeck, Sheldon. (2011). Predicting lawyer effectiveness: Broadening the basis for law school admission decisions. *Law and Social Inquiry*, 36, 620, 622–624. Snyder, Patricia. (2012, August 1). *Super women lawyers: A study of character strengths*. Unpublished master's thesis. Retrieved from http://repository.upenn.edu/mapp_capstone/38/. Sonsteng, John & Camarotto, David. (2000). Minnesota lawyers evaluate law schools, training and legal education. *William Mitchell Law Review*, 26, 327. Taylor, Irene E. (2002, November). Canada's Top 30 corporate dealmakers. *LEXPERT Magazine*. Taylor, Irene E. (2002, July). Canada's Top 25 corporate litigators. *LEXPERT Magazine*. Taylor, Irene E. (2004, November). Top 40 under 40. *LEXPERT Magazine*. Taylor, Irene E. (2003, September). Carpe diem! Canada's Top 25 women lawyers. *LEXPERT Magazine*. Taylor, Irene E. (2001, February 1). How smart are you really? *LEXPERT Magazine*. Wanser, Donna. (2012, February). *The emotional intelligence of general counsels in relation to lawyer leadership*. Unpublished doctoral dissertation, Pepperdine University Graduate School

each other," states law professor Susan Daicoff.[6] The studies can be categorized as being client-based or attorney-based. The client-based studies rely on surveys of a broad range of clients, from executives of publicly traded companies to prisoners serving long sentences. The attorney-based studies include large-scale surveys of attorneys in various practice settings, structured interviews with hiring partners, and analyses of law firm partners' evaluations of associate attorneys. Overall, there is a paucity of client-based studies, reflecting the profession's internal focus and the relative ease of locating attorneys and obtaining their consent to participate in studies.

The sections below summarize the most recent studies of essential lawyering skills. They are organized to present the five most recent client-based studies, followed by the five most recent attorney-based studies. Older studies are described in the appendix. Readers who do not wish to review the specific studies described below may proceed directly to the "Summary of Study Results Regarding Attorney Competencies" section of this chapter.

Most Recent Client-Based Studies

Directors of publicly traded companies/NYSE and Barker Gilmore (2016). This survey of 200 directors and officers at publicly traded companies in the United States asked them to identify the most valuable competencies for general counsel in 2020. "The bright spot," legal journalist Gabe Friedman notes, "is that in-house lawyers who have sound judgment and high integrity will be fine. Legal expertise – ehh, not as important."[7]

---

of Education and Psychology. Wawrose, Susan. (2013). What do legal employers want to see in new graduates?: Using focus groups to find out. *Ohio Northern University Law Review*, 39. 505. Zemans, Frances Kahn, & Rosenblum, Victor G. (1981). The making of a public profession. Chicago: American Bar Foundation. See also Shepherd, Lisa. (2016, December). What makes a star lawyer? New York: Thomson Reuters. After the book manuscript was submitted, Thomson Reuters released the results of a survey of corporate counsel. The survey indicates that exceptional attorneys exhibit the following qualities: expertise; commerciality (practicality, pragmatism, strategic viability); responsiveness (availability, meeting deadlines, and excelling at client service); integration (strong working relationship with client, client focused); being committed or hardworking; being innovative or creative; communicating well; breadth of knowledge; individual reputation; strong project management skills; competitive costs; and strong value for money.
6 Daicoff, Susan. (2015). Teaching relational skills: The evidence. In Maranville, Deborah, Bliss, Lisa Radtke, Kaas, Carolyn Wilkes, & Lopez, Antoinette Sedillo (Eds.). *Building on best practices* (p. 317). New Providence, New Jersey: LexisNexis. (Professor Daicoff's comment refers to studies in the 1988–2009 period.)
7 Friedman, Gabe. (2016, April 26). Being "innovative" not a winning trait for GCs, survey finds. *Bloomberg Law*. Retrieved from https://bol.bna.com/being-innovative-not-a-winning-trait-for-lawyers-survey-finds/.

The ten most important competencies and roles for 2020, as identified by the corporate directors and officers, are sound judgment, high integrity, legal expert, strategic perspective, problem solver, risk manager, forward thinker, powerful communicator, leadership, and global perspective.[8] In 2020, the five most important functions, "where GCs are expected to add the most value to the board," are acting as an advisor to the board; acting as an advisor to the CEO; promoting best governance practices; being unafraid to ask tough/sensitive questions; and serving as an ethical sounding board.

The competencies required in 2020 reflect a fundamental change in the role of in-house counsel. By 2020, their "most valuable functions will likely shift from serving as an ethical sounding board and ensuring the board adheres to best governance practices (which ranked first and second in 2015) to acting as adviser to the board and the CEO."[9] The role of advisor places a premium on soft skills like judgment, integrity, communication, and leadership. Although traditional legal expertise remains important, it now is "thought of as something that can be purchased as-needed."[10]

U.K. clients/LexisNexis (2015). LexisNexis sponsored a survey in the United Kingdom of more than 500 clients who had retained an attorney within the last two years. The most frequent client responses to the question "What are the three main things you look for in a lawyer/solicitor?" were as follows: provides clear indication of likely costs; provides regular updates on progress; explains billing system clearly at outset; fully appreciates client needs and expectations when taking the case on; personally responds to emails and calls within 24 hours; good at listening; keeps to a timetable/avoids case dragging on; demystifies the law/makes it understandable; explains the range of possible outcomes based on previous experience; and empathizes with client's situation.[11]

U.S. public and clients/Gerdy (2008). In this summary of various surveys and studies regarding client satisfaction, law professor Kristin Gerdy finds that clients "focused less on the lawyers' legal knowledge and expertise and more on the 'interpersonal skills and behaviors of the lawyers.' "[12] According to state bar surveys and academic studies, clients place greater weight on respect, regular communication from their attorneys, and attorneys' emotional involvement as shown by empathy, compassion, trust, and loyalty than on conventional legal skills. "What the client wanted," Gerdy declares, "was to know that their lawyer cared."[13]

---

[8] NYSE Governance Services & Barker Gilmore, *supra* note 5 at 5.   [9] Ibid. at 2.
[10] Ibid. at 4.   [11] LexisNexis, *supra* note 5 at 19.
[12] Gerdy, *supra* note 5 at 11. See Linder, Douglas, & Levit, Nancy. (2014). *The good lawyer* (pp. 7–8). New York: Oxford University Press.
[13] Gerdy, *supra* note 5 at 7, 11.

Corporate counsel/BTI Consulting Group (2008). BTI Consulting Group, Inc., interviewed more than 250 corporate counsel at large companies, asking them to identify the characteristics of the attorneys who deliver "the absolute best client service." They found that three abilities accounted for nearly 80 percent of the responses: client focus, understanding the client's business, and delivering results. Client focus "has been and continues to be the driving force" and includes responsiveness to client goals, strategic legal advice, and "going above and beyond the call of duty."[14] Illustrative comments about client focus include the following: "he really tries to anticipate the needs of the client;" "he is proactive;" "treats the client as part of the team;" "unprompted communication that she gives and the timeliness of her responses and results;" "he cares;" and "tries to get inside our heads and find out what is motivating us."[15] Understanding the client's business includes asking the right questions, listening to clients, and applying knowledge of the client's business to provide pointed advice. Delivering results means "no case churning, no changes in staffing, no science experiments – just laser focus on closure."[16]

An earlier BTI study asked corporate counsel, "What is the one thing your outside counsel does that just drives you crazy?" The majority of answers were "summarily categorized as poor communication" in four respects: failure to keep client adequately informed; lack of client focus as shown by failure to listen, non-responsiveness, and arrogance; making decisions without client authorization or awareness; and failure to give clear, direct advice.[17]

Male inmates at a maximum-security prison/Boccaccini, Boothby, and Brodsky (2002). Surveys were completed by 103 prison inmates who had been incarcerated for an average of 5.88 years and had an average of 21.68 years left to serve on their sentences. The ten most important attorney skills, as rated by the inmates in descending order, are: listening skills, courtroom speaking skills, comprehensive knowledge of criminal law, standing up for your rights, keeping you informed about your case, involving you in decision making, caring about what happens to you, getting your opinions about the case, spending time with you before court, and getting to know you.[18]

Psychology professors Marcus Boccaccini, Jennifer Boothby, and Stanley Brodsky found that both inmates and attorneys, who were surveyed concurrently, "viewed many client-relations skills as being as or more important than

---

[14]   BTI Consulting Group, *supra* note 5 at 6   [15]   Ibid. at 7.   [16]   Ibid. at 9.
[17]   Cunningham, Clark. (2013). What do clients want from their lawyers? *Journal of Dispute Resolution*, 2013(1), 143, 144.
[18]   Ibid.

legal skills." Attorneys and inmates ranked "caring about what happens to clients" and "involving clients in decision making" as more important than "legal skills such as being a good deal maker and establishing relationships with prosecutors and judges."[19]

Most Recent Attorney-Based Studies

U.S. lawyers/Institute for the Advancement of the American Legal System (IAALS) (2016). As noted briefly in Chapter 1, IAALS surveyed 24,137 attorneys in 37 states, asking them to evaluate 147 "Foundations" (skills, competencies, and characteristics). The attorneys represented a broad range of practice types: government (18 percent); business in-house (8 percent); solo private practice (19 percent); private practice with 2–100 attorneys (33 percent); private practice with 100+ attorneys (6 percent); public interest/nonprofit (1 percent); legal services/public defender (4 percent); and education (3 percent).[20]

Among the Foundations the attorneys ranked as "necessary immediately for the new lawyer's success in the short term," the highest priority was given to these ten skills, competencies, and characteristics, in descending order: keep information confidential; arrive on time for meetings, appointments, and hearings; honor commitments; integrity and trustworthiness; treat others with courtesy and respect; listen attentively and respectfully; promptly respond to inquiries and requests; diligence; have a strong work ethic and put forth best effort; and attention to detail.[21]

The "Top 10" Foundations, "not necessary in the short term but must be acquired over time," are as follows: develop expertise in a particular area; determine appropriate risk mitigation strategies; delegate to and manage support staff appropriately; objectively assess the soundness of a deal or proposed solution in terms of risks and rewards; prepare a case for trial; maintain knowledge of the relevant business, industry, and wider business landscape; provide quality in-court trial advocacy; determine ways to increase value to clients or stakeholders; assess possible courses of action and the range of likely outcomes in terms of risks and rewards; and manage meetings effectively.[22]

Alli Gerkman, the director of this IAALS project, states, "We were prepared to identify differences across practice settings, but what we have found is that

---

[19]   Ibid. at 112–113.
[20]   Gerkman & Cornett, *supra* note 5 at 10–11. Gerkman, Alli. (2015). "Foundations for Practice" PowerPoint presentation, on file with author.
[21]   Gerkman & Cornett, *supra* note 5 at 26.   [22]   Ibid. at 27.

there are more similarities. We were also prepared to see 'legal skills' populate the top of the list of Foundations that are necessary in the short term. Instead, we have seen 'characteristics,' like diligence, conscientiousness, and integrity and trustworthiness, command recognition at the top of the list."[23]

U.K. attorneys/LexisNexis (2015). LexisNexis surveyed 188 lawyers in the United Kingdom, asking them to rank the most important qualities that clients seek in attorneys. The ten most important qualities, ranked by the attorneys in descending order, are as follows: provides clear indication of likely costs; explains billing system clearly at outset; personally responds to emails and calls within 24 hours; demystifies the law/makes it understandable; appreciates client needs and expectations at case inception; treats client as a partner in the relationship; adheres to a timetable/avoids case dragging on; explains the range of possible outcomes; provides a tailored service versus a package solution; and provides regular updates on progress.

Lawyers and clients were surveyed concurrently in this study. The lawyers' priorities were quite different from the clients' priorities. Clients, for instance, ranked "providing regular progress reports" as their second priority, but lawyers placed it in the tenth position. "Good at listening" was ranked sixth by clients and twelfth by lawyers. Although clients placed "demystifying the law" in the eighth position, lawyers ranked it as the fourth highest priority.[24]

Minnesota lawyers/Hamilton (2014). Law professor Neil Hamilton asked lawyers in four different practice settings (large law firms, small law firms, county attorneys' offices, and legal aid offices) to rank the relative importance of various competencies. The ten most important competencies for all four types of legal employers were: integrity/honesty/trustworthiness; good judgment/common sense/problem solving; analytical skills; initiative/ambition/drive/strong work ethic; effective written/oral communication skills; dedication to client service/responsiveness to clients; commitment to the firm/department/office; strong work and team relationships; project management; and legal competency/expertise/knowledge of the law.[25]

Hamilton discovered that the ranking of some competencies varied with practice settings. Dedication to client service/responsiveness to clients, for example, was ranked first by legal aid offices, third by small firms, and sixth by large firms, but it was ranked seventeenth by county attorneys' offices.

[23] Gerkman, Alli. (2015, November 2). Beyond the conference: Foundations for practice and understanding tomorrow's lawyers. *IAALS Online.* Retrieved from http://iaals.du.edu/blog/beyond-conference-foundations-practice-and-understanding-tomorrow-s-lawyers.
[24] LexisNexis, *supra* note 5 at 18.   [25] Hamilton (2014), *supra* note 5 at 577.

Strong work and team relationships were ranked fourth by county attorneys' offices, but were ranked seventh by legal aid offices, tenth by small firms, and eleventh by large firms. Ability to work independently was ranked sixth by small firms and seventh by county attorneys' offices but was ranked sixteenth by large firms and eighteenth by legal aid offices.[26]

Legal employers/Wawrose (2013). Three legal research and writing professors organized focus groups of attorneys at law firms and organizations that had recently hired their law school's graduates. An independent moderator asked the attorneys questions like, "How would you describe the ideal recent law school graduate?" and "What strengths [and weaknesses] do you see in your recent hires?"[27] The attorneys' comments reflected a predominant "employer preference for attorneys who have well-developed professional or 'soft skills' such as a strong work ethic, willingness to take initiative, the ability to collaborate well with colleagues and clients, and the ability to adapt to the demands of supervisors."[28] The moderator, commenting on one focus group, said that the employers "spent most of the time ... on things I would assess as personality characteristics," and he "had to push the group for 'anything with respect to the more specific *legal* training that you regard as particular strengths and weaknesses?' "[29]

Associate evaluations by Minnesota law firms/Hamilton (2013). Professor Hamilton employed a unique research design to determine the most important associate attorney characteristics: he analyzed associate evaluation forms used by the 14 largest law firms in Minnesota. The evaluation forms indicate that the most important characteristics are the following: initiates and maintains strong work and team relationships; good judgment/common sense/problem solving; business development/marketing/client retention; analytical skills; effective written and oral communication skills; project management; legal competency/expertise/knowledge of the law; dedication to client service/responsive to client; initiative/ambition/drive/strong work ethic; and commitment to firm, its goals, and values.[30] Consistent with the other empirical studies, soft skills predominated over hard skills in importance.

Professor Hamilton also asked the ethics partner/general counsel of each firm to rank the relative importance of various competencies in the firm's decision to hire an associate. Their "top ten" list of competencies differed from that derived from the evaluation forms. The ethics partners/general counsel added four characteristics to their "top ten" list: integrity/honesty/

---

[26] Ibid. at 578–579. [27] Wawrose, *supra* note 5 at 518. [28] Ibid. at 522
[29] Ibid. at 522, fn. 91. [30] Hamilton (2013), *supra* note 5 at 9.

trustworthiness; inspires confidence; research skills; and commitment to professional development toward excellence. The ethics partners/general counsel dropped the following four characteristics from their top ten list: initiates and maintains strong work and team relationships; project management; legal competency/expertise/knowledge of the law; and business development/marketing/client retention.[31] The dominance of soft traits persisted in the ethics partners/general counsel's ranking of competencies.

SUMMARY OF STUDY RESULTS REGARDING ATTORNEY COMPETENCIES

The studies discussed above can be synthesized to reveal the most important attorney traits, qualities, characteristics, and habits. A consistent finding is that attorneys and clients place the highest priority on soft skills. "Law is human interaction in emotionally evocative climates," explains Yale University president and psychology professor Peter Salovey, whose pioneering work inspired decades of research on emotional intelligence. "Any lawyer who can understand what emotions are being presented and why," he asserts, "is at a tremendous advantage."[32]

When the study results are weighted to reflect their different sample sizes, it becomes clear that attorneys and clients have different concepts of attorney effectiveness, although both attorneys and clients indicate that soft skills are more important than hard skills. The ten competencies ranked as most important by clients, in descending order, are:

- Communicating regularly with clients; keeping clients informed and updated on the case/project status, progress, and new developments that could affect clients; promptly responding to client emails and telephone calls; asking questions and seeking information from clients
- Attentive listening skills
- Responsiveness to clients and their needs, interests, and goals; anticipation of client needs
- Explanation of fee arrangements; accurate estimates of fees and costs and range of variance from estimates
- Strategic problem solving, legal advice, and case/project management

---

[31] Ibid. at 15–16.

[32] Muir, Ronda. (2007, July/August). The importance of emotional intelligence in law firm partners. *Law Practice*, 33(5), 60.

- Understanding of client needs, expectations, and priorities, including need for closure
- Empathy and compassion
- Respectfulness
- Legal expertise/knowledge of the law
- Trust

Attorneys ranked the most important competencies, in descending order, as follows:

- Legal expertise/competence; knowledge of applicable law
- Honoring client confidentiality; keeping information confidential
- Punctuality/arriving on time for meetings, appointments, and hearings
- Ability to determine appropriate risk mitigation strategies
- Honoring commitments
- Ability to delegate to and manage support staff
- Integrity and trustworthiness
- Objective assessment of the soundness of a deal or proposed solution in terms of risks and rewards
- Treating others with courtesy and respect
- Ability to prepare a case for trial

The 20 most important competencies, as ranked by attorneys and clients, are shown in Table 2.1. Soft skills predominate in both the attorneys' and the clients' identification of the essential skills. The IAALS study skews the attorney results due to its large sample size of 24,137 attorneys, but the predominance of soft skills is consistent in nearly all of the studies summarized in this chapter and the appendix.

Comparing the attorney-based study results with the client-based study results, it is immediately apparent that they reflect different ideas about client service and disparate concepts of value. Clients emphasize communication, while attorneys emphasize legal expertise; clients are concerned about billing arrangements and fee estimates, yet attorneys concentrate on risk identification and assessments; clients appreciate empathy, compassion, and respect, but attorneys strive to be diligent, punctual, and technically proficient; and clients expect attorneys to anticipate their needs, but attorneys are trying to pay more attention to detail. Listening skills are the second most important competence for clients, but attorneys rank them as the eleventh most important competence. The side-by-side comparison of the attorney and client rankings of competencies in Table 2.1 evokes the title of law firm consultant Peter Zeughauser's book, *Lawyers Are From Mercury, Clients Are From Pluto*.

TABLE 2.1. *Comparison of attorneys' and clients' competency rankings*

Attorneys' rankings of competencies	Clients' ranking of competencies
Top ten competencies	
Legal expertise/competence; knowledge of applicable law	Ongoing communication with clients; keeping clients informed and updated on case status, progress, and new developments that could affect clients; promptly responding to client emails and telephone calls; asking questions and seeking information from clients
Honoring client confidentiality; keeping information confidential	Attentive listening skills
Punctuality/arriving on time for meetings, appointments, and hearings	Responsiveness to clients and their needs, interests, and goals; anticipation of client needs
Ability to determine appropriate risk mitigation strategies	Explanation of fee arrangements; accurate estimates of fees and costs and range of variance from estimates
Honoring commitments	Strategic problem solving, legal advice, and case/project management
Delegation to and management of support staff	Understanding of client needs, expectations, and priorities, including need for closure
Integrity and trustworthiness	Empathy and compassion
Ability to objectively assess the soundness of a deal or proposed solution in terms of risks and rewards	Respectfulness
Treating others with courtesy and respect	Legal expertise/thorough knowledge of law
Ability to prepare a case for trial	Trust
Next ten competencies	
Attentive listening skills	Loyalty
Maintain knowledge of the relevant business, industry, and wider business landscape	Judgment
Promptly respond to inquiries and requests	Results
Provide quality in-court trial advocacy	Integrity
Diligence	Management of case/project to expedite resolution
Ability to determine ways to increase value to clients or stakeholders	Ability to explain the law and range of outcomes
Have a strong work ethic and put forth best effort	Risk management skills

TABLE 2.1. *(cont.)*

Attorneys' rankings of competencies	Clients' ranking of competencies
Ability to assess possible courses of action and the range of likely outcomes in terms of risks and rewards	Courtroom skills
Attention to detail	Commitment to client
Effective meeting management	Client participation in decision making

ATTORNEYS' PROFICIENCY IN SOFT SKILLS

Having identified the essential soft skills for attorneys, based on the studies summarized in this chapter and the appendix, we now ascertain whether attorneys are proficient in those skills. A review of the data regarding client dissatisfaction, legal malpractice claims, disciplinary complaints, and attorneys' evaluations of associate attorneys demonstrates that attorneys' soft skills remain woefully underdeveloped. Soft skills, in contemporary law practices, are more of a concept than a feature, more of an aspiration than an effort.

Client Dissatisfaction

Client dissatisfaction with attorneys has been at epidemic levels for decades, perhaps centuries. Charles Dickens, writing in the mid-1800s, bemoaned ever filing his lawsuit against "literary pirates" who had published unauthorized versions of his books, *Christmas Carol* and *Chuzzlewit*. Lamenting that he had been treated as "the robber instead of the robbed," he was determined to avoid attorneys and their "mazes."[33] Writing to his attorney, Dickens mused, "It is better to suffer a great wrong than to have recourse to the much greater wrong of the law."[34] At the core of his disdain for attorneys was his conviction that attorneys mistreat clients and corrupt the practice of law so that its purpose "is to make business for itself, at their expense."[35]

Nearly two centuries later, 69 percent of respondents in an American Bar Association survey agree with the statement, "Lawyers are more interested in making money than in serving their clients;" and 57 percent agree with the statement, "Most lawyers are more concerned with their own self-promotion

[33] Gest, John Marshall. (1905, July). The law and lawyers of Charles Dickens. *The American Law Register (1898–1907)*, 53(7), 401, 405–406. Published by *The University of Pennsylvania Law Review*.
[34] Ibid. at 405. [35] Ibid. at 406.

than their client's best interests."[36] A survey of corporate counsel is similarly distressing: only 32 percent of corporate counsel would recommend their primary law firm.[37] "An arrogance has pervaded the profession for years," concedes an attorney. "There is a lack of understanding of what a customer is."[38]

Client dissatisfaction stems from multiple soft skills deficiencies. In the American Bar Association survey mentioned above, only 53 percent of clients were very satisfied with "how well the lawyer kept you informed of your case," and only 56 percent were very satisfied with "how quickly the lawyer worked to resolve the issue."[39] Less than two-thirds of the surveyed respondents were very satisfied with "how sensitive the lawyer was to your needs and concerns" and "how proactive the lawyer was in protecting and serving your interests."[40] When asked to think about "the things that lawyers and the legal profession might do to improve their reputation," 81 percent of respondents said it was important for lawyers to "do a better job of communicating with their clients."[41] Again citing soft skills as a paramount reason for client dissatisfaction, corporate counsel report that, of the four main reasons for firing outside counsel, "two are for deficiencies in soft skills – responsiveness and personality issues."[42]

It would be easy to conclude that attorneys are unconcerned about client dissatisfaction, but the problem actually is much deeper: attorneys think they are doing a superb job of meeting clients' expectations. The gap between client expectations and attorney performance, therefore, is not only substantive but perceptual as well. In one study of clients and their lawyers, for example, 80 percent of the lawyers said their service was "above average," but only 40 percent of the clients said that they were receiving service at that level.[43] The relation between clients' evaluations of their attorneys and attorneys' evaluations of their own performances, according to that study, was consistently divergent and persistently self-serving in other critical dimensions of client service. Ninety-one percent of attorneys thought they were doing "very well" or "quite well" in listening to clients, empathizing with clients, understanding client needs and expectations, and explaining the range of

[36] American Bar Association Section of Litigation. (2002, April). *Public perceptions of lawyers: Consumer research findings* (p. 7). Chicago: American Bar Association.
[37] BTI Consulting Group. (2006). How clients hire, fire and spend: Landing the world's best clients. BTI Consulting Group. (2007, March 27). How clients hire, fire and spend: Presentation to the Delaware Valley law firm marketing group.
[38] LexisNexis, *supra* note 5 at 15.
[39] American Bar Association Section of Litigation, *supra* note 36 at 20.   [40] Ibid. at 20.
[41] Ibid. at 32.   [42] Muir, *supra* note 32 at 61.   [43] LexisNexis, *supra* note 5 at 14, 22.

possible legal outcomes. But only 66 percent of clients thought the attorneys were performing those services at that level.[44] In another study, 62 percent of law firms gave themselves an "A" rating for overall performance, but only 19 percent of their clients thought they deserved an "A."[45] Noting that attorneys generally neglect client feedback and erroneously gauge their own reputations, BTI Consulting Group reports that "fewer than 15% of the self-perceptions held by a firm's attorneys are actually shared by the marketplace."[46]

Legal Malpractice Claims

Legal malpractice claims rates vary by insurer, ranging from one to five claims per year for every 100 lawyers.[47] When claims are paid, the average payment by insurers for large firms is "well over \$1 million."[48] Plaintiffs win 49 percent of malpractice cases against lawyers, compared with a win rate of 23 percent in actions against physicians and 39 percent in actions against other professionals.[49] The legal malpractice cases with the highest plaintiff win rates include cases that allege soft skills deficiencies, e.g., consultation, advice, settlement, and negotiation.[50]

Only 14 percent of legal malpractice claims allege a failure to know or properly apply the law. Deficient soft skills, rather than ignorance of the law, account for most of the activities that result in malpractice claims. These deficiencies include failure to follow client's instruction; failure to obtain client's consent or to inform client; failure to react to calendar notifications; misrepresentation; withdrawal from representation without proper communication to client; failure to recognize a conflict of interest; failure to initiate any kind of calendar entry when the attorney is aware of the existence of a time deadline; inadequate discovery of facts or investigation; planning or strategy errors; and procrastination or lack of follow-up in performance of services.[51]

[44] Ibid. at 21 (based on the average responses in those four categories).

[45] Kiser, Randall. (2010). *Beyond right and wrong: The power of effective decision making for attorneys and clients* (p. 165). Berlin, Heidelberg: Springer-Verlag.

[46] BTI (2006), *supra* note 57.

[47] Kritzer, Herbert, & Vidmar, Neil. (2015, June 29). When the lawyer screws up: A portrait of legal malpractice claims and their resolution (pp. 15–16). Retrieved from http://scholarship .law.duke.edu/faculty_scholarship/3491/.

[48] Ibid. at 51   [49] Ibid. at 44, 60.   [50] Ibid. at 44.

[51] American Bar Association Standing Committee on Lawyers' Professional Liability. (2012, September). *Profile of legal malpractice claims, 2008–2011*. Chicago: American Bar Association.

Legal malpractice claims data from Canada confirm the critical importance of soft skills in general and malpractice prevention in particular. Law
professors Kara MacKillop and Neil Vidmar analyzed the claims data compiled by The Lawyers' Professional Indemnity Company (LAWPRO), which
insures about 24,000 lawyers in Ontario, Canada.[52] (The American Bar
Association has compared its malpractice data with that of LAWPRO and
concluded that the results "show relatively similar claims experiences between
the two countries."[53]) Their analysis shows that the major cause of malpractice
claims has shifted from calendaring mistakes (usually failing to file an action
before it was barred by the statute of limitations) to "attorney/client communication and relationship issues."[54]

MacKillop and Vidmar found that communication and relationship problems were responsible for 46 percent of all claims and 51 percent of claims
costs.[55] The errors, they note, "fall into four categories: failure to follow
client instructions (13.7% of claims, 13.6% of costs), inadequate discovery
or investigation (12.9%, 15%), failure to inform or obtain consent (11.6%,
13.4%), and poor communication (8%, 9%)."[56] Similarly, in Australia, "the
most significant cause of professional negligence claims was not dissatisfaction with outcome but instead related to the handling of the client relationship; the most frequent problems were failure to listen to the client, failure to
ask appropriate questions, and failure to explain relevant aspects of the
matter."[57]

State Bar Discipline System Complaints

A comparable claims profile, indicating that soft skills deficiencies are at the
core of client dissatisfaction, is evident in state bar disciplinary records.
Although attorneys often associate state bar disciplinary actions with intentional wrongs like unauthorized trust account withdrawals, the reality is that
most state bar disciplinary actions involve soft skills deficiencies like neglect,
poor judgment, inadequate communication, and procrastination. Illustrative
state bar reports show that soft skills deficiencies predominate over intentional
misconduct claims:

---

[52] MacKillop, Kara, & Vidmar, Neil. (2006, June 29). Legal malpractice: A Preliminary inquiry.
      Unpublished manuscript. Retrieved from http://ssrn.com/abstract=912963.
[53] Ibid. at 21. See Kiser (2010), *supra* note 45 at 201.
[54] Ibid. at 15, 19–20. See Kiser, Randall. (2015). The emotionally attentive lawyer: Balancing the
      rule of law with the realities of human behavior. *Nevada Law Journal*, 15(2), 446–447.
[55] Ibid. at 19   [56] Ibid. at 19. See Kiser (2015), *supra* note 54 at 447.
[57] Cunningham, *supra* note 47 at 146.

- In Illinois, the Attorney Registration and Disciplinary Commission reports that "61% of grievances involved issues of poor attorney-client relations: neglect (38%), failure to communicate (12%) and disputes over fees (11%)."[58]
- In Washington State, the most common grievance allegation is "unsatisfactory performance" (38 percent), followed by "personal behavior" (20 percent).[59]
- In Utah, the violation most frequently found in discipline orders is lack of diligence (13.8 percent), followed by communication deficiencies (12.8 percent).[60]
- In Wisconsin, the Office of Lawyer Regulation's records show that the most common complaint against attorneys is lack of diligence (19.87 percent), followed by improper advocacy (16.2 percent), lack of communication (10.83 percent), misrepresentation and dishonesty (8.1 percent), and unreasonable fees (6.04 percent).[61]
- In California, "performance," which includes failure to perform and failure to communicate, is the most common ethics complaint (37 percent).[62] Eighty-nine percent of client claims against the Client Security Fund, established to compensate clients for attorney misconduct, are for "unearned fees," while only 11 percent of the claims are for intentional misappropriation.[63]

Depicting a gap between the priorities of clients and attorneys, law professor Anita Bernstein urges, "Check the disciplinary dockets in any state and you will find neglect, failure to communicate, and failure to represent clients diligently or competently heaped together at the top of the pile. In most jurisdictions these three offenses add up to more than half the total disciplinary volume – whether you count the number of complaints filed, the number of lawyers sanctioned, or the rules deemed violated in published disciplinary decisions."[64]

[58] *Attorney Registration and Disciplinary Commission annual report 2015* (p. 4). Chicago: Attorney Registration and Disciplinary Commission.
[59] Washington State Bar Association. *Discipline system 2015 annual report* (p. 8).
[60] Utah State Bar Office of Professional Conduct. *Annual report, August 2015* (p. 22).
[61] Office of Lawyer Regulation and Board of Administrative Oversight. *Report of the lawyer regulation system, fiscal year 2014–2015* (p. 47).
[62] The State Bar of California. (2010, April). *2009 report on the State Bar of California discipline* (p. 3).
[63] *The State Bar of California, client security fund – 2014 activities report.*
[64] Bernstein, Anita. (2003). What clients want, what lawyers need. *Emory Law Journal*, 52, 1053, 1056. See Brown, Jennifer Gerarda, & Wolf, Liana G. T. (2012) The paradox and promise of restorative attorney discipline. *Nevada Law Journal*, 12(2), 253, 259. (The "most common

Attorneys' Opinions About Associate Attorneys

Clients are not alone in thinking that attorneys lack the fundamental skills, talents, characteristics, and qualities necessary to practice law. When attorneys rated both the importance of certain soft skills and entry-level attorneys' actual proficiency in those soft skills, the performance gaps were glaring. Attorneys, for example, said that the level of competence "needed" for the ability to negotiate effectively is 4.18 (on a five-point scale), but the competence "observed" is 2.53 – only 61 percent of the necessary level of competence.[65] The shortfall for other soft skills was slightly better but certainly not reassuring: ability to ascertain facts through investigation or interrogation (66 percent); ability to interview clients and witnesses effectively (67 percent); understanding of the professional relationship between lawyers and judges and the ethical implications and responsibilities of that relationship (71 percent); capacity to organize work flow (72 percent); judgment (72 percent); understanding of the broader ethical implications of lawyers' conduct (72 percent); capacity to deal effectively with others (73 percent); and maturity (73 percent).[66]

The gap between skills needed and skills observed is exacerbated by over-confidence. When attorneys believe they already have achieved a high level of proficiency in a skill, they have few reasons and little motivation to improve their performance. A survey of about 1,500 law students, professors, and practicing attorneys, commissioned by the BARBRI Group, displays a consistent pattern of overconfidence in assessing practice proficiencies:[67]

- 76 percent of third-year law students believe "they are prepared to practice law 'right now.'" But only 56 percent of practicing attorneys, most of whom have practiced 20 years or more, think that recent law school graduates are prepared to practice law.
- 71 percent of third-year law students believe they currently have sufficient law practice skills. But only 23 percent of practicing attorneys believe that recent graduates have sufficient law practice skills.

---

complaints against lawyers include a failure to communicate with the client and neglect of the client's matters.")

[65] Mudd & LaTrielle, *supra* note 5 at 11.

[66] Ibid. at 7–14. Separately, Sonsteng observed a decline in attorney's "sensitivity to professional and ethical concerns." See Sonsteng, *supra* note 5 at 348.

[67] The BARBRI Group. (2015, March 5). *2014 state of the legal field survey.* The results from a LexisNexis survey of 300 hiring partners and senior associates show a harsher evaluation of new attorneys: "95% of hiring partners and associates whose practice has a transactional focus believed that new graduates are lacking practical transactional skills." LexisNexis. (2015). White paper: Hiring partners reveal new attorney readiness for real world practice.

- Nearly one-half of law professors believe that law students possess sufficient practice skills, but less than one-quarter of practicing attorneys think they have those skills.

Law professors and practicing attorneys share an identical view on one subject: "Only 18 percent of law school faculty members and the same number of practicing attorneys who work at companies that hire recent law school graduates believe recent law school graduates have the financial and business acumen required to practice law."[68] Considering that nearly all legal matters necessarily implicate clients' finances or businesses to some degree and require sound judgment in advising clients about those issues, our current system of legal education and professional development appears to be as unfair to new attorneys as it is to clients.

Reading data about these shortfalls in attorneys' skills can become numbing. One way of seeing these deficiencies as genuine problems instead of mere data is to imagine that your physician, like an attorney deficient in essential skills, has failed to ask critical questions, consult with colleagues, clearly communicate a diagnosis, explain the basis for that diagnosis, consider less risky alternatives, organize and lead a treatment team, and, perhaps most importantly, realize what he does not know and did not do. Deficiencies in attorneys' skills often have consequences as devastating for clients as those we would expect to see when doctors treat patients without adequate thought, training, experience, and preparation. The difference between attorneys' errors and physicians' errors is primarily their vividness, not their magnitude. As a leading California trial attorney remarked when recalling another attorney who belatedly recognized that his skills were inadequate, "That poor client – it may have cost them their business."[69]

---

[68] Ibid. [69] Kiser (2011), *supra* note 5 at 258.

3

Self-Awareness

For lawyers, self-awareness and self-development are concomitant responsibilities. The Fundamental Values of the Profession require lawyers to remain "constantly alert to the existence of problems that may impede or impair the lawyer's ability to provide competent representation."[1] This duty specifically includes awareness of "psychological or emotional problems."[2] The Model Rules of Professional Conduct, moreover, require attorneys to "strive to attain the highest level of skill."[3] To fulfill this duty attorneys must regularly evaluate their own performance, assessing its quality, the appropriateness of their reactions to unexpected events, and the accuracy of their assessment of "the likely perspectives, concerns and reactions of any individuals with whom one interacted."[4]

The Fundamental Values require an exceptionally high level of self-awareness. Attorneys must develop the capacity to replicate the effective aspects of their professional performance and prevent a repetition of ineffective aspects by learning and adopting specific practices:

(A) Methods of thinking or analysis that will make it possible to plan more effectively for performances;
(B) Methods of improving future performances, including one's applications of lawyering skills;
(C) Methods of improving one's own abilities to perceive or resolve ethical issues.[5]

[1] American Bar Association Section of Legal Education and Admissions to the Bar. (1992, July). *Legal education and professional development–An educational continuum* (p. 209). Chicago: American Bar Association.
[2] Ibid.
[3] Center for Professional Responsibility. (2007). *Model rules of professional conduct* (p. 2). Chicago, Illinois: American Bar Association.
[4] American Bar Association Section of Legal Education and Admissions to the Bar, *supra* note 1 at 218.
[5] Ibid. at 219.

This ongoing process of self-awareness and improvement, which necessitates self-evaluation and self-criticism, is a prerequisite to professional development. As David Shenk, author of *The Genius in All of Us*, explains, the most proficient professionals have "a daily grinding commitment to becoming better," and they effectuate that commitment through "a constant self-critique."[6]

Because lawyers have twin duties to assess and improve their performance, this chapter explains the difficulties encountered when we attempt to evaluate ourselves and identifies the beliefs, feelings, and practices that may impede or impair self-development. Building upon this foundation of self-awareness and self-assessment, the next chapter will describe and discuss the attitudes, traits, and habits that accelerate self-development.

BIASES AND DISTORTIONS IN EVALUATING OURSELVES

In his 1974 commencement address at the California Institute of Technology, Nobel Laureate Richard Feynman warned his audience, "The first principle is that you must not fool yourself – and you are the easiest person to fool. So you have to be very careful about that."[7] Our tendency to fool ourselves about our proficiency in various domains is so strong and so well documented that it has earned its own psychological label – "illusory superiority."[8] When illusory superiority has a firm grip on our sense of self-esteem, we not only overestimate our capabilities but also are woefully incapable of recognizing when other people are performing better than we are. Moreover, we don't seem to be aware that we are exaggerating our own capabilities; we are ignorant of our ignorance.[9]

One of the earliest studies of illusory superiority tested Cornell University undergraduate students on logical reasoning, humor, and English grammar.[10]

---

[6] Shenk, David. (2010). *The genius in all of us* (p. 55). New York: Doubleday.

[7] Feynman, Richard P. (1985). *Surely you're joking, Mr. Feynman!: Adventures of a curious character* (p. 343). New York: W.W. Norton & Company.

[8] See Buunk, Bram, & Oldersma, Frans. (2001). Social comparison and close relationships. In Fletcher, Garth, & Clark, Margaret (Eds.). *Blackwell handbook of social psychology* (p. 399). Malden, Massachusetts: Blackwell Publishers Ltd. Yamada, Makik., *et al.* (2013). Superiority illusion arises from resting-state brain networks modulated by dopamine. *Proceedings of the National Academy of Sciences*, 110(11), 4363–4367.

[9] Dunning, David, Johnson, Kerri, Ehrlinger, Joyce, & Kruger, Justin. (2003, June). Why people fail to recognize their own incompetence. *Current Directions in Psychological Science*, 12(3), 83, 86.

[10] Kruger, Justin, & Dunning, David. (1999). Unskilled and unaware of it: How difficulties in recognizing one's own incompetence lead to inflated self-assessments. *Journal of Personality and Social Psychology*, 77(6), 1121.

The students who scored in the bottom quartile "grossly overestimated their ability" on all tests. In one test, for example, the bottom-quartile participants scored in the bottom 10 percent on average, but they estimated their ability to be in the top 67th percentile.[11] When shown the test answers of their better-performing peers, they failed to see how their performance could have been improved and actually "tended to raise their already inflated self-estimates."[12] Ironically, the students who performed in the top quartile *under*estimated their ability and test performance.[13] They estimated their test performance to be in the 70th percentile (remarkably close to the bottom-quartile participants' estimate), but their actual average test performance was in the 89th percentile.[14]

Later research aimed at understanding why our perceived abilities are at odds with our actual performance indicates that we tend to make "top-down" performance estimates: "People start with their preconceived beliefs about their skill (e.g., 'I am good at logical reasoning') and use those beliefs to estimate how well they are doing on any specific test."[15] Unfortunately, these preconceived views lead people to make overinflated evaluations of their skills "that cannot be justified by their objective performance."[16] Given a conflict between our perceived abilities and our actual abilities, we choose, as Oscar Wilde reportedly said of first marriages, the "triumph of imagination over intelligence."

We hold onto the illusion that we are adept at multiple skills, despite contrary evidence, because it enhances our sense of well-being. Positive illusions increase self-confidence, foster optimism, intensify feelings of happiness, promote personal satisfaction, and amplify a sense of control over events.[17] These illusions sustain our psychological immune system. "Just as we possess a potent physical immune system that protects us from threats to our physical well-being," explains psychology professor Timothy Wilson, "so do we possess a potent psychological immune system that protects us from threats to our psychological well-being. When it comes to maintaining a sense of well-being, each of us is the ultimate spin doctor."[18]

Are lawyers – trained for years in objective, detached evaluation of facts and people – accurate judges of their own skills? The statistical evidence

---

[11]   Ibid. at 1126.   [12]   Ibid. at 1127.   [13]   Ibid. at 1131.   [14]   Ibid. at 1126.

[15]   Dunning (2003), *supra* note 9 at 86.   [16]   Ibid.

[17]   See Murray, Sandra L., Holmes, John G., & Griffin, Dale W. (1996, January). The benefits of positive illusions: Idealization and the construction of satisfaction in close relationships. *Journal of Personality and Social Psychology*, 70(1), 79. Makridakis, S., & Moleskis, A. (2015). The costs and benefits of positive illusions. *Frontiers of Psychology*, 6, 859.

[18]   Wilson, Timothy (2002). *Strangers to ourselves* (p. 38). Cambridge, Massachusetts: Belknap Press.

suggests not. In the Shultz/Zedeck study of lawyer effectiveness, discussed in Chapter 2, the attorneys ranked themselves on 26 effectiveness factors and provided the researchers with contact information for two supervisors and two peers.[19] The supervisors and peers, in turn, evaluated the attorneys on the same factors. Although the level of agreement on most personality traits is about .40 for the general population,[20] the level of agreement among the attorneys and their peers and supervisors was considerably lower at an average correlation of .28.[21]

When we examine the traits on which agreement was particularly low, we see that attorneys' evaluations of their soft skills differ markedly from those of their peers and supervisors. The lowest levels of agreement were evident in the evaluations of these skills: managing others (.12), integrity (.13), fact-finding (.13), ability to see the world through the eyes of others (.15), creativity (.15), and listening (.15).[22] Other soft skills for which the correlation was below the average correlation of .28 include practical judgment, advising clients, influencing and advocating, questioning and interviewing, negotiation, strategic planning, managing self, evaluating, developing and mentoring, developing relationships, stress management, diligence, self-development, and problem solving – nearly all of the critical soft skills.[23] Although clever attorneys will argue that the lack of agreement occurs because the attorneys themselves are the best judges of their traits and behavior and their peers and supervisors do not understand how great they really are, studies indicate that an individual's self-reports and predictions about future action are less accurate than other people's assessments and predictions.[24] Like the Cornell University undergraduates, many attorneys "overestimate their expertise and talent, thinking they are doing just fine when, in fact, they are doing quite poorly."[25]

Attorneys who overestimate their abilities find themselves in a large yet distinguished class. Eighty-eight percent of judges believe they are less likely to be overturned on appeal than the average judge.[26] Most judges believe that "the lawyers who appear in front of them feel much more fairly treated than is actually the case."[27] Bankruptcy court judges inaccurately see themselves as highly efficient adjudicators; 71 percent of judges report that they rule on final

---

[19] Shultz, Marjorie M., & Zedeck, Sheldon. (2009, January 30). Final report: Identification, development, and validation of predictors for successful lawyering. Retrieved from https://papers.ssrn.com/sol3/papers.cfm?abstract_id=1353554.

[20] Wilson, *supra* note 18 at 84.

[21] Shultz & Zedeck, *supra* note 19 at table 17: Inter-correlations of Raters.   [22] Ibid.

[23] Ibid.   [24] Wilson, *supra* note 18 at 85.   [25] Dunning, *supra* note 9 at 83.

[26] Guthrie, Chris, Rachlinski, Jeffrey J., & Wistrich, Andrew J. (2001). Inside the judicial mind. *Cornell Law Review*, 86(4), 814.

[27] Ibid. at 815.

fee applications at the hearing, but only 43 percent of the attorneys say they rule that quickly.[28] (The bankruptcy attorneys have their own problems: over 60 percent of the lawyers report that they "always" comply with local fee guidelines; but the judges report that only 18 percent of attorneys always comply.[29]) Professors, for their part, acknowledge that they have to be over-confident because "in some ways, we're all faking it." As one law professor concedes, "you're always teaching what you don't know."[30] Law appears to be one of the few domains that not only expects but rewards overconfidence and egocentric biases;[31] the distinction between projecting confidence and deluding oneself can be as fuzzy as an appellate court's plurality decision.

Recognizing that attorneys are vulnerable to the illusion of superiority, we now proceed to identify and examine specific beliefs, traits, and behaviors that impede self-development. As we examine these beliefs, traits, and behaviors, we are necessarily making private judgments about our own capabilities and vulnerabilities, possibly assuring ourselves that we already have overcome any challenges and are performing at exceptional levels of proficiency. But to be successful at self-development, we must be ruthlessly objective and place accuracy above superficial self-esteem. As psychology professor K. Anders Ericsson advises, "The journey to truly superior performance is neither for the faint of heart nor for the impatient. The development of genuine expertise requires struggle, sacrifice, and honest, often painful self-assessment."[32]

IMPEDIMENTS TO SELF-DEVELOPMENT

Extensive research into human performance demonstrates that specific attitudes, emotions, feelings, traits, and behaviors tend to impede self-development, while others accelerate self-development. The balance of this chapter identifies and explains impediments that affect thousands of attorneys and obstruct their professional development – often without attorneys' awareness of the impediment and its consequences. The 12 impediments highlighted in this chapter are emotional numbing; high moral

---

[28] Eisenberg, Theodore. (1994). Differing perceptions of attorney fees in bankruptcy cases. *Washington University Law Quarterly*, 72, 979, 984.

[29] Ibid. at 987.

[30] Huston, Therese. (2009). *Teaching what you don't know* (p. 12). Cambridge, Massachusetts: Harvard University Press.

[31] See Medwed, Daniel S. (2014, February 3). The good fight: The egocentric bias, the aversion to cognitive dissonance, and the American criminal law. *Journal of Law and Policy*, 22(1), 135–145.

[32] Ericsson, K. Anders, Prietula, Michael J., & Cokely, Edward T. (2007, July–August). The making of an expert. *Harvard Business Review*, pp. 114–121.

identity; static self illusion; omniscience; stress/anxiety; aggressiveness; extrinsic motivation; procrastination; impostor syndrome; alcohol and drug impairment; narcissism; and status, affluence, and power.

Emotional Numbing

Conventional wisdom dictates that emotions must be kept out of the workplace. Law schools inject steroids into this concept by training lawyers "to think precisely, to analyze coldly, to work within a body of materials that is given, to see, and see only, and manipulate, the machinery of the law."[33] Empirical research, however, now informs us that effective performers are aware of their emotions, knowledgeable about the effects of emotions, and confident in their ability to capture the benefits of emotions.[34] And as a practical matter, it is futile to suppress and hide our emotions because this cannot be done without damaging our problem-solving skills and harming our relationships with the people who invariably see that we're faking it.

Does this mean that we give free rein to whatever we feel at the workplace? No, it means that we should be continually aware of our emotions and modulate them as necessary to facilitate an authentic yet empathetic relationship with others. Some unregulated propensities – constant expression of intense anger and continual rumination about distressing events, for example – are detrimental to the individual expresser, and suppressing those propensities benefits both the expresser and the target.[35]

We are frequently unaware of our feelings and emotions for at least three reasons. First, we suppress emotions and feelings that make us uneasy or uncomfortable; at least temporarily, we choose to disregard rather than acknowledge sensations that threaten our sense of equilibrium. Second, we are simply inattentive. Due to situational distractions or personal insensitivity, we fail to attend to emotions and feelings because we are unaware that they have changed. Third, we reject feelings and emotions that conflict with our beliefs, schemas, rules, and standards about how and what we should think

---

[33] Llewellyn, Karl N. (1996). *The bramble bush: On our law and its study* (p. 116). New York: Oceana Publications.

[34] See David, Susan, & Congleton, Christina. (2013, November). Emotional agility. *Harvard Business Review*, p. 125. Gilkey, Roderick, Caceda, Ricardo, & Kilts, Clinton. (2010, September). When emotional reasoning trumps IQ. *Harvard Business Review*, p. 27. Blackman, Andrew. (2014, April 27). The inner workings of the executive brain. *The Wall Street Journal*.

[35] See Butler, Emily, & Gross, James. (2004). Hiding feelings in social contexts: Out of sight is not out of mind. In Philippot, Pierre, & Feldman, Robert (Eds.). *The regulation of emotion* (p. 113). Mahwah, New Jersey: Lawrence Erlbaum Associates.

and feel in certain circumstances. Feeling miserable on your wedding day, for instance, defies a cultural feeling rule and, for that reason, it must be dragged into the mind's equivalent of the trash icon.[36]

Whether it occurs by repression, inattention, or rejection, our neglect of feelings and emotions limits our capacity to handle negative emotions, optimize positive emotions, enjoy interactions with friends, build trust with colleagues and clients, and remember critical events. Suppression of feelings and emotions is correlated with increased negative emotion experience; decreased positive affect; heightened alienation from yourself and social partners; less responsive conversational behavior; and higher levels of distraction during conversations. Suppression also is associated with reduced memory about what was said during social interactions; less rapport, liking, and affiliation on the part of social partners; decreased relationship satisfaction and closeness; and elevated physiological stress (e.g., blood pressure increases) in both the persons suppressing affect and their social partners.[37] People who suppress their emotions report that they feel inauthentic and alienated; ironically, they perceive their social partners to be similarly inauthentic and alienated.[38] Suppression, in sum, intensifies negative feelings, diminishes positive sensations, and eviscerates social relationships.

Even when suppression of emotions and feelings seems to be desirable, it cannot be accomplished credibly or constructively. Events that trigger an emotional response also raise an expectation by others that we will express that emotional response.[39] When we fail to express the anticipated response, we convey an unintentional message, "I want you to know that I am hiding something from you" or "I am withholding my emotions from you."[40] This lack of expression is perceived to be deceptive and inauthentic. It diminishes trust, raises the other person's blood pressure, and forces them to search for reasons for the reticence and secrecy.[41] Although we may think of the lack of an expected behavior as simply an absence, "it is registered and interpreted by observers as a meaningful act in its own right."[42]

---

[36]   The three circumstances are identified and described in Wilson, *supra* note 18 at 134. Emotional numbing in acute stress disorder is described in Bryant, R.A., Friedman, M.J., Spiegel, D., Ursano, R., & Strain, J. (2011). A review of acute stress disorder in DSM-5. *Depression And Anxiety* 28(9), 802–817.

[37]   Butler & Gross, *supra* note 35 at 112. Butler, Emily, Egloff, Boris, Wilhelm, Frank, Smith, Nancy, Erickson, Elizabeth, & Gross, James. (2003). The social consequences of expressive suppression, *Emotion*, 3(1), 48. Gross, James. (2002). Emotion regulation: Affective, cognitive, and social consequences. *Psychophysiology*, 39, 281–291.

[38]   Butler & Gross, *supra* note 35 at 106.

[39]   See Rock, David. (2009). *Your brain at work* (p. 112). New York: HarperCollins.

[40]   Butler & Gross, supra note 35 at 107, 109.   [41]   Ibid. at 108–110.   [42]   Ibid. at 109.

High Moral Identity

At an early age we develop a self-definition, a series of beliefs about who we are and the attributes that distinguish us from other people.[43] These beliefs center on our personal traits and social roles and strongly affect our self-esteem.[44] Although both high self-esteem and low self-esteem people aspire to maintain a positive self-concept, they differ in their self-definitions, and as a result, differ in their strategies for coping with possible failures and other threats to their self-esteem.[45]

People who have high self-esteem "are quite certain that they have positive attributes and do not have negative attributes, and it is important to them to have positive attributes."[46] To maintain a consistently positive self-definition and enhance their self-concept, high self-esteem people rely on self-serving biases more than low self-esteem people and are more likely to "seek self-enhancement intrapsychically," that is, in their own mind.[47] Consistent with the self-deception required to maintain an invariably positive view of their virtues, high self-esteem people are more resistant to feedback, more likely to question the credibility of people who evaluate them, and more likely to distort the reasons for their failures and successes.[48] Conversely, low self-esteem people are more likely to acknowledge the possibility of failure, and, when they do fail, they "spend more free time practicing at tasks at which they have failed than at tasks at which they have succeeded."[49]

When we form our self-definition, we frequently imbue these beliefs about ourselves with a sense of constancy, giving our virtues a permanence that defies the realities of our behavior and the insights of neuroscience.[50] This sense of

[43]   See Baumeister, Roy (Ed.). (1999). *The self in social psychology*. Philadelphia: Psychology Press.

[44]   See Baumeister, Roy (Ed.). (1993). *Self-esteem*. New York: Plenum Press.

[45]   Blaine, Bruce, & Crocker, Jennifer. (1993). Self-esteem and self-serving biases in reactions to positive and negative events. In Baumeister, *supra* note 44 at 75.

[46]   Ibid. at 80   [47]   Ibid. at 75, 80

[48]   Ibid. at 78–79. See Crocker, Jennifer, & Nuer, Noah. (2003). The insatiable quest for self-worth. *Psychological Inquiry*, 14(1), 1. Ludeman, Kate, & Erlandson, Eddie. (2004, May). Coaching the alpha male. *Harvard Business Review*, p. 60. Argyris, Chris. (1991). Teaching smart people how to learn. *Harvard Business Review*, 69(3), 99.

[49]   Blaine & Crocker, *supra* note 45 at 78. Blaine & Crocker cite Baumeister, Roy, & Tice, Dianne. (1985). Self-esteem and responses to success and failure: Subsequent performance and intrinsic motivation. *Journal of Personality*, 53, 450–467. See Sonnenfeld, Jeffrey, & Ward, Andrew. (2007). *Firing back: How great leaders rebound after career disasters*. Boston, Massachusetts: Harvard Business School Press.

[50]   See Auerbach, John, Levy, Kenneth, & Schaffer, Carrie. (Eds.). (2005). Relatedness, self-definition and mental representation. New York: Routledge. Kagan, Jerome, & Snidman, Nancy. (2009). *The long shadow of temperament*. Cambridge, Massachusetts: Belknap Press.

constancy – the illusion of a unitary self – is pernicious. It leads us to perceive and respond to new challenges by superimposing our self-definition over them instead of recognizing the nuances of the challenges and the multiple ways in which our minds are actually reacting to them. To paraphrase Anais Nin, we see the world as we think we are, not as it is and certainly not as we really are.[51]

Persistent, unitary self-definitions have an extraordinary effect on our decision making in general and our ethical behavior in particular. People who define themselves as having high morals ("high moral identity") and believe they have acted morally in the past ("moral credentials") actually act less morally than other people.[52] As psychologist Sonya Sachdeva and her colleagues have demonstrated in numerous experiments, "affirming a moral identity leads people to feel licensed to act immorally."[53] "Moral licensing," she explains, "lowers the bar of what is considered to be an amoral activity so that people are more likely to do immoral things that yield various types of secular benefits."[54] Whether this occurs because people with a perceived moral surplus feel entitled to engage in immoral behavior or they misconstrue their own behavior so that it seems moral is unclear; but for the victims of the immoral behavior that inquiry is inconsequential.[55]

People with high moral identity and moral credentials act as though a durable self-definition can override a dissonant self-revelation. The tendency of self-defined virtuous people to act without virtue has been demonstrated in multiple experiments by independent psychologists.[56] The results of these experiments reveal the self-delusion that attends high moral identity:

Cf. Aquino, Karl, & Reed, Americus. (2002). The self-importance of moral identity. *Journal of Personality and Social Psychology*, 83(6), 1423–1440.

[51] Anais Nin is reputed to have said, "We do not see things as they are. We see things as we are." Lack, Jeremy. (2011). The neurophysiology of ADR and process design: A new approach to conflict prevention and resolution? In Rovine, Arthur (Ed.). *Contemporary issues in international arbitration and mediation* (p. 341). Leiden, The Netherlands: Martinus Nijhoff Publishers. This phrase also has been attributed to *The Talmud*. See Myers, David G. (2002). *Intuition: Its powers and perils* (p. 73). New Haven, Connecticut: Yale University Press.

[52] See Robbennolt, Jennifer, & Sternlight, Jean. (2012). *Psychology for lawyers* (p. 399). Chicago: American Bar Association.

[53] Sachdeva, S., Iliev, R., & Medin, D. L. (2009). Sinning saints and saintly sinners: The paradox of moral self-regulation. *Psychological Science*, 20(4), 523.

[54] Ibid.

[55] Merritt, Anna C., Effron, Daniel A., & Monin, Benoît. (2010). Moral self-licensing: When being good frees us to be bad. *Social and Personality Psychology Compass*, 4 (5), 344–357.

[56] Ibid. See Jordan, Jennifer, Leliveld, Marijke, & Tenbrunsel, Ann. (2015, December 15). The moral self-image scale: Measuring and understanding the malleability of the moral self. *Frontiers in Psychology*, 6, Article 1878. Quintanilla, Victor D., & Kaiser, Cheryl R. (2016). The same-actor inference of nondiscrimination: Moral credentialing and the psychological and legal licensing of bias. *California Law Review*, 104(1), 1, 15.

- Study participants, who were asked to recall a time when they had acted morally, cheated more often on a math exam and expressed less willingness to engage in altruistic activities like donating blood, volunteering, and giving money to a charity when compared with participants who were asked to recall a time when they had acted *im*morally.[57]

- Study participants given a set of positive words (e.g., fair, generous, kind) to use in a brief story about themselves were comparatively stingy in making charitable donations, more likely to breach agreements, and relatively confident that they would not be caught breaching the agreement. After they wrote their story, using the positive words to describe themselves, they were asked to make a small donation to a charity of their choice. The amount they chose to donate was one-fifth of the amount selected by study participants given negative words (e.g., mean, selfish, greedy) to include in their story. The study participants in the positive-traits condition also were more likely than the participants in the negative-traits condition to surreptitiously violate an agreement they had reached with other business owners in a simulated environmental dispute. The positive-trait condition participants also were convinced that they were less likely to get caught when they failed to perform that agreement.[58]

- In a simulated employment decision, men who were given an opportunity to establish their aversion to sexist attitudes (by expressing their objections to blatantly sexist statements) were more likely to discriminate against female candidates in subsequent hiring decisions.[59] Similarly, the act of recommending a black person for a job, and thereby establishing moral credentials in their minds, increased study participants' subsequent willingness to discriminate against a black job candidate. It also increased the participants' likelihood of expressing attitudes "of a sexist or racist disposition."[60]

Ironically, viewing ourselves as moral actors seems to increase our tendency to act immorally, and the specific process of credentialing ourselves as

---

[57] Jordan, Jennifer, Mullen, Elizabeth, & Murnighan, J. Keith. (2011). Striving for the moral self: The effects of recalling past moral actions on future moral behavior. *Personality and Social Psychology Bulletin*, XX(X), 1–13. In another study, moral credentialing, effectuated through four hypothetical moral dilemmas, was correlated with higher cheating levels on math problems. Brown, Ryan. (2011). Moral credentialing and the rationalization of misconduct. *Ethics and Behavior*, 21(1), 1–12.

[58] Sachdeva, Iliev, & Medin, *supra* note 53 at 523.

[59] Monin, B., & Miller, D. T. (2001). Moral credentials and the expression of prejudice. *Journal of Personality and Social Psychology*, 81, 33–43.

[60] Ibid. at 40.

nonprejudiced actors increases the likelihood of acting with prejudice. Moral credentialing, whether it involves real or imagined behavior, "can free people to behave according to their 'darker' impulses, loosening the bonds of self-restraint imposed by a socially tuned conscience."[61]

Static Self Illusion

The static self illusion is the belief that our behavior is invariant and that some people are consistently good and others are consistently bad. This belief in a unified, constant self is flattering and alluring, especially if you see yourself in the good person bloc. But our perceived virtue is a poor predictor of actual behavior.[62] The circumstances that precede our decisions and actions exert a powerful yet imperceptible effect on behavior and demonstrate that we rarely have the dispositional fortitude that we represent to the world. Psychology professor Karl Aquino describes how the realties of human behavior clash with our simplistic views of a unified, morally intransigent self:

> But dividing the people of the world into the wicked or the virtuous does not fully capture the contingent nature of human morality. Even the most pious person sometimes violates moral standards he or she claims to hold dear, and even the meanest scoundrel sometimes displays acts of kindness and gener- osity. That we vacillate from abandoning our moral principles in one situa- tion to acting on them with extraordinary will and determination in another is merely to recognize that in the messy, imperfect world of everyday morality, the situations in which we find ourselves can often be decisive in determining the direction toward which our moral compass turns.[63]

When we underestimate the strong and insidious effects of circumstances and fail to acknowledge the complexities of human decision making and behavior, we set ourselves up for large-scale failures. Fooling ourselves into thinking that we are not vulnerable to the attractions and rationalizations that have misled others – "I'm not the sort of person who would do that" – is the ultimate self-conceit.

Believing that we have a unified, constant self also reflects a serious mis- understanding of how our brains are structured and how our minds actually make decisions. Although we fondly imagine that we are the captains of our

---

[61] Brown, *supra* note 57 at 2.

[62] For a discussion of whether personality in general is an unreliable predictor of behavior see Wilson, *supra* note 18 at 70–73, discussing Walter Mischel's research.

[63] Aquino, Karl, Freeman, Dan, Reed, II, Americus, Lim, Vivien, & Felps, Will. (2009). Testing a social-cognitive model of moral behavior: The interactive influence of situations and moral identity centrality. *Journal of Personality and Social Psychology*, 97(1), 123.

souls, it would be more realistic to see ourselves as continually struggling with a mutinous crew. This follows from the fact that the brain has about 100 billion neurons, and each neuron is making up to 10,000 connections through synapses.[64] "Given these figures," explains neuroscientist V.S. Ramachandran, "it's been calculated that the number of possible brain states – the number of permutations and combinations of activity that are theoretically possible – exceeds the number of elementary particles in the universe."[65] At any moment, millions of local processors are making decisions, and the critical networks are distributed troughout the brain.[66] Although we can discern some hierarchy *within* the brain's modules, "it's looking like there is no hierarchy *among* the modules. All these modules are not reporting to a department head, it is a free-for-all, self-organizing system."[67]

Recognizing that the brain consists of multiple structures constantly competing with each other for dominance, we can better understand why we prefer to acknowledge and define ourselves by certain characteristics and disregard the existence of other characteristics. When a judge says she is inclined to deny our client's motion at a hearing, for example, we may simultaneously entertain the idea of hurling a laptop at the judge while mentally rehearsing a deferential, sophisticated argument that will overcome the court's tentative decision. Neither reaction is less authentic than the other or less representative of who we actually are at that moment. But attorneys will tell you about their arguments and forget the seconds they felt unsettled by the intensity of their visceral reactions.

When we indulge the illusion of a static self with permanent traits, we choose to ignore the fact that our brains are wildly complex mechanisms without a central command center, requiring a continually high level of awareness and attention from us. The static self illusion invites us to disregard our two minds or selves – the static self, which is easy to define and control, and the dynamic self, which is largely unknown and typically unruly – to present a concordant person to ourselves and everyone else. Our emphasis on the static self, to the exclusion of the dynamic self, is deceptive and inconsistent with scientific knowledge indicating that we "are literally remaking our brains – who we are and how we think, with all our actions, reactions, perceptions, postures, and positions – every minute of the day and every day of the week and every month and year of our entire lives."[68]

[64] Epley, Nicholas. (2014). *Mindwise* (p. 24). New York: Knopf. [65] Ibid.
[66] Gazzaniga, Michael S. (2011). *Who's in charge* (p. 44). New York: Ecco Press.
[67] Ibid. at 69–70. (Emphasis provided).
[68] Andreasen, Nancy. (2005). *The creative brain* (p. 146). New York: Penguin Group.

Antonio Damasio, a renowned neurologist and professor of neuroscience, has discovered that our dynamic self is indeed our core self, "a transient entity, ceaselessly re-created for each and every object with which the brain interacts."[69] Since we are more comfortable with our static self and can never quite get a grip on our dynamic self, we tend to define ourselves by our static self, as Damasio explains:

> Our traditional notion of self, however, is linked to the idea of identity and corresponds to a nontransient collection of unique facts and ways of being which characterize a person. My term for that entity is the *autobiographical self*. The autobiographical self depends on systematized memories of situations in which core consciousness was involved in the knowing of the most invariant characteristics of an organism's life – who you were born to, where, when, your likes and dislikes, the way you usually react to a problem or a conflict, your name, and so on. I use the term *autobiographical memory* to denote the organized record of the main aspects of an organism's biography.[70]

This static self – the autobiographical self – delimits many attorneys' self-knowledge. For that reason, they have a "good person" self-definition that is more constructed than discovered.[71] They are highly susceptible to the decision-making errors and ethical shortcomings that characterize people with high moral identity and moral credentials. Self-discerning attorneys, in contrast, learn a skill that Damasio calls the "orderly enhancement of both kinds of consciousness," attending to both the transient core self and the static autobiographical self.[72]

Omniscience

When you are charging $250–$1,250 per hour, it is difficult to admit that you don't know the answer to a client's inquiry. After a few years of providing opinions that are only partly correct or are stated with a degree of certainty unmatched by our knowledge or the state of the law itself, we develop chronic overconfidence. Our initial belief that partial answers or overstatements can be corrected later by some quick legal research yields to a growing conviction that we actually know more than we realized.

---

[69] Damasio, Antonio. (1999). *The feeling of what happens* (p. 17). Orlando, Florida: Houghton Mifflin.

[70] Ibid.

[71] Siebert, Al. (2010). *The survivor personality* (p. 106). New York: Penguin Group. (The good person "has a constructed personality, not a discovered personality.")

[72] Ibid.

The American Bar Association cautions against this tendency to overestimate our knowledge and underestimate its limitations. The Fundamental Values of the Profession urge attorneys to develop "a realistic sense of the limits of the lawyer's own skills and knowledge."[73] Recognizing a duty to objectively assess our own competence, the American Bar Association also instructs attorneys to advise clients "of the limits of the lawyer's skills" and to "refrain from handling matters that are beyond the lawyer's range of competence."[74] In the abstract, it seems that attorneys would want to avoid practice areas outside their expertise. But as a practical matter attorneys "feel pressured to take cases outside their focal areas of practice" and, as a result, increase their exposure to malpractice claims.[75] "Always remember," write professional liability experts Mark Bassingthwaighte and Reba Nance, "that we don't know what we don't know and therein lies the problem."[76]

Knowing what we don't know – and being upfront about it with clients – is particularly difficult for attorneys who have succeeded in an educational system that rewards quick answers and treats hesitancy as a scholastic deficiency. Our reluctance to acknowledge that we do not have adequate information or skills is compounded by five propensities: (1) lack of awareness of our ignorance ("we are bad at knowing we don't know");[77] (2) delusions about the quality of our knowledge ("the same process that makes you know less also makes you satisfied with your knowledge");[78] (3) reticence to ask questions that might reveal our ignorance ("we don't ask for clarification because we fear what we might hear");[79] (4) a belief that any answer is better than none ("we are very, very good at making stuff up");[80] and (5) the habit of responding to a complex question by seeing only the part we understand ("when faced with a difficult question, we often answer an easier one instead").[81] Collectively,

---

[73] American Bar Association Section of Legal Education and Admissions to the Bar, *supra* note 1 at 208.

[74] Ibid. at 208–209.

[75] Jaffee, Lisa. Ten tips to assist in avoiding a malpractice claim. *CNA Professional Counsel* (p. 3). See Pinnington, Daniel. (2010, July/August). Avoiding malpractice – Are you at risk? *Law Practice*, 36(4), 29.

[76] Bassingthwaighte, C. S., & Nance, Reba J. (2006). The top ten causes of malpractice – and how you can avoid them. Program materials presented at ABA TECHSHOW® 2006, April 20–22, 2006, Chicago, Illinois.

[77] Schulz, Kathryn. (2011). *Being wrong* (p. 82). New York: Ecco Press.

[78] Taleb, Nassim. (2010). *The black swan* (p. 147). New York: Random House.

[79] DeLong, Thomas. (2011). *Flying without a net* (p. 57). Brighton, Massachusetts: Harvard Business Review Press.

[80] Schulz, *supra* note 77 at 70.

[81] Kahneman, Daniel. (2011). *Thinking fast and slow* (p. 12). New York: Farrar, Straus and Giroux.

these propensities hide our ignorance and maintain the illusion that we already have sufficient knowledge and expertise. They halt self-development because, as Alfred North Whitehead observed, "ignorance of ignorance is the death of knowledge."[82]

Stress/Anxiety

Stress management is a critical skill for lawyers. This skill may be increasingly important because lawyers suffer disproportionately from anxiety and depression and appear to have ineffective coping skills. A recent survey of 12,825 attorneys confirms that attorneys show a unique susceptibility to behavioral health problems: "Levels of depression, anxiety, and stress among attorneys reported here are significant, with 28 percent, 19 percent, and 23 percent experiencing mild or higher levels of depression, anxiety, and stress, respectively. In terms of career prevalence, 61 percent reported concerns with anxiety at some point in their career and 46 percent reported concerns with depression."[83] Notably, 11.5 percent of the attorneys "reported suicidal thoughts at some point during their career,"[84] an incidence that compares favorably with an earlier study finding that 11 percent of attorneys experienced suicidal ideation at least once a month.[85] This survey data and other studies indicate that the incidence of mental health disorders among attorneys ranges from two times to six times that of the general population.[86]

The survey indicates that depression, anxiety, and stress are associated with specific personal and professional characteristics:

- Men reported higher levels of depression, while women had higher anxiety levels.
- Junior and senior associates were more likely to suffer from anxiety and stress than junior and senior partners.

[82] Burton, Robert. (2008). *On being certain* (p. 216). New York: St. Martin's Press.
[83] Krill, Patrick R., Johnson, Ryan, & Albert, Linda. (2016, January/February). The prevalence of substance use and other mental health concerns among American attorneys. *Journal of Addiction Medicine*, 10(1), 51.
[84] Ibid. at 50.   [85] Keeva, Steven. (2006, January). Depression takes a toll. *ABA Journal*, p. 38.
[86] McQueen, M. P. (2016, February 4). The legal profession's drinking problem is worse than we thought. *The Am Law Daily*. See Weiss, Debra Cassens. (2007, December 13). Lawyer depression comes out of the closet. *ABA Journal, Law News Now*. Jones, Leigh. (2008, March 12). ABA law student group tackles depression. *National Law Journal Online*. Daicoff, Susan. (1997). Lawyer know thyself: A review of empirical research on attorney attributes bearing on professionalism. *American University Law Review*, 46, 1337, 1378, 1379. Daicoff, Susan. (2004). *Lawyer, know thyself* (pp. 99–139). Washington, DC: American Psychological Association.

- Attorneys employed in government, in-house, public, or nonprofit organizations reported lower levels of depression, anxiety, and stress than attorneys in private practices.
- Senior partners in firms reported the lowest levels of depression, anxiety, and stress.[87]

Patrick Krill, an attorney and one of the study coauthors, believes that mental health impairment may be attributable to the type of person attracted to the legal profession in the first place – "competitive, driven, ambitious, hardworking people who prioritize success and accomplishment way above personal health and well being."[88]

Anxiety not only damages attorneys' mental health but also seriously impairs their professional performance and harms their client relations. This source of stress alters brain function, releasing cortisol, adrenaline, norepinephrine, and other hormones and neurotransmitters that impair memory, learning, attention, judgment, empathy, and impulse control.[89] Stress also reduces self-confidence and the ability to distinguish between relevant and irrelevant information, while increasing defensiveness and perseveration (the repetition of an action after it has ceased to be appropriate).[90] Although a moderate amount of stress increases attention, alertness, and efficiency, chronic stress can lead to dementia, atrophy of the frontal cortex, and other forms of permanent brain damage.[91]

The high-quality analysis and deliberation that clients justifiably expect from their attorneys disappear under stress. The brain reverts to a more primitive mode of processing information under pressure, forcing us to overemphasize initial information, disregard later, contradictory information, underestimate side effects and long-term consequences of decisions, rely on

---

[87] Krill, *supra* note 83 at 50.   [88] McQueen, *supra* note 86.

[89] Mora, F., Segovia, G., Del Arco, A., de Blas, M., & Garrido P. (2012, October 2). Stress, neurotransmitters, corticosterone and body-brain integration. *Brain Research*, 1476, 71–85. Southwick, Steven, & Carney, Dennis. (2012). *Resilience* (p. 140). New York: Cambridge University Press. Sapolsky, Robert. (2015, January 16). When stress rises, empathy suffers. *The Wall Street Journal.*

[90] For effects of stress on self-confidence, see Gino, Francesca, Brooks, Alison, & Schweitzer, Maurice. (2012). Anxiety, advice, and the ability to discern: Feeling anxious motivates individuals to seek and use advice. *Journal of Personality and Social Psychology*, 102(3), 497–512.

[91] McEwen, B. S. (2000, December 15). The neurobiology of stress: From serendipity to clinical relevance. *Brain Research*, 886(1–2), 172–189. Fryer, Bronwyn. (2005, November). Are you working too hard? A conversation with mind/body researcher Herbert Benson. *Harvard Business Review*. Sapolsky, Robert. (2014, July 24). Stress hormones that leave marks on trading floors. *The Wall Street Journal.* Southwick & Carney, *supra* note 89.

stereotypes, overlook nuance, dismiss conflicting viewpoints, and elevate the need for closure over the duty of competent representation.[92] Stress overrides the deliberative functions of the brain, as psychology professor Gary Marcus explains: "as the demands on the brain, so-called *cognitive load*, increase, the ancestral system continues business as usual – while the more modern deliberative system gets left behind. Precisely when the cognitive chips are down, when we most need our more evolved (and theoretically sounder) faculties, they can let us down and leave us less judicious."[93] Stress, then, is more than an uncomfortable sensation; it cordons off an entire range of faculties required for competent performance.

Stress has been treated effectively by cognitive behavioral therapy (CBT).[94] CBT therapists, law professor Larry Cunningham relates, teach patients to ask three questions about thoughts and conditions generating stress: "(1) 'What is the evidence for and against the belief?;' (2) 'What are alternative interpretations of the event or situation?;' and (3) 'What are the real implications, if the belief is correct?'"[95] Using a law student's anxiety about an upcoming oral argument as an example, Cunningham identifies these steps in applying CBT principles:[96]

- Acknowledge and talk about anxiety and ways of reducing it and recognize that anxiety often is a normal reaction.
- Correct unrealistic thoughts, discuss why judges ask questions during oral agreement, identify techniques for handling judges' questions, and redirect anxiety by focusing on positive aspects of the experience.
- Learn deep breathing exercises. ("When you know how to breathe, the word 'stress' is not in the dictionary," says 80-year-old clarinet player Giora Feidman.)[97]

---

[92] Holmes, Jaime. (2015). *Nonsense* (pp. 13, 75). New York: Crown. Dorner, Dietrich. (1997). *The logic of failure* (p. 33). New York: Perseus Books. Bonner, Sarah. (2007). *Judgment and decision making in accounting* (pp. 247–248). London: Pearson. Brown, Jeff, & Fenske, Mark. (2010). *The winner's brain* (pp. 112, 204). Boston, Massachusetts: Da Capo Lifelong Books.

[93] Marcus, Gary. (2008). *Kluge* (p. 146). New York: Houghton Mifflin Co.

[94] Many forms of anxiety disorders are identified in the American Psychological Association's *Diagnostic and Statistical Manual of Mental Disorders* (DSM-5). Any person seeking treatment for anxiety, of course, should consult a mental health professional, as this book's brief discussion of CBT can only highlight some features that may not be advisable or helpful in treating various forms of anxiety.

[95] Cunningham, Larry. (2015). Using principles from cognitive behavioral therapy to reduce nervousness in oral argument or moot court. *Nevada Law Journal*, 15(2), 599.

[96] Ibid. at 603–604.

[97] Wollan, Malia. (2016, July 24). How to breathe. *The New York Times Magazine*, p. MM21.

- Prepare thoroughly for the oral argument to build confidence, antici-pate questions, and develop materials that could provide comfort, e.g., a document binder or argument summary.
- Simulate the argument in a small group presentation and practice in an office, conference room, moot courtroom, or a vacant courtroom.
- Consider how qualified you are to make the argument (knowledge of record, familiarity with argument, legal research to support argument) and set realistic expectations.
- Acknowledge nervousness but do not dwell on it, allowing it to pass.

These steps are consistent with the CBT methods employed by Joseph Bankman, a law professor who is also trained as a clinical psychologist.[98] His successful programs, designed to reduce anxiety and depression, teach legal professionals to "(1) notice and identify negative automatic thoughts; (2) ques-tion automatic thoughts for accuracy or utility; (3) identify inaccuracy, exag-geration, or error (also referred to as cognitive distortions or unhelpful thoughts); and (4) challenge cognitive distortions and reframe automatic thoughts to interrupt the cycle and change emotions, physical sensations, and behaviors."[99]

Aggressiveness

Aggressiveness looms large in clients' expectations of attorneys. When clients are sued, their press releases typically proclaim, "We are absolutely certain that it is without merit and we will defend ourselves aggressively against any of the claims."[100] In response to these expectations, attorneys question whether they are projecting the requisite aura of aggressiveness to impress and retain clients. For many attorneys, this question is answered by defaulting to familiar behaviors that actually are pathological; attorneys display higher rates of hostile personality disorder than the general population, and they "feel a lot of hostility and anger and experience more paranoia than most people."[101] Hostility is the only symptom of psychological distress, according to one study,

[98] Fenner, Randee. (2015, April 7). Stanford law professor creates new way to help students deal with the stress of it all. *Stanford News*.

[99] Bankman, Joseph. Psychoeducation about anxiety – for you and your students. (Unpublished course materials on file with author).

[100] See, for example, Krolicki, Kevin (2009, August 13). Chrysler creditors win approval for Daimler suit. *Reuters*. Retrieved from www.reuters.com/article/retire-us-daimler-chrysler-idUSTRE57C4ZX20090813.

[101] Daicoff, *supra* note 86 at 10, 151. See Kiser, Randall (2010). *Beyond right and wrong* (p. 184). Berlin, New York: Springer.

that is *not* more common among male attorneys than female attorneys.[102] Hostility, it appears, is the most democratic disorder afflicting attorneys, degrading male attorney and female attorney performance with equal force.

The tension between projecting an aggressive image and being an effective attorney is described by Mark Herrmann, Vice President and Chief Counsel – Litigation at Aon, one of the world's largest insurance brokerages:

> I've recently heard several tales of business folks (or in-house lawyers) worrying that outside counsel is not aggressive enough. What prompts the concern is the lawyer's performance during a conference call or at a meeting: The lawyer is civilized. The lawyer speaks quietly, asks probing questions, gives intelligent advice, and appears to be an effective advocate.
>
> After the meeting, one of the participants says: "Are you sure we should use that guy? He doesn't seem very aggressive."
>
> Remarkably (at least to me), I've heard the same thing at law firms. I've heard transactional lawyers wonder about litigators who are calm and intelligent at the lunch table: "He's such a nice guy. I'm not sure I'd trust him in court."[103]

Herrmann says he has three reactions to these concerns about an attorney's aggressiveness. First, being a good litigator does not mean that you are aggressive; some of the best litigators, he states, "have been low-key people who would quietly and methodically unearth great legal theories and disembowel witnesses on cross."[104] Second, attorneys display different personality traits in different situations and should not be judged as aggressive or unaggressive based on a single encounter. Third, "being a blowhard can in fact undermine a lawyer's effectiveness. As a client, I really don't need to spend money on tangential discovery disputes caused by lawyers with too much testosterone being unable to get along."[105]

When we closely examine aggressiveness, we find that it has little value to clients or attorneys. In negotiations, attorneys who display an aggressive, competitive style generally obtain worse results than attorneys who adopt a cooperative, problem-solving style.[106] In one study, for example, "only

---

[102]   Daicoff, *supra* note 86 at 10.

[103]   Herrmann, Mark. (2012, February 16). Inside straight: Is our lawyer aggressive enough? *Above the law*. Retrieved from http://abovethelaw.com/2012/02/inside-straight-is-our-lawyer-aggressive-enough/?rf=1

[104]   Ibid.   [105]   Ibid.

[106]   Schneider, Andrea K. (2002). Shattering negotiation myths: Empirical evidence on the effectiveness of negotiation style. *Harvard Negotiation Law Review*, 7, 143–233. See Craver, Charles. (2002). *The intelligent negotiator* (pp. 3–19). Roseville, California: Prima Publishing.

9 percent of the attorneys perceived to be effective negotiators by their peers exhibited combative, inflexible, self-centered and arrogant behavior, while 91 percent of the attorneys perceived to be effective negotiators displayed trustworthy, personable, communicative, perceptive and adaptable behavior."[107] In another study, 59 percent of "Cooperators" were considered to be effective negotiators, but only 25 percent of "Adversarial" negotiators were regarded as proficient.[108] Recognizing that he achieves better results by avoiding an aggressive negotiation style, a noted civil litigation attorney remarks, "Braying, bragging, threatening, expressly or implicitly, will draw a conclusion that you are not as good as you want them to think you are. Understatement creates more anxiety in your opponent than braggadocio and will produce a better settlement."[109]

Law professor Charles Craver, who has taught negotiation skills for about 40 years, finds that cooperative/problem-solving negotiators are more likely than their competitive/adversarial colleagues to achieve results that maximize the benefits to all parties. When negotiators simultaneously attempt to maximize their own client's returns and attempt to enhance opponent's interests, he asserts, they are more likely to reach an agreement and are "more likely to obtain the best settlement for their own clients."[110] Professor Craver dismisses the idea that aggressiveness is essential to effective negotiation: "The notion that one must be uncooperative, selfish, manipulative, and even abrasive to be successful is erroneous. One must simply possess the capacity to say 'no' forcefully and credibly in order to achieve beneficial negotiation results. They can do so courteously and quietly – and be as effective as those who do so more demonstrably."[111]

The IAALS survey of 24,137 attorneys, discussed in Chapter 2, also suggests that aggressiveness is considerably less important than nuanced, subtle skills like adaptability, flexibility, foresight, and anticipation. Although the IAALS study does not specifically evaluate the importance of aggressiveness, it does measure the importance of scaled-down concepts like "assertiveness" and "confidence."[112] As shown in Table 3.1, assertiveness and confidence are ranked below more complex problem-solving skills like assessing likely

[107] Kiser, Randall. (2011). *How leading lawyers think* (pp. 170–171). Heidelberg, New York: Springer.

[108] Craver (2002), *supra* note 106 at 10.   [109] Kiser (2011), *supra* note 107 at 198.

[110] Craver, Charles. (2009). *Effective legal negotiation and settlement* (6th ed.) (pp. 11, 13). Newark, New Jersey: Matthew Bender.

[111] Craver (2009), *supra* note 110 at 11.

[112] Gerkman, Alli, & Cornett, Logan. (2016, July). *Foundations for practice: The whole lawyer and the character quotient* (p. 16). Denver, Colorado: Institute for the Advancement of the American Legal System.

TABLE 3.1. *Comparative importance of confidence, assertiveness, flexibility, foresight, and anticipation in IAALS 2016 survey*

Quality/Skill	Necessary immediately (%)	Necessary over time (%)	Necessary immediately or over time (%)
Adopt work habits to meet demands and expectations	70.8	26.9	97.7
Understand when to engage a supervisor or seek advice in problem solving	75.2	22.3	97.5
Exhibit flexibility and adaptability regarding unforeseen, ambiguous, or changing circumstances	58.1	39.0	97.1
Anticipate case, project, or workload needs	42.5	54	96.5
Assess possible courses of action and the range of likely outcomes in terms of risks and rewards	33.1	62.6	95.7
Think strategically	46.2	48.7	94.9
Proactively provide status updates to those involved on a matter	73.5	19.8	93.3
Take ownership	70.4	23.0	93.4
Confidence	38.6	54.5	93.1
Show initiative	74.8	17.7	92.5
Assertiveness	31.9	46.5	78.4

Source: IAALS, Foundations for Practice (2016)

outcomes of possible courses of action, adapting to changing circumstances and demands, anticipating needs, taking ownership of problems, and thinking strategically.[113] Assertiveness is ranked nearly 20 percentage points below "flexibility and adaptability regarding unforeseen, ambiguous or changing circumstances."[114]

Although attorneys stereotypically project obstinacy and aggressiveness, it appears that those characteristics are overrated and frequently counterproductive. Attorneys today need complex problem-solving skills that emphasize adaptability, flexibility, foresight, and anticipation – skills considerably more difficult to develop than those exhibited by aggressive

[113] Ibid. at 8, 11, 13, 14, 16, 17, 21   [114] *Ibid.* at 16, 17.

attorneys' expensive, protracted iterations of primate ground slapping, screaming, and vegetation tearing. Aggressiveness is an easy diversion from problem solving and a provocative, dangerous strategy; it tends to appease clients in the short term and harm their interests in the long term. When deployed, its insult is deep and lasting, decimating the trust necessary to establish a constructive working relationship with opposing parties.

Looking back on his mistaken reliance on aggressiveness in the early phase of his career, a noted New York City trial attorney recalls his realization that his style was ineffectual:

> When I first started practicing, the idea was you had to be tough – yelling, fighting. When I would talk with my dad about my work – he was a defense attorney – he would ask, "Why are you yelling?" Of course, I didn't pay any attention to him because he was my dad. Then a few years into my career, I had a trial with one of the best trial attorneys in the City – the Top 1 or 2. I saw him talking to them [jurors] like they were family. I thought, "Holy Shit! This is what my father has been telling me. Look at what I could do by being calm and assertive." It just hit me – Holy Mackerel.[115]

Although the realization was sudden, his evolution was slow. Recalling his difficulties in adopting a less antagonistic style, he muses, "it took a while to learn." But over time, he told himself, "You cannot be nasty. You cannot be cynical."[116]

Extrinsic Motivation

We often characterize people as motivated or unmotivated. For lawyers, the more important distinction might be whether they are driven by intrinsic motivation or extrinsic motivation. Intrinsic motivation is the drive to achieve a goal or accomplish a purpose because it has meaning and value independent of tangible rewards.[117] Extrinsic motivation, in contrast, is centered on the direct, tangible rewards (usually money) that can be obtained by completing a task or being promoted to a new position. An intrinsically motivated person would ask, "How can I solve this problem," while an extrinsically motivated person would ask, "What will solving this problem do for me?"[118] For

---

[115] Transcript of Attorney Interview P34 for study reported in Kiser (2011), *supra* note 107.

[116] Ibid.

[117] Runco, Mark A. (2007). Motivation, competence, and creativity. In Elliot, Andrew J., & Dweck, Carol S. (Eds.). *Handbook of competence and motivation* (p. 613). New York: The Guilford Press.

[118] Colvin, Geoff. (2008). *Talent is overrated* (p. 188). New York: Penguin Group.

intrinsically motivated people, the work is inherently interesting and challenging. For extrinsically motivated people, the work is instrumental; it must lead to something else.[119]

The source of your motivation turns out to be strongly determinative of your attitude toward your work and your actual performance.[120] People who have extrinsic motivation display consistently higher levels of anxiety and depression and lower levels of cooperation, ethical behavior, and complexity in problem solving than people whose motivation is intrinsic.[121] Ironically, trying to motivate people with more tangible rewards like increased compensation tends to result in worse performance and more cheating, risk-taking, and short-term decision making.[122] Extrinsic rewards also undermine our sense of autonomy, drain our sense of enthusiasm, and quickly become addictive, generating a downward spiral of dependence and resentment.[123] Like mice in a sucrose addiction experiment, extrinsically motivated people compulsively seek external rewards long after reaching a state of plenitude.[124]

For clients working with extrinsically motivated attorneys, the most detrimental impact may be the loss of their attorneys' problem-solving abilities. Extrinsic motivation is correlated with a narrow focus and diminished creativity in problem solving, while intrinsic motivation is correlated with breadth of analysis and enhanced creativity.[125] The drive for money, prestige, and

---

[119] Deci, Edward, & Moller, Arlen. (2007). The concept of competence. In Elliot, Andrew J., & Dweck, Carol S. (Eds.). *Handbook of competence and motivation* (p. 579–589). New York: The Guilford Press.

[120] See Wrzesniewski, Amy, Schwartz, Barry, Cong, Xiangyu, Kane, Michael, Omar, Audrey, & Kolditz, Thomas. (2014). Multiple types of motives don't multiply the motivation of West Point cadets. *Proceedings of the National Academy of Sciences of the United States of America*, 111(30), 10990, 10993–10994. Wrzesniewski, Amy, & Schwartz, Barry. (2014, July 4). The secret of effective motivation. *The New York Times*.

[121] Pink, Daniel H. (2009). *Drive* (pp. 50, 141–142). New York: Riverhead Books. Deci, Edward. (1995). *Why we do what we do* (pp. 51, 128). New York: Penguin Group.

[122] Pink, *supra* note 121 at 37–38, 57. Ryan, Richard, & Brown, Kirk. (2007). Legislating competence. In Elliot, Andrew J., & Dweck, Carol S. (Eds.). *Handbook of competence and motivation* (pp. 361–362.). New York: The Guilford Press. Deci and Moller, *supra* note 119 at 584–588. See Brafman, Ori, & Brafman, Rom. (2008). *Sway* (pp. 132–148). New York: Doubleday.

[123] Deci, *supra* note 121 at 27, 31.

[124] For an illustrative experiment with mice, see Nieh, Edward, *et al.* (2015). Decoding neural circuits that control compulsive sucrose seeking. *Cell*, 160(3), 528–541. Even after being fed, the mice in that experiment "behaved bizarrely, gnawing on the bottom of the cage and pantomiming the motions of bringing a food nugget to the mouth and chewing it." Decoding sugar addiction: Separate neural circuits control sugar cravings and healthy eating, researchers find. (2015, January 29). *MIT News*.

[125] Colvin, *supra* note 118 at 191. Pink *supra* note 121 at 50, 54–55.

power, which characterizes extrinsic motivation, appears to crush creativity, as psychologist Jeff Brown and neuroscientist Mark Fenske report:

> It seems that productivity and external reward are inversely proportional after a certain threshold. To begin with, extrinsic rewards tend to encourage people to focus narrowly on a task, to do it as quickly as possible, and to take few risks. They focus on getting the prize and less on the creative process of reaching the goal. Second, they often begin to feel as if they are being controlled by the reward, so they tend to be less invested and less performance-oriented than if they were doing it for the sense of accomplishment or even a compliment from the boss. The less self-determined they feel, the more their creative juices dry up.[126]

A notable exception to the research demonstrating that extrinsic rewards undermine performance is evident in studies of dull or boring tasks. Rewards for accomplishing those tasks appear to be effective "because there is little or no intrinsic motivation to be undermined."[127]

Are attorneys vulnerable to the performance deficiencies resulting from extrinsic motivation? The sparse evidence on the subject suggests that many, perhaps most, attorneys are primarily motivated by extrinsic rewards. In a national survey of law students conducted by the American Bar Association Young Lawyers' Division, about one-third of law students identified extrinsic motivations (family pressure, financial opportunity, no attractive alternative, and escaping family background) as their primary reason for attending law school.[128] Similarly, 33 percent of the students in the Class of 2010 at the National University of Singapore identified extrinsic factors (money, job security, social status and prestige, parents and friends) as their primary reason for studying law.[129] This emphasis on external rewards is consistent with a profession that has fostered *The American Lawyer*'s annual ranking of law firms by gross revenue and profits per partner, arguably the most visible shrine to extrinsic motivation ever erected by any profession.

When he was Dean of the University of San Diego Law School, Sheldon Krantz interviewed pre-law and law students to assess their motivations. He

---

[126]   Brown, Jeff, & Fenske, Mark. (2010). *The winner's brain* (p. 76). Cambridge, Massachusetts: Da Capo Press.

[127]   Pink, *supra* note 121 at 60.

[128]   ABA Young Lawyers Division. (1990). *The state of the legal profession–1990*. Chicago: American Bar Association.

[129]   Tan, Seow Hon. (2009, December). Law school and the making of the student into a lawyer: Transformation of first year law students in the National University of Singapore. *Legal Ethics*, 12(2), 131.

found that "a much higher percentage of the students expressed interest in law for reasons related not to altruism, but to money, status or access to power."[130] A student's interview remarks illustrate the differences between intrinsic motivation and extrinsic motivation and how lawyers often resolve that conflict in favor of extrinsic motivation:

> I first wanted to go into oceanography. It seemed like an interesting field to me. I think it was my Mom who said to me one day that I could work hard through school and become an oceanographer and make nothing or I could work just as hard and become an attorney and make money. So my first instinct to become a lawyer was based on greed.[131]

Krantz concluded that students' reasons for selecting a legal career "were primarily materialistic and were linked more to 'helping self' than to 'helping others.'"[132]

This discussion of intrinsic and extrinsic motivation may be unsettling to attorneys who see their personal motivation as tilting toward the extrinsic side. The takeaway from the research, however, is that motivation is context-dependent and people are not permanently intrinsically or extrinsically motivated.[133] When people emphasize external rewards to the exclusion of personal fulfillment they lose interest in their work and develop workarounds to achieve the highest reward with the lowest level of time, attention, and commitment. Over time, this attitude destroys attorneys' professional pride and deprives them of their distinct identity and significance. Since we are driven by "a specifically human longing to find meaning and value,"[134] attorneys who have already lost themselves in external rewards will benefit from discovering an aspect of their current work or possible future work that evokes a sense of curiosity, engagement, excitement, and fulfillment independent of financial compensation. If this approach seems too esoteric or impractical in the real world of law practice, bear in mind the fact that 88 percent of practicing attorneys believe "an *internalized* commitment to developing

---

[130] Krantz, Sheldon. (2013). *The legal profession: What is wrong and how to fix it* (p. 18). Dayton, Ohio: LexisNexis.
[131] Ibid. at 17.   [132] Ibid. at 18.
[133] See Urdan, Tim, & Turner, Julianne. (2007). Competence motivation in the classroom. In Elliot, Andrew J., & Dweck, Carol S. (Eds.). *Handbook of competence and motivation* (pp. 300–301). New York: The Guilford Press. Kanfer, Ruth, & Ackerman, Phillip. (2007). Work competence. In Elliot, Andrew J., & Dweck, Carol S. (Eds.). *Handbook of competence and motivation* (pp. 339–350). New York: The Guilford Press.
[134] Zohar, Danah, & Marshall, Ian. (2000). *SQ: Connecting with our spiritual intelligence* (p. 4). New York: Bloomsbury.

toward excellence" is a trait that must be acquired immediately or over time "for the lawyer's continued success."[135]

Procrastination

"Lawyers are genetically prone to procrastination," quips Craig Riemer, a Superior Court judge in Riverside County, California.[136] If Judge Riemer is correct, lawyers will find themselves in a rapidly expanding crowd of fellow procrastinators. The ranks of "dedicated ditherers," as psychologist Roy Baumeister calls procrastinators, have increased sharply during the last four decades. About 20 percent of adults internationally "consider procrastination to be a defining personal characteristic."[137] In the United States, most Americans characterize themselves as chronic procrastinators, and they waste about one-quarter of their work time procrastinating or thinking about procrastinating.[138]

Although procrastination is frequently regarded as a personal quirk, in reality it caps attorneys' careers at an early stage and frequently prevents them from re-establishing credibility and trust within a firm even after they have overcome procrastination. What starts in adolescence as mildly annoying, sometimes humorous slacking manifests in adulthood as unacceptable neglect and irresponsibility. Many attorneys do not seem to notice or change their habits when the consequences of procrastination shift from being minor, curable, and self-contained in their youth to being serious, irreparable, and uncontrollable in their professional lives. Their first acknowledgment that procrastination is more than a personal idiosyncrasy often occurs when a legal malpractice claim or a state bar disciplinary action is filed.

The consequences of attorney procrastination are sufficiently severe to be addressed specifically in the Comments on the Model Rules of Professional Conduct:

> Perhaps no professional shortcoming is more widely resented than procrasti-
> nation. A client's interests often can be adversely affected by the passage of
> time or the change of conditions; in extreme instances, as when a lawyer
> overlooks a statute of limitations, the client's legal position may be destroyed.
> Even when the client's interests are not affected in substance, however,
> unreasonable delay can cause a client needless anxiety and undermine
> confidence in the lawyer's trustworthiness.[139]

[135] Gerkman & Cornett, *supra* note 112 at 14.
[136] Noblin, Logan. (2016, May 5). Stickler for rules. *San Francisco Daily Journal*, p. 2.
[137] Baumeister, Roy, & Tierney, John. (2011). *Willpower* (p. 240). New York: Penguin Group.
[138] Ibid.   [139] ABA Model Rules of Prof'l Conduct R. 1.3 cmt. 3.

Procrastination not only violates an attorney's ethical responsibilities to clients; it is also a major cause of legal malpractice lawsuits. About 10 percent of legal malpractice actions allege procrastination errors, making it the second most common type of error after "failure to know/properly apply law."[140] The number of malpractice claims alleging procrastination nearly quadrupled in the most recent four-year reporting period.[141]

Since each of us procrastinates occasionally and many of us are chronic procrastinators, it is helpful to identify and dismiss the myths that we tell ourselves about procrastinators. These myths include: (1) procrastinators do their best work under pressure; (2) procrastinators are more relaxed than their deadline-obsessed peers; (3) procrastinators' performance improves when they can set their own deadlines; (4) procrastinators are perfectionists and avoid completing their work until it meets their high standards; and (5) procrastinators tend to be rebellious, neurotic, and less intelligent than their peers. Studies indicate that these myths are widespread and misleading. In fact, the quality of procrastinators' work is generally worse than the quality of non-procrastinators' work; procrastinators' stress, as measured by blood pressure readings and other physical symptoms like frequency of illnesses, is greater than non-procrastinators' stress; procrastinators do not meet their own deadlines when given an opportunity to set them; externally imposed deadlines are more effective than internally imposed deadlines; procrastinators are less likely to be perfectionists than non-procrastinators; the association between procrastination and neuroticism and procrastination and rebelliousness varies from weak to nonexistent; and intellectual ability is unrelated to procrastination.[142]

Research also indicates that procrastinators exhibit higher levels of depression, impulsiveness, distractibility, and creativity and lower levels of

[140] American Bar Association Standing Committee on Lawyers' Professional Liability. (2012). *Profile of legal malpractice claims, 2008–2011* (p. 11). Chicago: American Bar Association.
[141] Ibid.
[142] Baumeister, *supra* note 137 at 240–243. van Eerde, Wendelien. (2003). A meta-analytically derived nomological network of procrastination. *Personality and Individual Differences*, 35, 1401–1418. Steel, Piers. (2007). The nature of procrastination: A meta-analytic and theoretical review of quintessential self-regulatory failure. *Psychological Bulletin*, 133(1), 65–94. Tice, D. M., & Baumeister, R. F. (1997). Longitudinal study of procrastination, performance, stress, and health: The costs and benefits of dawdling. *Psychological Science*, 8, 454–458. Ariely, D., & Wertenbroch, K. (2002). Procrastination, deadlines, and performance: Self-control by precommitment. *Psychological Science*, 13, 219–224. Reuben, Ernesto, Sapienza, Paola, & Zingales, Luigi. (2015, July). Procrastination and impatience. *Journal of Behavioral and Experimental Economics*, 58, 63–76. van Eerde, Wendelien. (2000). Procrastination: Self-regulation in initiating aversive goals. *Applied Psychology: An International Review*, 49(3), 372–389.

self-esteem, self-efficacy, conscientiousness, self-regulation, emotional hardiness, achievement motivation, discipline, and persistence.[143] A strong relationship exists between procrastination and "self-handicapping" (protecting our sense of self-competence by raising impediments to our own performance).[144] People who self-handicap through procrastination hope that their evaluators will think that the cause of any performance shortcomings is lack of effort rather than lack of ability.[145] They invite failure through procrastination but preserve their self-image by intimating that, under the right circumstances, their performance would have been exemplary.

Procrastination ultimately causes more procrastination. Disliking a task initially causes anxiety, which increases the likelihood of procrastination; procrastination then causes inferior performance, which lowers self-efficacy and self-esteem; and lower levels of self-efficacy and self-esteem, in turn, cause more procrastination.[146] We could call this a vicious cycle, but to be candid with ourselves, we should acknowledge that, more importantly, it is a form of self-sabotage. The fallout from serial procrastination includes inferior grades, health, finances, and career progression.[147] The overall effect of procrastination is to "chip away at the most valuable resource in the world: time."[148]

Procrastination generally decreases with experience.[149] But attorneys cannot meet their current professional responsibilities with a wait-and-see approach. Instead, they would benefit from adopting the following methods empirically proven to reduce procrastination:[150]

- Make email and other distractions less visible or delay your access to them.
- Work or study regularly in a specific location not associated with distractions.

[143] van Eerde, Wendelien (2000) and van Eerde, Wendelien (2003), *supra* note 142. Steel, *supra* note 142. van Eerde, Wendelien. (2003). Procrastination at work and time management training. *The Journal of Psychology*, 137(5), 422.
[144] Jones, E. E., & Berglas, S. (1978). Control of attributions about the self through self-handicapping strategies: The appeal of alcohol and the role of underachievement. *Personality and Social Psychology Bulletin*, 42(2), 200–206. Ferrari, J. R., & Tice, D. M. (2000). Procrastination as a self-handicap for men and women: A task-avoidance strategy in a laboratory setting. *Journal of Research in Personality*, 34, 73–83. Steel, *supra* note 142 at 77.
[145] Jaffe, Eric. (2013, April). Why wait? The science behind procrastination. *Observer*, 26(4). Van Eerde, Wendelien. (2003), *supra* note 142 at 1404.
[146] Steel, *supra* note 142 at 71, 75.   [147] Ibid. at 80.   [148] Jaffe, *supra* note 145.
[149] Steel, *supra* note 142 at 71. van Eerde (2003), *supra* note 142 at 1409.
[150] Steel, *supra* note 142 at 82–83. Jaffe, *supra* note 145. van Eerde, Wendelien (2003), *supra* note 143 at 422. Ferrari & Tice, *supra* note 144 at 80.

- Develop work habits that eliminate personal choices about whether to work; each choice creates an opportunity to procrastinate.
- Set well-defined goals and deadlines and surround yourself with reminders of these goals and deadlines; inform your friends and colleagues of your goals and deadlines to heighten your sense of accountability.
- Allow other people to set deadlines for you.
- Break difficult tasks into discrete components so that the tasks appear less daunting.
- Forgive yourself for previous procrastination; don't ruminate about prior lapses but change your habits for future challenges.
- Take time management courses that, at a minimum, show how your time is presently spent, pinpoint distractions and self-defeating habits, and demonstrate how to prioritize assignments by distinguishing between importance and urgency.

Timothy Pychyl, a psychologist who has studied procrastination extensively, says procrastination is "not getting on with life itself. You only get a certain number of years. What are you doing?"[151]

Impostor Syndrome

Earlier in this chapter we explored the dangers of overconfidence and its tendency to obstruct self-development as we become convinced we know more than we actually know. There is an equally pernicious, seemingly opposite belief that undermines self-development. Psychologists call this the "impostor syndrome." It occurs when we become convinced that we lack the skills required for a particular position or assignment – and everyone is very close to discovering the deception we have perpetrated upon them.

The impostor syndrome is characterized by a sense of "intellectual phoniness" – the conviction that our achievements are undeserved and unrelated to our abilities, accompanied by the fear that we will be exposed as a fraud.[152] "Impostors" cannot internalize their success and, instead, relate their achievements to external factors like luck, personal connections, and working harder to accomplish the same results that other people achieve with nominal effort.[153] The three key features of the impostor syndrome are: "(1) the belief

[151] Jaffe, *supra* note 145.
[152] Sakulku, Jaruwan, & Alexander, James. (2011). The impostor phenomenon. *International Journal of Behavioral Science, 6*(1), 74.
[153] Ibid. at 76. Vergauwe, Jasmine, Wille, Bart, Feys, Marjolein, De Fruyt, Filip, & Anseel, Frederik. (2014, October). Fear of being exposed: The trait-relatedness of the impostor phenomenon and its relevance in the work context. *Journal of Business Psychology, 30*(3), 568.

that he/she has fooled other people, (2) fear of being exposed as an impostor, and (3) inability to attribute own achievement to internal qualities such as ability, intelligence, or skills."[154] The existence and severity of these factors are assessed by subjects' responses to statements like these: "I'm afraid people important to me may find out that I'm not as capable as they think I am" and "When people praise me for something I've accomplished, I'm afraid I won't be able to live up to their expectations of me in the future."[155]

The impostor syndrome afflicts about 20 percent of the general population, 30 percent of people who recently started a new job, and 40 percent of students.[156] Seven in ten people, psychologists estimate, will experience a major episode of the impostor syndrome in their adult lives.[157] The syndrome is evident in both men and women and throughout different cultures and levels of an organization.[158] High-achieving individuals are particularly vulnerable to the impostor syndrome; "impostors have often been in the top of the class throughout their school years."[159] Consistent with the correlation between the impostor syndrome and high academic achievement, the syndrome is particularly prevalent in academia and medicine;[160] and it is "especially common in the legal profession."[161]

Impostors experience a cycle of anxiety, over-preparation, and self-doubt whenever they undertake a new assignment:

> [I]mpostors are usually plagued with worry, self-doubt, and anxiety. In order to deal with these feelings, they either extremely over-prepare a task or initially procrastinate followed by frenzied preparation. Mostly, they succeed, and they experience temporary feelings of elation and relief. However, their success reinforces the feelings of fraudulence rather than weakening them, because in their mind, this success does not reflect true ability. Once a new task is assigned, feelings of anxiety and self-doubt reoccur, a phenomenon referred to as the "impostor cycle."[162]

[154]   Sakulku, *supra* note 152 at 78.   [155]   Vergauwe, *supra* note 153 at 571.

[156]   The personality traits that hold us back. (2016, January–February). *Harvard Business Review*, p. 32. Berinato, Scott. (2015, October 22). The personality traits that make us feel like frauds. *Harvard Business Review*. Sonnak, C., & Towell, T. (2001). The impostor phenomenon in British university students: Relationship between self-esteem, mental health, parental rearing style and socioeconomic status. *Personality and Individual Differences*, 31, 863–874. Vergauwe, *supra* note 153 at 568.

[157]   Sakulku, *supra* note 152 at 73.   [158]   Ibid.   [159]   Ibid. at 77.

[160]   Ibid. at 73. See Oriel, K., Plane, M. B., & Mundt, M. (2004). Family medicine residents and the impostor phenomenon. *Family Medicine*, 36, 248–252. Henning, K., Ey, S., & Shaw, D. (1998). Perfectionism, the impostor phenomenon and psychological adjustment in medical, dental, nursing and pharmacy students. *Medical Education*, 32(5), 456–464.

[161]   Sells, Benjamin. (1994). *The soul of the law* (p. 130). Rockport, Massachusetts: Element.

[162]   Vergauwe, *supra* note 153 at 569.

Even when impostors receive positive feedback after completing an assignment, they dismiss or discount it and develop arguments to prove their work
does not merit credit or praise.[163] If they have expended substantial time to
achieve an outstanding result, for example, they rationalize away their success
with the idea that "accomplishment through hard work does not reflect true or
real ability."[164]

Impostors lead difficult lives. They thwart their own development and
deprive themselves of the sense of fulfillment, pride, and happiness that
would normally follow from their good work. They experience fear, stress,
guilt, shame, depression, self-criticism, job dissatisfaction, and self-doubt at
levels significantly higher than their peers.[165] Both a sense of inadequacy and
a loss of intrinsic motivation pervade impostors' lives.[166] Because they have an
extreme need to appear to be perfectly capable and competent and are fearful
of detection, they avoid interacting with others and are less inclined than their
colleagues to participate in organizational activities outside their narrow job
description.[167] They also are reluctant to advance within an organization or
pursue employment in another organization; these career changes, in their
mind, heighten the risk that their incompetence will be discovered.[168]

The impostor syndrome is strongly correlated with perfectionism, the habit
of setting impossibly high standards, and then admonishing yourself for not
achieving them.[169] Like perfectionism, the impostor syndrome is difficult to
overcome without supportive colleagues, individual coaching, and professional intervention. If you see some features of the impostor syndrome in
your own life and are inclined to try self-improvement before seeking outside
help, these techniques may be helpful: (1) recognize and acknowledge the
sensation of being an impostor and track the circumstances that provoke that
sensation; (2) develop realistic expectations about yourself, including the
possibility of transient ignorance, setbacks, and failures; (3) define goals by
focusing on what is practicable instead of what is ideal; (4) avoid generalizing
and catastrophizing about mistakes and shortcomings; (5) allow yourself the
freedom to make mistakes, and if you need a justification for this freedom,

---

[163]   Sakulku, *supra* note 152 at 77. Kets de Vries, Manfred. (2005, September). The dangers of
        feeling like a fake. *Harvard Business Review*, p. 110.
[164]   Sakulku, *supra* note 152 at 76.
[165]   Vergauwe, *supra* note 153 at 570–578. Sakulku, *supra* note 152 at 83–88.
[166]   Sakulku, *supra* note 152 at 86.
[167]   The personality traits that hold us back. (2016, January–February). *Harvard Business Review*
        (p. 32). Sakulku, *supra* note 152 at 85.
[168]   Vergauwe, *supra* note 153 at 579. Berinato, *supra* note 156.
[169]   Sakulku, *supra* note 152 at 84. Vergauwe, *supra* note 153 at 573–574. Berinato, *supra* note 156.

treat mistakes as educational opportunities; and (6) accept praise at face value and consider all the reasons the source is credible and the praise is accurate.[170]

Overcoming the impostor syndrome may be especially difficult for inexperienced attorneys. In the early stages of attorneys' careers, the unrealistic fears that characterize impostor syndrome are aggravated by the realistic fears that accompany genuine encounters with our own ineptitude. Douglas Litowitz, a lawyer, author, and law professor, contends that attorneys' feeling of faking it begins in law school, continues in law practice, and eventually becomes part of the attorney persona:

> At the time that I passed the bar exam, I had never actually seen a trial from start to finish, let alone participated in one, and I had never worked on a transaction or drafted a document that had actually been signed. I had no idea what to say to a client, what to charge a client, what a retainer agreement looked like, or how to find my way around a courthouse. I felt like a doctor who had bluffed his way through medical school without learning how to take a pulse or start an intravenous line. I felt like a fraud, because I was a fraud. But I was a *licensed* fraud.[171]

Law school, Litowitz asserts, "sets the tone for the fronting and fakery which will be expected of the lawyer in the future. To this day, when I hear lawyers bluster with their phony tone of self-assurance and pretension, I know that it can be traced back to law school."[172] If Litowitz is correct, lawyers face exceptional challenges in identifying and recovering from the impostor syndrome; they must distinguish between the anxiety caused by unrealistic self-assessment in the impostor syndrome and the anxiety caused by inexperience and chronic hyperbole in law practice.

Alcohol and Drug Impairment

One in every five attorneys is impaired by alcohol or drugs.[173] This impairment is more than a lifestyle choice or a bad habit; it directly violates the ethical duty

---

[170] See Richards, Carl. (2015, October 26). Learning to deal with the imposter syndrome. *The New York Times.* Corkindale, Gill. (2008, May 7). Overcoming imposter syndrome. *Harvard Business Review.* Retrieved from https://hbr.org/2008/05/overcoming-imposter-syndrome.

[171] Litowitz, Douglas. (2005). *The destruction of young lawyers* (p. 58). Akron, Ohio: University of Akron Press.

[172] Ibid. at 48. See Sells, *supra* note 161 at 130–133.

[173] Krill, Johnson, & Albert, *supra* note 83 at 51. See Beck, Connie, Sales, Bruce, & Benjamin, G. Andrew. (1996). Lawyer distress: Alcohol-related problems and other psychological concerns among a sample of practicing lawyers. *Journal of Law & Health,* 10(1), 1–60.

of competence.[174] Attorneys must remain "constantly alert to the existence of problems that may impede or impair" their ability to provide competent representation, including alcohol abuse and drug abuse.[175] When their competence is impaired or impeded, they should seek treatment and enlist "whatever aid is necessary" to competently represent clients until they have regained competence.[176] Despite these clear duties to clients and strong admonitions against impairment, the rate of alcoholism among attorneys is at least twice that of the general population – a substantial danger to clients, motorists, law firm employees, families, and the attorneys themselves.[177]

Three decades of research demonstrate that attorneys suffer disproportionately from alcoholism and drug abuse.[178] The legal profession, however, has failed to acknowledge and adequately address what is arguably the statistically distinguishing feature of the profession. This degree of alcoholism and drug abuse would be considered a substantial threat to public welfare in any other context in which people entrust their lives, assets, and reputations to licensed professionals. In the legal profession, though, impairment is treated as an occupational hazard instead of a public harm. Its pervasiveness leads attorneys to minimize its damage.

The stereotype of impairment is an older, wizened attorney whose cynicism, weariness, and depression have finally overwhelmed the convention of sobriety. This stereotype is misleading and encourages younger attorneys to overlook their own impairment. The most recent research reveals that attorneys in their first ten years of practice have the highest rate of problematic alcohol use (29 percent), followed by attorneys practicing for 11–20 years (21 percent).[179] Attorneys 30 years of age and younger have the highest rates of problematic drinking (32 percent), and attorneys aged 31–40 have the next highest rate (26 percent).[180] Among the attorneys who believe that their alcohol use has been a problem in the past, 27 percent report that their problematic use began

---

[174] ABA Model Rules of Prof'l Conduct R. 1.1.
[175] American Bar Association Section of Legal Education and Admissions to the Bar. (1992). Legal education and professional development – An educational continuum (p. 209). Chicago: American Bar Association. (The quoted section is from the Fundamental Values of the Profession, 1.2(d)(i), (ii).)
[176] Ibid.   [177] Krill, *supra* note 173 at 46. Daicoff, *supra* note 86 at 129.
[178] Krill, *supra* note 173. Weiss, *supra* note 86. Allan, Rick B. (1997). Alcoholism, drug abuse and lawyers: Are we ready to address the denial? *Creighton Law Review*, 31, 26. Schiltz, Patrick J. (1999) On being a happy, healthy, and ethical member of an unhappy, unhealthy, and unethical profession. *Vanderbilt Law Review*, 52, 871. Daicoff, Susan, *supra* note 177. Benjamin, G. A., Darling, E., & Sales, B. (1990). The prevalence of depression, alcohol abuse, and cocaine abuse among United States lawyers. *International Journal of Law and Psychiatry*, 13, 233–246.
[179] Krill, *supra* note 173 at 51.   [180] Ibid.

before law school, and 14 percent said it began during law school.[181] The initial phase of a legal career, thus, "is strongly correlated with a high risk of developing an alcohol use disorder."[182]

Attorneys' substance abuse is not limited to alcohol. About one-third of attorneys show a significant risk of drug abuse.[183] Among the attorneys who report drug use during the last 12 months, "those using stimulants had the highest rate of weekly usage (74.1 percent), followed by sedatives (51.3 percent), tobacco (46.8 percent), marijuana (31.0 percent), and opioids (21.6 percent)."[184] Drug use on this scale presents a high risk of impairing "brain functions such as decision-making, attention, and impulse control."[185]

Alcoholism and drug abuse cause distinct, sometimes irreversible, physical changes in attorneys.[186] The effects on attorneys' clients can be equally certain and severe. Although missed deadlines and court appearances may appear to be the most common problems resulting from impairment, the most serious effects often relate to attorneys' judgment and advice. Specific effects of impairment include: narrow focus of attention; inability to develop creative ideas; difficulty in processing language; short- and long-term memory loss; reluctance to deal with negative information; and poor performance in analytical thinking, critical reasoning, and simple math problems.[187] An impaired attorney cannot provide the knowledge, discernment, foresight, objectivity, and sense of proportion essential to professional judgment.

The consequences of chronic alcoholism and drug abuse are aggravated by attorneys' reluctance to seek treatment. Attorneys adopt a "tough it out" attitude, reflecting their tendency to "feel isolated, alone, and lacking in social support."[188] Although attorneys generally have superior health insurance and coverage for substance abuse treatment, only seven percent of attorneys report that they have previously sought treatment for alcohol or drug use."[189] The most commonly cited reason for resisting treatment is "not wanting others to find out they needed help."[190] This is a particularly unfortunate attitude because treatment programs designed specifically for attorneys are usually confidential and relatively successful.[191]

---

[181] Ibid. at 48.   [182] Ibid. at 51.

[183] Ibid. at 49. See Benjamin, *supra* note 178. McQueen, M.P. (2014, July 18). More lawyers ask for help for alcohol, drug abuse. *The Am Law Daily*.

[184] Krill, *supra* note 173 at 49.

[185] Austin, Debra. (2015). Drink like a lawyer: The neuroscience of substance use and its impact on cognitive wellness. *Nevada Law Journal*, 15, 871.

[186] Ibid. at 853–867.

[187] Kiser, Randall. (2010). *Beyond right and wrong* (p. 187). Berlin, London: Springer.

[188] Daicoff, *supra* note 177 at 130.   [189] Krill, *supra* note 173 at 50.   [190] Ibid.   [191] Ibid.

It would be easy, and in some circumstances accurate, to attribute alcoholism and drug abuse to the pressures of law practice. But causation is problematic:

> While some individuals may drink to cope with their psychological or emotional problems, others may experience those same problems as a result of their drinking. It is not clear which scenario is more prevalent or likely in this population, though the ubiquity of alcohol in the legal professional culture certainly demonstrates both its ready availability and social acceptability, should one choose to cope with their mental health problems in that manner. Attorneys working in private firms experience some of the highest levels of problematic alcohol use compared with other work environments, which may underscore a relationship between professional culture and drinking. Irrespective of causation, we know that co-occurring disorders are more likely to remit when addressed concurrently.[192]

Long work hours in any occupation are correlated with alcoholism,[193] and when excessive work is compounded by the anxiety and depression prevalent in the legal profession, the outcome frequently is devastating for attorneys and their clients.

Alcoholism and drug abuse warrant professional intervention and treatment. For those attorneys who are concerned about substance abuse but not presently affected by it, some preventative measures might be helpful. Exercise, time management, adequate sleep, reduction of dietary fats and sugars, meditation, mindfulness, cognitive reappraisal (reinterpreting the meaning and significance of events), aligning work with values, reducing comparisons with other people, and socializing with friends and family can be effective in overall stress reduction.[194] Whatever measures are taken, it is imperative to maintain an objective perspective on yourself – regularly assess your reactions to stressful events and avoid self-serving excuses about your reactions.

Don Jack, a prominent litigation attorney practicing in Toronto, tells new clerks at his firm to "take a good look around this profession. A lot of people my

---

[192]   Ibid. at 51.
[193]   Virtanen, Marianna, *et al.* (2015, January 13). Long working hours and alcohol use: Systematic review and meta-analysis of published studies and unpublished individual participation data. *BMJ*, 350, g7772.
[194]   See Pirtle, Jennifer. (2006, September). Stressing yourself sick. *ABA Journal*, pp. 35–40. Levit, Nancy, & Linder, Douglas. (2010). *The happy lawyer* (pp. 78–111). New York: Oxford University Press. Freshman, Clark, Hayes, Adele, & Feldman, Greg. (2002). The lawyer-negotiator as mood scientist: What we know and don't know about how mood relates to successful negotiation. *Journal of Dispute Resolution*, 2002(1), 75–79

age just look like shit. If you want to stay on top, you have to avoid the burnout that gets to many great lawyers."[195] "I've seen everything," he says. "Divorces, heart attacks, alcoholism, you name it. Nothing is worth that and, more importantly, you can't stay on top, however good you are, if you are not mentally and physically strong."[196] He advises the firm's clerks "to start good habits early, to develop hobbies and interests outside of law, to get a fitness plan and follow it and to plan vacations well in advance so they have things to look forward to."[197]

Narcissism

Self-centered, uncaring, selfish, and egotistical – these are words we use to describe people whose attention is limited to their own appearance, acquisitions, needs, and actions. Although the degree of self-absorption may vary from mild conceit to extreme self-obsession, the catchall term for this preoccupation with self is narcissism. At a pathological level – Narcissistic Personality Disorder – narcissism "is characterized by a pervasive pattern of grandiosity, need for admiration, interpersonal exploitiveness, and lack of empathy."[198] In a non-pathological but nevertheless detrimental form – narcissistic personality, sometimes called "subclinical" or "normal" narcissism – it manifests as an inflated sense of self and a disregard of others' rights and feelings.[199]

For attorneys, who may perceive their self-absorption to be the source of their determination and success,[200] the critical question is: Has my sense of self-importance and focus on self-achievement become maladaptive, diminishing my sense of self-esteem, interfering with my career and possibly alienating my colleagues? Since this question is fundamentally personal, it is best answered by each attorney's efforts to (1) understand narcissism and how it is assessed; (2) learn how narcissism affects relationships with other people; and

---

[195]   Taylor, Irene. (2001, February 1). How smart are you–really? *LEXPERT Magazine*.
[196]   Ibid.   [197]   Ibid.
[198]   Stinson, Frederick, *et al.* (2008, July). Prevalence, correlates, disability and comorbidity of DSM-IV Narcissistic Personality Disorder: Results from the Wave 2 national epidemiologic survey on alcohol and related conditions. *Journal of Clinical Psychiatry*, 69(7), 1034.
[199]   Twenge, Jean, & Foster, Joshua. (2010). Birth cohort increases in narcissistic personality traits among American college students, 1982–2009. *Social Psychological and Personality Science*, 1(1), 99. Twenge, J. M., & Campbell, W. K. (2009). *The narcissism epidemic: Living in the age of entitlement* (p. 4). New York: Free Press. Bushman, Brad, & Baumeister, Roy. (1998). Threatened egotism, narcissism, self-esteem, and direct and displaced aggression: Does self-love or self-hate lead to violence? *Journal of Personality and Social Psychology*, 75(1), 221.
[200]   See Wallace, Harry, Ready, C. Beth, & Weitenhagen, Erin. (2009). Narcissism and task persistence. *Self and Identity*, 8(1), 78–93.

(3) decide whether it is advisable to start to mitigate the detrimental effects of narcissism. Those topics frame the discussion below.

Narcissism has six key components: grandiosity (self-centeredness, condescension, sense of superiority, and belief that others are envious); attention seeking (excessive efforts to attract attention and be the focus of others' attention); need for admiration (preoccupation with power and success, excessive admiration seeking, and setting goals primarily to gain approval from others); lack of empathy (inability to recognize others' feelings and needs unless perceived as directly relevant to self, misperception of effect on others, minimal interest in others, and lack of genuine rapport and intimacy in relationships); exploitation (taking advantage of others to achieve personal objectives); and sense of entitlement (expectation of favorable treatment from others and automatic compliance by others with that expectation).[201] Narcissists, in short, "are grandiose self-promoters who continually crave attention."[202]

To assess narcissism, psychologists often administer the Narcissistic Personality Inventory, asking people to read paired statements and choose the statement that most closely matches their feelings. Examples of these paired statements are:

A. I expect a great deal from other people.
B. I like to do things for other people.
A. I can usually talk my way out of anything.
B. I try to accept the consequences of my behavior.
A. I insist upon getting the respect that is due me.
B. I usually get the respect that I deserve.
A. I get upset when people don't notice how I look when I go out in public.
B. I don't mind blending into the crowd when I go out in public.[203]

"A" responses to these statements are suggestive of narcissism.

---

[201] American Psychiatric Association. (2013). *Diagnostic and statistical manual of mental disorders* (5th ed.). Kluger, Jeffrey. (2014). *The narcissist next door.* New York: Riverhead Books.

[202] Paulhus, Delroy. (2014, December). Toward a taxonomy of dark personalities. *Current Directions in Psychological Science, 23*(6), 421.

[203] Kluger, *supra* note 201. See Raskin, Robert, & Terry, Howard. (1988). A principal components analysis of the Narcissistic Personality Inventory and further evidence of its construct validity. *Journal of Personality and Social Psychology, 54*(5), 890–902. Raskin, R. N., & Hall, C. S. (1981). The narcissistic personality inventory: Alternative form reliability and further evidence of construct validity. *Journal of Personality Assessment, 45,* 159–16. Miller, Joshua, Price, Joanna, & Campbell, W. Keith. (2011). Is the Narcissistic Personality Inventory still relevant? A test of independent grandiosity and entitlement scales in the assessment of narcissism. *Assessment 19*(1), 8–13.

Assessments of narcissism during the last 40 years indicate that the incidence of narcissism has increased significantly among college students.[204] "You can look at individual scores of narcissism, you can look at data on lifetime prevalence of Narcissistic Personality Disorder, you can look at related cultural trends, and they all point to one thing," asserts psychologist W. Keith Campbell. "Narcissism is on the rise."[205] Attorneys, in general, and litigators, in particular, appear to "have generous helpings of narcissism,"[206] and a recent study of corporate counsel reveals high scores on positive impression management consistent with narcissism.[207]

The clinical form of narcissism, Narcissistic Personality Disorder (NPD), affects about 7 percent of the adult population.[208] Over their lifetimes, 1 in 16 Americans is expected to be clinically impaired by this disorder.[209] Men are more likely to be diagnosed with NPD than women, and narcissism is more prevalent among younger adults than older adults.[210] Men with NPD have higher rates of substance use disorders and anti-social personality disorders, while women with NPD have higher rates of major depression and anxiety disorders.[211]

Although narcissists project a sense of superiority, their self-esteem and tolerance for criticism and social rejection turn out to be relatively low. "Narcissists care passionately about being superior to others," explain psychologists Brad Bushman and Roy Baumeister, "even if they are not yet convinced that they have achieved this superiority."[212] Narcissists rate themselves as having high levels of self-esteem, but their self-reports are belied by more sophisticated psychological tests revealing "underlying feelings of low

[204] Twenge, Jean, Konrath, Sara, Foster, Joshua, Campbell, W. Keith, & Bushman, Brad. (2008, August). Ego inflating over time: A cross-temporal meta-analysis of the narcissistic personality inventory. *Journal of Personality*, 76(4), 875–902. Twenge & Campbell, *supra* note 199. Westerman, James. (2012). Are universities creating millennial narcissistic employees? An empirical examination of narcissism in business students and its implications. *Journal of Management Education*, 36(1), 5–32. See Baumeister & Tierney, *supra* note 137 at 192–194. Cai, Huajian, Kwan, Virginia S. Y., & Sedikides, Constantine. (2012). A sociocultural approach to narcissism: The case of modern China. *European Journal of Personality*, 26, 529–535.

[205] Dingfelder, Sandie. (2011, February). Reflecting on narcissism. *Monitor*, 43(2), 64. Cf. Quenqua, Douglas. (2013, August 5). Seeing narcissists everywhere. *The New York Times*.

[206] Burger, Arthur. (2008, August 25). Why do lawyers lie? One word: Narcissism. *New Jersey Law Journal*.

[207] Wanser, Donna. (2012, February). *The emotional intelligence of general counsels in relation to lawyer leadership*. Unpublished doctoral dissertation, Pepperdine University Graduate School of Education and Psychology.

[208] Stinson, *supra* note 198.   [209] Twenge & Campbell, *supra* note 199 at 23.

[210] Stinson, *supra* note 198.   [211] Ibid.   [212] Bushman & Baumeister, *supra* note 199 at 220.

self-worth."[213] Narcissists, in brief, "may not feel as good about themselves as they often claim."[214] And when rejected or insulted, narcissists lash out and display exceptionally aggressive reactions.[215] They are intolerant of criticism and seek to "punish or defeat someone who has threatened their highly favorable views of themselves."[216]

Brain scans of narcissists substantiate the findings of low self-esteem and high aggressiveness and hostility in responding to criticism and rejection. Narcissists' low self-esteem is associated with a "neural disconnect between the self and reward."[217] The areas of the brain responsible for processing rewards (ventral striatum) and stimuli (medial prefrontal cortex) show weaker structural connectivity in narcissists' brains than non-narcissists' brains. The "narcissistic motivation to secure external admiration and affirmation," researchers conclude, "may arise from a deficit in neural pathways that connect self-relevant processing with reward."[218] Brain scans of narcissists also assist in understanding their overreactions to criticism and social rejection. These overreactions, fMRI brain scans show, "may be a function of hypersensitivity in brain systems associated with social pain."[219]

Because narcissists lack empathy, their relationships with other people tend to be superficial, manipulative, and unstable; they "have relatively little interest in forming warm, emotionally intimate bonds with others."[220] The lack of empathy is exacerbated by narcissists' inflated sense of self and their

---

[213]   Cascio, C. N., Konrath, S. H., & Falk, E. B. (2015, March). Narcissists' social pain seen only in the brain. *Social Cognitive and Affective Neuroscience,* 10(3), 336. See Zeigler-Hill, Virgil. (2006, February). Discrepancies between implicit and explicit self-esteem: Implications for narcissism and self-esteem instability. *Journal of Personality,* 74(1), 119–144. Brummelman, E., Thomaes, S., & Sedikides, C. (2016). Separating narcissism from self-esteem. *Current Directions in Psychological Science,* 25(1), 8–13. Orth, Ulrich, & Luciano, Eva. (2015, October). Self-esteem, narcissism, and stressful life events: Testing for selection and socialization. *Journal of Personality and Social Psychology,* 109(4), 707–721.

[214]   Myers, Erin, & Zeigler-Hill, Virgil. (2011, November). How much do narcissists really like themselves? Using the bogus pipeline procedure to better understand the self-esteem of narcissists. *Journal of Research in Personality,* 46(1), 102.

[215]   Twenge & Foster, *supra* note 199 at 100. Twenge, *supra* note 204 at 877.

[216]   Bushman & Baumeister, *supra* note 199 at 227. See Burton, James, & Hoobler, Jenny. (2011). Aggressive reactions to abusive supervision: The role of interactional justice and narcissism. *Scandinavian Journal of Psychology,* 52, 389–398.

[217]   Chester, David, Lynam, Donald, Powell, David, & DeWall, C. Nathan. (2016). Narcissism is associated with weakened frontostriatal connectivity: A DTI study. *Social Cognitive and Affective Neuroscience,* 11(7), 1036–1040.

[218]   Ibid.

[219]   Cascio, Konrath & Falk, *supra* note 213 at 338. See Schulze, Lars, *et al.* (2013, October). Gray matter abnormalities in patients with narcissistic personality disorder. *Journal of Psychiatric Research,* 47(10), 1363–1369.

[220]   Twenge & Foster, *supra* note 199 at 100.

exploitation of others to achieve their own goals. The impact on their relationships with coworkers is described by Jeffrey Kluger, author of *The Narcissist Next Door*:

> Narcissists thrive when there's an opportunity for glory but are uninterested in the collaborative work that leads to greater good for a larger group; they bristle and bitch when their talents are challenged, but never consider the possibility that those talents may be less than they believe them to be or that there is at least room for improvement. For narcissists, setbacks are not opportunities to learn; they're problems caused by somebody else who got in their way or sabotaged their plans.[221]

Despite these problems, narcissists frequently occupy leadership positions. Since they project strong confidence in their opinions, "other people tend to believe them and the narcissists become disproportionately more influential in group situations."[222]

For those attorneys who either see some correlation between narcissism and their own behavior or are working with a narcissist receptive to change, the question arises, "What methods are successful in mitigating narcissism?" Surprisingly, narcissism is one of the few disorders for which there is no specifically tailored medication, although antidepressants and antipsychotics may be prescribed. But behavioral therapy, based on perspective taking, is promising. In a study of 300 students, narcissists shown a video depicting the breakup of a romantic relationship predictably showed less empathy and emotional reactivity as measured by changes in heart rate.[223] The narcissists then watched a different video in which a woman described a domestic violence experience. Those narcissists who were instructed to take the woman's perspective ("imagine how she is feeling about what is happening") changed their responses significantly; they displayed normal levels of empathy and reactivity (raised heart rate).

The narcissists who had displayed the highest levels of entitlement, exhibitionism, and exploitation in that study showed the most significant changes in empathy when they assumed the woman's perspective. These results suggest that narcissists "are capable of change" and their lack of empathy "is not due to

---

[221] Kluger, *supra* note 201.
[222] Gladwell, Malcolm. (2002, July 22). The talent myth. *The New Yorker*. See Brunell, A. B., Gentry, W.A., Campbell, W.K., Hoffman, B.J., Kuhnert, K.W., & Demarree, K.G. (2008). Leader emergence: The case of the narcissistic leader. *Personality and Social Psychology Bulletin*, 34, 1663–1676.
[223] Hepper, Erica G., Hart, Claire M., & Sedikides, Constantine. (2014, June). Moving Narcissus: Can narcissists be empathic? *Personality and Social Psychology Bulletin*, 40(6), 1079.

lack of capacity, but more to do with lack of motivation."[224] Summarizing the results of this study, Erica Hepper, a psychologist and the lead researcher, states, "If we encourage narcissists to consider the situation from their team-mate or friend's point of view, they are likely to respond in a much more considerate or sympathetic way."[225]

Status, Affluence, and Power

"Success is a lousy teacher," observes Microsoft founder Bill Gates. "It seduces smart people into thinking they can't lose."[226] Success, unfortunately, also seduces smart people into thinking they don't need to listen to other people and that they should not complicate their lives with conventional ethics. Retaining your openness to other people and your ethical bearings, therefore, is an immense challenge as you become more successful, affluent, and influential. You cannot rely on colleagues to tell you when you have become a bothersome, self-important jerk; by the time you have devolved to that point, you will be living in a bubble, surrounded by people whose deference is seen as wise counsel.

The phenomenon of distancing yourself from other people and relying on your own opinions, as you advance through the hallowed halls of success, is known as the paradox of power. The paradox appears when "the very traits that helped leaders accumulate control in the first place all but disappear once they rise to power. Instead of being polite, honest and outgoing, they become impulsive, reckless and rude."[227] Jim Collins, a leadership consultant and author of the bestseller *How the Mighty Fall*, uses the term "hubris born of success" to describe how successful people unknowingly plot their own demise. "Stage 1," he says, "kicks in when people become arrogant, regarding success virtually as an entitlement and they lose sight of the true underlying factors that created success in the first place."[228] When you attribute success to your own superior qualities and disregard the role luck and chance may have played, Collins asserts, "you have succumbed to hubris."[229]

---

[224] The British Psychological Society. (2014, June 4). Narcissists can be taught to empathise. *BPS Research Digest*.

[225] Society for Personality and Social Psychology. (2014, May 30). Can narcissists be moved to show empathy? *ScienceDaily*.

[226] Gates, Bill. (1996). *The road ahead* (p. 38). New York: Penguin Group.

[227] Lehrer, Jonah. (2010, August 14–15). The power trip. *The Wall Street Journal*. See Keltner, Dacher. (2016). *The power paradox*. New York: Penguin Press.

[228] Collins, Jim. (2009). *How the mighty fall* (p. 21). New York: Harper Collins.   [229] Ibid.

Power and status adversely affect behavior in three aspects important to attorneys: empathy, ethics, and decision making. "More powerful people tend to be less likely to take the perspective or feel the emotions of another person,"[230] state law professors Jennifer Robbennolt and Jean Sternlight. "In particular, powerful people are less likely to take into account another person's visual perspective, less likely to adjust for the fact that others lack access to their private information, and are less accurate at identifying emotions in others."[231] As a result of this lack of empathy and inability to sense and understand others' emotions, many attorneys are inattentive to clients' needs and susceptible to ethical violations ranging from failure to communicate with clients to outright disregard of clients' interests.[232]

Although we might assume that people with less money are driven to compromise their ethics when necessary to improve their financial status, research indicates the opposite is true: wealthy people are more likely to conceal essential information, lie, cheat, and otherwise obtain an advantage than people of lower socio-economic status.[233] The results of four experiments,

[230] Sternlight, Jean R., & Robbennolt, Jennifer K. (2013). Behavioral legal ethics. *Arizona State Law Journal*, 45, 1144.

[231] Ibid. See Grewal, Daisy. (2012, April 10). How wealth reduces compassion. *Scientific American*. Kraus, Michael, Piff, Paul, Mendoza-Denton, Rodolfo, Rheinschmidt, Michelle, & Keltner, Dacher. (2012). Social class, solipsism, and contextualism: How the rich are different from the poor. *Psychological Review*, 119(3), 546–572. Ma-Kellams, Christine. (2012). The ironic effect of financial incentive on empathic accuracy. *Journal of Experimental Social Psychology*, 49(1), 65–71. Kraus, Michael. (2010). Social class, contextualism, and empathic accuracy. *Psychological Science*, 21(11), 1716–1723. Akinola, Modupe, & Mendes, Wendy. (2014). It's good to be king: Neurobiological benefits of higher social standing. *Social Psychological and Personality Science*, 5(1), 43–51. Curhan, Jared, & Pentland, Alex. (2007). Thin slices of negotiation: Predicting outcomes from conversational dynamics within the first 5 minutes. *Journal of Applied Psychology*, 92(3), 802–811. Hogeveen, Jeremy, Inzlicht, Michael, & Obhi, Sukhvinder. (2014, April). Power changes how the brain responds to others. *Journal of Experimental Psychology*, 143(2), 755–762.

[232] Ibid. See O'Grady, Catherine Gage. (2015). Behavioral legal ethics, decision making, and the new attorney's unique professional perspective. *Nevada Law Journal*, 15(2), 671–697.

[233] Kouchaki, Maryam, Smith-Crowe, Kristin, Brief, Arthur, & Sousa, Carlos. (2013, May). Seeing green: Mere exposure to money triggers a business decision frame and unethical outcomes. *Organizational Behavior and Human Decision Processes*, 121(1), 53–61. Piff, Paul K., Stancato, Daniel M., Cote, Stephane, Mendoza-Denton, Rodolfo, & Keltner, Dacher (2012, March 3). Higher social class predicts increased unethical behavior. *Proceedings of the National Academy of Sciences*, 109(11), 4086–4091. (2010, May). Powerful people are better liars. *Harvard Business Review* (p. 32–33). Giridharadas, Anand. (2016, February 1). How wealth plays into politics at a personal level. *The New York Times*. Whitson, Jennifer, Liljenquist, Katie, Galinsky, Adam, Magee, Joe, Gruenfeld, Deborah, & Cadena, Brian. (2013, May). The blind leading: Power reduces awareness of constraints. *Journal of Experimental Social Psychology*, 49(3), 579–582. Grewal, *supra* note 231. Lammers, J., Stapel,

published in the *Proceedings of the National Academy of Sciences*,[234] illustrate the differences in ethics and altruism between upper-class and lower-class individuals:

- Study participants in a negotiation simulation assumed the role of an employer and were instructed to negotiate as low a salary as possible with a job candidate. They also were informed that (1) the candidate desires to remain in the same job for at least two years and will accept a lower starting salary in return for a verbal commitment of job stability; and (2) the job for which the candidate is applying will be eliminated in six months due to an organization restructuring, but the job candidate does not have this information. Upper-class individuals were more likely to conceal the fact that the job would be eliminated in six months: "Social class negatively predicted probability of telling the truth . . . and positively predicted favorable attitudes toward greed."[235] Favorable attitudes toward greed, in turn, "negatively predicted probability of telling the truth."[236]

- Study participants were told they were playing a "game of chance" in which a computer screen would display the random results of five separate rolls of dice. They were told that higher rolls would increase their chances of winning a $50 cash price. Unbeknownst to the participants, the computer screen showed each participant the same side of a six-sided die, and the "die rolls were predetermined to sum up to 12."[237] Upper-class people were more likely to report scores exceeding 12; "social class positively predicted cheating."[238]

- After completing part of an experiment, study participants were shown a jar of wrapped candies. They were informed that the candies were for children in a nearby laboratory, but they could take some candies if they wanted them. Upper-class participants "took more candy that would otherwise go to children than did those in the lower-rank condition."[239]

- At a traffic intersection, researchers recorded the number of cars failing to yield to a pedestrian or another car already in the intersection. The cars were categorized in five groups based on make, age, and appearance. Nearly 50 percent of the highest ranked vehicles proceeded through the crosswalk without yielding to a pedestrian, while none of the lowest

D.A., & Galinsky, A.D. (2010, May). Power Increases hypocrisy: Moralizing in reasoning, immorality in behavior. *Psychological Science*, 21(5), 737–744.
[234] Piff, *supra* note 233.   [235] Ibid. at 4088.   [236] Ibid.   [237] Ibid.   [238] Ibid.
[239] Ibid. at 4087

ranked vehicles failed to yield. In addition, "drivers of higher-end auto-mobiles were four times more likely to cut off other vehicles before waiting their turn at a busy, four way-intersection with stop signs on all sides."[240]

Reviewing the study results, lead researcher Paul Piff concludes, "The relative privilege and security enjoyed by upper-class individuals gives rise to inde-pendence from others and a prioritization of the self and one's own welfare over the welfare of others – what we call 'greed.' This is likely to cause someone to be more inclined to break the rules in his or her favor, or to perceive themselves as, in a sense, being 'above the law.'"[241]

It is critical to note that simply contemplating the benefits of economic superiority can induce the lack of ethics and altruism shown in these studies; objective superiority in economic status is not required to dull our sense of fairness and compassion. When asked to list three benefits of greed before participating in an experiment, for example, "lower-class participants exhib-ited high levels of unethical behavior comparable to their upper-class counterparts."[242] As the researchers report, "lower-class individuals were as unethical as upper-class individuals when instructed to think of greed's ben-efits, suggesting that upper- and lower-class individuals do not necessarily differ in terms of their capacity for unethical behavior but rather in terms of their default tendencies toward it."[243] This finding is substantiated by other research indicating that "individuals primed with money were more likely to demonstrate unethical intentions."[244]

In addition to influencing our ethical behavior, social status and affluence affect our receptiveness to others' opinions and the overall quality of our decisions. An unfortunate byproduct of success is overconfidence in our judgment and an attendant resistance to eliciting others' opinions and revising our judgments on the infrequent occasions when we obtain other

---

[240] National Science Foundation. (2012, March 7). Upper class people more likely to behave unethically. *ScienceDaily*. Retrieved from www.sciencedaily.com/releases/2012/03/12030714 5432.html. Another variant of automobile status behavior is described by Robert Cialdini:

> Drivers wait significantly longer before honking their horns at a new, luxury car stopped in front of a green traffic light than an older, economy model. The motorists had little patience with the economy car driver: Nearly all sounded their horns, and the majority of these did so more than once; two simply rammed into his rear bumper. . . . 50 percent of the motorists waited respectfully behind it [the prestige automobile], never touching their horns, until it drove on.

Cialdini, Robert. (1984). *Influence* (p. 229). New York: William Morrow and Company.
[241] National Science Foundation, *supra* note 240. [242] Piff, *supra* note 233 at 4088.
[243] Ibid. [244] Kouchaki, *supra* note 233. See Whitson *et al.*, *supra* note 233.

opinions.[245] This resistance is indiscriminate; powerful people "discount advice from experts and novices equally."[246]

Since high-power people rely on their own opinions and fail to incorporate or properly weight other opinions, the quality of their decisions tends to be inferior. Their decisions are less accurate than those made by low-power people because they are "less open to factual advice, even when that advice can help achieve accuracy objectives and improve performance."[247] Although high- and low-power people may start off with judgments of equivalent accuracy, high-power people ultimately perform worse due to their deliberate disregard of disconfirming information; "when presented with input from others, those with greater power are likely to improve less (in terms of ultimate accuracy) than those lacking power."[248] The decision-making deficiencies of high-power people are exacerbated when they perform tasks requiring careful deliberation and accuracy;[249] and in experiments with financial incentives "greater power was associated with a significantly greater loss of money."[250] Being overconfident and impermeable, thus, turns out to have a detrimental effect on your finances and a harmful impact on your relationships with other people.

When powerful people are required to work with other powerful people in groups, their reluctance to elicit and incorporate other viewpoints shifts from being ineffective to dysfunctional. They perform poorly relative to groups of low-power individuals and cannot complete tasks because they are reluctant to share information and spend their time fighting over their relative status in the group.[251] (Anyone who has attended a law firm executive committee meeting or a law school faculty meeting will no doubt have more vivid depictions of this phenomenon than any experiment can conjure up.) Although powerful people may believe that seeking and taking advice is a sign of weakness and

---

[245] See, Kelly E., Morrison, Elizabeth Wolfe, Rothman, Naomi B., & Soll, Jack B. (2011, August 2). The detrimental effects of power on confidence, advice taking, and accuracy. *Organizational Behavior and Human Decision Processes*, 116(2), 272–285.

[246] Tost, Leigh, Gino, Francesca, & Larrick, Richard. (2012, January). Power competitiveness, and advice taking: Why the powerful don't listen. *Organizational Behavior and Human Decision Processes*, 117(1), 53.

[247] Kelly, *supra* note 245 at 282.   [248] Ibid.

[249] Fast, Nathanael, Sivanathan, Niro, Mayer, Nicole, & Galinsky, Adam. (2011). Power and overconfident decision-making. *Organizational Behavior and Human Decision Processes*, 117(2), 257.

[250] Ibid. at 255

[251] Hildreth, John, & Anderson, Cameron. (2016, February). Failure at the top: How power undermines collaborative performance. *Journal of Personality and Social Psychology*. 110(2), 261–286. (2016, May). Collaboration: Powerful people perform badly on teams. *Harvard Business Review*, p. 28.

undermines their projection of confidence, there is a "strong positive relationship between reported advice taking and being seen as a good leader."[252] Resistance to others' opinions, therefore, leads to both poor decision-making processes and flawed leadership.

CHAPTER CAPSULE

Self-awareness is a threshold requirement for improving soft skills. The Model Rules of Professional Conduct and the Fundamental Values of the Profession require attorneys to be self-aware – constantly alert to mental and physical conditions that may impede or impair attorneys' performance and, specifically, "the lawyer's ability to represent the client."[253] Attorneys also must objectively analyze their performance to identify the positive aspects that can be replicated and the negative aspects that should not be repeated.

In evaluating their performance, attorneys frequently succumb to biases and distortions that convince them that their performance is exemplary when it actually is suboptimal. Fulfilling the duty of self-awareness thus requires not only an ethical commitment but also a personal commitment to detached self-assessment and self-improvement. Our tendency to be affected if not overcome by "illusory superiority" must yield to a more balanced evaluation of our own performance and the habits, traits, motivations, propensities, emotions, and delusions that undermine our performance.

As we evaluate our performance and commit ourselves to self-improvement, we benefit from considering whether 12 conditions could be subverting our careers and relationships: emotional numbing; high moral identity; static self illusion; omniscience; stress/anxiety; aggressiveness; extrinsic motivation; procrastination; impostor syndrome; alcohol and drug impairment; narcissism; and status, affluence, and power. Each of these conditions can deprive attorneys of the professional fulfillment that they would otherwise achieve and rob clients of the full set of skills that the attorney would otherwise employ. Fortunately, as discussed earlier in this chapter, each of these impediments and impairments to performance can be effectively managed or successfully overcome.

---

[252] See Kelly, *supra* note 245 at 276.   [253] ABA Model Rules of Prof'l Conduct R. 1.16.

4

Self-Development

Louis Terman was a man on a mission in 1921. A psychology professor at Stanford University, he was determined to prove that "there is nothing about an individual as important as his IQ, except possibly his morals."[1] Funded by a large research grant from the Commonwealth Foundation, Terman tested elementary school students throughout California and then selected 1,470 students with an IQ above 135. The lives of those students – later called "Terman's Termites" – were tracked for decades to confirm Terman's thesis that, from the ranks of high-IQ children, "and nowhere else, our geniuses in every line are recruited."[2]

Terman enmeshed himself in the lives of his Termites, checking up on them regularly, providing advice, and writing letters of recommendation for them. Even after the students became adults, Terman referred to them as "my gifted children."[3] Observing their successes over 35 years, he was delighted to find that their median income was nearly twice that of men in white-collar jobs and they had published reams of scientific and technical papers and articles.[4]

But Terman was wrong in thinking that IQ was the dispositive factor in career achievement. It turns out that Terman's "A" group achievers (professors, scientists, doctors, and lawyers) had an average IQ of 157, compared to an average IQ of 150 for his "C" group achievers (sales clerks, technicians, police, carpenters, and pool cleaners).[5] This difference in IQ scores is "meaningless"

---

[1] Gladwell, Malcolm. (2008). *Outliers* (p. 75). New York: Little, Brown and Company.
[2] Dubey, Mohan. (2005). *Gifted and talented education* (p. 23). New Delhi: Mittal Publications.
[3] Leslie, Mitchell. (2000, July/August). The vexing legacy of Lewis Terman. *Stanford Magazine*.
[4] Eysenck, Hans (2009). *The structure and measurement of intelligence* (p. 98). New Brunswick, New Jersey: Transaction Publishers. Leslie, *supra* note 3.
[5] Leslie, *supra* note 3. Goleman, Daniel. (1995, March 7). 75 years later, study still tracking geniuses. *The New York Times*.

in this upper IQ range, according to Stanford psychologist Al Hastorf, a former director of the Terman Study of the Gifted.[6] The factor that stood out in predicting career achievement was not IQ but motivation. Students in the C group "showed a lack of persistence in pursing their goals, whether in school or work," while students in the A group, at an early age, were more engaged and displayed greater "will power, perseverance and desire to excel."[7]

Terman also erred in measuring the gross productivity of his students instead of their relative productivity. Although the Termites who became scientists were productive scholars, for instance, their output was markedly below that of eminent scientists. Dean Simonton, an international expert on intelligence and creativity, explains how the productivity of Terman's scientists compares with that of Nobel laureates:

> [O]n average, Terman's notable scientists produced about 29 publications by the time they had reached their mid-40s. In contrast, American Nobel laureates in the sciences averaged about 38 publications by the time they were 39 years old, and claimed about 59 publications by their mid-40s. That amounts to a twofold disparity in output. Hence, Terman's intellectual elite was not of the same caliber as the true scientific elite of the same nation and era.[8]

Two of the students Terman deemed to be insufficiently intelligent to participate in his study, Luis Alvarez and William Shockley, won the Nobel Prize in Physics. None of the Termites received a Nobel Prize or a Pulitzer Prize.[9] Nor did any of the Termites become world-class musicians like Isaac Stern and Yehudi Menuhim – two other students rejected by Terman for insufficient IQ scores.[10] "All in all," writes David Shenk, the author of *The Genius in All of Us*, "Terman's epic studies in genius turned out to be studies in disappointment."[11]

Terman's study reminds us that one of life's most intriguing questions is why highly intelligent people fail to make contributions to society commensurate with their intellectual abilities while people of average or below average intelligence advance to positions of leadership, responsibility, and influence incommensurate with their measured intelligence. Exceptional ability, it seems, is not consistently transformed into exceptional performance. Intelligence does not appear to be reliably predictive of maturity,

---

[6] Goleman, *supra* note 5.   [7] Ibid.

[8] Simonton, Dean. (1994). *Greatness: Who makes history and why* (p. 222). New York: The Guilford Press.

[9] Leslie, *supra* note 3.

[10] Shenk, David. (2010). *The genius in all of us* (p. 74). New York: Doubleday.   [11] Ibid.

judgment, or success, indicating that other skills, traits, and attitudes like motivation, self-discipline, and perseverance play major roles in influencing if not determining our achievements. In professional practices, for example, the determinants of competence and achievement tend to involve "noncognitive skills, including communication (language, empathy, integrity, compassion), collaboration (responsibility, respect, duty), and continuous improvement (recognition of limitations, motivation to improve)."[12]

Because noncognitive skills may be more important than cognitive skills in determining individual fulfillment and career success, this chapter explores some of the most important noncognitive skills. These soft skills, powerful in their practical effects but generally neglected in traditional education, include resilience, willpower, self-efficacy, optimism, emotional granularity, feedback elicitation, curiosity, goal achievement, embodied cognition, and mindfulness.

RESILIENCE

Resilience is the capacity to bounce back from setbacks and become a more capable and adaptive person after the setback.[13] It has three features: (1) an ability to absorb stress and continue functioning despite adversity; (2) an ability to recover from untoward events; and (3) an ability to learn and grow from previous episodes of resilient action.[14] Resilient people tend to have "a staunch acceptance of reality; a deep belief, often buttressed by strongly held values, that life is meaningful; and an uncanny ability to improvise."[15]

A resilient person emerges from difficult circumstances by forming more elaborate response capabilities rather than more defenses.[16] Fragile people, in contradistinction, build elaborate defenses in a vain effort to prevent problems from occurring and are ill-equipped to handle problems when they inevitably penetrate those defenses.[17] The most resilient people learn to thrive under adverse circumstances, while most people, including attorneys, freeze, fret,

---

[12]　Kirk, Lynne. (2007, January). Professionalism in medicine: Definitions and considerations for teaching. *Proceedings (Baylor University Medical Center)*, 20(1), 3–16.

[13]　See Duhigg, Charles. (2012). *The power of habit* (p. 124). New York: Random House. Harford, Tim. (2011). *Why success always starts with failure*. New York: Farrar, Straus and Giroux.

[14]　Weick, Karl E., & Sutcliffe, Kathleen. (2001). *Managing the unexpected* (p. 71). San Francisco, California: Jossey-Bass.

[15]　Coutu, Diane. (2002, May). How resilience works. *Harvard Business Review*.

[16]　See Taleb, Nassim Nicholas. (2012). *Antifragile*. New York: Random House.

[17]　Weick & Sutcliffe, *supra* note 14 at 72.

and fail.[18] Many professionals, business professor Chris Argyris observes, "have extremely 'brittle' personalities. When suddenly faced with a situation they cannot immediately handle, they tend to fall apart."[19]

Your level of resilience can be assessed by responses (true/very much like me vs. false/not like me at all) to these types of statements:

> If I am being considered for an important professional award or promotion and it goes to someone I consider less qualified, I can usually move on quickly.[20]
>
> If I make a mistake at work and get reprimanded for it, I can shrug it off and take it as a learning experience.[21]
>
> I finish whatever I begin.[22]
>
> I have overcome setbacks to conquer an important challenge.[23]

People who agree with statements like these score higher on resilience. In extreme cases, these highly resilient people may be too adaptable (e.g., inappropriately tolerant of objectionable behavior) or too perseverant (e.g., disregarding negative feedback and other information signaling a need for reappraisal).[24] Ultra high resilience also may reflect a lack of empathy and kindness, as when exceptionally tenacious people refuse to understand why tasks are hard for ordinarily tenacious people.[25]

Resilience is a critical trait for attorneys. Fifty-six percent of attorneys report that the ability to "exhibit resilience after a set-back" is immediately necessary for a new attorney's success; an additional 40 percent of attorneys state that it is a necessary trait that "must be acquired for the lawyer's continued success over

[18]   See Ripley, Amanda. (2008). *The unthinkable* (pp. 163–178). New York: Three Rivers Press. Kiser, Randall. (2011). *How leading lawyers think* (p. 99). Heidelberg, New York: Springer. ("Although realism may seem to be a logical and ordinary response to a catastrophic event, only 10%–20% of victims can pull themselves together to plan their recovery. Many people 'go numb' and wander around in a daze. Others delay, procrastinate, retreat to a state of denial and become lethargic. Rather rapidly they become resigned, disintegrate psychologically, tidily arrange their personal belongings and lie down to die quietly or, if at sea, slip over the side of an inflatable boat, saying 'I'll be back in a few.' ")

[19]   Argyris, Chris. (1991, May–June). Teaching smart people how to learn. *Harvard Business Review*.

[20]   Davidson, Richard, & Begley, Sharon. *The emotional life of your brain* (p. 46). New York: Penguin Group.

[21]   Ibid.

[22]   Duckworth, Angela, Peterson, Christopher, Matthews, Michael, & Kelly, Dennis. (2007). Grit: Perseverance and passion for long-term goals. *Journal of Personality and Social Psychology*, 92(6), 1087–1101.

[23]   Ibid.   [24]   Davidson & Begley, *supra* note 20 at 44.

[25]   Tough, Paul. (2012). *How children succeed* (p. 99). Boston: Houghton Mifflin Harcourt.

time."[26] Similarly, 59 percent of attorneys identify the ability to "enjoy over-coming challenges" as an immediately necessary trait, and 22 percent regard it as a necessary trait that must be acquired over time.[27] For clients, an attorney's ability to respond constructively to criticism and setbacks is an essential part of a successful attorney–client relationship, as Gregory Gilman, General Counsel of Science Media LLC, explains:

> I don't think anyone has ever provided me with work that I was 100 percent satisfied with all of the time. For every firm that we've worked with, and we've worked with probably a dozen or more, there were times when we had to go back and retread some issues. For me, it will be important to see their ability to get it right after discussion, their willingness to remedy any errors and the speed with which they can remedy those errors.[28]

Despite the importance of resilience for attorneys and clients, lawyers have notoriously low levels of resilience. Larry Richard, a psychologist and former trial lawyer who has studied attorney personality extensively, reports that 90 percent of attorneys score below average in resiliency.[29] Noting that resilience-building may be the most important skill for attorneys, Richard describes the advantages to be gained from enhancing resilience:

> Lawyers today need to learn how to build their Resilience skills. Doing so has a double benefit – first, it reduces their poor response to change, stress, and adversity, and further it helps toughen them so that they don't have as many setbacks in the first place. It also helps them recover faster when they do have a setback. But the second benefit is the more important one – the very same Resilience-building techniques that protect you from adversity also build positive resources. Lawyers who have learned how to boost their psychologi-cal Resilience are more likely to be collaborative, grateful, friendly, less critical, more open-minded, more social and more optimistic. And these characteristics, in turn, are all predictors of greater success in the workplace, and greater life satisfaction.[30]

[26] Gerkman, Alli, & Cornett, Logan. (2016, July). *Foundations for practice: The whole lawyer and the character quotient* (p. 17). Denver, Colorado: Institute for the Advancement of the American Legal System.
[27] Ibid. at 13.
[28] Brisbon, Melanie. (2016, May 3). Business builder. *San Francisco Daily Journal*, p. 4.
[29] Richard, Larry. (2012, September 19). Resilience and lawyer negativity. Retrieved from www.lawyerbrainblog.com/2012/09/resilience-and-lawyer-negativity/. See Richard, Larry. (2008). Herding cats: The lawyer personality revealed. *LAWPRO*, 7(1), 2–5.
[30] Richard, Larry. (2013, November 14). The psychologically savvy leader. Retrieved from: www.lawyerbrainblog.com/2013/11/the-psychologically-savvy-leader/.

The most resilient lawyers distinguish themselves in four respects, according to Richard and his colleagues Paula Davis-Laack and David Shearon:[31]

- *They are inspired.* They build resilience and heighten their professional engagement by finding meaning, value, and impact in their work. They see their work as more of a calling than a task.
- *They think differently under stressful conditions.* Although many people under stress catastrophize and fixate on worst-case scenarios, resilient people maintain a flexible, objective thinking style. They try to find some aspect of a problem over which they have control, influence, or leverage.
- *They connect with others when stressed.* Instead of isolating themselves under adversity, resilient people moderate their stress and others' stress by relating and providing help to others.
- *They tend to be givers rather than takers.* Resilient people focus on others' needs and find meaning in determining what other people need from them. They are driven more by a desire to maintain strong bonds with others than to achieve an equal balance between giving and taking.

These behaviors, Richard asserts, "reinforce and support each other. For example, when you focus on creating better relationships, you also increase meaning in your life because the interactions you have with the people who matter most are more high quality."[32]

Resilience, like all of the attitudes, traits, and habits discussed in this chapter, is not a fixed feature of our personality and can be learned and enhanced. It also can be lost, as occurred in Primo Levi's life. He survived and wrote about his life in the concentration camp at Auschwitz but committed suicide 40 years later, saying his depression was "worse than Auschwitz, because I'm no longer young and I have scant resilience."[33] Building and maintaining resilience requires attorneys to assess their current capacities and commit themselves to continuous self-evaluation and improvement in these eight dimensions of adaptability, flexibility, and versatility: (1) solving problems creatively; (2) learning new technologies,

---

[31] Davis-Laack, Paula, Richard, Larry, & Shearon, David. (2016, June 14). Four things resilient lawyers do differently. *Law Practice Today.* See Richard, Larry, Davis-Laack, Paula, & Shearon, David. (2013, Summer). Increasing lawyer resilience: New remedies from the front lines. *PDC Linkletter,* 2(1).

[32] Ibid.

[33] Wood, James. (2015, September 28). The art of witness. *The New Yorker.* See Levi, Primo. (1995). *Survival in Auschwitz.* New York: Simon & Schuster.

tasks, and procedures; (3) demonstrating interpersonal adaptability in communicating and working with others; (4) adjusting physically to fit into and excel in the work environment; (5) changing plans, goals, actions, and priorities to deal with uncertain and unpredictable work situations; (6) handling work stress; (7) demonstrating cultural adaptability; and (8) handling emergencies and crisis situations.[34] Each of these dimensions of resilience is predictive of professional success.[35]

Building resilience ultimately requires a difficult assessment of how we reacted to previous setbacks and how we can develop flexibility and improve our performance in the future. Although this self-assessment is uncomfortable, sometimes painful in the short term, it promotes growth and resilience in the long term and establishes a new model of continuous performance, evaluation, goal setting, and execution. Our initial resistance to introspection and evaluation, however, stymies most efforts to build resilience. Attorneys committed to building resilience, therefore, need to overcome these common, self-protective practices: projecting perpetual success and infallibility to deny failures and quash criticism; impugning the motives of detractors instead of considering the merits of their opinions; presenting diversionary explanations to obscure what actually happened and avoid remedial actions; and believing that responding to criticism and accepting advice from others is a sign of weakness.[36] As Henry Ford observed, "failure is only the opportunity more intelligently to begin again. There is no disgrace in honest failure; there is disgrace in fearing to fail."[37]

WILLPOWER/SELF-REGULATION

Self-regulation is not tested on any state bar examination, but 97 percent of attorneys believe the ability to "regulate emotions and demonstrate self-control"

[34] Shadrick, Scott B., & Lussier, James W. (2009). Training complex cognitive skills: A theme-based approach to the development of battlefield skills. In Ericsson, K. Anders. (Ed.). *Development of Professional Expertise* (p. 287). New York: Cambridge University Press.

[35] Pulakos, E.D., Arad, S., Donovan, M.A., & Plamondon, K.E. (2000). Adaptability in the workplace: Development of a taxonomy of adaptive performance. *Journal of Applied Psychology*, 85(4), 612–624. Pulakos, E.D., Schmitt, N., Dorsey, D.W., Arad, S., Borman, W. C., & Hedge, J.W. (2002). Predicting adaptive performance: Further tests of a model of adaptability. *Human Performance* 15(4). 299–323. Burtscher, M. J., Wacker, J., Grote, G., & Manser, T. (2010). Managing nonroutine events in anesthesia: The role of adaptive coordination. *Human Factors*, 52(2), 282–294.

[36] Sonnenfeld, Jeffrey, & Ward, Andrew. (2007). *Firing back: How great leaders rebound after career disasters* (pp. 61–77). Boston, Massachusetts: Harvard Business School Press.

[37] Berns, Gregory. (2008). *Iconoclast* (p. 125). Boston, Massachusetts: Harvard Business Press.

is required for an attorney's success.[38] That self-regulation is essential to professional achievement and a fulfilling life is demonstrated by multiple studies showing that "willpower is the single most important keystone habit for individual success."[39] Consistent with these findings, research indicates that self-regulation is more predictive of human performance than IQ.[40] Despite its importance in achievement and fulfillment, self-regulation is the characteristic we are *least* likely to identify as one of our virtues and most likely to identify as a personal failing.[41] Our lack of willpower, moreover, is "the most commonly cited barrier to making lifestyle changes."[42]

When we talk about "willpower," "self-control," "self-discipline," and "self-regulation," each of us has a specific concept in mind – possibly derived from a recent personal shortcoming – that may be more idiosyncratic than instructive. When psychologists use those terms, they are referring to "the capacity to suppress thoughts, inhibit impulses, overcome temptations or change habits."[43] This capacity usually "takes the form of overriding one response or behavior and replacing it with a less common but more desired response."[44] Neuroscientist Antonio Damasio offers a more succinct definition: "Willpower is just another name for the idea of choosing according to long-term outcomes rather than short-term ones."[45]

Willpower generally has three components: (1) a commitment to standards and goals; (2) a continuous process of monitoring our emotions and behavior; and (3) the capacity to make personal changes by overriding initial responses and redirecting behavior.[46] Willpower, by definition, requires a standard or goal because willpower is a purposeful attempt to control motivation and behavior to meet a standard or goal. A standard may include "ideals,

[38] Gerkman & Cornett, *supra* note 26 at 14.   [39] Duhigg, *supra* note 13 at 131.

[40] Duckworth, Angela L., & Seligman, Martin E.P. (2005). Self-discipline outdoes IQ in predicting academic performance of adolescents. *Psychological Science*, 16(12), 939–44. See Coyle, Daniel. (2009). *The talent code* (p. 150). New York: Bantam Dell. Brooks, David. (2011). *The social animal* (pp. 123–124). New York: Random House.

[41] Baumeister, Roy, & Tierney, John. (2011). *Willpower* (p. 2). New York: Penguin Press.

[42] American Psychological Association. (2015, February 4). *Stress in America: Paying with our health*, p. 10.

[43] Chatzisarantis, Nikos L.D., & Hagger, Martin S. (2015). Illusionary delusions. Willingness to exercise self-control can mask effects of glucose on self-control performance in experimental paradigms that use identical self-control tasks. *Appetite* 84, 322.

[44] Baumeister, Roy F., Schmeichel, Brandon J., & Vohs, Kathleen D. (2007). Self-regulation and the executive function: The self as controlling agent. In Kruglanski, A.W., & Higgins, E.T. (Eds.). *Social psychology: Handbook of basic principles* (2nd ed.) (p. 517). New York: Guilford.

[45] Damasio, Antonio. (1994). *Descartes' error* (p. 175). New York: Quill.

[46] Baumeister, Roy, & Heatherton, Todd. (1996). Self-regulation failure: An overview. *Psychological Inquiry*, 7(1), 1–15. Baumeister, Schmeichel & Vohs, *supra* note 44 at 516–539.

expectations, goals, values and comparison targets" (e.g., the status quo or what other people have achieved).[47] Monitoring is accomplished through ongoing awareness of our emotions and behavior; assessment of our progress and the rate of progress toward a goal; detection of discrepancies between our current behavior and intended behavior; and recall of conditions that previously diverted us from goal-fulfillment so that we avoid those conditions in the future.[48] Making personal changes occurs when we recognize a gap between the current state and the standards and then take conscious action to override our current behavior or rely on a prior "implementation intention" that automatically triggers specific plans and actions when a specific event occurs or a time arrives.[49]

Higher levels of self-control are correlated with numerous qualities and conditions that facilitate achievement and enhance personal well-being: physical health, sound personal finances, better grades, higher self-esteem, increased empathy, superior conflict resolution skills, fewer psychological problems, and higher ratings from coworkers and supervisors.[50] Lower levels of self-control, in contrast, have been linked to financial instability, binge eating, dysfunctional social relationships, poor health, alcohol abuse, juvenile delinquency, and adult criminal activity.[51] Although we cannot conclusively determine whether different levels of self-control are the cause or the result of differences in outcomes, "most theorists assume that personality traits precede behaviors and are therefore more likely the cause than the consequence."[52]

People with strong self-control, we imagine, have extraordinary reservoirs of willpower that enable them to resist the temptations that ensnare ordinary

---

[47] Baumeister, Schmeichel, & Vohs, *supra* note 44 at 523.   [48] Ibid. at 524–525.
[49] Ibid. at 525, 528.
[50] Moffitt, T.E., *et al.* (2011). Gradient of childhood self-control predicts health, wealth, and public safety. *Proceedings of the National Academy of Sciences*, 108, 2693–2698. Tangney, J., Baumeister, R., & Boone, A.L. (2004). High self-control predicts good adjustment, less pathology, better grades, and interpersonal success. *Journal of Personality*, 72, 271–324. Mischel, Walter, Shoda, Yuichi, & Rodriguez, Monica. (1989). Delay of gratification in children. *Science*, 244, 933–938. Mischel, W., & Ayduk, O. (2004). Willpower in a cognitive-affective processing system: The dynamics of delay of gratification. In Baumeister, R.F., & Vohs, K.D. (Eds.). *Handbook of self-regulation: Research, theory, and applications*. New York: Guildford. King, K., Fleming, C.B., Monahan, K.C., & Catalano, R.F. (2011). Changes in self-control problems and attention problems during middle school predict alcohol, tobacco, and marijuana use during high school. *Psychology of Addictive Behaviors*, 25, 69–79. de Ridder, D. T., Lensvelt-Mulders, G., Finkenauer, C., Stok, F.M., & Baumeister, R.F. (2012). Taking stock of self-control: A meta-analysis of how trait self-control relates to a wide range of behaviors. *Personality and Social Psychology Review*, 16, 76–99.
[51] Ibid.   [52] Baumeister, Schmeichel, & Vohs, *supra* note 44 at 517.

people. The reality, however, is that willpower is exercised more in avoidance than extrication, as psychologist Roy Baumeister explains:

> [P]eople with strong self-control spent less time resisting desires than other people did ... These people have less need to use willpower because they're beset by fewer temptations and inner conflicts. They're better at arranging their lives so that they avoid problem situations ... people with good self-control mainly use it not for rescue in emergencies but rather to develop effective habits and routines in school and at work ... people with high self-control consistently report less stress in their lives. They use their self-control not to get through crises but to avoid them. They give themselves enough time to finish a project; they take the car to the shop before it breaks down; they stay away from all-you-can-eat buffets. They play offense instead of defense.[53]

Baumeister's thesis is consistent with management expert Peter Drucker's observation that, for sound reasons grounded in human nature, the Lord's Prayer implores, "lead us not into temptation" instead of seeking divine intervention once tempted.[54] Prospective resistance, it seems, is more likely to be successful than remedial intercession.[55]

LOCUS OF CONTROL AND SELF-EFFICACY

"Locus of control" is a belief about how the world works.[56] People with an *external* locus of control believe that their lives are largely determined by luck, fate, powerful people, and events beyond their control, while people with an *internal* locus of control believe they exercise control over their lives and the outcomes of their decisions and behavior.[57] A statistically correlated concept, "self-efficacy," refers to our perceived ability to "cope, perform and be

---

[53] Baumeister & Tierney, *supra* note 41 at 239.

[54] Peter Drucker's remarks are paraphrased based on the author's recollections from attending his lectures in 2002 at the Peter F. Drucker and Masatoshi Ito Graduate School of Management, Claremont Graduate University.

[55] Ent, Michael R., Baumeister, Roy F., & Tice, Dianne M. (2015, February). Trait self-control and the avoidance of temptation. *Personality and Individual Differences, 74,* 12–15.

[56] Twenge, Jean. (2007). Locus of control. In Baumeister, Roy, & Vohs, Kathleen (Eds.). *Encyclopedia of social psychology* (Vol. II) (p. 530). Thousand Oaks, California: SAGE Publications.

[57] Twenge, Jean, Zhang, Liqing, & Im, Charles. (2004). It's beyond my control: A cross-temporal meta-analysis of increasing externality in locus of control, 1960–2002. *Personality and Social Psychology Review, 9*(3), 308, 309. Caliendo, Marco, Cobb-Clark, Deborah, & Uhlendorff, Arne. (2010, February). *Locus of control and job search strategies* (Discussion paper No. 4750) (p. 2). Institute for the Study of Labor. Van Liew, Julia. (2013). Locus of control. In Gellman, Marc, & Turner, Rick (Eds.). *Encyclopedia of behavioral medicine* (p. 1171). Berlin: Springer.

successful" – our ability, in short, to produce effects.[58] Locus of control and self-efficacy are considered together in this section because they are "among the best dispositional predictors of job satisfaction and job performance," and they display a strong positive correlation, that is, people who have an internal locus of control also tend to score high on self-efficacy assessments.[59]

Locus of Control

Since people with an internal locus of control take individual responsibility for outcomes rather than attributing them to external forces, they monitor and change their behavior to achieve their objectives. They increase their efforts when they are performing below their expectations or when they perceive a discrepancy between their current performance and the required performance. Conversely, people with an external locus of control tend to lower their aspirations or withdraw from the task when faced with negative feedback or other signals indicating that their performance is inadequate.[60] Not surprisingly, an internal locus of control is associated with higher levels of educational attainment, income, openness, conscientiousness, extraversion, and innovation. An external locus of control, in contrast, is correlated with "poor school achievement, helplessness, ineffective stress management, decreased self-control and depression."[61]

In law firms, attorneys' locus of control affects both their attitude and performance, as Lori Berman and Heather Bock, professional development directors at Hogan Lovells, explain:

> People with a high internal locus of control feel they have a great deal of influence over their environment. Conversely, people with a high external locus of control feel that they have no impact on the environment, but rather that external forces affect them. In a law firm, this is likely to mean that attorneys with a high internal locus of control will continue striving to complete a challenging assignment, since they would consider success on that assignment to stem mainly from their effort and intelligence. Attorneys

[58] Judge, Timothy A. & Bono, Joyce E. (2001). Relationship of core self-evaluation traits–self-esteem, generalized self efficacy, locus of control, and emotional stability–with job satisfaction and job performance: A meta-analysis. *Journal of Applied Psychology*, 86(1), 80. Bandura, Albert. (1994). Self-efficacy. In Ramachandran, Vilayanur S. (Ed.). *Encyclopedia of human behavior*, 4, 71. San Diego, California: Academic Press.
[59] Judge & Bono, *supra* note 58 at 86.   [60] Ibid. at 82.
[61] Twenge, Zhang, & Im (2004), *supra* note 57 at 308. Caliendo, Cobb-Clark, & Uhlendorff, *supra* note 57 at 10. Miller, D., Kets de Vries, M., & Toulouse, J. (1982, June 1). Top executive locus of control and its relationship to strategy-making, structure and environment. *Academy of Management Journal*, 25(2), 237–253.

with a high external locus of control may feel that their skills cannot help them to overcome external obstacles, and would consider success on an assignment to result from luck or the impact of other people, rather than from their own skills. Thus, they may be less persistent in attempting to achieve a task in the face of difficulties.[62]

Although studies refer to people as having an internal or external locus of control, it is critical to understand that an individual's locus of control may vary based on roles, assignments, and other contextual factors.[63] The attorney who appears to be fatalistic in undertaking an assignment in one law firm may exhibit a different level of motivation, responsibility, and accountability on another assignment or in a different law firm. These attitudinal differences may result from changes in the work environment, new practice group leaders, attorneys' fluctuating perceptions of their autonomy, and the long-term consequences of blaming adverse events on external conditions.[64]

If you are wondering about the location of your own locus of control, you might benefit from completing the Rotter Internal-External Locus of Control Scale or alternative assessments like the Levenson IPC Scale and the Reid-Ware Three-Factor Internal-External Scale.[65] Illustrative questions from the Rotter assessment, requiring a choice between two alternative statements, are:

a. When I make plans, I am almost certain that I can make them work.
b. It is not always wise to plan too far ahead because many things turn out to be a matter of good or bad fortune anyhow.

a. Becoming a success is a matter of hard work, luck has little or nothing to do with it.

---

[62] Berman, Lori, & Bock, Heather. (2012). Developing attorneys for the future: What can we learn from the fast trackers? *Santa Clara Law Review*, 52(3), 879.

[63] Twenge, Zhang, & Im (2004), *supra* note 57 at 309.

[64] See Lefcourt, Herbert. (1982). *Locus of control: Current trends in theory & research* (2nd Ed.) (p. 163). Hillsdale, New Jersey: Lawrence Erlbaum Associates, Inc.

[65] These scales, with scoring tools, are available online. The Levenson IPC Scale and the Reid-Ware Scale are shown in Halpert, Rita, & Hill, Russ. (2011). *28 measures of locus of control*. Beach Haven, New Jersey: Will To Power Press. For research regarding the validity of these scales, see Lange, R.V., & Tiggemann, M. (1981, August). Dimensionality and reliability of the Rotter I-E locus of control scale. *Journal of Personality Assessment*, 45(4), 398. Lao, Rosina. (1978). Levenson's IPC (Internal-External Control) Scale: A comparison of Chinese and American students. *Journal of Cross-Cultural Psychology*, 9(1), 1113. Zerega, William, Greever, Kathryn, & Tseng, M.S. (1976, July). Stability and concurrent validity of the Rotter Internal-External Locus of Control Scale. *Educational and Psychological Measurement* 36(2), 473. Loas, G., Dardennes, R., Dhee-Perot, P., Leclerc, V., & Fremaux, D. (1994, August–September). Locus of control: Initial validation of a French translation of Levenson's IPC Scale. *Annales Médico-Psychologiques*, 152(7), 466. Lefcourt *supra* note 64.

b. Getting a good job depends mainly on being in the right place at the right time.
a. People are lonely because they don't try to be friendly.
b. There's not much use in trying too hard to please people, if they like you, they like you.

People choosing (b)-type responses to these questions receive scores indicating an external locus of control.[66]

Scores on locus of control assessments since 1960 show a steady increase in the percentage of children and college students with an external locus of control.[67] The ironic result, according to psychology professor Jean Twenge, is that "[a]s individualism has increased, locus of control has become more external."[68]

Self-Efficacy

An internal locus of control is predictive of job satisfaction and job performance as well as a high level of self-efficacy.[69] Although an internal locus of control and high self-efficacy are correlated, they are different concepts: locus of control represents a personal belief about causation in one's life, while self-efficacy is a measure of how well we think we can perform in different situations.[70] Locus of control effects spring from our beliefs about the relative power of external and internal factors, while self-efficacy effects are determined by our perceived "ability to perform across a variety of different situations."[71]

High self-efficacy promotes superior performance by providing a platform of experience and confidence. From this platform, challenges are invited, evaluated, refined, and surmounted. Albert Bandura, a psychology professor, describes the interactions among self-efficacy, confidence, goal setting, and commitment:

> The stronger the perceived self-efficacy, the higher the goal challenges people set for themselves and the firmer is their commitment to them . . .

---

[66]   Rotter, J. B. (1966) Generalized expectancies for internal versus external control of reinforcement. *Psychological Monographs: General and Applied*, 80, 1–28. (Different versions of the Rotter assessment contain a different number of questions and sometimes change the answer format to a scale from 1 ("I do not agree at all") to 7 ("I fully agree")).

[67]   Twenge, Zhang, & Im (2004), *supra* note 57 at 313–314.   [68]   Ibid. at 315.

[69]   Judge & Bono, *supra* note 58 at 86.

[70]   Scherbaum, Charles, Cohen-Charash, Yochi, & Kern, Michael. (2006, December). Measuring self-efficacy: A comparison of three measures using item response theory. *Educational and Psychological Measurement*, 66(6), 1047–1063.

[71]   Ibid. at 1048.

Those who have a high sense of efficacy, visualize success scenarios that provide positive guides and supports for performance. Those who doubt their efficacy, visualize failure scenarios and dwell on the many things that can go wrong. It is difficult to achieve much while fighting self-doubt.[72]

Our self-efficacy beliefs, Bandura asserts, "determine the goals people set for themselves, how much effort they expend, how long they persevere in the face of difficulties, and their resilience to failures."[73] Consequently, attorneys with high self-efficacy are more likely to set challenging goals and persist despite intermediate failures. Attorneys with low self-efficacy, however, tend to question their abilities and "are likely to reduce their efforts and give up quickly when faced with obstacles."[74]

People with a high sense of self-efficacy do not regard their failures as reflections on their abilities. Instead, they see failures as being caused by insufficient effort.[75] As a prominent medical malpractice plaintiffs' attorney explains, "If a case does not turn out the way I expected, it's usually because of not paying attention to details at the beginning of the case. When you hear something from a juror that you had not considered, you didn't prepare. You should never hear something you hadn't expected from a juror."[76]

To assess self-efficacy, psychologists employ measures like Sherer's General Self-Efficacy Scale, Schwarzer and Jerusalem's General Perceived Self-Efficacy Scale, and Chen's New General Self-Efficacy Scale.[77] The Chen scale, which is considered slightly advantageous in at least one study, contains statements with scaled responses (strongly disagree–strongly agree) like these:[78]

When facing difficult tasks, I am certain that I will accomplish them.
I believe I can succeed at most any endeavor to which I set my mind.
I am confident that I can perform effectively on many tasks.

Responses evidencing agreement with these statements are correlated with high self-efficacy. High self-efficacy, in turn, is correlated with higher task

---

[72]   Bandura, *supra* note 58 at 71.
[73]   Bandura, Albert (Ed.). (1995). *Self-efficacy in changing societies* (p. 8). New York: Cambridge University Press. See Druckman, Daniel, & Bjork, Robert A. (Eds.). *Learning, remembering, believing* (p. 173). Washington, DC: National Academies Press.
[74]   Berman & Bock, *supra* note 62 at 880.   [75]   Bandura *supra* note 58.
[76]   Kiser, *supra* note 18 at 12.
[77]   Scherbaum, Cohen-Charash, & Kern, *supra* note 70 at 1049. See Chen, Giliad, Gully, Stanley, & Eden, Dov. (2001, January). Validation of a new general self-efficacy scale. *Organizational Research Methods*, 4(1), 62–83. Panc, Teofil, Mihalcea, Alexandru, & Panc, Ioana. (2012). Self-efficacy survey: A new assessment tool. *Procedia–Social and Behavioral Sciences*, 33, 880–884.
[78]   Scherbaum, Cohen-Charash, & Kern, *supra* note 70 at 1050.

TABLE 4.1. *Comparative importance of positivity based on attorney experience level*

Years in law practice	Positivity necessary immediately (%)	Positivity necessary over time (%)	Positivity necessary immediately or over time (%)
1–10 years	57.5	12.1	69.6
11–20 years	63.1	12.8	75.9
21–30 years	67.2	13.4	80.6
30+ years	69.8	16	85.8

Source: IAALS, Foundations for Practice, Explore the Data

performance, better strategic decision making, and improved organizational performance.[79] But, as a note of caution for confident, goal-driven transactional and litigation attorneys, high self-efficacy also has been linked to "escalating commitment to a losing course of action."[80] In the perpetual battle between prudence and perseverance, prudence is often miscast as a lack of confidence and perseverance is often mistaken for perspicacity.

OPTIMISM

Optimism is enjoying a resurgence among desirable attorney traits. In the IAALS survey, 65 percent of attorneys report that "positivity" is a quality that is necessary in the short term for an attorney's success, while an additional 14 percent regard it as "not necessary in the short term but must be acquired for the lawyer's continued success over time."[81] Only 2 percent of attorneys regard positivity as being irrelevant to an attorney's success.[82] As shown in Table 4.1, attorneys' ratings of positivity's importance are directly related to attorneys' experience levels; the longer an attorney has been practicing, the greater the importance they attach to positivity.[83] The attorneys' ratings do not

[79] Soane, Emma, & Nicholson, Nigel. (2008). Individual differences and decision making. In Hodgkinson, Gerard, & Starbuck, William. (Eds.). *The Oxford handbook of organizational decision making* (p. 345). New York: Oxford University Press.
[80] Ibid.
[81] Gerkman & Cornett, *supra* note 26 at 16. See Lane, Fred, & Lane, Scott. (2004). *Lane's Goldstein trial technique* (3rd ed) (Chapter 7A, p. 6). Eagan, Minnesota: Thomson West. ("While it is important to be realistic with the client, at the same time counsel must never hesitate expressing optimism if the facts justify it. Sincere expressions of optimism are very helpful in establishing a healthy attorney-client relationship.")
[82] Gerkman & Cornett, *supra* note 26.
[83] The data in Table 4.1 does not appear in the IAALS report referenced in fn. 26. It was derived from the "Explore the Data" page of the IAALS website, available at http://iaals.du.edu/foundations/survey.

vary significantly by practice type. Sixty-four percent of litigation attorneys think positivity is necessary in the short term, while a slightly higher percent of transactional attorneys (67.3 percent) regard it as necessary in the short term.

The importance of positivity is again shown in legal employers' consistent emphasis on upbeat attitudes and enthusiasm. Structured interviews with legal employers regarding ideal attorney characteristics reveal a strong demand for optimistic, resilient attorneys:

> Employers from diverse practice backgrounds stressed the importance of bringing a positive attitude to the workplace. This includes the ability to "stay positive" or "pretty steady" in the face of challenging work assignments or difficult cases and being able to "go on to your next case" and "not dwell" after an unfavorable outcome in court. For some employers, a positive attitude means new hires who are "excited about the work that [they] do."[84]

Legal employers depict positive attitudes as an attorney being "enthusiastic and personable," wanting "to be involved in the case," asking "what else can I do on this case?," "stepping up to help without being asked," and generally "wanting to come to work, and being 'excited to be there and excited to accept the challenges that there may be.' "[85]

The current enthusiasm for optimism runs counter to earlier research indicating that optimistic law students perform worse in law school than pessimistic law students.[86] After analyzing law students' psychological assessments and their academic performance at the University of Virginia School of Law, psychologist Martin Seligman and his colleagues found that pessimistic law students outperformed optimistic law students on grade point averages (GPAs) and executive board membership on a law review. Seligman noted that the legal profession is unique in rewarding pessimism "because seeing trouble as pervasive and permanent is a component of what the law profession deems prudence."[87] Pessimism, he observes, may make an attorney professionally successful but personally miserable.[88]

---

[84] Wawrose, Susan, (2013). What do legal employers want to see in new graduates?: Using focus groups to find out. *Ohio Northern University Law Review*, 39. 529

[85] Ibid. at 524–528

[86] Satterfield, J.M., Monahan, J., & Seligman, M.E. (1997, Winter). Law school performance predicted by explanatory style. *Behavioral Sciences and the Law*, 15(1), 95–105. See Seligman, M.E. Verkuil., P. R. & Kang, T. H. (2001, November). Why lawyers are unhappy. *Cardozo Law Review*, 23(1), 33–54. Weiss, Debra. (2007, November 9). Pessimistic law students more successful, study finds. *ABA Journal*.

[87] Seligman, Martin. (2004). *Authentic happiness* (p. 178). New York: Free Press.

[88] Ibid. at 181. (Attorneys will be "depressed, anxious, and angry a lot of the time.")

Seligman's research regarding pessimism and law school performance has been questioned, but his research has not been substantively disputed during the 20 years after its publication. A possible limitation of this research, how-ever, is that the results should not be extrapolated from law school to law practice. Since the correlation between law school grades and success in law practice is weak or nonexistent, as discussed in Chapters 1 and 2, the positive correlation between pessimism and law school achievement may not extend to law practice success. None of the studies of essential attorney skills examined in Chapter 2 and the appendix indicates that attorneys or clients regard pessimism as a desirable trait – despite its apparent correlation with higher law school grades. The pessimism that underpins high performance in law school does not appear to promote high performance in law practice.

Although attorneys and clients regard optimism as a desirable trait, they have a specific type of optimism in mind – called "flexible" or "complex" optimism – and are not seeking the barrister version of Pollyanna. Flexible optimism requires judgment; it is a "psychological strategy to be exercised when appropriate as opposed to a reflex or habit over which we have no control."[89] Its underlying premise is that "people should be optimistic when the future can be changed by positive thinking but not otherwise."[90]

The strategic judgment required for flexible optimism is intended to cap-ture the benefits of optimism (e.g., positive mood, perseverance, popularity, effective problem solving, and good health) while simultaneously avoiding the inaccurate risk assessments that result from indiscriminate optimism and wishful thinking.[91] In flexible optimism, both optimism and pessimism have legitimate roles:

> Pessimism has a role to play, both in society at large and in our own lives; we must have the courage to endure pessimism when its perspective is valuable. What we want is not blind optimism but flexible optimism – optimism with its eyes open. We must be able to use pessimism's keen sense of reality when we need it, but without having to dwell in its dark shadows.[92]

Learning how and when to employ flexible optimism "does not erode your sense of values or your judgment. Rather it frees you to use a tool to better achieve the goals you set."[93]

When attorneys are obdurately pessimistic they undermine their own psy-chological well-being and become an impediment to client problem solving. The pervasive pessimism that characterizes many attorneys is associated with a

---

[89] Peterson, Christopher. (2000). The future of optimism. *American Psychologist*, 55(1), 51.
[90] Ibid. [91] Ibid. at 44, 50. [92] Seligman, Martin. (2004), *supra* note 87 at 292. [93] Ibid.

tendency to generalize from a single negative event to all related occurrences.[94] This comprehensive negativity – often expressed by attorneys as a weary cynicism that is intended to pass for worldly wisdom – stifles creativity, quashes motivation, and effectively halts problem-solving efforts. Flexible optimism overcomes this tendency by seeing setbacks as temporary, specific, instructive, and solvable.[95] "Every case has problems," a prominent plaintiffs' personal injury attorney muses. "It's a question of how you deal with them. If you think positively about the problems, you can come up with a way of dealing with it."[96]

EMOTIONAL GRANULARITY

Learning not to suppress emotions, as discussed in the previous chapter, is a first step toward a durable sense of well-being and sound relationships with friends, colleagues, and clients. The next, steeper step is learning how to identify emotions with precision, a process called "emotional differentiation" or "emotional granularity." Being able to distinguish general emotional states (e.g., upset and happy) from specific states (angry vs. frustrated and contentment vs. joy) results in what psychologists call "larger repertoires of emotion-regulation strategies"[97] – in human-speak, less distractibility and better problem-solving skills and coping abilities.

People who can identify emotions with precision and specificity are healthier, more resilient, less likely to suffer from depression and alcohol dependence, and better at evaluating complex information and options.[98] Despite these benefits of emotional granularity, only 36 percent of people can accurately identify their emotions as they happen.[99] "This means," psychologist Travis Bradberry explains, "that two thirds of us are typically controlled by our

---

[94] Robbennolt, Jennifer, & Sternlight, Jean. (2012). *Psychology for lawyers* (p. 428). Chicago: American Bar Association. Rosen, Corie. (2011). Creating the optimistic classroom: What law schools can learn from attribution style effects. *McGeorge Law Review*, 42, 328.

[95] Rosen, *supra* note 94 at 329.   [96] Kiser (2011), *supra* note 18 at 103.

[97] Tugade, M. M., Fredrickson, B. L., & Barrett, L. F. (2004). Psychological resilience and positive emotional granularity: Examining the benefits of positive emotions on coping and health. *Journal of Personality*, 72(6), 1161, 1176.

[98] Ibid. at 1175–1184. Smidt, Katharine, & Suvak, Michael. (2015). A brief, but nuanced, review of emotional granularity and emotion differentiation research. *Current Opinion in Psychology*, 3, 48–51. Kashdan, Todd, Barrett, Lisa, & McKnight, Patrick. (2015). Unpacking emotion differentiation: Transforming unpleasant experience by perceiving distinctions in negativity. *Current Directions in Psychological Research*, 24(1), 10–16.

[99] Bradberry, Travis, & Greaves, Jean. (2009). *Emotional intelligence 2.0* (p. 13). San Diego, California: TalentSmart.

emotions and are not yet skilled at spotting them and using them to our benefit."[100]

Although we sometimes think that getting closer to our emotions and labeling them will make us feel worse, research indicates the opposite is true: our ability to understand and modulate our emotions depends on our capacity "to classify experiences into discrete emotional categories."[101] Identifying emotions with precision ("I am angry") enables the brain to respond with more specific actions, while generalized emotions ("I feel miserable") fail to evoke effective responses.[102] Like legal research software, our brains process inputs more efficiently and effectively when the critical issues are precisely identified.

Fortunately, we can readily expand our emotional vocabulary and use this enhanced vocabulary to differentiate among emotions.[103] "The good news," says psychology professor Lisa Barrett, "is that emotional granularity is a skill." As we learn more about different emotional states and become more aware of our emotions, she contends, we achieve higher levels of emotional granularity. Her findings are supported by extensive research with children and adults, demonstrating that emotional granularity "is a simple, easily trainable skill."[104] To remind yourself to identify emotions with specificity, you might find it helpful to remember the psychologists' phrase, "name it to tame it."[105]

FEEDBACK AND ADVICE

"Feedback" was not part of philosopher John Stuart Mill's lexicon when he wrote *On Liberty* in 1859. Yet his insights succinctly capture the benefits of feedback:

> In the case of any person whose judgment is really deserving of confidence, how has it become so? Because he has kept his mind open to criticism of his opinions and conduct. Because it has been his practice to listen to all that could be said against him; to profit by as much of it as was just . . . The steady habit of correcting and completing his own opinion by collating it with those of others, so far from causing doubt and hesitation in carrying it into practice, is the only stable foundation for a just reliance on it.[106]

---

[100]   Ibid.
[101]   Smidt & Suvak, *supra* note 98 at 48. See Rock, David. (2009). *Your brain at work* (p. 114). New York: HarperCollins.
[102]   Barrett, Lisa Feldman. (2016, June 3). Are you in despair? That's good. *The New York Times.* See Rock, *supra* note 101 at 114–115. New York: HarperCollins.
[103]   Kashdan, Barrett, & McNight, *supra* note 98 at 13.   [104]   Ibid.
[105]   Daniel, Siegel. (2010). *Mindsight* (p. 116). New York: Bantam Books.
[106]   Mill, John Stuart, (1859). *On Liberty*, Chapter II, Of the Liberty of Thought and Discussion.

The part that John Stuart Mill left out – and probably the reason feedback is no more popular today than it was in 1859 – is that feedback often hurts and makes us feel uncomfortable. Even seemingly confident people avoid feedback; in a survey of 70,000 business leaders, the activity ranked as the least frequent among 30 leadership behaviors was "asks for feedback on how his/her actions affect others' performance."[107]

Feedback, paradoxically, remains the most valuable and the most irritating source of self-development. It has "its greatest effect when a learner expects a response to be correct and it turns out to be wrong" – making it most effective when it is least expected.[108] Since feedback does not reliably confirm what we want to hear, our tendency is to forgo the benefits of feedback whenever it threatens to impinge upon our self-esteem. When it comes to knowing what other people think about us or our performance, ignorance is not only bliss; it may be essential to preserving our illusion of competence until our self-esteem can handle another piece of advice from a well-intentioned colleague.[109]

We also are reluctant to seek feedback or ask for advice because we think we are bothering other people and imagine that they will think less of us or assume that we are incompetent.[110] Research, however, indicates that our apprehensions may be baseless. People who ask for advice are perceived to be more competent than people who do not seek advice.[111] The "robust relationship between advice seeking and judgments of competence" is even stronger when (1) the task is difficult rather than easy; (2) the person evaluating the advice seeker's competence is the same person whose advice is sought instead of a third party; and (3) people seek advice from an expert on the subject rather than someone who is unfamiliar with the subject.[112] An additional benefit of seeking advice is that "being asked for advice caused advisors to feel more self-confident and, in turn, to view the advice seeker more positively."[113] By asking someone to provide advice, business professor Francesca Gino explains, "advice seekers stroke the

---

[107] Rhode, Deborah. (2013). *Lawyers as leaders* (p. 27). New York: Oxford University Press. See Jackman, Jay, & Strober, Myra. (2003, April). Fear of feedback. *Harvard Business Review*, p. 101.

[108] Hattie, John, & Timperley, Helen. (2007, March). The power of feedback. *Review of Educational Research*, 77(1), 95.

[109] Crocker, Jennifer, & Nuer, Noah. (2003). The insatiable quest for self-worth. *Psychological Inquiry*, 14(1), 31–34. DeLong, Thomas. (2011). *Flying without a net* (p. 199). Boston, Massachusetts: Harvard Business Review Press. ("Deep down inside, we worry that if someone tells us what he thinks of us and it's not flattering, it might shatter how we see ourselves.")

[110] Brooks, Alison, Gino, Francesca, & Schweitzer, Maurice. (2015, June). Smart people ask for (my) advice: Seeking advice boosts perceptions of competence. *Management Science*, 61(6), 1424–1425, 1432.

[111] Ibid. at 1431.   [112] Ibid. at 1431–1433.   [113] Ibid. at 1431.

adviser's ego and can gain valuable insights."[114] And the advisors "do not think less of you – they actually think you're smarter."[115]

Despite our reluctance to seek feedback and advice, those inputs have proven to be essential components of self-development. Expert performers distinguish themselves by proactively seeking feedback and advice from colleagues with a higher level of expertise.[116] The continual elicitation of feedback is particularly important in professions, like law, where the effects of decisions and actions are not immediately available or directly traceable to a single person or organization.[117] "The most effective strategy to foster self-development in professional formation," writes law professor Neil Hamilton, "is to internalize the habit of actively seeking feedback and reflecting on it."[118] Even some judges welcome and integrate criticisms, as Santa Barbara County Superior Court Judge Michael Carrozzo explains: "I've learned in life that trying to defend your actions oftentimes stifles you from learning and getting better. I have no problem reconsidering issues if something's been pointed out to me."[119]

The good news and bad news about feedback is that it presents problems in only two circumstances: giving feedback and receiving feedback. Both are awkward, strained, stressful, and subject to misunderstandings.[120] Giving feedback often is ineffective because people in superior positions jump to conclusions about the reasons for a subordinate's behavior, ignore or underestimate the impact of external conditions on a subordinate's performance, and try to manage the communication to gain and maintain control.[121] Receiving feedback is equally problematic because subordinates tend to remember positive feedback, forget negative feedback, and rationalize their behavior as necessary to preserve their positive self-image.[122] Some corrective steps are described below to overcome these tendencies and upgrade how we give and respond to feedback.

[114] Korkki, Phyllis. (2015, September 5). Smart workers seek out advice, study suggests. *The New York Times.*
[115] Ibid.
[116] Rosen, Michael, Salas, Eduardo, Lyons, Rebecca, & Fiore, Stephen. (2008). Expertise and naturalistic decision making in organizations: Mechanisms of effective decision making. In Hodgkinson, Gerard, & Starbuck, William (Eds.). *The Oxford handbook of organizational decision making* (p. 218). New York: Oxford University Press.
[117] Ibid.
[118] Hamilton, Neil. (2013). The qualities of the professional lawyer. In Haskins, Paul (Ed.). *Essential qualities of the professional lawyer* (pp. 1–18). Chicago: ABA Publishing.
[119] Keys, Laurinda. (2015, October 15). An officer and a judge. *San Francisco Daily Journal*, p. 2.
[120] Manzoni, Jean-Francois. (2002, September). *Harvard Business Review*, pp. 114–119.
[121] Ibid. at 118.
[122] Russo, J. Edward, & Schoemaker, Paul. (2002). *Winning decisions* (p. 200). New York: Random House. Oettingen, Gabriele. (2014). *Rethinking positive thinking* (p. 112). New York: Penguin Random House.

Giving Feedback

Organizations do a lousy job of providing employee evaluations and feedback. Surveys show that 55–75 percent of employees think performance reviews are unfair or inaccurate, and about half of all employees say they are surprised by their ratings.[123] One in four employees say that they dread performance reviews "more than anything else in their other working lives."[124] The widespread dissatisfaction with evaluations indicates that they are failing to meet three basic requirements: (1) the person providing the evaluation must be perceived to be reliable and to have good intentions in making the evaluation; (2) the feedback development process must be perceived to be fair by reflecting all available information and incorporating the employee's explanations, clarifications, and opinions; and (3) the feedback communication process must be perceived to be fair by showing respect for the employee, supporting the employee despite disagreements, and paying careful attention to the employee's ideas.[125]

Quick, effective methods of improving formal and informal evaluations and feedback include the following:

- *Respect privacy.* Make sure that evaluation and feedback are delivered in a private environment free from distractions. Allow ample time for the meeting. If negative feedback was voiced in a meeting, apologize and assure the person receiving the negative feedback that in the future those discussions will be one-on-one.[126]
- *Increase frequency.* Frequent, informal evaluations are more effective than annual, formal evaluations. Many companies – Microsoft Corp., Eli Lilly & Co., Adobe Systems, General Electric, and Accenture, for example – have abandoned annual evaluations in favor of ongoing evaluations.[127] People "tend to become less defensive if they receive frequent feedback."[128]

---

[123] Rock, David, Davis, Josh, & Jones, Beth. (2014, August 8). Kill your performance ratings. *Strategy + Business.* Schoenberger, Chana. (2015, October 26). How performance reviews can harm mental health. *The Wall Street Journal.* Heen, Sheila, & Stone, Douglas. (2014, January–February). Find the coaching in criticism. *Harvard Business Review,* p. 109.

[124] Heen & Stone, *supra* note 123.

[125] Manzoni, Jean-Francois. (2002, September). A better way to deliver bad news. *Harvard Business Review,* p. 118.

[126] Garvin, David, & Margolis, Joshua. (2015, January–February). The art of giving and receiving advice. *Harvard Business Review,* p. 66. Shellenbarger, Sue. (2014, June 18). How to take criticism well. *The Wall Street Journal.* See Stone, Douglas, & Heen, Sheila. (2014). *Thanks for the feedback: The science and art of receiving feedback well.* New York: Viking.

[127] See Weber, Lauren. (2016, August 21). At Kimberly-Clark, "dead wood" workers have nowhere to hide. *The Wall Street Journal.* Rock, Davis & Jones, *supra* note 123.

[128] Shellenbarger, *supra* note 126.

- *Be specific.* Avoid generalized personal feedback like "great job" or "good work." These phrases contain insufficient information to increase engagement, instill confidence, and direct future behavior.[129] Also avoid general characterizations of behavior like "you lack motivation" or "you seem to be distracted." If you tell someone, "You're irresponsible," for example, "he or she may argue about that statement." But if you describe specific actions like, "You forgot to check on Mrs. Jones' lab work, and the results weren't available when we needed to use them to take care of her," you provide feedback that guides future action.[130] By focusing on the behavior instead of the perceived trait, the feedback shifts from accusing someone of having a character flaw to indicating "that he or she didn't exhibit the ideal behavior in that instance but is likely to do so next time."[131]

- *Highlight goals.* Effective feedback answers three questions: What are the goals? What progress is being made toward the goals? What activities need to be undertaken to make better progress?[132] Goal-oriented evaluations often are tied to "guided conversations" instead of the stilted interchange that characterizes formal evaluations. A guided conversation "focuses on the goals people set for themselves and how they are progressing toward those goals, along with their contribution, past and present to the company."[133] The process of emphasizing goals and relating the feedback to accomplishment of those goals depersonalizes the feedback, reduces defensiveness, and orients the participants to future action.[134]

- *Provide process and outcome feedback.* Specificity in evaluations is beneficial, but it sometimes leads to an overemphasis on results. Although results are critical and can serve as objective measures of performance, they frequently provide ambiguous information and little guidance about improving performance. For that reason, decision scientist Gary Klein finds that "outcome feedback – knowledge of results – doesn't improve our performance as much as process feedback, which helps us understand how to correct flaws."[135] By emphasizing processes as much as outcomes, he asserts, people can "learn to connect their actions to consequences, learn to sort out the relevant causal

---

[129]   Hattie & Timperley, *supra* note 108 at 96.   [130]   Kirk, *supra* note 12 at 14.
[131]   Ibid. at 15.   [132]   Hattie & Timperley, *supra* note 108 at 86.
[133]   Rock, Davis, & Jones, *supra* note 123.   [134]   Hattie & Timperley, *supra* note 108 at 86–87.
[135]   Klein, Gary. (2009). *Streetlights and shadows* (p. 166). Cambridge, Massachusetts: MIT Press.

threads and the coincidental ones."[136] Discussing the processes that preceded results enables people to identify and understand behavior, assumptions, and conditions that must be modified or accommodated to achieve better results in the future.

- *Avoid numerical ratings.* Many performance evaluation systems rank people on a 1–3 or 1–5 scale. These numerical rankings seem to invite misunderstandings and decrease employee motivation. If an evaluation system has a 1–5 scale, for example, "a manager might give an employee a 4 out of 5. The manager might see this as positive feedback, but an employee might see this as negative if he or she is striving for a 5 out of 5."[137] Numerical rankings also provoke "an overwhelming 'fight or flight' response that impairs good judgment."[138] Because they incite aggressive reactions or passive resignation, rankings "are ill-suited for the kind of thoughtful, reflective conversation that allows people to learn from a performance review."[139]

- *Present alternatives.* If the person providing the evaluation or feedback requires an action to be taken by the person receiving the evaluation, it is important to present several choices, including hybrid choices.[140] This forces the evaluator to consider a broader range of alternatives before meeting with the person being evaluated and engages that person in a collaborative problem-solving effort instead of a confrontation. Business professors David Garvin and Joshua Margolis suggest that, if you are the evaluator, "think of yourself as a driving instructor. While you provide oversight and guidance, your ultimate goal is to empower the [advice] seeker to act independently."[141]

Successful evaluation and feedback compel an adroit balance between directness and tact, clarity and sensitivity, and hope and realism. "Communicating feedback effectively," states Tony Schwartz, author of *The Way We're Working Isn't Working*, "requires holding each of these seemingly opposite poles – honesty and compassion – and continuously moving between them as circumstances demand."[142]

---

[136] Ibid. at 172.
[137] Kansas State University. (2014, February 24). Better job performance review built by researcher. *ScienceDaily.* Retrieved from www.sciencedaily.com/releases/2014/02/14022412 3800.htm.
[138] Rock, Davis, & Jones, *supra* note 123.   [139] Ibid.
[140] Garvin & Margolis, *supra* note 126 at 67.   [141] Ibid. at 70.
[142] Schwartz, Tony, (2015, October 16). Why great leaders see more and exclude less. *The New York Times.*

TABLE 4.2. *Recovering from poor responses to feedback*

Your response to feedback	Effect on person providing feedback	Your quick recovery	Your talking points
Getting angry	Becomes angry and mistrustful	Calm yourself; ask for another meeting, if necessary; apologize at next meeting; ask for more information and examples	"I want to be sure I understand. Is this what you're saying?"
Denying criticism	Doubts your credibility and self-knowledge	Ask to meet again; explain that you failed to see the big picture or were too defensive; ask for specifics	"This comes as a surprise. Could you give me some examples?"
Blaming others	Loses respect for you and your judgment; wonders who you're criticizing in other contexts	Analyze yourself and your actions; find what's accurate in the feedback; ask to meet again	"I hadn't considered looking at it that way. Could you tell me a little more about how you see that?"

Source: Sue Shellenbarger, "How to Take Criticism Well," *The Wall Street Journal*, 2014, June 18

Responding to Feedback

Receiving feedback is difficult because it "strikes at the tension between two core human needs – the need to learn and grow, and the need to be accepted just the way you are. As a result, even a seemingly benign suggestion can leave you feeling angry, anxious, badly treated, or profoundly threatened."[143] Typical responses to negative feedback – getting angry, denying criticism, and blaming others – and ways of recovering from our negative reactions and constructively responding to the feedback are shown in Table 4.2.

When feedback is rejected or poorly received, it usually has set off a *truth trigger* (the content is inaccurate, incomplete, biased, or unhelpful); a *relationship trigger* (the person providing the feedback lacks credibility, is untrustworthy, has improper motives, or is otherwise unqualified to provide feedback); or an *identity trigger* (the feedback makes you feel "overwhelmed, defensive or off balance").[144]

---

[143] Heen & Stone, *supra* note 123 at 109.   [144] Ibid.

Some effective techniques for dealing with these triggers and improving our response to feedback include the following:

- *Avoid defensiveness.* The most common obstacle to receiving and responding to feedback is defensiveness. Being good at receiving feedback means maintaining an open attitude and being genuinely curious about the feedback.[145] When people find that they are overwhelmed by defensiveness or anger, it's prudent to refrain from reacting and continue to listen. Asking for additional time to respond may be the best alternative when defensiveness is overwhelming: "Say, thank you very much for the feedback. What I'd like to do is think about it."[146]

- *Be vulnerable.* Learning from feedback requires receptiveness and vulnerability – two characteristics not usually associated with attorneys. As a lawyer in a major London-based law firm said to Thomas DeLong, author of *Flying Without a Net*, "the last thing a smart lawyer wants to be seen as is incompetent or stupid. Embarrassment is devastating. We lawyers will do anything to make sure that we save face, that we manage our environment so that we don't look foolish."[147] This preoccupation with impression management makes advice and feedback antithetical to lawyers. Although lawyers say they want feedback, "they are unwilling to make themselves sufficiently vulnerable to take it in objectively and deeply; they fail to display the resilience to learn from the feedback and improve how they handle similar situations the next time."[148]

- *Be open about difficulties.* The tension that attends evaluation and feedback can be eased by an early acknowledgement that you are having difficulties with some aspect of your performance. Consider asking questions like "Can you help me?," "What would you do if you were running this project?," "How would you make it better?," or "How do you think I can really improve this?"[149]

- *Ask for specifics.* When evaluators use general or conclusory terms, ask for a more specific description of the problem and examples. If an evaluator says, "You need to be a better team player," you might say,

---

[145] Shellenbarger, Sue. (2016, June 28). What does your boss really think about you? *The Wall Street Journal.* (Lunch break with Tanya Rivero–The Wall Street Journal Video.) Retrieved from: www.wsj.com/video/what-does-your-boss-really-think-about-you/3EF2C6D5-9D28-45F7-8E73-FA2577540A4C.html).

[146] Ibid.   [147] DeLong, *supra* note 109 at 18.   [148] Ibid. at 15.

[149] Shellenbarger (2016), *supra* note 145.

"I know that's important, but what does that look like? What are two or three things you'd do differently if you were in my shoes?"[150]

- *Ask for clarification.* Douglas Stone, coauthor of *Thanks for the Feedback*, recalls a meeting where a client threw a report he had written with coauthor Sheila Heen on the table and exclaimed, "This is a piece of s–!" Stone remembers that his heart sank, but Heen recovered quickly, saying, "When you say s–, could you be more specific? What do you mean?"[151] Her question launched a productive, extensive discussion with the client. Asking clarification questions usually is perceived as a genuine effort to understand and solve a problem and provides additional time to explore the reasons behind a seemingly hostile evaluation.

- *Relate responses to goals.* Linking questions and responses to a shared goal defuses tension and facilitates cooperation. By first identifying what the common goals are and then linking those goals to the performance issues, feedback shifts from a competitive or combative stance to a collaborative effort. Expressing mutual goals and seeking feedback to achieve those goals – e.g., "It's important for me to deliver the high-quality work product that clients expect from this firm, and I want to know when I'm not meeting that standard" – shows your commitment and confirms your capabilities.

- *Give the evaluator a workaround.* If evaluators seem reluctant to provide substantive information, they might be more comfortable talking about what other people in the organization think. These types of questions may draw out evaluators and allow them to voice their own opinions by using other people as proxies: What do other people think? How do you think I'm seen around here? How does the senior team think of me? Who do you think is doing a good job around here? Are there examples of other people's work you'd like me to emulate?[152]

- *Identify the accurate part.* When your tendency to reject the advice or feedback is particularly strong, try to identify what part of it is right. "Too often we use all that is wrong with the feedback we get to cancel out the possibility that there is anything right about it," assert Stone and Heen in *Thanks for the Feedback*. "Your feedback might be 99% wrong, but that 1% that's right might be just the insight you need."[153]

[150]   Shellenbarger, Sue. (2016, June 28). How to find out what the boss really thinks of you. *The Wall Street Journal.*

[151]   Shellenbarger (2014), *supra* note 126.   [152]   Shellenbarger (2016), *supra* note 145.

[153]   A conversation with Douglas Stone and Sheila Heen, authors of *Thanks For The Feedback: The Science and Art of Receiving Feedback.* Retrieved from: http://stoneandheen.com/sites/ tbook.hairpin.org/files/QA_Heen_and_Stone_web_version.pdf

- *Follow up*. Evaluations can be so stressful that the best outcome seems to be surviving it rather than using the information to enhance future performance. Attorneys committed to self-development, though, will recognize that feedback is a gift and should be facilitated with ongoing advice and guidance. Law professor Neil Hamilton recommends that attorneys seek out lawyers, professors, and judges who will "challenge your current assumptions, beliefs and performance, and support you to reflect and try again."[154] He urges attorneys to form a "personal board of directors" for this purpose.[155] If the personal board of directors seems too ambitious, ask one or two people to act as your advisors, schedule regular meetings with them, assure them that you need them to speak the truth, and take time later to reflect on these conversations.[156]

"We each have more control of our future than we recognize," states Barbara Mistick, president of Wilson College and coauthor of *Stretch: How to Future-proof Yourself for Tomorrow's Workplace*. "One of the most powerful ways we can take charge of developing new skills is to ask for feedback. If I had known how much I would benefit from asking for genuine feedback, I would have done it much earlier."[157]

CURIOSITY

Curiosity and open-mindedness are essential traits for attorneys. In the IAALS survey, 79 percent report that "intellectual curiosity" is required for an attorney's success.[158] Nineteen percent of attorneys believe that intellectual curiosity is advantageous but not required; and only 1.4 percent of attorneys think that intellectual curiosity is not relevant to an attorney's success.[159]

This emphasis on curiosity is displayed again in PricewaterhouseCoopers' survey of 1,322 CEOs in 77 countries. The CEOs "cited 'curiosity' and 'open-mindedness' as leadership traits that are becoming increasingly critical in challenging times."[160] In that survey, business leaders explained why curiosity and open-mindedness – a receptive, inquiring frame of mind for anticipating change, solving problems, and observing people, conditions, and events – have moved to the forefront of required skills:

---

[154] Hamilton, *supra* note 118.   [155] Ibid.   [156] Delong, *supra* note 109 at 196–197.
[157] Mistick, Barbara. (2016, January 30). Leadership means learning to look behind the mask. *The New York Times*.
[158] Gerkman & Cornett, *supra* note 26 at 16.   [159] Ibid.
[160] Berger, Warren. (2015, September 11). Why curious people are destined for the C-Suite. *Harvard Business Review*.

- "The one attribute CEOs need in the future to succeed, that I would place my bet on, is curiosity. From curiosity comes learning and new ideas. In businesses that are changing very rapidly, if you're not curious, if you're not learning, if you don't have new ideas, you're going to have a real problem."[161] (Michael Dell, Chairman and Chief Executive Officer, Dell Inc., U.S.)

- "In today's world, which is becoming more global and multicultural, whether you like it or not, industries overlap and penetrate each other. If you don't know how to learn, you will not survive."[162] (Alexey Marey, Chief Executive Officer, Alfa Bank, Russia)

- "If I was to point out one thing that CEOs need to have, to be successful in the future, I think it is the characteristic – around learning – of being a student and a teacher. CEOs simultaneously, I believe, especially in order to survive the world of tomorrow, have to be … lifelong teachers and lifelong students … in having a curiosity. The day we stop being curious is the day that we stop growing. In effect, it is the day we die."[163] (Vishal Sikka, Chief Executive Officer & Managing Director, Infosys, India)

Although attorneys and business leaders place an increasingly high value on curiosity and open-mindedness, this trend runs counter to the typical course of human development. As we age and gain a sense of control over our environment, our curiosity diminishes. Consistent with our diminishing curiosity, "question-asking peaks at age 4 or 5 and then steadily drops off."[164] By the time we become adults, asserts Warren Berger, author of *A More Beautiful Question*, "many of us have gotten out of the habit of asking fundamental questions about what's going on around us. And some people worry that asking questions at work reveals ignorance or may be seen as slowing things down."[165]

Can we counter this trend of diminishing curiosity? Can our sense of curiosity and open-mindedness at least be stabilized or, ideally, increased? How would our thinking change if we could become more curious and open-minded? To address those questions, it is instructive to understand what it means to be curious and open-minded, determine whether genes strongly

---

[161] PricewaterhouseCoopers. (2015). *18th Annual Global CEO Survey: A marketplace without boundaries?* (p. 35).

[162] Ibid. at 34.

[163] Ibid. at 38. The quote is based on Dr. Sikka's videotaped survey interview retrieved from: www.pwc.com/gx/en/ceo-agenda/ceosurvey/2015/interviews/vishal-sikka.html.

[164] Berger, Warren. (2016, July 2). The power of "why?" and "what if?" *The New York Times*.

[165] Ibid.

affect our sense of curiosity and open-mindedness, explain how curiosity and open-mindedness affect performance, and identify some techniques for enhancing those characteristics.

Definition and Assessment

Curiosity has been defined as "a desire for acquiring new knowledge and new sensory experience that motivates exploratory behavior."[166] It is a "drive to know" and a "drive to experience and feel."[167] Psychologists recognize two different types of curiosity: "trait" or "individual" curiosity (a relatively stable dispositional propensity to experience interest or curiosity) and "situational" or "specific" curiosity (a transitory curiosity about a particular stimulus).[168] Curiosity is measured by an individual's responses to statements like these: "I like to listen to new and unusual kinds of music;" "It excites me to have a new idea that leads to even more new ideas;" "I would like to read any magazine that reports new scientific discoveries;" and "I am interested in discovering how things work."[169]

Open-mindedness, a trait related to curiosity, refers to the "ability and tendency to seek, detect, comprehend, utilize, and appreciate complex patterns of information, both sensory and abstract."[170] Psychologist Martin Seligman defines open-mindedness as "the willingness to search actively for evidence against one's favored beliefs, plans, or goals, and to weigh such evidence fairly when it is available."[171] Closed-minded people, in contrast, "cease seeking additional information once a preferred position is

---

[166] Litman, Jordan, & Spielberger, Charles. (2003). Measuring epistemic curiosity and its diversive and specific components. *Journal of Personality Assessment*, 80(1), 75–86. See Litman, Jordan. (2007). Curiosity as a feeling of interest and feeling of deprivation: The I/D model of curiosity. In Zelick, Paula R. (Ed.). *Issues in the psychology of motivation* (pp. 149–156). New York: Nova Science Publishers.

[167] von Stumm, Sophie, Hell, Benedikt, & Chamorro-Premuzic, Tomas. (2011). The hungry mind: Intellectual curiosity is the third pillar of academic performance. *Perspectives on Psychological Science*, 6(6), 576.

[168] Littman & Spielberger, *supra* note 166 at 76. Guthrie, Chris. (2009, July). Be curious. *Negotiation Journal*, 25(3), 401–406.

[169] Littman & Spielberger, *supra* note 166 at 79, 80, 84.

[170] DeYoung, C. G. Openness/intellect: A dimension of personality reflecting cognitive exploration. In Cooper, M. L., & Larsen, R. J. (Eds.). (2014). *APA handbook of personality and social psychology: Personality processes and individual differences* (Vol. 4) (pp. 369–399). Washington, DC: American Psychological Association. See DeYoung, Colin, Quilty, Lena, Peterson, Jordan, & Gray, Jeremy. (2014). Openness to experience, intellect, and cognitive ability. *Journal of Personality Assessment*, 96(1), 46.

[171] Peterson, Christopher, & Seligman, Martin E. P. (2004). *Character strengths and virtues: A handbook and classification* (p. 144). New York: Oxford University Press.

adopted."[172] Like curiosity, open-mindedness entails exploration and "encompasses engagement with perceptual and aesthetic domains."[173] To measure open-mindedness, psychologists evaluate scaled responses to statements like these: "I actively look for information that challenges my opinions and values;"[174] "I do not usually consult many different opinions before forming my own views;"[175] "I feel irritated when one person disagrees with what everyone else in a group believes;"[176] and "I tend to make snap judgments."[177]

Genes

Curiosity and open-mindedness have a strong genetic determinant. Professor Scott Shane contends that the personality trait of openness to experience – which is correlated with imagination, creativity, curiosity, and inventiveness – "is largely in your DNA, with studies showing that genetics accounts for between 45 percent and 61 percent of the variance in this characteristic."[178] The effect of genes on curiosity and open-mindedness is stronger than the effect of genes on some other personality characteristics like altruism (30 percent); self-efficacy (32 percent); and stress reaction (43–45 percent).[179] Shane, however, argues persuasively that your genes are not your destiny and do not cause or determine any behavior.[180] In his view, a genetic predisposition is only a tendency, and understanding your tendencies enables you to overcome them when they are a disadvantage and to exploit them when they are beneficial.[181]

Performance Effects

Curiosity and open-mindedness are distinct traits. They are not the same thing as being highly intelligent in a conventional sense, and some studies indicate

---

[172] Wastell, Colin. (2013). The impact of closed-mindedness on the assessment of threat: An empirical study. *The Open Psychology Journal*, 6, 10–19.

[173] DeYoung, *et al. supra* note 170 at 46.

[174] Fortier, Alexandre, & Burkell, Jacquelyn. *Influence of need for cognition and need for cognitive closure on three information behavior orientations.* Paper submitted to the 77th ASIS&T Annual Meeting, October 31–November 5, 2014, Seattle, Washington.

[175] Holmes, Jamie. (2015). *Nonsense* (p. 87). New York: Crown.

[176] Roets, Arne, & Van Hiel, Alain. (2011, January). Item selection and validation of a brief 15-item version of the Need for Closure Scale. *Personality and Individual Differences*, 50, 90–94.

[177] Seligman (2002), *supra* note 87 at 143.

[178] Shane, Scott. (2010). *Born entrepreneurs, born leaders* (p. 157). New York: Oxford University Press.

[179] Ibid. at 50, 60, 61.   [180] Ibid. at 7.   [181] Ibid. at 201.

that "intelligence is negligibly related to open-mindedness."[182] Conventionally smart people, thus, can be closed-minded, and people of ordinary or low intelligence may be quite open-minded. This distinction is important because the effects of curiosity and open-mindedness are not identical to the effects of high intelligence. Being smart does not necessarily provide the benefits – being able to handle ambiguity and uncertainty, for example – linked to high levels of curiosity and open-mindedness.[183]

Curiosity and open-mindedness are correlated with multiple advantages that enhance the general well-being of attorneys and their professional performance: better decision-making outcomes;[184] higher academic performance;[185] increased creativity in problem solving;[186] less reliance on stereotyping;[187] superior problem solving under complexity;[188] interpersonal closeness;[189] improved diagnostic accuracy;[190] longevity;[191] decreased vulnerability to cognitive biases;[192] and more accurate forecasting of future events.[193]

Improvement Techniques

We can enhance our sense of curiosity and open-mindedness by changing the contexts in which we hope to be curious and the ways in which we think. Changing the context means that we become more aware of the effects of moods, anxiety, depression, other people, and perceptions. Research demonstrates that we are more likely to be curious when we are in a good

[182] Sorrentino, Richard, & Roney, Christopher. (2000). *The uncertain mind* (p. 17). Philadelphia, Pennsylvania: Psychology Press.
[183] Holmes, *supra* note 175 at 11.
[184] Baron, Jonathan. (2000). *Thinking and deciding* (p. 203). Cambridge, United Kingdom: Cambridge University Press. Holmes, *supra* note 175 at 88.
[185] Von Stumm, *supra* note 167.
[186] Andreasen, Nancy. (2006). *The creative brain* (p. 31). New York: Plume.
[187] Gigerenzer, Gerd. (2014). *Risk savvy* (p. 20). New York: Penguin Group.
[188] Dorner, Dietrich. (1997). *The logic of failure* (pp. 175–180). New York: Basic Books.
[189] Kashdan, Todd B., & Roberts, John E. (2004). Trait and state curiosity in the genesis of intimacy: Differentiation from related constructs. *Journal of Social and Clinical Psychology*, 23(6), 792–816.
[190] Norman, Geoff, Eva, Kevin, Brooks, Lee, & Hamstra, Stan. (2006). Expertise in medicine and surgery. In Ericsson, K. Anders (Ed.). *Cambridge handbook of expertise and expert performance* (p. 349). New York: Cambridge University Press.
[191] Swan, G. E. & Carmelli, D. (1996). Curiosity and mortality in aging adults: A 5-year follow-up of the Western Collaborative Group study. *Psychology and Aging*, 11, 449–453.
[192] Brest, Paul, & Krieger, Linda Hamilton. (2010). *Problem solving, decision making, and professional judgment* (p. 633). New York: Oxford University Press.
[193] Tetlock, Philip, & Gardner, Dan. (2015). *Superforecasting* (p. 125). New York: Crown Publishers.

mood,[194] are working with other people,[195] and perceive an object or problem to be new, novel, or complex but also comprehensible.[196] Our curiosity is diminished when we feel anxious or depressed and lack self-esteem.[197] Curiosity, it appears, is not a fixed trait that we apply uniformly to every new encounter but rather is a variable characteristic that is dependent on our emotions, self-confidence, and whether we are working alone or with others.

Apart from context, we can enhance curiosity and open-mindedness with three strategies suggested by Chris Guthrie, Dean of Vanderbilt University Law School.[198] For any task, he asserts, we can heighten our interest in three ways:

- *Increasing the challenge (the "challenge" strategy).* The challenge strategy promotes curiosity, interest, and engagement by requiring us to set goals or otherwise perform at a higher level than we are currently performing.
- *Focusing on the purposes to be served by completing the task (the "purpose" strategy).* The purpose strategy enhances curiosity by focusing on and reminding ourselves of the purposes that will be served and the goals that will be achieved by performing the task.
- *Varying the task or process (the "variety strategy").* The variety strategy helps to maintain interest in a task by varying the methods used to accomplish it.[199]

This three-step program, in summary, requires us to set higher goals, remember purposes, and introduce variety.

When attorneys can develop an enhanced sense of curiosity and open-mindedness, they significantly increase their value to clients, as David Maister, a respected law firm management consultant, relates:

---

[194] Murray, Noel, Sujan, Harish, Hirt, Edward, & Sujan, Mita. (1990, September). The influence of mood on categorization: A cognitive flexibility interpretation. *Journal of Personality and Social Psychology, 59*(3), 411–425.

[195] Isaac, J. D., Sansone, C., & Smith, J. (1999). Other people as a source of interest in an activity. *Journal of Experimental Social Psychology, 35*, 239–265. See Guthrie, *supra* note 168.

[196] Silvia, Paul. (2008). Interest–the curious emotion. *Current Directions in Psychological Science, 17*(1), 57–60.

[197] Rodrigue, James R., Olson, Kenneth R., & Markley, Robert P. (1987, February). Induced mood and curiosity. *Cognitive Therapy and Research, 11*(1), 101–106. Kashdan, T. B. (2002). Social anxiety dimensions, neuroticism, and the contours of positive psychological functioning. *Cognitive Therapy and Research, 26*, 789–810. Keller, J.A. (1987). Motivational aspects of exploratory behavior. In Gorlitz, D., & Wohlwill, J.E. (Eds.). *Curiosity, imagination and play* (pp. 25–42). London: Lawrence Erlbaum Associates.

[198] Guthrie, *supra* note 168.   [199] Ibid.

The key is to focus not on what we know, but on what we don't know. And that is curiosity: the constant asking of questions. "What's behind that?" "Why is this the case?" "How does this fit in?"

As curiosity does its work, problem definitions evolve. Patterns emerge, connections are made, and positions soften and re-form. Perspectives migrate, and richness of insight is gained. The "right answer" is never as right at the outset as it is after it has evolved, informed by inquiry.[200]

Maister encourages attorneys to recognize that they must work closely with clients to earn their trust and merit their confidence, and he believes that "curiosity is the attitude that drives the opportunity to contribute."[201]

GOAL SETTING AND ACHIEVEMENT

Attorneys are "competitive, aggressive, and achievement-oriented."[202] A large part of their lives, consequently, is spent on setting goals and attempting to achieve them. A remarkably small part of their lives, however, is spent on learning about the most successful methods of establishing and achieving those goals. This oversight is unfortunate because, like all other aspects of attorneys' lives and practices, goal setting and achievement can be better understood and more effectively performed. To start that process, this section discusses the importance of goals, describes methods to improve goal setting, and identifies attitudes and methods that facilitate goal achievement.

Goal Importance

Two of the most influential psychologists in the United States, Martin Seligman and Daniel Kahneman, find that goals are an integral component of well-being.[203] After studying what he calls the "striking evidence of the lifelong effects of the goals that young people set for themselves,"[204] Kahneman has modified his earlier views on goals and well-being:

---

[200]   Maister, David, Green, Charles, & Galford, Robert. (2000). *The trusted advisor* (p. 57). New York: Free Press.

[201]   Ibid. at ix, 57.

[202]   Daicoff, Susan. (1997). Lawyer, know thyself: A review of empirical research on attorney attributes bearing on professionalism. *American University Law Review.* 46, 1337.

[203]   Seligman, Martin. (2011). *Flourish* (pp. 238–239). New York: Free Press. Kahneman, Daniel. (2011). *Thinking, fast and slow* (pp. 401–402). New York: Farrar, Straus and Giroux.

[204]   Kahneman, *supra* note 203 at 401.

In part because of these findings I have changed my mind about the definition of well-being. The goals that people set for themselves are so important to what they do and how they feel about it that an exclusive focus on experienced well-being [momentary or daily assessments of feelings and emotions] is not tenable. We cannot hold a concept of well-being that ignores what people want.[205]

"One recipe for a dissatisfied adulthood," Kahneman finds, "is setting goals that are especially difficult to attain."[206]

Seligman, too, places a high emphasis on setting and achieving goals. Although extensive research indicates that well-being has three core features (positive emotions, engagement, and meaning) and six additional features (self-esteem, optimism, resilience, vitality, self-determination, and positive relationships),[207] Seligman thinks this model is insufficient without *accomplishment*. "I would suggest that accomplishment be added as an element," Seligman writes, "so that being in the upper range of positive emotion, and engagement, and meaning, and positive relationships, and positive accomplishment would be my criteria for flourishing."[208] Seligman's stress on accomplishment is supported by research showing that goal progress is associated with positive affect and well-being.[209]

Goal Setting

The essential elements of effective goal setting are specificity, autonomy, compatibility, and realism. An alternative paradigm, suggested by some organizational psychologists, is based on the SMART acronym (Specific, Measurable, Attainable, Relevant, and Time-bound).[210] Although people can readily list goals, they often fail to achieve them because their goals do not satisfy these threshold requirements.

Specificity in goal setting requires a precise definition of the goal to be achieved and the action to be taken. The daily "to do" list, the simplest form of goal setting, usually fails because the tasks are neither accurately

[205] Kahneman, *supra* note 203 at 402. For definitions and measurements of experienced well-being, see Stone, Arthur A., & Mackie, Christopher (Eds.). (2013). *Subjective well-being: Measuring happiness, suffering, and other dimensions of experience* (pp. 29–68). Washington, DC: National Academies Press.

[206] Kahneman, *supra* note 203 at 402.   [207] Seligman, *supra* note 203 at 27.

[208] Seligman, *supra* note 203 at 239.

[209] Koestner, Richard. (2008). Reaching one's personal goals: A motivational perspective focused on autonomy. *Canadian Psychology*, 49(1), 65.

[210] Oettingen, Gabriele. (2014). *Rethinking positive thinking* (pp. 150–151). New York: Current.

visualized nor adequately described. Lacking any concrete representation of action, sequence, and duration, the daily list "contains more work than could be done the entire week."[211] The takeaway for specifying goals "is that difficult and specific goals yield better performance on a given work task than easy and vague goals. If you aim to simply 'do your best' on a given day, you'll accomplish far less than if you seek to complete 75 percent of your presentation, for example, or to make twenty phone calls to customers."[212]

Autonomy in goal setting is frequently overlooked, but it has a powerful effect on whether goals are achieved. Goal setting is autonomous when it "reflects an individual's interests and personal values versus whether it is adopted because of social pressures or expectations of what an individual 'should do.' "[213] When goals are developed autonomously, people are more motivated to achieve them and more likely to exert a sustained effort; non-autonomous goals, in contrast, generate intrapersonal conflict.[214]

Although people quickly enumerate goals, they give little thought to compatibility among the goals. The sole criterion for many goals is desirability, e.g., spend more time on career and family, and the desirability of the goals obscures their basic incompatibility. Psychologists Robert Emmons and Laura King have studied conflicting goals, and they observe three major, detrimental consequences:[215]

- *You worry.* You ruminate about the competing demands; the more conflicting demands you face, the more you worry.
- *You get less done.* Instead of taking action, people faced with conflicting goals are beset with worry and get stuck.
- *Your physical and mental health deteriorates.* People with incompatible goals experience more depression and anxiety; they have a higher number of self-reported illnesses and visits to a doctor.

Conflicting goals, unless resolved by a candid acknowledgment of values and priorities, often cancel each other out, restoring the status quo and the dissatisfaction that preceded the goal setting.

In addition to being specific, autonomous, and compatible, goals must be realistic. Psychologist Gabriel Oettingen has studied goal setting and achievement, and she finds that people adopt one of three goal-setting strategies.[216] Optimists envision the future they hope to achieve and its

[211] Baumeister, Roy. (2011). *Willpower* (p. 63). New York: Penguin Press.
[212] Oettingen, *supra* note 210 at 151. [213] Koestner, *supra* note 209 at 60.
[214] Ibid. at 62, 63. [215] Baumeister, *supra* note 211 at 67. [216] Tough, *supra* note 25 at 92.

attendant benefits – accolades, status, success, and fulfillment.[217] Pessimists think of the obstacles that will prevent them from achieving their goals. And people who employ "mental contrasting" combine both strategies, "concentrating on a positive outcome and simultaneously concentrating on the obstacles in the way."[218] Only the mental contrasting method is correlated with actual achievement.

Goal Achievement

To achieve goals, we need a method that has been proven to be effective and a deadline that can be met. We also might want to know why other people fail to achieve their goals, so that we can avoid the problems that deterred them. Looking first at why people do not achieve their goals, research points to three main causes: "(a) they lack clear, specific goals; (b) they fail to monitor their progress toward the goal; and (c) they do not possess sufficient self-regulatory strength [self-control] to maintain goal pursuit in the face of obstacles and distractions."[219]

Turning next to effective methods to achieve goals, we find that current research supports Oettingen's WOOP method (Wish, Outcome, Obstacle, Plan).[220] People following this model identify and describe a wish or goal, depict the outcome desired, anticipate and define the main obstacles to be encountered, and then create an "if obstacle, then action to overcome" plan.[221] In her study of students applying for graduate school, for instance, Oettingen found that recognizing obstacles and developing plans to counter them actually increased their goal commitment:

> Students in the mental contrasting [WOOP] group who saw present realities more sharply as obstacles expressed a greater sense of responsibility for whether they would get into graduate school, and those who saw present realities less sharply as obstacles were less inclined to take personal responsibility for achieving this wish. Mental contrasting thus shaped participants' view of reality, helping them become more aware of the elements standing in their way, and in the process leading them to feel more strongly about pursuing a wish.[222]

Despite popular conceptions, positive thinking alone does not appear to facilitate goal achievement. As Oettingen points out, "by fooling our brains into thinking we're already successful, we lose motivation and energy to do what it takes to actually become successful."[223]

---

[217] Ibid.   [218] Ibid. at 93.   [219] Koestner, *supra* note 209 at 61.
[220] Oettingen, *supra* note 210 at xv, 118–140, 166.   [221] Ibid. at 166.   [222] Ibid. at 109.
[223] Ibid. at 50.

The final phase of goal achievement is setting a realistic deadline. Even when goals are properly defined and an effective implementation plan is selected, we may fail to formulate an appropriate timeline, monitor our progress, and adjust the schedule as necessary to maintain motivation and accomplish the goal. The biggest obstacle in this respect may be our own lack of willpower rather than the challenges presented by the goal itself. In an experiment regarding time management and procrastination, for example, Kahneman offered three groups of students a monetary reward for completing and returning a survey. One group was given five days to complete the survey, another was given 21 days, and the third group had no deadline. Two-thirds of the students in the first group returned the survey on time, 40 percent of the students in the second group finished the survey on time, and only 25 percent of the students with no deadline completed the survey at any time.[224] As author Gary Belsky notes, "The reality is that the more time you have to do a task – any task – the less pressure you feel to 'get with it,' and the frequent result is that you never get to it at all."[225]

EMBODIED COGNITION

"The world belongs to those who fake it," said Anna Dickinson, an impassioned orator who spoke against slavery and for women's suffrage in the 1860s.[226] A national celebrity whose stump speeches attracted thousands of listeners, she eventually earned speaker fees of $300,000 per year in today's currency.[227] Mark Twain exclaimed, "My what houses she used to draw!" as he recalled her "pouring out the lava of her blistering eloquence upon the enemy."[228] Whether she was faking it until she became a distinguished orator nobody knows, but she was prescient in recognizing that enacting a role often precedes proficiency in that role. "One of the most enduring

---

[224] Belsky, Gary, & Gilovich, Thomas. (1999). *Why smart people make big money mistakes and how to correct them* (p. 87). New York: Simon & Schuster.

[225] Ibid. at 87–88.

[226] Anna Elizabeth Dickinson, 1842–1932. Portrait, head and shoulders, facing left; autographed "The World belongs to those who fake it." Library of Congress Control Number 2004679213. Reproduction Number LC-USZ62-59772 (b&w film copy neg.). Retrieved from: www.loc .gov/item/2004679213/

[227] See Gallman, J. Matthew. (2006). *America's Joan of Arc: The life of Anna Elizabeth Dickinson*. New York: Oxford University Press.

[228] Twain, Mark. (2009). *Who is Mark Twain?* New York: HarperCollins. See Book Excerpt, "Who Is Mark Twain?" (2009, April 17). *The Wall Street Journal*.

lessons of social psychology," states psychologist Timothy Wilson, "is that behavior change often precedes changes in attitudes and feelings."[229]

"Embodied cognition" reflects the radical idea that Anna Dickinson was right – we can fake ourselves into behaving differently by assuming the body postures and creating the environment that would exist if we actually had the expertise, power, confidence, and status to which we aspire.[230] Embodied cognition challenges the conventional concept that our minds direct our bodies and shows that the sequence can be reversed: our bodies and sensations direct our minds, at least some of the time. Psychology professor Joshua Davis says that we previously thought that "sensory inputs and motor outputs were secondary," but now we "see them as integral to cognitive processes."[231]

An underlying premise of embodied cognition is "do the behavior first and let the feelings follow."[232] People who are depressed, for example, are encouraged to overcome social isolation and lack of intimacy by taking concrete action to interact with people rather than wait for a change in mood or motivation. These actions, if repeated, change self-concepts: "Small changes in behavior can lead to small changes in one's self-concept, however, and small changes in one's self-concept can make the next behavior change easier."[233]

Applying embodied cognition principles, we can provoke changes in our self-concept and behavior in three distinct ways: priming our self-perception to embody and animate a preferred role; changing our appearance to make it compatible with a preferred role; and changing our environment to promote or represent a preferred role. In one study regarding priming, for example, people who were required to remember and describe an incident in which they exercised power over another person "spoke earlier and more assertively than their teammates" during a subsequent meeting.[234] In a related study, priming for power significantly increased the participants' chances of acceptance in practice interviews for business school admissions.[235] In another study, participants who were primed by recalling previous power incidents changed their voices (less

[229]   Wilson, Timothy, (2002). *Strangers to ourselves* (p. 212). Cambridge, Massachusetts: The Belknap Press.
[230]   See Wilson, Andrew, & Golonka, Sabrina. (2013, February). Embodied cognition is not what you think it is. *Frontiers in Psychology*, 4, Article 58. Angier, Natalie. (2010, February 2). Abstract thoughts? The body takes them literally. *The New York Times*.
[231]   McNerney, Samuel, (2011, November 4). A brief guide to embodied cognition: Why you are not your brain. *Scientific American*.
[232]   Wilson, *supra* note 229 at 214.   [233]   Ibid.
[234]   Galinsky, Adam, & Kilduff, Gavin. (2013, December). Be seen as a leader. *Harvard Business Review*, p. 129.
[235]   Ibid.

pitch and more volume) to sound more authoritative – and they were perceived to be more authoritative than their teammates.[236] These priming effects lasted for days, "even though those mind-sets were no longer being primed and the tasks had changed."[237]

Similar results occur when people assume "power poses" like putting their feet on a desk and folding their hands behind their head or standing behind a desk, placing two hands on the desk, and leaning forward:

> Simply holding one's body in expansive, "high-power" poses for as little as two minutes stimulates higher levels of testosterone (the hormone linked to power and dominance in the animal and human worlds) and lower levels of cortisol (the "stress" hormone that can, over time, cause impaired immune functioning, hypertension, and memory loss). The result? In addition to causing the desired hormonal shift, the power poses led to increased feelings of power and a greater tolerance for risk.[238]

Both females and males assuming the power poses reported a heightened sense of power and authority, supporting a gender-neutral "fake it till you make it" approach.[239]

Wearing different types of clothes also has an impact on our behavior, especially in competitive events. Dressing up generally makes the wearer feel more powerful, increases abstract thinking, and improves complex and long-term problem solving.[240] In a negotiation study, for example, men were assigned to three groups: one group wore business suits, a button-down shirt, and dress shoes ("Suits"); the second group wore sweatpants, T-shirts, and sandals ("Sweats"); and the third group wore the clothes they were wearing when they arrived for the experiment ("Neutrals").[241] All of the men assumed the role of the buyer in the purchase of a factory and were informed of its fair

[236] Ibid. [237] Ibid. at 130.
[238] Hanna, Julia. (2010, September 20). Power posing: Fake it until you make it. *Harvard Business School Working Knowledge Newsletter*.
[239] Ibid. See Galinsky, Adam, & Huang, Li. (2011, January 4). How you can become more powerful by literally standing tall. *Scientific American*. Cf. Simmons, Joseph P., & Simonsohn, Uri. (2016, September 26). Power posing: P-curving the evidence. *Psychological Science*, forthcoming. Retrieved from https://ssrn.com/abstract=2791272.
[240] See Hutson, Matthew, & Rodriguez, Tori. (2016, January 1). Dress for success: How clothes influence our performance. *Scientific American*. Pinsker, Joe. (2015, April 30). Wearing a suit makes people think differently. *The Atlantic*. Slepian, Michael, Ferber, Simon, Gold, Joshua, & Rutchick, Abraham. (2015). The cognitive consequences of formal clothing. *Social Psychological and Personality Science*, 6(6), 661–668.
[241] Kraus, Michael W., & Mendes, Wendy Berry. (2014, December). Sartorial symbols of social class elicit class-consistent behavioral and physiological responses: A dyadic approach. *Journal of Experimental Psychology: General*, 143(6), 2330–2340.

market value. The Suits negotiated a sale price that resulted in an average profit, relative to fair market value, of $2.1 million, with an average concession of $830,000 from their initial offer. The Sweats gained an average profit of $680,000, only a third of the profit obtained by the suits, and their average concession off their initial offer was $2.8 million.[242] The Neutrals' performance was between the Suits and the Sweats. During the negotiation, the testosterone levels of the Sweats dropped 20 percent while the testosterone levels of the Suits and Neutrals showed little or no changes.[243]

Wearing a white lab coat, according to another study, also seems to change behavior by increasing carefulness and attentiveness, two characteristics associated with physicians.[244] But this beneficial effect only occurs when the study participant is informed the lab coat is a doctor's coat; no increase in carefulness and attentiveness is observed when the study participant is informed that the same lab coat is a painter's coat.[245] This study, notes coauthor Adam Galinsky, "reminds people that clothes aren't just a device of perception, but a tool that can really affect how you perceive yourself."[246]

Altering our physical environment – and the physical space around us, in particular – is yet another example of how embodied cognition affects our self-perception and alters our behavior. In a series of experiments, Andy Yap, an organizational behavior professor, finds that expanding our physical space increases our sense of power and emboldens us to make unethical decisions that we would not make when operating in a smaller space. "These spaces allow you to have an expansive posture, and that's what makes you feel more powerful," he says. "And the feelings of power are what alter your behavior."[247]

In one of Yap's experiments, students were randomly assigned to two different configurations in a driving simulator: the "expansive" driver's seat was 22.5 inches from the steering wheel, while the "contractive" driver's seat was 17 inches from the steering wheel. Once seated, students participated in

---

[242] Smith, Ray. (2016, February 21). Why dressing for success leads to success. *The Wall Street Journal.*

[243] Kraus & Mendes, *supra* note 241.

[244] Blakeslee, Sandra. (2012, April 2). Mind games: Sometimes a white coat isn't just a white coat. *The New York Times.*

[245] Adam, Hajo, & Galinsky, Adam. (2012, July). Enclothed cognition. *Journal of Experimental Social Psychology: General,* 48(4), 918–925. See Van Stockum, Jr., Charles, & DeCaro, Marci. (2014). Enclothed cognition and controlled attention during insight problem-solving. *Journal of Problem Solving,* 7, 73–83.

[246] McGregor, Jena. (2012, March 10). New study: What you wear could affect how well you work. *The Washington Post.*

[247] Williams, Alison. (2013, November). Big chairs create big cheats. *Harvard Business Review,* p. 36.

simulated races with clear rules (e.g., stop and count-to-ten after any collision). The race results showed that drivers in expansive seats drove more recklessly and were involved in more "hit and run" accidents – and they felt more powerful than drivers in contractive seats.[248] In another experiment, researchers identified double-parked vehicles in New York City and classified them by volume (determined by wheelbase, height, and width of the car). Car length was strongly correlated with driver's seat size, and "vehicles with larger driver's seats were more likely to be double parked."[249] Yap reaches two conclusions: (1) environments that allow us to expand our body can lead us to feel more powerful; and (2) feelings of power can lead to dishonest behavior. The space that we occupy, therefore, serves as both a symbol and a source of power, fostering an illusory sense of dominance, autonomy, and invincibility.

MINDFULNESS, EQUANIMITY, AND WELL-BEING

For some attorneys, the terms "mindfulness," "equanimity," and "well-being" may have a spiritual, metaphysical, or mystical connotation. Although the transcendent versions of those terms are important to many people, this section focuses on the functional aspects of mindfulness, equanimity, and well-being – what do they mean to practicing attorneys, what benefits do they confer, and how can attorneys enhance those qualities if they can have a verifiably positive effect on law practice?

Meaning and Concepts

The most popular definition of mindfulness is expressed by Jon Kabat-Zinn, author of the bestseller *Full Catastrophe Living*. He regards mindfulness as "paying attention in a particular way: on purpose, in the present moment, and non-judgmentally."[250] Psychologist Ruth Baer contends that mindfulness has five component skills: observing, describing, acting with awareness, nonjudging of inner experience, and nonreactivity to inner experience.[251] She elaborates on these skills and the related attitudes and actions:

---

[248] Yap, Andy, Wazlawek, Abbie, Lucas, Brian, Cuddy, Amy, & Carney, Dana. (2013). The ergonomics of dishonesty: The effect of incidental posture on stealing, cheating, and traffic violations. *Psychological Science, 24*(11), 2281–2289.

[249] Ibid.

[250] Kabat-Zinn, J. (1990). *Full catastrophe living: How to cope with stress, pain and illness using mindfulness meditation.* New York: NY: Bantam Dell.

[251] Baer, Ruth, Smith, Gregory, Lykins, Emily, & Williams, J. Mark. (2008). Construct validity of the five facet mindfulness questionnaire in meditating and nonmeditating samples. *Assessment, 15*(3), 329.

Observing includes noticing or attending to internal and external experiences, such as sensations, cognitions, emotions, sights, sounds, and smells. Describing refers to labeling internal experiences with words. Acting with awareness includes attending to one's activities of the moment and can be contrasted with behaving mechanically while attention is focused elsewhere (often called automatic pilot). Nonjudging of inner experience refers to taking a nonevaluative stance toward thoughts and feelings. Nonreactivity to inner experience is the tendency to allow thoughts and feelings to come and go, without getting caught up in or carried away by them.[252]

Definitions of mindfulness uniformly include the concept of being "nonjudgmental" or "non-evaluative." But this form of acceptance "should not be equated with passivity or resignation. Rather, acceptance in this context refers to the ability to experience events fully, without resorting to either extreme of excessive preoccupation with, or suppression of, the experience."[253]

"Equanimity" is often associated with mindfulness, but it is a conceptually different state of mind. It has been defined as "an even-minded mental state or dispositional tendency toward all experiences or objects, regardless of their affective valence (pleasant, unpleasant or neutral) or source."[254] In this definition, "even-minded" means being calm, stable, and composed.[255] Equanimity is different from mindfulness because mindfulness "emphasizes the ability to remain consciously aware of what is happening," while equanimity "allows awareness to be even and unbiased by facilitating an attitude of non-attachment and non-resistance."[256] If a reckless driver veered in front of us, for example, we might be mindful of a surge of anger, but we may not reach a state of equanimity, allowing us to detach from our initial sense of anger.[257]

"Well-being" is a concept more easily discussed than defined. Psychologist Martin Seligman contends that "no single measure defines it," although he has identified measurable elements that contribute to it.[258] In his theory of well-being, the five essential elements are: positive emotion, engagement, meaning, accomplishment, and positive relationships.[259] Alternative models of well-being focus on the "components of enduring success" (happiness, achievement, significance, and legacy)[260] and the experiences "central to

---

[252]   Ibid. at 330.
[253]   Keng, Shian-Ling. (2011, August). Effects of mindfulness on psychological health: A review of empirical studies. *Clinical Psychology Review*, 31(6), 1042.
[254]   Desbordes, Gaelle, *et al.* (2015, April). Moving beyond mindfulness: Defining equanimity as an outcome measure in meditation and contemplative research. *Mindfulness*, 6(2), 356–372.
[255]   Ibid.   [256]   Ibid.   [257]   Ibid.   [258]   Seligman (2011), *supra* note 203 at 15.
[259]   Ibid. at 16–20.   [260]   Rhode, *supra* note 107 at 207.

making a person thrive" (security, autonomy, authenticity, relatedness, competence, and self-esteem).[261]

Benefits of Mindfulness, Equanimity, and Well-Being

Well-being – as measured by relatively high levels of life satisfaction, vitality, self-actualization, autonomy, and competence and low levels of depression, hostility, anxiety, and impulsivity – is positively correlated with mindfulness.[262] Additional benefits of mindfulness, all of which enhance attorney performance, include increased empathy and self-awareness; lower levels of the stress hormone cortisol; improved communication skills and relationship satisfaction; less reactivity; and more effective emotion regulation.[263]

The specific practice of mindfulness meditation is associated with reduced rumination; heightened compassion; better counseling skills; increased working memory; stronger ability to focus attention; and faster information processing speed.[264] Preliminary research indicates that meditation practice may alter brain activity and structure, developing cortical thickness, decreasing amygdala activation, increasing prefrontal cortex activation, and expanding

[261] Levit, Nancy, & Linder, Douglas. (2010). *The happy lawyer* (p. 44). New York: Oxford University Press.

[262] See de Vibe, M., Bjorndal, A., Tipton, E., Hammerstrom, K.T., & Kowalski, K. (2012). Mindfulness based stress reduction (MBSR) for improving health, quality of life and social functioning in adults. *The Campbell Collaboration Library of Systematic Reviews*, 8(3). Brown, K.W., Ryan, R.M., & Creswell, J.D. (2007). Mindfulness: Theoretical foundations and evidence for its salutary effects. *Psychological Inquiry*, 18(4), 211–237. Khoury, B., *et al.* (2013). Mindfulness-based therapy: A comprehensive meta-analysis. *Clinical Psychology Review*, 33, 763–771. Brown, Kirk, & Ryan, Richard. (2003). The benefits of being present: Mindfulness and its role in psychological well-being. *Journal of Personality and Social Psychology*, 84(4), 822–848.

[263] Davis, Daphne, & Hayes, Jeffrey. (2011). What are the benefits of mindfulness? A practice review of psychotherapy-related research. *Psychotherapy*, 48(2), 198–208. Grossman, P., Niemann, L., Schmidt, S., & Walach, H. (2004). Mindfulness-based stress reduction and health benefits: A meta-analysis. *Journal of Psychosomatic Research*, 57, 35–43. See Huang, Peter. (2017). Can practicing mindfulness improve lawyer decision-making, ethics and leadership? *Houston Law Review*, 55 (forthcoming).

[264] Davis & Hayes, *supra* note 263. Southwick, Steven, & Charney, Dennis. (2012). *Resilience* (p. 153). New York: Cambridge University Press. Cf. Goyal, Madhav, *et al.* (2014, March). Meditation programs for psychological stress and well being: A systematic review and meta-analysis. *JAMA Internal Medicine*, 174(3), 357–368. The Goyal meta-analysis found "low evidence of no effect or insufficient evidence of an effect of meditation programs on positive mood, attention, sleep, and weight. We also found insufficient evidence that meditation programs had an effect on health-related behaviors affected by stress, including substance use and sleep."

volumes of the hippocampus (implicated in memory).[265] Describing the neurobiological mechanisms associated with meditation, psychiatrists Steven Southwick and Dennis Charney note that modulation of the amygdala assists emotional regulation, and activation of the anterior cingular cortex (ACC) helps to "regulate attention, partly by enhancing cognitive control over distracting memories and external events."[266]

Mindfulness, Equanimity, and Well-Being Practices

Mindfulness, equanimity and well-being are not the first qualities that come to mind when most people think of attorneys. Being a lawyer, at times, seems to require a lack of awareness of ourselves and other people. "You have to do things, be part of things, you don't want to be part of," an attorney remarks in *Lawyerland*. "We all know there are times when you're working on some deal that, if you were to think it through, you'd realize that it was going to ruin the lives of thousands of people and their families."[267] The conflict between who we think we are and what we do can lead to a deliberate, practiced mindlessness.

Unless we are mindful, disassociation from ourselves starts as a temporary method of coping with a case or client and eventually becomes a habit. The habit of neglecting or overriding personal feelings and values is the antithesis of mindfulness; it undermines well-being and eventually renders us unaware of our unawareness.[268] The incremental disassociation that begins with a sense of unease and ends with a sense of resignation is portrayed by Timothy Tosta, a preeminent land use and environmental law lawyer:

> The world of a lawyer is, at times, brutal. At first, the brutality is shocking – the lawyer who intentionally exacerbates the personality conflicts at the price of obscuring the substantive issues, the rich and powerful party who, irrespective of the merits, manipulates the system to vanquish a weaker opponent. But, as you proceed in this career, you enure yourself to brutality. You avoid it, you

[265] Brown, Jeff, & Fenske, Mark. (2010). *The winner's brain* (p. 176). Cambridge, Massachusetts: Da Capo Press. Luders, Eileen, Toga, Arthur, Lepore, Nathasha, & Gaser, Christian. (2009, April). The underlying anatomical correlates of long-term meditation: Larger hippocampal and frontal volumes of gray matter. *Neuroimage, 45*(3), 672–678. Southwick & Charney, *supra* note 264.

[266] Southwick & Charney, *supra* note 264.

[267] Joseph, Lawrence. (1997). *Lawyerland* (p. 41). New York: Farrar, Straus and Giroux. See Litowitz, Douglas, (2005). *The destruction of young lawyers* (p. 111). Akron, Ohio: The University of Akron Press. ("At the end of the day, you are simply delaying lawsuits, forcing people into unfair contracts, helping the rich avoid taxation and making life miserable for workers and consumers. That's no way for a young person to live.")

[268] See Wilson, *supra* note 229.

minimize it, you rationalize it, and some surrender to practicing it. But, we all are affected. Brutality chips away not only at our profession's stature, but to a greater or lesser degree on our individual well being and on that of our families and communities.[269]

When attorneys' professional actions conflict with their personal values, they often resolve the conflict by disengaging from themselves and following rules, procedures, and protocols that are familiar and devoid of personal significance. As organizational behavior expert Karl Weick explains, "When people function mindlessly they don't understand either themselves or their environments, but they feel as though they do. They feel that because they have routines to deal with problems, this proves that they understand what's up."[270] Detached from their values and mindlessly following rules and routines, attorneys forfeit what has proven to be one of the strongest determinants of work satisfaction for attorneys: their satisfaction with the value of their work to society.[271]

For attorneys who can risk the dissonance that often attends mindfulness, the following practices and techniques may be helpful in promoting mindfulness and enhancing well-being:

- *Think in conditionals instead of absolutes.* Ellen Langer, author of *Mindfulness*, contends that we become more mindful as we shift from thinking in absolute terms to conditional terms: "When you think conditionally you tell yourself, 'Well, it could be this way, it could be that way' – so you stay attentive. You don't end up with this illusion of certainty. The illusion of certainty is mindless."[272]

- *Define work/life priorities.* When attorneys are asked to rate their satisfaction with various aspects of their career, "satisfaction with balance of work and family/private life" is ranked last among nine aspects (e.g., intellectual challenge of work and control over work).[273] To achieve a work/life allocation that promotes well-being, you must "be willing to sacrifice income if necessary," state Nancy Levit and Douglas Linder, coauthors of *The Happy Lawyer*.[274] The trade-off between well-being and income is palpable: "people who earned more tended to report more moments of anger, anxiety, and excitement, suggesting that

[269] Tosta, Tim. (2010, June 3). Working with angels. *San Francisco Daily Journal*, p. 5.

[270] Weick, & Sutcliffe, *supra* note 14 at 43.

[271] Chambers, David L. (2013, May 1). Satisfaction in the practice of law: Findings from a long-term study of attorneys' careers. (University of Michigan Public Law Research Paper No. 330.) Retrieved from http://ssrn.com/abstract=2274162.

[272] Ayala, Nick. (2014, April 16). Ellen Langer, Harvard University psychology professor, author of "Mindfulness." *J. Walter Thompson Intelligence*.

[273] Chambers, *supra* note 271.   [274] Levit & Linder, *supra* note 261 at 110.

high-paying jobs may produce higher levels of arousal, which are more often than not of the negative kind."[275]

- *Keep a gratitude diary.* People who record experiences in which they felt gratitude exhibit a stronger sense of conscientiousness and connectedness with other people and report higher levels of positive affect and optimism.[276] They also display less stress and hopelessness, lower blood pressure, and better blood-glucose management.[277]

- *Gaze at nature.* Viewing a computer screen with a flowering meadow for 40 seconds increases concentration levels, promotes sustained attention, and decreases errors. "The theory is that because nature is effortlessly fascinating, it captures your attention without your having to consciously focus on it," explains researcher Kate Lee. "So gazing at natural environments provides you with an opportunity to replenish your stores of attention control."[278] Ideally, you can look at nature outside a window or while walking through it, but even a simulated view of nature restores attention.

- *Develop a sense of awe.* The feeling of being in awe may be more effective in promoting happiness and reducing inflammation in the body than other emotions like amusement, compassion, contentment, joy, love, and pride.[279] Being in awe also slows down our sense of time and makes us more patient.[280] On average, people report feeling a sense of awe at least three times per week. "Some people feel awe

---

[275] Sharot, Tali. (2012). *The optimism bias* (p. 79). New York: Vintage Books. See Whillians, Ashley, Weidman, Aaron, & Dunn, Elizabeth. (2016). Valuing time over money is associated with greater happiness. *Social Psychological and Personality Science*, 7(3), 213–222. Krieger, Lawrence, & Sheldon, Kennon. (2015, February). What makes lawyers happy?: A data-driven prescription to redefine professional success. *The George Washington Law Review*, 83(2), 554.

[276] Emmons, Robert, & McCullough, Michael. (2003). Counting blessings versus burdens: An experimental investigation of gratitude and subjective well-being in daily life. *Journal of Personality and Social Psychology*, 84(2), 377–389. See Brooks, Arthur. (2015, November 21). Choose to be grateful. It will make you happier. *The New York Times*.

[277] Pinker, Susan. (2015, December 17). When does gratitude bring better health? *The Wall Street Journal*.

[278] Torres, Nicole. (2015, September). Gazing at nature makes you more productive: An interview with Kate Lee. *Harvard Business Review*. See Clay, Rebecca, (2001, April). Green is good for you. *Monitor on Psychology*, 32(4), 40. Berman, M. G., Jonides, J., & Kaplan, S. (2008). The cognitive benefits of interacting with nature. *Psychological Science*, 19(12), 1207–1212.

[279] Reynolds, Gretchen. (2015, March 26). An upbeat emotion that's surprisingly good for you. *The New York Times*.

[280] Rudd, Melanie, Aaker, Jennifer, & Vohs, Kathleen. (2012). Awe expands people's perception of time, alters decision making, and enhances well-being. *Psychological Science*, 23(10), 1130–1136.

listening to music," psychologist Dacher Keltner remarks, while others may feel awe "watching a sunset or attending a political rally or seeing kids play."[281]

- *Exercise regularly.* An exercise program "can increase attentional focus, improve learning and memory, reduce impulsivity, enhance mood, lower stress, and increase the volume of important structures in the brain."[282] The effects of exercise on your brain are so positive that "it almost makes the benefits to the heart, lungs and muscles seem incidental."[283]

It is important to remember that mindfulness does not require meditation. As Tony Schwartz writes in his column Life@Work, "There is a difference between mindfulness meditation and simple mindfulness. The latter isn't a practice separate from everyday life. Mindfulness just means becoming more conscious of what you're feeling, more intentional about your behaviors and more attentive to your impact on others."[284]

CHAPTER CAPSULE

High intelligence is not a reliable predictor of professional success. Other skills – notably, resilience, grit, perseverance, motivation, and willpower – exert a stronger effect on professional success than high intelligence. Although these "soft skills" appear to be intangible and difficult to measure, studies demonstrate that people in general and attorneys in particular can improve their soft skills and gauge their progress in expanding and enhancing their soft skills.

Resilience is, arguably, the most important soft skill. It enables attorneys to recover from setbacks and not only restore their equilibrium but become more adaptable and proficient as they learn valuable lessons from those setbacks. Despite its critical importance, resilience is in short supply among attorneys; studies indicate that attorneys are markedly less resilient than other people. Attorneys' low level of resilience results in professional performances that do not improve over time and a defensiveness that retards personal growth and discourages colleagues from providing the candid, constructive feedback essential to career development. In trying to make themselves less vulnerable to criticism, attorneys may unknowingly render themselves less adaptable, flexible, and resilient.

---

[281] Reynolds, *supra* note 279. [282] Brown, & Fenske, *supra* note 265 at 176. [283] Ibid.
[284] Schwartz, Tony. (2014, January 31). More mindfulness, less meditation. *The New York Times.*

In addition to developing resilience, attorneys may benefit from assessing and enhancing these important soft skills: willpower, self-efficacy, optimism, emotional granularity, feedback receptiveness, curiosity, goal setting and achievement, embodied cognition, and mindfulness. Although these soft skills may seem elusive, squishy, or impalpable to attorneys projecting a brittle image of professional competence, they turn out to be more determinative of professional success and personal fulfillment than attorneys' technical competencies. Each of these soft skills, as shown in this chapter, can be defined, assessed, and enhanced; and they are as amenable to ongoing improvement as our technical competencies.

5

Social Proficiency

When people respond to the question, "Which super powers do you wish you had?" the most popular choice is the "ability to read people's minds." That form of clairvoyance is tied with "ability to time travel" and followed by "ability to fly," "ability to teleport," and "invisibility."[1] The minds we want to read are not those of political leaders, film stars, or business magnates, but rather those of our friends, employers, family members, neighbors, and, most of all, spouses and dating partners.[2] The ability to read the minds of the people around us may be an astute choice among super powers because understanding people is the foundation for relating to them, and we are stunningly inept at understanding what other people are thinking and feeling. We cannot accurately predict their sentiments and intentions when we are working with them, and we usually are mistaken about the most basic notions – whether they like us, believe we are intelligent, or find us attractive.

Since most work today is performed by teams, our ignorance of other people and our oversights in relating to them put us at a serious disadvantage. We simply cannot afford to continue our social illiteracy. The shift from solo performances to group endeavors began a few decades ago and continues to change organizations and the nature of work itself. In 1987, for example, 28 percent of Fortune 1000 companies reported that they used self-directed teams. By 1995, the percent of Fortune 1000 companies using self-directed teams had increased to 67 percent, and by 2004, the percentage had risen to 79 percent.[3]

---

[1] Epley, Nicholas. (2014). *Mindwise* (p. xviii). New York: Alfred A. Knopf. Marist Poll. (2011, February 8). Holy super powers, Batman! Mind reading and time travel top list. Press release. Retrieved from http://maristpoll.marist.edu/28-holy-super-powers-batman-mind-reading-and-time-travel-top-list/.

[2] Epley, *supra* note 1 at 5.

[3] See Lawler, E., Mohrman, S., & Benson, G. (2001). *Organizing for high performance: Employee involvement, TQM, reengineering, and knowledge management in the Fortune 1000*. San

In academia, long known for solitary scholarship, the average number of authors per paper has increased from one author per paper in 1913 to more than five authors per paper in 2013.[4] In the field of psychology, 63 percent of papers had a single author in the 1950s; by 2010, only 7 percent of papers had a single author.[5] The trend from individual to collaborative scholarship also reflects a rapid increase in international collaborations. In scientific papers, for example, the number of articles with lead authors in the United States and co-authors outside the United States nearly doubled from 1996 to 2008.[6]

For lawyers, the general trend toward collaboration is stymied by a professional ethos that exalts individual accomplishment and personality traits that impede collegial, cooperative relationships.[7] The personal nature of the attorney–client relationship appears to promote individualism,[8] and law firm partners "vigorously defend their rights to autonomy and individualism, well beyond what is common in other professions."[9] Attorney personality assessments, moreover, indicate that attorneys score markedly above the general population in skepticism, autonomy, and urgency and significantly below the general population in sociability.[10] To that baneful concoction of personality traits add attorneys' low levels of interpersonal sensitivity.[11]

Despite lawyers' personal and cultural aversion to working collaboratively, most attorneys now acknowledge that teamwork is essential to professional success. Ninety-one percent of attorneys believe that the ability to "work cooperatively and collaboratively as part of a team" is necessary for a lawyer's

Francisco: Jossey-Bass. Lawler, Edward E., Mohrman, Susan A., & Ledford, Jr., Gerald E. (1995). *Creating high performance organizations*. San Francisco: Jossey-Bass. Lawler, Edward E., Mohrman, Susan, & Ledford, Gerald E, Jr. (1992, September). The Fortune 1000 and total quality. *The Journal for Quality and Participation*, 15(5), 6–10. Druskat, Vanessa, & Wheeler, Jane. (2004, Summer). How to lead a self-managing team. *MIT Sloan Management Review*, 65.

[4] Aboukhalil, Robert. (2014). The rising trend in authorship. *The Winnower*, 3: e141832.26907.

[5] Piocuda, Jorge E., Smyers, John O., Knyshev, Elena, & Harris, Richard J. (2015). Trends of internationalization and collaboration in U.S. psychology journals 1950–2010. *Archives of Scientific Psychology*, 3, 82–92.

[6] Gilbert, Natasha. (2011). Research sans frontiers. *Nature*, 471, 559.

[7] See Sturm, Susan. (2013, December 4). Law schools, leadership, and change. *Harvard Law Review*, 127, 49, 50. Meyerson, Michael. (2015). Law school culture and the lost art of collaboration: Why don't law professors play well with others? *Nebraska Law Review*, 93, 547.

[8] Schmidt, Sally. (2004). *Marketing the law firm: Business development techniques* (pp. 4–6). New York: Law Journal Press.

[9] Maister, David. (2006, April). Are law firms manageable? *The American Lawyer*.

[10] Altman Weil. (2002, August). *Report to management*.

[11] Foster, Jeff, Richard, Larry, Rohrer, Lisa, & Sirkin, Mark. (2010). Understanding lawyers: The personality traits of successful practitioners. Hildebrandt Baker Robbins.

success.[12] An even greater percentage of attorneys contend that the related skills of "expressing disagreement thoughtfully and respectfully" and "maintaining positive professional relationships" are essential to an attorney's success.[13] Reflecting attorneys' ambivalence about interpersonal relationships, however, only 69 percent of attorneys think that "sociability" is an essential skill.[14] A paradox of attorney success, then, is how does one become socially proficient in working with teams, expressing disagreements diplomatically, and maintaining congenial relationships without being sociable? It's like expecting an Olympic athlete to be fast but not agile; it could possibly occur in some context but the very fact that someone thought it could be done means that they probably missed the point.

Recognizing the importance of working with other people and the difficulties attorneys encounter in establishing productive relationships with other people, attorneys need to put as much effort into building their social skills as they put into developing their legal skills. The highest level of legal skills will not compensate for the lowest level of social skills that frequently characterize attorneys.[15] Thorough legal research and brilliant arguments, for example, flounder when attorneys do not understand the perceptions, values and objectives of adverse parties, opposing counsel, judges and juries and do not notice when they have failed to establish credibility, trust, and rapport. For these reasons, this chapter focuses on social proficiency and discusses its major components: understanding others' perceptions, perspectives, and beliefs; knowing how to communicate, persuade, listen, share stories, empathize, build trust, apologize, and work within teams; and developing cultural competence.

UNDERSTANDING OTHER PEOPLE

"Theory of mind" is the ability to understand the beliefs, desires, intentions, and emotions that cause actions in the lives of other people.[16] It is "one of the quintessential abilities that makes us human" because it means we have

---

[12] Gerkman, Alli, & Cornett, Logan. (2016, July). *Foundations for practice: The whole lawyer and the character quotient* (p. 20). Denver, Colorado: Institute for the Advancement of the American Legal System.

[13] Ibid. (Ninety-five percent contend that "expressing disagreement thoughtfully and respectfully" is an essential skill, and 94 percent contend that "maintaining positive professional relationships" is an essential skill.)

[14] Ibid. at 16.

[15] See Guthrie, Chris. (2001, Spring). The lawyer's philosophical map. *Harvard Negotiation Law Review 6*, 145.

[16] Baron-Cohen, Simon. (2001). Theory of mind in normal development and autism. *Prisme*, 34, 174.

the capacity to look at someone's face, listen to them, and comprehend the contents of their mind – to know and anticipate their thoughts, feelings, and actions.[17] "When you are thinking about whether your supervisor knows that you missed your deadline because you went out last night rather than stayed in to finish your assignment," explains neuroscientist Tali Sharot, "you are engaging in theory of mind. Theory of mind includes contemplating what other people know, assessing other peoples' motivations and feelings, and considering what others expect from you."[18]

How accurate are we at reading others' minds? In experiments testing "empathic accuracy" (the degree to which a perceiver's inferences match another person's actual thoughts and feelings),[19] psychologist William Ickes finds that men and women who have not previously met and are seeing each other's expressions for the first time are accurate in only one of every five tests:

> The average empathic accuracy score was only 22% on our scale from 0 to 100. The worst of the "amateur mind readers" in our sample scored right at 0%, displaying absolutely no empathic insight whatsoever. On the other hand, the best of these amateur mind readers was still far from perfect, scoring only 55%. Although the average level of empathic accuracy was well above a chance baseline, which we estimated to be around 5%, it is clear that the opposite-sex strangers in our study were only modestly successful in reading each other's thoughts and feelings.[20]

For those people who are concerned that new acquaintances may know more about them than they would prefer, Ickes assures them: "my advice would be to relax; it's likely that the person you are with knows only a fraction of what's going on inside your head."[21]

Empathic accuracy scores increase from 22 percent in the opposite-sex stranger experiments to 30 percent when close friends are tested and 35 percent when married couples are tested.[22] This relatively small increase in accuracy, however, is accompanied by a large increase in confidence. When couples predicted how their partners would rate them on a variety of characteristics, for instance, they believed their predictions were accurate 82 percent of the time.

---

[17] Ibid.   [18] Sharot, Tali. (2011). *The optimism bias* (p. 53). New York: Vintage Books.
[19] Ickes, William. (1993). Empathic accuracy. *Journal of Personality* 61(4), 596.
[20] Ickes, W. (2003). *Everyday mind reading: Understanding what other people think and feel.* Amherst, New York: Prometheus Books.
[21] Ibid.
[22] Ickes, William. (2016). Empathic accuracy: Judging thoughts and feelings. In Hall, Judith, Mast, Marianne, & West, Tessa (Eds.). *The social psychology of perceiving others accurately* (p. 55). New York: Cambridge University Press.

In fact, they were accurate in only 30–40 percent of their predictions.[23] "These couples hit a double," behavioral scientist Nicholas Epley quips, "but they thought they'd hit a home run."[24]

Although we have a high level of confidence in our ability to understand what other people are thinking and feeling – especially when they are friends or romantic partners – our perceptions of other people are consistently inaccurate. Surveying 50 years of his research, Ickes says, "there are no empathic superstars," and the "highest empathic accuracy scores we have seen in our research are in the general range of 50–60 percent."[25] These low levels of empathic accuracy, unfortunately, are not matched by a commensurately low level of confidence in our ability to discern others' thoughts and emotions. The correlation between our accuracy and our confidence in reading minds, in fact, is low or non-existent – placing us in the "often in error but never in doubt" class of predictors.[26] In one study, for instance, "those in the lowest quartile in interpersonal sensitivity greatly overestimated their relative ability, often by as much as 40 or more percentile points. Indeed, across our tasks, 85–90 percent of participants in the lowest quartile thought they were at or above average."[27] The least sensitive people, it turns out, are the most likely to be "substantially ignorant of their limitations."[28]

In addition to generally misunderstanding what other people are thinking and feeling, we misperceive them in four specific respects: (1) we think other people are thinking about us and evaluating us more frequently than they really are; (2) we imagine that they like us more often than they actually do; (3) we think they see us as we would like to see ourselves; and (4) we infer their beliefs and experiences by transposing our own onto them. Our egocentric bias misleads us by:

[23] Epley, *supra* note 1 at 10–11. In a study of couples who had been married six years on average, in which they reported their perception of their partner's level of sexual desire, men "consistently underestimated their female partner's desire, while the women had an accurate read on whether or not their partner was interested in sex." Bernstein, Elizabeth. (2016, May 30). Women are more interested in sex than you think studies show. *The Wall Street Journal*. The study is reported in Muise, Amy, Stanton, Sarah, Kim, James, & Impett, Emily. (2016, May). Not in the mood? Men under- (not over-) perceive their partner's sexual desire in established intimate relationships. *Journal of Personality and Social Psychology*, 110(5), 725–742.

[24] Epley, *supra* note 1 at 10.

[25] Kovacs, Elaine. (2011, October 28). Beyond the 40 acres: UT-Arlington. *Longhorn Life*.

[26] Goleman, Daniel. (2000). *Working with emotional intelligence* (p. 261). New York: Bantam. Myers, David. (2004). *Intuition* (p. 43). New Haven, Connecticut: Yale University Press.

[27] Ames, Daniel, & Kammrath, Lara. (2004). Mind-reading and metacognition: Narcissism, not actual competence, predicts self-estimated ability. *Journal of Nonverbal Behavior*, 28(3), 205.

[28] Ibid.

- enlarging our perceived effect on other people, leading us to believe that they are thinking about us as much as we are thinking about ourselves when, in fact, they are preoccupied with their own lives.[29]
- fostering the presumption that, if we like someone, they surely must like us, despite the evidence that only about 50 percent of people reciprocate our affinity or friendship.[30]
- supporting the illusion that other people perceive us to be as competent, ethical, and personable as we would like them to believe we are, although there is scant evidence that our self-perceptions and the features of our image management match what other people actually think of us.[31]
- disregarding the individuality of other people by presuming that their experiences, preferences, and priorities are the same as ours or would be the same as ours if they could choose.[32]

These egocentric biases encourage us to see other people not just through our own perspectives but also as reflections of our own perspectives.

To more accurately discern other people's thoughts and feelings, conventional wisdom urges us to engage in "perspective taking." The concept is that if we just put more effort into understanding the circumstances that preceded an action, opinion, or emotion, we could more accurately understand people. Epley refutes this conventional wisdom, asserting, "We've now looked many times for evidence that perspective taking – actively trying to imagine being in another person's circumstances – systematically increases mind reading and have yet to find any supportive evidence."[33] As an alternative to perspective taking, he urges us to engage in "perspective getting:"

> The science is clear. You don't try to adopt another person's perspective and guess better. Instead, you adopt a different approach. You have to actually *get*

[29] Gilovich, Thomas, Kruger, Justin, & Medvec, Victoria. (2002). The spotlight effect revisited: Overestimating the manifest variability of our actions and appearances. *Journal of Experimental Social Psychology*, 38, 93–99. Epley, *supra* note 1 at 96–97.

[30] Almaatouq, Abdullah, Radaelli, Laura, Pentland, Alex, & Shmueli, Erez. (2016, March 22). Are you your friends' friend? Poor perception of friendship ties limits the ability to promote behavioral change. *PLOS ONE*, 11(3), e0151588. Murphy, Kate. (2016, August 6). Do your friends actually like you? *The New York Times*.

[31] Wilson, Timothy. (2002). *Strangers to ourselves* (pp. 194–202). Cambridge, Massachusetts: The Belknap Press. Epley, *supra* note 1 at 6–7.

[32] Ubel, Peter. (2012). *Critical decisions* (p. 88). New York: HarperCollins. Gilovich, Thomas. (1991). *How we know what isn't so* (pp. 114–122). New York: The Free Press. Thaler, Richard. *Misbehaving* (p. 280). New York: W.W. Norton.

[33] Epley, *supra* note 1 at 170.

the other person's perspective, and perhaps the only way to do that is to ask . . . Recognizing the limits of your sixth sense suggests a different approach to understanding the minds of others: trying harder to *get* another person's perspective instead of trying to *take* it. As the old reminder to doctors trying to understand their patients goes, "The patient is trying to tell you what's wrong with him. You have to shut up and listen."

It is remarkably difficult for people to ask for information that they think they should already possess. The fact that they do not have the information seems to strengthen their determination to act autonomously and intuitively rather than obtain the missing information. The problem with this reliance on intuitive judgment, Epley observes, "is that the confidence we have in this sense far outstrips our actual ability, and the confidence we have in our judgment rarely gives us a good sense of how accurate we actually are."[34]

INFLUENCE AND COMMUNICATION

To become socially proficient, we need to do more than understand others' thoughts and feelings; we also need to communicate effectively with them. To become effective communicators, we must identify the factors that influence human behavior and the best methods for establishing rapport, credibility, and meaning in interpersonal relationships. This section, accordingly, first examines the psychology of influence and then shows how we can get beyond our reticence in relating to people and establish effective, durable, and enjoyable professional relationships.

Influence

The most popular model of influence is Robert Cialdini's six principles of persuasion. He has distilled his research regarding psychology and marketing into these "weapons of influence:"

- *Consistency/commitment.* We feel obligated to act in a manner consistent with our prior attitudes, beliefs, actions, and commitments.[35] "After committing themselves to a particular position – especially when the commitment is active, public, and freely chosen – people are more likely to behave in ways that are congruent with that position," Cialdini

[34] Ibid. at 12.
[35] Robbennolt, Jennifer, & Sternlight, Jean. (2012). *Psychology for lawyers* (p. 129). Chicago: American Bar Association.

asserts. "As a consequence, future behavior is likely to resemble past behavior."[36]

- *Social proof/conformity*. People determine appropriate behavior by noticing and then imitating other people. People "tend to behave as their friends and peers have behaved."[37] When they see other people doing something, especially if it is enjoyable but ethically problematic, the message that runs through their minds is, "Why not me?"

- *Liking*. We prefer to work with people we like, and we like people who are attractive and look similar to us. We imbue attractive people with various characteristics that, in reality, have no relation to their attractiveness: talent, kindness, honesty, and intelligence.[38]

- *Reciprocation*. The reciprocity rule requires us to "repay, in kind, what another person has provided us."[39] In negotiations this means that, when an adverse party makes a concession, we are expected to respond in kind. Ironically, the obligation to respond can seem so burdensome that "we may be willing to agree to perform a larger favor than we received, merely to relieve ourselves of the psychological burden of debt."[40]

- *Authority*. We are highly deferential to authority figures like doctors, police, employers, judges, government leaders, and teachers.[41] Even when they make a mistake, "no one lower in the hierarchy will think to question it – precisely because, once a legitimate authority has given an order, subordinates stop thinking in the situation and start reacting."[42]

- *Scarcity*. We determine the quality of a service or product by its scarcity. We make the assumption that scarce items are better than non-scarce items, and scarcity then becomes a proxy for quality.[43] When our access to an item is restricted, the desirability of the item increases and "we assign it positive qualities to justify the desire."[44]

These six principles have evolved over centuries, Cialdini believes, to enable people to function in social groups. It is generally adaptive, efficient, and productive, he writes, "to repay favors, behave consistently, follow the lead of similar others, favor the requests of those we like, heed legitimate authorities and value scarce resources."[45] But we also need to be aware when these norms

[36] Cialdini, Robert. (2010). Compliance with a request in two cultures: The differential influence of social proof and commitment/consistency on collectivists and individualists. *Personality and Social Psychology Bulletin*, 25(1), 1244.
[37] Ibid. at 1243.   [38] Cialdini, Robert. (1993). *Influence* (p. 171). New York: William Morrow.
[39] Ibid. at 17.   [40] Ibid. at 35.   [41] Ibid. at 218.   [42] Ibid. at 219.   [43] Ibid. at 244.
[44] Ibid. at 251.
[45] Cialdini, Robert. (2001). The science of persuasion. *Scientific American*, 284(2), 76.

are being used to manipulate us for improper purposes. "It is so easy to be a patsy," says Charles Munger, Vice Chairman of Berkshire Hathaway, describing the importance of Cialdini's work in detecting and understanding our compliance with the six sources of social influence.[46]

Communication

"Surprisingly large numbers of professionals do less than their best," asserts management professor Keith Rollag, "because they haven't mastered three basic yet critical getting-to-know you skills: introducing themselves, remembering people's names and asking questions."[47] Despite the simplicity of the three basic skills, attorneys stumble early and often in their interactions with other people. Part of the problem is a sense of unease about initiating contact with others – "networking" is the word that appears to provoke alternating displays of disdain and anxiety in attorneys – and the other part is a lack of communication skills or, more precisely, the lack of practice in using those skills.

In a study that included 154 lawyers in a large law firm, organizational behavior professor Tiziana Casciaro and her colleagues discovered that many lawyers were ambivalent about or disgusted by professional networking.[48] Although the lawyers who disliked networking had lower billable hours than those who liked networking, the reluctant attorneys could not overcome their aversion to networking and recognize that "their success depended on their ability to network effectively both internally (to get themselves assigned to choice clients) and externally (to bring business into the firm)."[49] The reluctant attorneys had deep-seated beliefs that networking was inauthentic, exploitative, and morally repugnant. "They feel so impure," says Casciaro, "that they literally wish to take a shower."[50]

In working with the attorneys, Casciaro found that four strategies were effective in changing their attitudes about networking and enabling them to overcome their aversion to it:

---

[46] Munger, Charlie. On the psychology of human misjudgment. Speech given at Harvard University in June 1995. (Transcribed and edited by Whitney Tilson).

[47] Rollag, Keith. (2015, December). Managing yourself: Succeed in new situations. *Harvard Business Review*, p. 113.

[48] Casciaro, Tiziana, Gino, Francesca, & Kouchaki, Maryam. (2016, May). Learning to love networking. *Harvard Business Review*.

[49] Ibid.

[50] Chen, Vivia. (2016, June 9). Tips on overcoming that dirty feeling about networking. *The American Lawyer*.

- *Focus on learning*. People who see networking as an opportunity for personal growth, rather than an obligation to be completed with a minimum of effort, approach it with a sense of curiosity and excitement. "Concentrate on the positives – how it's going to help you boost the knowledge and skills that are needed on your job – and the activity will begin to seem much more worthwhile," advises Casciaro.[51]
- *Identify common interests*. Before networking events, conduct research regarding the people you will be meeting. Once shared interests and common goals are identified, networking "will feel more authentic and meaningful and is more likely to lead to relationships that have those qualities too."[52]
- *Think broadly about what you can give*. A reluctance to network may reflect an underestimation or exceedingly narrow view of your possible contributions to other people and organizations. Think creatively about tangible and intangible contributions you could make.
- *Find a higher purpose*. Lawyers' attitudes and effectiveness were affected by how they defined the primary purpose of networking. Casciaro found that "attorneys who focused on the collective benefits of making connections ('support my firm' and 'help my clients') rather than on personal ones ('support or help my career') felt more authentic and less dirty while networking, were more likely to network, and had more billable hours as a result."[53]

For attorneys who have made their peace with networking and can see the connections between networking and choice clients, stimulating work, billable hours, and career satisfaction, the next step is to make sure you have mastered Rollag's three basic getting-to-know-you skills (introducing yourself, remembering names, and asking questions). These skills apply to any new situation, from social functions to new jobs.

Rollag's first skill, introducing yourself, enables professionals to overcome their reluctance to initiate conversations. This is accomplished by considering how you would feel if you were in the other person's position; experimenting with and practicing your initial remarks; thinking about what you want to say about yourself; and planning what you want to ask about the other person.[54]

Rollag's second basic skill is remembering names. Names are best recalled by listening very intently when people introduce themselves; focusing on a person's name instead of your next comment; saying the name out loud after the introduction; writing or typing the name at the earliest opportunity;

---

[51] Casciaro, *supra* at note 48.   [52] Ibid.   [53] Ibid.   [54] Rollag, *supra* note 47 at 113–114.

testing your recall while imagining the face; and associating the person's name with a mental image that triggers recall.[55]

Lastly, Rollag explains how to ask better questions. Questions are most effective when we have considered and clarified what we want to ask and why we are asking; eliminated confusing, multipart questions; determined who is the most qualified person to answer the questions; selected the best time to present the questions; and expressed gratitude for the answers that have been provided so that the person will be receptive to future questions.[56] And never ask insincere questions designed to showcase your knowledge or intelligence; people will detect the insincerity immediately and remember you as being both immature and untrustworthy.

Communication becomes more challenging, complex, and nuanced as we move from new relationships to ongoing relationships. Although Rollag's three skills remain pertinent in ongoing relationships, a more sophisticated model of communication is necessary to expand and refine our communication skills. This additional model can be based on speech communication professor Julien Mirivel's "positive communication" principles: greeting, asking, complimenting, disclosing, encouraging, listening, and inspiring, as summarized below:[57]

- *Greeting.* Mirivel reminds us that communication is more than exchanging information; our communication defines and is an integral part of our relationships. The act of greeting – initiating contact, acknowledging people and inviting them into our world – renews and reconstructs relationships and is especially important when tension has disrupted a relationship. To better understand the purpose, content, and effects of our greetings, Mirivel suggests we ask ourselves these questions: How often do you initiate contact instead of waiting for the other person to greet you? When do you resist greeting another person? When do you feel most comfortable initiating contact? When do you hesitate?[58]
- *Asking.* Questions serve at least two purposes: they may lead to information and, perhaps most importantly, they enable us to discover more about the other person and whether we can trust them. Questions, therefore, invariably have both explicit and implicit purposes. "The more a question is open-ended," Mirivel notes, "the more it will dig beneath the surface and foster relationships."[59]
- *Complimenting.* Our communication affects the development of the person to whom it is directed – and it affects our development as well.

[55] Ibid. at 114.   [56] Ibid. at 115.
[57] Mirivel, Julien. (2014). *The art of positive communication.* New York: Peter Lang.
[58] Ibid. at 162.   [59] Ibid.

When we compliment others, we necessarily focus on their positive aspects and counter our tendencies to criticize and focus on problems. To gain more insights into ourselves, Mirivel recommends that we ask ourselves these questions about compliments: "Who do you compliment? Is your natural tendency to criticize or to compliment? What kinds of compliments do you share? Do you sometimes resist your impulse to compliment someone?"[60]

- *Disclosing.* Communication tests our capacity for intimacy and vulnerability. Even in a professional context, as discussed in Chapter 4, communication in the form of feedback makes us feel vulnerable and can provoke angry, defensive reactions. When we have the courage to be vulnerable and to disclose, though, it generally enhances trust, deepens relationships, and promotes self-development. To better understand ourselves and how we communicate, Mirivel poses these questions: "When do you disclose? When do you not? What pieces of information do you wish you could share with others but hesitate to reveal? What forces prevent you from opening yourself up to others?"[61]

- *Encouraging.* Communication imparts substantive information, and through words, intonation, pitch, and timbre, it simultaneously and sometimes unintentionally transmits our opinions about the status, education, predicaments, and prospects of the persons receiving the communication. Despite their tremendous impact, our messages frequently lack the thoughtfulness and encouragement that people need and expect. This occurs because we focus on another person's literal, expressed needs rather than their faint intimations of confusion, discouragement, and dismay. Since communication is an act of giving as well as informing, Mirivel presents these questions to promote encouragement in communication: "What are the people around me doing? Do they need words of encouragement? Can I say something that will make a difference in their ability to move forward to make better decisions?"[62]

- *Listening.* When we listen, Mirivel asserts, we "transcend human separateness."[63] To determine whether we have developed the art of listening, he advises us to ask four questions: "How much do I talk? How much do I listen? Am I judging or evaluating the other? Am I inviting conversation by listening deeply to others?"[64]

- *Inspiring.* We readily acknowledge that we communicate to influence other people, but somehow we find it more difficult to acknowledge that influencing them can be a form of inspiring them. "If our

---

[60] Ibid. at 163. [61] Ibid. [62] Ibid. at 164. [63] Ibid. at 165. [64] Ibid.

communication has ripple effects of influence," asserts Mirivel, "then we can choose to inspire others. From my perspective, to inspire is the pinnacle of positive communication."[65] Instead of choosing to merely influence people, why not inspire them?

LISTENING

We briefly discussed listening in the previous section. Because listening is arguably the most important yet most difficult aspect of human communication, this section explores listening in greater depth. The questions addressed in this section are: What is listening? What happens when we don't listen? Why do we neglect our listening skills? How do we assess listening skills? How can we improve our listening skills?

Listening is the discipline of hearing and comprehending explicit and tacit messages when someone else is talking. To be effective, listening must meet objective and subjective requirements in at least two ways. First, our understanding of what we hear must be an objectively reasonable interpretation of the message, *and* it must subjectively resonate with and be accepted by the person who expressed it. Second, to be effective listeners, we have to listen in an objectively supportive manner as shown by our discernible attention, consideration, reflection, and comprehension; *and* the person transmitting the message must believe that we are listening, acknowledging, understanding, and reacting in a manner that meets their subjective expectations. Unlike other expert skills, listening requires both an objectively proficient performance and a subjectively satisfying experience. The objective and subjective criteria must be met not only in the moment of listening but for as long as the memory of that conversation affects the parties' relationship. If, for instance, you are initially convinced that someone understood what you were saying but you discover months later that they misunderstood or are now disregarding a critical aspect of the conversation, your initial satisfaction is rapidly eclipsed by your current dismay.

Commenting on the vagaries of human interactions, George Bernard Shaw said, "The single biggest problem in communication is the illusion that it has taken place."[66] The illusion of communication occurs when we are convinced that we expressed ourselves clearly but subsequently learn that we were neither heard nor understood – that our partner in conversation was not actually listening. Our reaction upon learning that our partner was not listening tells

---

[65] Ibid.
[66] Oliver, Robert. (2015, October 30). Communication is what it's all about. *San Francisco Daily Journal*, p. 2.

us that not listening to someone is considerably more than a communication failure; not listening incites frustration, alienation, and anger, indicating that not being listened to violates our cultural norms and abases our sense of self-worth. Listening, therefore, is considerably more than an acknowledgment of another person's ideas. It is a time-honored ritual that, when undertaken attentively and compassionately, serves to honor people and, if undertaken superficially and impatiently, offends them. Listening is fundamentally an affirmation that another person merits attention and respect.

We fail to listen and neglect our listening skills for four primary reasons: we prefer to talk about ourselves; we think that listening to people with opinions different from ours is a waste of our time; listening is physically exhausting; and engaging with people triggers a sense of vulnerability. Talking about ourselves, rather than listening to or thinking about other people, makes us feel extraordinarily good. When people are talking about themselves neuroscientists observe "heightened activity in brain regions belonging to the meso-limbic dopamine system, which is associated with the sense of reward and satisfaction from food, money or sex."[67] In experiments where financial incentives are offered to people if they will talk about someone else, most people "willingly gave up between 17% and 25% of their potential earnings" so they could continue talking about themselves.[68]

Apart from the exhilaration we experience when "banging on about No. 1," we avoid listening to other people because they might disagree with us, and listening, even when it reinforces what we want to hear, is tiring.[69] For most of us, hearing dissonant information or opinions activates an impulse to ignore or suppress the data rather than exploit the opportunity to acquire new and potentially valuable facts and perspectives. We share John Francis' approach to disconfirming evidence:

> [M]ost of my adult life I have not been listening fully. I only listened long enough to determine whether the speaker's ideas matched my own. If they didn't, I would stop listening, and my mind would race ahead to compose an argument against what I believed the speaker's idea or position to be.[70]

---

[67] Hotz, Robert. (2012, May 7). Science reveals why we brag so much. *The Wall Street Journal*. See Tamir, Diana, & Mitchell, Jason. (2012, May 22). Disclosing information about the self is intrinsically rewarding. *Proceedings of the National Academy of Sciences*, 109(21), 8038.

[68] Hotz, *supra* note 67.

[69] Luscombe, Belinda. (2012, May 8). Why we talk about ourselves: The brain likes it. *Time*.

[70] Francis, John. (2005). *Planetwalker: 22 years of walking. 17 years of silence* (p. 46). Washington, DC: National Geographic Society.

And even when people have the good sense to agree with us, listening to them quickly tires us. When fatigued, our attention shifts away from the speaker, our reaction times slow, and we disassociate from our listening goals.[71] As communications professor Paul King explains, "If you're really concentrating, critical listening is a physically exhausting experience."[72]

Listening also makes us feel vulnerable. When we stop talking about ourselves and ask about someone else, we are concerned that it may be perceived as a sign of weakness or vulnerability.[73] As Edgar Schein, an organizational behavior expert, explains, "It implies the other person knows something that I need to or want to know. It draws the other person into the situation and into the driver's seat; it enables the other person to help or hurt me and, thereby, opens the door to building a relationship."[74] We also fear that listening may create an expectation or implication that we might change as a result of another person's ideas, opinions, and feelings, a possibility that is prospectively barred by signaling that we will not listen or are not listening. Even when we do not fully understand what someone else is communicating, our sense of vulnerability prevents us from seeking clarification. "We don't ask for clarification because we fear what we might hear," states Thomas DeLong, a management professor and former Managing Director of Morgan Stanley Group, Inc. "We don't want to discover that the nod we received was in fact a nod of disappointment."[75]

Although we resist listening, nearly all of us (96 percent) think we are good listeners.[76] Research, however, shows that we remember less than 10 percent of what people tell us.[77] To assess whether you are a good listener, law professor Neil Hamilton has developed a Listening Strengths and Weaknesses Inventory and a Listening Preference Profile, available in his law review article, "Effectiveness Requires Listening: How to Assess and

[71] See Boksen, Marteen, Meijman, Theo, & Lorist, Monicque. (2005, September). Effects of mental fatigue on attention: An ERP study. *Cognitive Brain Research, 25,* 107–116.

[72] Gallo, Carmine. (2014). *Talk like TED* (p. 185.) New York: St. Martin's Press.

[73] Schein, Edgar. (2013). *Humble inquiry* (p. 81). San Francisco: Berrett-Koehler Publishers.

[74] Ibid. at 9.

[75] DeLong, Thomas. (2011). *Flying without a net* (p. 58). Boston, Massachusetts: Harvard Business Review Press.

[76] Cole, Samantha (2015, February 26). New research shows we're all bad listeners who think we work too much. *Fast Company.* Accenture. (2015). *#ListenLearnLead Global Research* (p. 5).

[77] See Shellenbarger, Sue. (2014, July 22). Tuning in: Improving your listening skills. *The Wall Street Journal.*

Improve Listening Skills."[78] To get a sense for your own listening skills, consider what your responses, on a five-point scale from 1 (Never) to 5 (Always), would be to these statements from Hamilton's Listening Strengths and Weaknesses Inventory:

> I ask questions to help the speaker clarify and reflect.
>
> I confirm my understanding of what the speaker is communicating by paraphrasing what the speaker has said.
>
> I use pauses and silence in conversation to allow the speaker to formulate a response.
>
> During conversation, I step back and reflect on all communication, verbal and nonverbal, to determine what is really going on.

For these statements, higher scores indicate stronger listening abilities. Hamilton suggests that you ask a friend, family member, or colleague to evaluate you on his complete 20-statement inventory, so that you can compare their assessment with your own.

Michael Nichols, a psychologist and author of *The Lost Art of Listening*, offers a different assessment tool. He asks us to think of a conversation with a family member or a colleague and then rank ourselves on a scale (1-Almost Never and 4-Almost Always) in responding to these types of questions:[79]

> When someone is talking to you, do you:

> Think about what you want to say while others are talking?
>
> Share similar experiences of your own rather than inviting the speaker to elaborate on his or her experience?
>
> Assume you know what someone is going to say before he or she is finished?

For these questions, lower scores indicate better listening skills. If your score on Nichols' 25-statement assessment shows poor listening skills, he suggests that you "pick out one bad habit at a time and practice letting others finish talking, and then let them know what you think they're saying before you say what's on your mind."[80]

As we move from assessment to performance, we need to identify techniques for improving listening skills and flag the attitudes and remarks that invariably irritate others. This task is more difficult than we might expect because, just as "there is no generally accepted definition of listening," there is

---

[78] Hamilton, Neil. (2012, Winter). Effectiveness requires listening: How to assess and improve listening skills. *Florida Coastal Law Review*, 13, 120, 123. Retrieved from http://papers.ssrn.com /sol3/papers.cfm?abstract_id=1917059

[79] Nichols, Michael. (2009). *The lost art of listening* (pp. 67–68). New York: The Guilford Press.

[80] Ibid. at 69.

no empirically validated body of research identifying successful listening techniques for attorney–client interactions.[81] Nevertheless, we can synthesize ideas and research from other fields and present ten recommendations for effective listening:[82]

1. Prepare for a meeting or conversation by thinking about and writing down issues, questions, and what you want to say and accomplish.
2. Set a listening goal of speaking 25 percent of the time and listening 75 percent of the time.
3. Turn off phones, computers, and other devices.
4. Make eye contact and maintain a relaxed yet alert posture, exhibiting sincerity, focus, and receptiveness.
5. Ask clarifying questions throughout the conversation.
6. Make expressions, comments, and noises to show you are paying attention, e.g., "hmmm," "oh," "I see."
7. Take notes to indicate interest and attention but know when to stop taking notes if they become a distraction.
8. Restate, repeat, or paraphrase what the speaker has said and ask whether you have accurately understood the speaker.
9. Pay keen attention to facial expressions, body positioning, and changes in speaking volume, tone, and speed to detect the feelings behind the content.
10. Develop a tolerance for pauses and silence so that people can collect their thoughts and see you as a patient listener.[83]

The "not to do list" is shorter and hopefully these errors are easily recognized due to their frequency and consistently annoying effects:[84]

---

[81] Hamilton, *supra* note 78 at 111, 116–117.
[82] The ten ideas are distilled from a variety of sources. See Shellenbarger, *supra* note 77. Hamilton, *supra* note 78. Richards, Carl. (2015, November 2). Start listening to burnish your reputation as a trusted advisor. *The New York Times*. Goleman, Daniel. (2013). *Focus*. New York: HarperCollins. Bryant, Adam. (2015, December 17). Melanie Whelan of SoulCycle: Find the questions in every answer. *The New York Times*. Goulston, Mark. (2010). *Just listen*. New York: American Management Association. Nichols, *supra* note 79.
[83] For an excellent article on the meaning and effects of silence in communication, see Bassett, Debra Lyn. (2015). Silencing our elders. *Nevada Law Journal*, 15, 519.
[84] Sources for the five recommendations listed here include those in footnote 82 and Isaac Prilleltensky, Dean, School of Education and Human Development, University of Miami. Dean Prilleltensky's PowerPoint presentation, "Well-Being, Fun, Fitness and Fairness," at the University Colorado Law School conference, "Mindfulness and Thriving Legal Practices," on August 9, 2016, includes three of the five recommendations.

1. *Don't be a "story topper."* Story toppers always have a better story – a greater accomplishment, a funnier event, a smarter insight, a more grateful client. Toppers act like they share your experiences and feelings ("That reminds me of the time ...")[85] but leave you with the sense you have been put down.

2. *Don't provide advice unless asked.* No matter how clear a problem and the solution is to you, resist the temptation to say, "If I were you I would ..."[86] or "This is what you should tell them." Well-intentioned advice, when unsolicited, can be seen as intrusive, rude, and belittling.

3. *Don't tell people to change or how they should change.* Listening "is not about offering advice or solutions, and it is not about persuading the other person. It is simply holding the other person's story, and honoring it, and valuing what that person is offering in that moment."[87]

4. *Don't minimize through glib reassurance.* When other people's problems generate anxiety, we attempt to reduce their anxiety and ours with well-meaning but thoughtless comments like, "Don't worry about it, I am sure everything will work out" or "There really is nothing to be concerned about." This has the effect of minimizing or dismissing their problems and creating the impression we are not listening to them.

5. *Don't diagnose.* It's hard to resist conveying your perceptive analysis of other people's problems and diagnosing them with statements like, "Your problem is that you ..." But most people are seeking understanding, acceptance, affinity, and empathy and do not want to hear your analysis of their professional or personal shortcomings. Your diagnosis may look like you are insensitive to the other person's vulnerability in disclosing their problems.

Perhaps the clearest path to effective listening is laid out by Sam Palmisano, the former President and Chief Executive Officer of IBM. When asked how his early experience in Japan affected his self-development, he replied, "I learned to listen by having only one objective: comprehension. I was only trying to understand what the person was trying to convey to me. I wasn't listening to critique or object or convince."[88]

---

[85] Nichols, *supra* note 79 at 82.   [86] Ibid. at 84.

[87] Brooks, Susan. (2015). Cultivating students' relational skills. In Maranville, Deborah, Bliss, Lisa Radtke, Kaas, Carolyn Wilkes, & Lopez, Antoinette Sedillo (Eds.). *Building on best practices: Transforming legal education in a changing world* (p. 330). New Providence, New Jersey: LexisNexis.

[88] Fleming, Thomas. (2012, April). Why I'm a listener: Amgen CEO Kevin Sharer. *McKinsey Quarterly*.

STORYTELLING/NARRATIVE REASONING

Storytelling, also called narrative reasoning, is premised on the idea that we learn more from stories and anecdotes than facts and logic. It recognizes that tales and folklore rather than statistics and reasoning have transmitted human knowledge for centuries. Consequently, we are primed to respond to stories, and modern learning methods often fail because they reflect a fundamental misunderstanding of how humans learn. As applied to law practice, this means that lawyers' penchant for logic and abstract reasoning frequently results in communication breakdowns that could have been prevented by learning the art of storytelling. Stories, not logic, captivate and motivate people.

Andrew Stanton, the writer of *Toy Story*, tells us why stories have the power to crystallize emotions, values, and aspirations and connect us to universal themes:

> We all love stories. We're born for them. Stories affirm who we are. We all want affirmations that our lives have meaning. And nothing does a greater affirmation than when we connect through stories. It can cross the barriers of time, past, present and future, and allow us to experience the similarities between ourselves and through others, real and imagined.[89]

We understand the events in our lives through stories, and we construct stories about other people's lives in an effort to reconcile personalities, motivations, actions, and outcomes with our expectations. Stories add content and context to fill in the interstices in our knowledge, enabling us to create credible sequences of events and plausible cause and effect relationships. We also use stories to help us remember; facts are easily forgotten but stories "stick."[90]

Stories literally connect us with other people. When a person is relating an unrehearsed personal story, for instance, the brain scans of both the speaker's and the listener's brains show similar activation patterns. "The listener's brain activity," neuroscientists report, "mirrors the speaker's brain activity with temporal delays."[91] As the story evolves, the listener develops the capacity to anticipate the speaker's thoughts. This predictive capacity is displayed in "a subset of brain regions in which the activity in the listener's brain preceded the

---

[89] Gallo, *supra* note 72 at 52.

[90] McKee, Robert. (2003, June). Storytelling that moves people. *Harvard Business Review.* p. 52. See Heath, Chip, & Heath, Dan. (2007). *Made to stick: Why some ideas survive and others die.* New York: Random House.

[91] Stephens, Greg, Silbert, Lauren, & Hasson, Uri. (2010, August 10). Speaker-listener neural coupling underlies successful communication. *Proceedings of the National Academy of Sciences,* 107(2), 14428.

activity in the speaker's brain, suggesting that the listeners were actively predicting the speaker's upcoming utterances."[92] Minds, in short, meld with stories.

Because stories quickly convey ideas, inspire people, and incite action, lawyers need to know when and how to shift away from their linear, literal, and rational communication styles and adopt a storytelling approach. They need to understand and acknowledge that their positions and arguments do not fail for lack of logic but instead fail for lack of emotion.[93] This shift from logic to affect requires lawyers to overcome the assumption that human conduct is governed by rules, laws, and principles and the application and extension of court opinions revered as *stare decisis*. Neuroscience research demonstrates that this legalistic, rational view of human behavior is both erroneous and misleading; it lacked scientific support from its inception and is an artifact of seventeenth-century philosophy. Contrary to the syllogistic logic taught and reasonable person models espoused in law school, humans feel first, act second, and think later.[94] We are overpowered by emotions very early in the process of considering information and perceiving sensations, and we remain largely unaware of the fact that our reasoning and decision making are being governed by our emotions.[95] As neuroscientist Joseph LeDoux explains in *The Emotional Brain*, "the wiring of the brain at this point in our evolutionary history is such that connections from the emotional systems to the cognitive systems are stronger than connections from the cognitive systems to the emotional systems."[96]

When attorneys doggedly stick with a communication style that is exclusively rational, it is a disservice to their clients. They are electing to allocate all of their persuasive efforts to a secondary level of neural processing and are ignoring the most basic tenets of neuroscience. "If stories trigger brain-to-brain 'coupling,'" states Carmine Gallo, author of *The Storyteller's Secret*, "then part of the solution to winning people over to your argument is to tell more stories."[97]

---

[92] Patel, Ushma. (2011, December 5). Hasson brings real life into the lab to examine cognitive processing. *News at Princeton*.
[93] See McKee, *supra* note 90.
[94] See Rock, David. (2009). *Your brain at work*. New York: Harper Collins. Hill, Dan. (2010). *Emotionomics*. Philadelphia, Pennsylvania: Adams Business & Professional. LeDoux, Joseph. (1996). *The emotional brain*. New York: Simon & Shuster.
[95] See Janicki, Karol. (2015). *Language and conflict* (pp. 60–62). London: Palgrave Macmillan.
[96] LeDoux, *supra* note 94.
[97] Gallo, *supra* note 72 at 51. Cf. Johansen, Steven. (2006). This is not the whole truth: The ethics of telling stories to clients. *Arizona State Law Journal*, 38, 961.

Once you are convinced that storytelling might be effective, three questions come to mind: Why don't we tell more stories? How do you find stories to tell? What exactly is a story anyway? The threshold question – why don't we tell more stories if they're so effective? – is easily answered: it takes considerable time and is very hard work. As Robert McKee, author of *Story: Substance, Structure, Style and the Principles of Screenwriting*, observes, "It takes rationality but little creativity to design an argument using conventional rhetoric. But it demands vivid insight and storytelling skill to present an idea that packs enough emotional power to be memorable."[98]

If we are willing to take on the hard work of storytelling, the next step is to find stories to tell by identifying the grand themes in our clients' conflicts. These themes are "not imposed on the story but evoked from within it."[99] Themes may embrace personal hopes, desires, and dreams and frequently highlight classic conflicts like "good v. evil, justice v. injustice, pride v. humility, greed v. generosity"[100] and the tensions between "character and candor, power and weakness, deception and vulnerability."[101]

Themes, once identified, underpin the story, and the story itself should fit the classic arc:

> Essentially, a story expresses how and why life changes. It begins with a situation in which life is relatively in balance ... But then there's an event – in screenwriting, we call it the "inciting incident" – that throws life out of balance. ... The story goes on to describe how, in an effort to restore balance, the protagonist's subjective expectations crash into an uncooperative objective reality. A good storyteller describes what it's like to deal with these opposing forces, calling on the protagonist to dig deeper, work with scarce resources, make difficult decisions, take action despite risks, and ultimately discover the truth. All great storytellers since the dawn of time – from the ancient Greeks through Shakespeare and up to the present day – have dealt with this fundamental conflict between subjective expectation and cruel reality.[102]

Compelling stories have drama, empathy, wisdom, plausibility, consistency, and uniqueness.[103] They incorporate a "reversal of fortune and a lesson

---

[98] McKee, *supra* note 90 at 52.
[99] Meyer, Philip. (2015, January). Telling unfinished stories. *ABA Journal*, p. 28.
[100] Berg, David. (2006). *The trial lawyer* (p. 3). Chicago: American Bar Association.
[101] McElhaney, Jim. (2008, March). Stuck in the rut. *ABA Journal*, p. 24.
[102] McKee, *supra* note 90 at 52.
[103] Klein, Gary. (1999). *Sources of power* (pp. 182–183). Cambridge, Massachusetts: The MIT Press.

learned."[104] When stories falter, a common cause is the tendency to focus on accomplishments and ignore or gloss over struggles, difficulties, and vulnerabilities. The obstacles and setbacks, however, are what people relate to in human drama, and a story without challenges is empty and unbelievable.[105] If we are relating a story to communicate who we are, for instance, it must reveal both strengths and vulnerabilities.[106]

Exceptional attorneys have learned how to persuade judges and jurors with stories. They describe how they rely on storytelling and develop their storytelling strategies in these comments:

- "Whether I'm arguing to a jury or to a court, I start thinking about my story and how it's going to flow. I start thinking like a non-lawyer. I think that's a good way to think when preparing a case, especially one you've lived with for some time, and to see it through new eyes."[107]

- "I look at, 'Where is the hook?' because you need a hook for the jury to identify with your client and make them want to make your client whole. It's very difficult for a jury to give a big award to someone they don't identify with, and plaintiffs' attorneys don't understand this. Whether you're the plaintiff or the defendant, it comes down to making the jury look at your client and think, 'there but for the grace of God go I.' "[108]

- "The state's case is a narrative: the story of a crime. The defense has only to cast doubts on the coherence of that story. The 'why' elements of the story must make sense – what would have motivated this person to hurt that person – before you can engage the jurors' empathy, put them in the shoes of the accused or the victim, as needed: make them feel the cold blade held against their necks, or the pang of unappreciated devotion that might drive someone to steal from a former employer. It is the particulars that make a story real."[109]

- "The one constant? I learned this from a federal judge who gave me this sage advice very early on in my career: 'Don't bore the jury.' Always come knowing you're a storyteller."[110]

[104] Denning, Stephen. (2004, May). Telling tales. *Harvard Business Review*, p. 124.
[105] McKee, *supra* note 90 at 53.   [106] Denning, *supra* note 104 at 126.
[107] (2010, May 12). The list. *San Francisco Daily Journal.*
[108] Kiser, Randall. *How leading lawyers think* (p. 138). Heidelberg, New York: Springer. (Part of this quotation does not appear on p. 138; it is excerpted from the transcript of Attorney Interview D2, one of the 78 interviews completed for the *How Leading Lawyers Think* study.)
[109] Sotomayor, Sonia. (2013). *My beloved world* (pp. 269–270). New York: Random House.
[110] Greene, Jenna. (2015, September 27). Randy Mastro on teddy bears, bridgegate and how he'll beat you in court. *The AmLaw Litigation Daily.*

The central element in attorneys' stories is the theme, the through-line that connects people, facts, and events, as these attorneys' comments illustrate:

- "A theme is not what you want. It is why you are entitled to what you want. That is, you cannot decently ask the jurors to give you a money judgment, to give you a verdict of no liability, or to acquit your client unless they have a reason to do it. And that reason is your theme."[111]
- "Step back from the details of your case. Some deeper meaning had to have emerged from the testimony of witnesses and the conduct of the lawyers during trial. Not from the documents or the graphics – but from the people involved. That 'big theme,' whatever it might be, should come early in your argument, to get the jurors' attention, and to point the way to a just decision."[112]
- "I tell even some of the best attorneys they need a theme. Attorneys to this day still think of an argument instead of a theme. Most attorneys are so darned focused on – to use that expression we used ten years ago, anal-retentive – they want to dominate all the facts. But you have to do something with the facts. You have to have an equitable, resonating theme."[113]

Although these attorneys' comments show the value of themes and story-telling in litigation, narratives have equal force in transactional matters. When a party with superior bargaining power is trying to impose onerous terms in contract negotiations, for example, it may be more effective to relate a story than to reject outright their demand for unreasonable terms. Describing a previous client who acquiesced to harsh pricing terms and then realized weeks later that he could not perform the contract and stay in business, resulting in a bankruptcy filing and rejection of the contract, might be more effective in conveying the importance of reasonable pricing than flatly rejecting a party's pricing demand.

EMPATHY

Clients and law firms place an increasingly high priority on empathy. As discussed in Chapter 2, both clients and attorneys consider empathy to be an essential skill for successful attorneys. In the 2016 IAALS survey, 69 percent of attorneys stated that the ability to "demonstrate tolerance, sensitivity and compassion" was "necessary immediately" for a lawyer's success, and an

[111] Tigar, Michael. (2010). *Persuasion* (p. 80). Chicago: American Bar Association.
[112] Berg, *supra* note 100 at 279. [113] Kiser, *supra* note 108 at 47.

additional 19 percent thought that ability "must be acquired for the attorney's continued success over time."[114]

Despite this urgent need for empathy, at least in the legal profession, people have become less empathetic during the last 30 years.[115] Consistent with this downward trend, medical students are less empathetic, and physicians exhibit lower levels of empathy as they advance from their initial clinical experiences into medical residency.[116] Law students exhibit a similar pattern; after the first year, they show "decreased sociability and interest in people, and decreased altruism."[117]

In an abstract sense, nearly everyone would agree that empathy is desirable, and we would like to receive more empathy and probably should show more empathy to others. But when we try to move beyond platitudes to action we stumble – uncertain about what we should do and whether we can handle the emotional burden of becoming more empathetic. This section provides some tools to better understand empathy and guide our efforts to be empathetic. It addresses four basic questions: What is empathy? What does it mean to be empathetic? How do we express empathy? When are we least likely to be empathetic?

Empathy is the ability to understand another person's situation, perspective, and feelings and to communicate that understanding.[118] Stated differently, empathy is "the ability to accurately recognize the immediate emotional perspective of another person while maintaining one's own perspective."[119]

---

[114]   Gerkman & Cornett, *supra* note 12 at 9.

[115]   See Konrath, Sara, O'Brien, Edward, & Hsing, Courtney. (2011, May). Changes in dispositional empathy in American college students over time: A meta-analysis. *Personality and Social Psychology Review*, 15(2), 180–198. Zaki, Jamil. (2011, January 1). What, me care? Young are less empathetic. *Scientific American*.

[116]   See Marcus, E. R. (1999). Empathy, humanism and the professionalization process of medical education. *Academic Medicine*, 74, 1211–1215. Hojat, Mohammadreza, *et al.* (2004). An empirical study of decline in empathy in medical school. *Medical Education*, 38, 934–941. Neumann, M., *et al.* (2011, August). Empathy decline and its reasons: A systematic review of studies with medical students and residents. *Academic Medicine*, 86(8), 996–1009.

[117]   Daicoff, Susan. (1997). Lawyer, know thyself: A review of empirical research on attorney attributes bearing on professionalism. *The American University Law Review*, 46, 1387.

[118]   Coulehan, John, *et al.* (2001, August 7). "Let me see if I have this right...": Words that help build empathy. *Annals of Internal Medicine*, 135(3), 221. See Clark, Kenneth. (1980, February). Empathy: A neglected topic in psychological research. *American Psychologist*, 35(2), 187–190. Clark defines empathy as "the unique capacity of the human being to feel the experiences, needs, aspirations, frustrations, sorrows, joys, anxieties, hurt, or hunger of others as if they were his/her own."

[119]   Shea, Shawn Christopher. (1988). *Psychiatric interviewing: The art of understanding* (p. 14). Philadelphia: W.B. Saunders Company.

There are three types of empathy (cognitive, emotional, and empathic), as summarized below:

- *Cognitive empathy.* Cognitive empathy is the ability to perceive and understand another person's mental state while maintaining our own perspective. We are aware of and think about another person's feelings, but we do not feel them directly ourselves.[120]
- *Emotional empathy.* Emotional empathy is the "ability to feel what someone else feels" – we literally feel his or her pain.[121] It is a largely automatic response by which our feelings start to resonate with those of another person.[122] In a sense, we become their emotional surrogate.[123]
- *Empathic concern.* Empathic concern, the "action item" part of empathy, is the "ability to sense what another person needs from you."[124] It has been described as a "double-edged feeling"[125] because it is both visceral and deliberative. We intuitively recognize another person's distress, yet we rationally evaluate the importance of that person's well-being to us in deciding whether and how to help them.[126]

Although each type of empathy displays a different aspect or function of human understanding and compassion, they collectively reflect the idea that "empathy is being in the heart of another person."[127] Empathy, when effectively expressed, connects one person's response to another person's experience.[128]

Like listening, empathy has both objective and subjective components. If we are listening or empathizing, but the other person does not sense that we understand and empathize, our efforts fail by a subjective standard. Conversely, if we are not actually listening or empathizing, and yet the other person feels that we are because we have done a good job of pretending, our efforts fail by an objective standard. In that regard, listening and empathy require us to continually monitor and complete the communication loop from ourselves through another person and then back to ourselves.[129]

To be empathetic or empathic means that we possess two skills: the ability to understand another person's emotional state and the ability to relate to them

[120] Goleman, Daniel (2013, December). The focused leader. *Harvard Business Review*, p. 55.
[121] Ibid. [122] Goleman, Daniel. (2013). *Focus* (p. 98). New York: HarperCollins.
[123] Coulehan, *et al., supra* note 118 at 221. [124] Goleman, *supra* note 120 at 55.
[125] Ibid. at 56. [126] Goleman, *supra* note 122 at 98.
[127] Bernstein, Elizabeth. (2016, May 2). Why you should have more empathy. *The Wall Street Journal.*
[128] Davis, Mark. (2015). Empathy. In Stets, Jan, & Turner, Jonathan. (Eds.). *Handbook of the sociology of emotions* (p. 443). New York: Springer.
[129] Coulehan, *supra* note 118 at 222.

based on their emotional state.[130] Although many people are wary about emotional involvement with other people, they should recognize that empathy does not require them to internalize another person's emotions. The distinction between understanding and internalizing emotions is explained by physician Shawn Shea, referring to medical patients: "Thus a simple but important lesson to be learned from the study of empathy is that most patients are not searching for a person who feels as they do; they are searching for someone who is trying to understand what they feel."[131]

Two additional qualities – self-awareness and motivation – may be necessary for attorneys to function as empathic professionals. Self-awareness is essential because we have to understand our reactions to other people as well as we understand their feelings. If we are emotionally overwhelmed by compassion for clients and lose our self-awareness we "may take on their interests as our own."[132] Studies indicate that, when we are overtaken by another person's hurt and distress, we become excessively aggressive and are more likely to act unethically to help that person.[133] As psychologist Michael Poulin notes, "The irony is that the effects of empathy overload might undercut the very things for which empathy evolved in us – mutually beneficial cooperation and collaboration."[134] For attorneys, this means that our empathy for clients can lead to unethical conduct and ineffective negotiation and advocacy tactics.

Motivation also may be necessary for empathic professionals because empathy is not a permanent trait or a static ability; only 30–40 percent of the variation in empathy and altruism is genetic.[135] Our capacity for empathy varies with our motivation to empathize and develop our empathic skills.[136]

[130] Goleman, Daniel. (2004, January). What makes a leader? *Harvard Business Review*, p. 88.
[131] Shea, *supra* note 119 at 14.
[132] Waytz, Adam. (2016, January–February). The limits of empathy. *Harvard Business Review*, p. 72.
[133] Ibid. See Buffone, Anneke E. K., & Poulin, Michael J. (2014). Empathy, target distress, and neurohormone genes interact to predict aggression for others–even without provocation. *Personality and Social Psychology Bulletin*, 40(11), 1406. Batson, C. Daniel, Klein, Tricia, Highberger, Lori, & Shaw, Laura. (1995). Immorality from empathy-induced altruism: When compassion and justice conflict. *Journal of Personality and Social Psychology*, 68(6), 1042. Bloom, Paul. (2016). *Against empathy: The case for rational compassion.* New York: Ecco.
[134] Young, Emma. (2016, May 11). How sharing other people's feelings can make you sick. *New Scientist*, 3073.
[135] Shane, Scott. *Born entrepreneurs, born leaders* (pp. 50, 52). New York: Oxford University Press.
[136] See Keysers, C., & Gazzola, Valeria. (2014, April). Disassociating the ability and propensity for empathy. *Trends in Cognitive Sciences*, 18(4), 163–166. Weng, Helen, et al. (2013, July). Compassion training alters altruism and neural responses to suffering. *Psychological Science*, 24(7), 1171–1180.

We choose whether to be empathic and the extent of our empathy, as writer Leslie Jamison informs us in *The Empathy Exams*:

> Empathy isn't just something that happens to us – a meteor shower of synapses firing across the brain – it's also a choice we make: to pay attention, to extend ourselves. It's made of exertion, that dowdier cousin of impulse. Sometimes we care for another because we know we should or because it's asked for, but this doesn't make our caring hollow. The act of choosing simply means we've committed ourselves to a set of behaviors greater than the sum of our individual inclinations.[137]

Empathy, in short, is a conscious choice. We elect to be empathetic and, absent motivation, we can quickly succumb to indifference.

Once we decide to be empathetic, we express empathy verbally and non-verbally through intonation, tempo, facial expressions, gestures, and our ability to encapsulate another person's feelings in our words and phrases. "Relational skills," assert law professors Larry Gantt and Benjamin Madison, "may be viewed as empathy in action."[138] In attempting to express empathy, however, we sometimes heighten our anxiety and misunderstand the nature of empathy by focusing more on empathic accuracy than empathic sincerity. In fact, we do not need perfect perception when we have genuine interest. Even awkward attempts to understand people are appreciated when undertaken with care, humility, and concern.

Our general unease with asking open-ended questions undermines our capacity to empathize, as few people can accurately predict how someone else is feeling without an expansive conversation. "The missing ingredients in most conversations," organizational behavior professor Edgar Schein states, "are curiosity and willingness to ask questions to which we do not already know the answer."[139] To nudge attorneys' willingness to ask questions that elicit candid answers rather than the controlled responses typical of a cross-examination, some sample phrases are listed below.[140] They are used in physician/patient interactions – where openness and honesty are paramount

[137] Jamison, Leslie. (2014). *The empathy exams* (p. 23). Minneapolis, Minnesota: Graywolf Press. See Garner, Dwight. (2014, March 27). Contemplating other people's pain. *The New York Times*.

[138] Gantt, Larry, & Madison, Benjamin. (2015). Teaching knowledge, skills, and values of professional identity formation. In Maranville, Deborah, *et al.* (Eds.). *Building on best practices: Transforming legal education in a changing world* (p. 261). New Providence, New Jersey: LexisNexis.

[139] Schein, *supra* note 73 at 4.

[140] The phrases appear in Coulehan, *supra* note 118 at 222–223, 225. Some of the phrases have been modified.

for diagnosis and treatment – and are easily modified by attorneys to convey empathy in client and peer interactions. For attorneys who look at these phrases and think, "I could never say that to a client," consider how you can modify them to accommodate the clients' different levels of sophistication and then experiment with some phrases to test whether your apprehension is realistic. If the phrases work in life-and-death medical contexts, they may be more effective than you imagine in legal contexts.

Queries

"Would you (or could you) tell me a little more about that?"
"What has this been like for you?"
"Tell me how you're feeling about this."
"Are you OK with that?"
"Is there anything else?"
"Did I miss anything? Anything I left out?"

Clarifications

"Let me see if I have this right . . ."
"I want to make sure that I understood what you're telling me. I am hearing that . . ."
"I don't want us to go further until I'm sure I've gotten it right."
"I have the sense that you feel strongly, but I'm not sure I understand exactly what the feeling is. Can you tell me?"
"When I'm done, if I've gone astray, I'd appreciate it if you would correct me. OK?"

Responses

"That sounds very difficult."
"Sounds like . . ."
"That's great! I bet you're feeling pretty good about that."
"I can imagine that this might feel . . ."
"Anyone in your situation would feel that way . . ."
"I can see that you are . . ."
"That situation really got to you, didn't it? I can imagine how angry I'd feel if that happened to me."

When asking these questions and making these comments, it is critical to be comfortable with silence and quiescent during pauses. Remind yourself of the medical school adage, "Don't just do something, stand there."

In developing our empathy skills, it also is instructive to understand when we are least likely to be empathetic. As it turns out, we are not particularly accurate in predicting our own insensitivity. We are least empathetic, for example, when another person is undergoing an experience that we successfully endured. If we experienced unemployment, for example, we are less empathic toward someone who is currently unemployed. Summarizing the results of five separate empathy studies, researchers report:

> When struggling to endure an emotionally distressing event, it would seem that people should turn to those who have endured that same experience. Yet it appears that this intuition may be misguided, as it fails to take into account the psychological consequences of enduring these distressing events. Across five studies, we demonstrated that previously enduring an emotionally distressing event led to more negative evaluations of those who failed to endure a similar emotionally distressing event.[141]

This research has serious implications for both the person expecting empathy and the person from whom empathy is elicited. The person expecting empathy "would be wise to pause before immediately seeking compassion from someone who has had a similar experience. He might, in fact, get a better reaction from someone who has never gone through the same ordeal."[142] The person who is expected to be empathic, explains management professor Loran Nordgren, should recognize that prior experience creates a bias and that, "in a situation like this where someone is struggling to deal with a situation that we got through earlier, we may be callous."[143]

APOLOGIES

Apologies are an under-utilized tool in extricating ourselves from shortsightedness, insensitivity, and poor judgment. Our resistance to making an apology, unfortunately, is often directly proportional to the benefits of making the apology – the more grievous our actions have been, the harder it is to make an apology.[144] Conversely, when the weight of our misbehavior is trivial, we can be quite generous with our apologies. This occurs because an apology creates dissonance by revealing a gap between our self-image and our actual behavior.[145] The wider the gap, the greater the dissonance.

Apologies have proven to be immensely helpful in healing relationships and resolving conflicts. Jennifer Robbennolt, a psychology and law professor who

[141] Ruttan, Rachel, McDonnell, Mary-Hunter, & Nordgren, Loran. (2015, April). Having "been there" doesn't mean I care: When prior experience reduces compassion for emotional distress. *Journal of Personality and Social Psychology*, 108(4), 610–622.
[142] (2015, October 5). I don't feel your pain. *Kellogg Insight.*   [143] Ibid.
[144] See Weeks, Holly. (2003, April). The art of the apology. *Harvard Management Update.*
[145] See Tavris, Carol, & Aronson, Elliot. (2007). *Mistakes were made (but not by me)* (pp. 11–39). San Diego, California: Harcourt. Schumann, Katrina. (2014, September). An affirmed self and a better apology: The effect of self-affirmation on transgressors' responses to victims. *Journal of Experimental Social Psychology*, 54, 89–96.

has studied apologies extensively, describes their benefits: "more favorable attributions, more positive and less negative emotion for both apologizer and recipient, improved physiological responses for both parties, improved future relations, decreased need to punish, and more likely forgiveness."[146] Apologies, she asserts, also are effective in "improving expectations about the future conduct and relationship of the parties, changing negotiation aspirations and fairness judgments, and increasing willingness to accept an offer of settlement."[147]

Apologies are so successful in resolving conflicts that many hospitals have adopted a policy of disclosing and apologizing for medical errors.[148] These policies – requiring the hospital to "take responsibility, apologize and discuss preventive measures with the patient or the family"[149] – reduce the number of claims, the amount of payments and defense costs, and delays in claim resolution. The claims experiences at the University of Michigan Health System, Stanford Hospital, and the VA Medical Center in Lexington, Kentucky, are illustrative:

- *Michigan Health System.* Comparing liability claims for a six-year period before and after instituting a disclosure program, the University of Michigan Health System found that the number of claims and the costs per claim decreased by 50 percent. The average time to settle a claim decreased from 20 months to eight months, and annual litigation costs decreased from $3 million to $1 million.[150]
- *Stanford Hospital.* After adopting its PEARL (Process for Early Assessment, Resolution and Learning) program, the frequency of

---

[146] Robbennolt, Jennifer. Apologies and settlement. *Court Review, 45*, 90–96.

[147] Robbennolt, Jennifer. (2008). Attorneys, apologies, and settlement negotiation. *Harvard Negotiation Law Review, 13*, 349. See Robbennolt, Jennifer. (2006, July). Apologies and settlement levers. *Journal of Empirical Legal Studies, 3*(2), 333.

[148] To encourage physician apologies, most states have adopted apology laws barring the admission of expressions of sympathy, explanations, and, less commonly, admissions of responsibility or fault. See Mastroianni, Anna, Mello, Michelle, Sommer, Shannon, Hardy, Mary, & Gallagher, Thomas. (2010, September). The flaws in state "apology" and "disclosure" laws dilute their intended impact on malpractice suits. *Health Affairs, 29*(9), 1611–1619. McDonnell, William, & Guenther, Elisabeth. (2008, December 2). Narrative review: Do state laws make it easier to say "I'm sorry?" *Annals of Internal Medicine, 149*(11), 811–815. MacDonald, Noni, & Attaran, Amir. (2009, January 6). Medical errors, apologies and apology laws. *Canadian Medical Association Journal, 180*(1), 11.

[149] Jain, Manoj. (2013, May 27). Medical errors are hard for doctors to admit, but it's wise to apologize to patients. *The Washington Post.*

[150] Ibid. Curtis, Diane. (2010, July). Sometimes an apology can deter a lawsuit. *California Bar Journal.* See Tavris & Aronson, *supra* note 145 at 219. Epley, *supra* note 1 at 182–183.

lawsuits decreased by 50 percent, and the costs in paid cases decreased by 40 percent.[151]

- *VA Medical Center.* In a 13-year period, the Center resolved more than 170 claims at an average cost of $36,000. This average claim cost compares favorably with average claim costs at VA hospitals nationwide ($98,000 average pretrial settlement, $248,000 average trial settlement, and $413,000 average malpractice judgment).

These programs not only reduce "hard" costs but also ameliorate the sense of anger, loss, and grief that frequently attend medical errors. One study of 958 patients enrolled in a large health plan, for instance, found that "full disclosure after a medical error reduces the likelihood that patients will change physicians, improves patient satisfaction, increases trust in the physician, and results in a more positive emotional response."[152]

What makes an apology successful? To be effective, an apology must contain at least three elements: "acknowledgment of a fault or an offense, regret for it, and responsibility for the offense."[153] Steven Mehta, a Los Angeles mediator, adds five components: "a detailed account of the situation;" "recognition of your role in the event;" "asking for forgiveness;" "promise that it won't happen again;" and "restitution if possible."[154] The timing of the apology also is important; some research indicates that the offended person must first have "the opportunity to express themselves and feel heard by the other party."[155] But delaying an apology also is dangerous, as psychologist Cynthia Frantz explains: "Apologies that come too late, like those that come too early, are likely to fail; the sweet spot is somewhere between the two." Determining the ideal time, she notes, "depends entirely on the circumstances and the nature of the relationship."[156]

In addition to understanding the elements and timing of an apology, we need to understand the difference between a real apology and a partial apology. A real apology is candid, expresses genuine remorse about specific behavior, and demonstrates a commitment to change.[157] A partial apology

[151] Landro, Laura. (2016, February 1). Hospitals find a way to say, "I'm sorry." *The Wall Street Journal.*
[152] Mazor, Kathleen, *et al.* (2004, March 16). Health plan members' views about disclosure of medical errors. *Annals of Internal Medicine*, 140(6), 409–518.
[153] Weeks, *supra* note 144.
[154] Mehta, Steven. (2010, February 26). The art of apologizing. *San Francisco Daily Journal*, p. 6.
[155] Urist, Jacoba. (2016, February 23). The art and science of apologizing. *The Atlantic.*
[156] Ibid.
[157] Schweitzer, Maurice, Brooks, Alison, & Galinsky, Adam. (2015, September). The organizational apology. *Harvard Business Review*, p. 50.

168 Social Proficiency

hedges in acknowledging an offense and often shifts responsibility from the
apologizer to the offended party. Typical partial apologies include:

I'm sorry if you were offended by ...
I'm sorry for any misunderstanding caused by ...
I'm sorry you're upset by ...
I'm sorry that you feel that way.[158]

Each of these partial apologies evades responsibility and suggests that the
injured party is overly sensitive and may have contributed to the problem.
Partial apologies are harmful: "while good apologies have the power to heal,
bad ones only make things worse."[159]

Jennifer Robbennolt's research, discussed earlier, demonstrates that real
apologies and partial apologies have materially different effects on people.
In a study designed to test the effects of apology on settlement decision
making in a hypothetical claim involving a pedestrian–bicycle accident,
she compared settlement decisions under three different scenarios.[160]
In the full apology scenario, the bicyclist said, "I am so sorry that you were
hurt. The accident was all my fault. I was going too fast and not watching
where I was going until it was too late." In the partial apology scenario, the
bicyclist said, "I am so sorry that you were hurt. I really hope that you feel
better soon." In the third scenario, no apology was offered. Although each
study participant read an identical description of the claim and the settlement offer, their willingness to accept the settlement offer varied dramatically with the type of apology:

When no apology was offered 52% of respondents indicated that they would
definitely or probably accept the offer, while 43% would definitely or probably reject the offer and 5% were unsure. When a partial apology was offered,
only 35% of respondents were inclined to accept the offer, 25% were inclined
to reject it, and 40% indicated that they were unsure. In contrast, when a full
apology was offered, 73% of respondents were inclined to accept the offer,
with only 13–14% each inclined to reject it or remaining unsure.[161]

The study participants who received the partial apology thus were less willing
to accept the settlement offer than those who received the full apology or no
apology.

---

[158] See McCall, Bruce. (2001, April 22). The perfect non-apology apology. *The New York Times*.
[159] Urist, *supra* note 155.
[160] Robbennolt, Jennifer K. (2003). Apologies and legal settlement: An empirical examination. *Michigan Law Review*, 102, 460–516.
[161] Ibid. at 484–485.

When asked about their perceptions of the offender, the study participants "expressed greater sympathy and less anger at the offender who offered a full apology than they did at offenders who offered either a partial or no apology."[162] The full apology offender "was seen as experiencing more regret, as more moral, and as more likely to be careful in the future than one offering a partial or no apology."[163] The study participants also were more inclined to forgive the full apology offender whose offer, though identical in all three scenarios, "would better make up for their injuries."[164]

Reviewing the results of Robbennolt's research and assessing contemporary, ineffective apologies by errant politicians and business executives, journalist Lisa Belkin observes, "A botched apology not only taints the act of apology but the ability to accept an apology as well."[165] The loss of that opportunity to restore dignity and grant forgiveness, she explains, may prevent both parties from moving on: "When an apology fails, two things are lost – the victims are not asked for forgiveness, nor are they given a chance to grant it."[166]

TRUST

"When you're a lawyer, what you're selling, at the end of the day, is trust," states Joshua Wayser, a California Superior Court judge and former managing partner of Katten Muchin Rosenman LLP's Los Angeles office. "And how you communicate with people reflects trust."[167] Although trust may be the most important element in establishing credibility, instilling confidence, and attracting clients, lawyers are regarded as the least trustworthy professionals. When ranked by honesty and ethics, medical doctors are at the top of the professions, followed by high school teachers, accountants, journalists, bankers, and lawyers.[168] During the last 40 years the percentage of Americans ranking attorneys as "low" or "very low" in honesty and ethics has ranged from 26 percent to 46 percent.[169] In the most recent survey, only 4 percent of Americans ranked attorneys' honesty and ethics as "very high."[170]

Lawyers are generally regarded as competent but not trustworthy. They fall into the same category as other "high-competence, low-warmth" professionals who are respected but not trusted: chief executive officers, engineers,

---

[162] Ibid. at 488. [163] Ibid. at 487. [164] Ibid. at 488.

[165] Belkin, Lisa. (2010, July 2). Why is it so hard to apologize well? *The New York Times*.

[166] Ibid.

[167] Sullivan, Casey. (2011, November 18). Perception is reality when managers decide who makes partner. *San Francisco Daily Journal*.

[168] Gallup. (2015, December 2-6). Honesty/ethics in professions. [169] Ibid. [170] Ibid.

accountants, scientists, and researchers.[171] Being seen as competent might seem to be an acceptable consolation prize until we recognize that "communicator credibility requires not just status and expertise (competence) but also trustworthiness (warmth)."[172] In other words, attorneys' effectiveness as communicators will be seriously and persistently impaired unless they can establish trust with other people.

The public's distrust of attorneys is rivaled by attorneys' distrust of each other. The amalgam of cynicism, skepticism, and faultfinding that distinguishes many attorneys' personalities seems to generate a pervasive distrust in law firms. David Maister, a law firm consultant and author of *The Trusted Advisor*, shares his experiences in working with law firm partners and dealing firsthand with their lack of trust:

> It is hard to unbundle which is the cause and which is the effect, but the combination of a desire for autonomy and high levels of skepticism make most law firms *low-trust environments.*
>
> Recently, I was advising a firm on its compensation system. They didn't like my recommendations. Finally, one of the partners said, "David, all your recommendations are based on the assumption that we trust each other and trust our executive or compensation committees. We don't. Give us a system that doesn't require us to trust each other!"
>
> A former managing partner with whom I have discussed this says, "It's not that I don't trust my partners. They're good people, mostly. It's that I don't want to have to trust them. Why give up any degree of control over your own affairs if you don't have to?"[173]

This distrust among lawyers in law firms makes it difficult for them to establish and implement mutual goals, accept sacrifices that benefit the whole firm but not necessarily the individuals making the sacrifice, and delegate decision-making authority to law firm leaders. They cannot achieve long-term goals that are critical to the firm's continued success but unimportant to an individual attorney's success.[174] This distrust leads directly to the myopic focus on personal compensation that pervades law firms and incites acute dissension and disruptive defections among partners.

---

[171] Fiske, Susan, & Dupree, Cydney. (2014, September 16). Gaining trust as well as respect in communicating to motivated audiences about science topics. *Proceedings of the National Academy of Sciences*, 111(4), 13595.

[172] Ibid.

[173] Maister, *supra* note 9. See Maister, David, Green, Charles, & Galford, Robert. (2001). *The trusted advisor.* New York: Touchstone.

[174] See Maister (2006), *supra* note 173.

But if lawyers "deal with each other so poorly," Maister asks, "why do they do so well financially?" His answer: "The greatest advantage lawyers have is that they compete only with other lawyers. If everyone else does things equally poorly, and clients and recruits find little variation between firms, even the most egregious behavior will not lead to a competitive disadvantage."[175]

Although lawyers' compensation and law firms' profits are not sufficiently low to provoke broad concerns about the absence of trust, this malady does take a toll on attorneys' reputations, law firms' stability, and the public's faith in the legal system. For those attorneys who recognize that distrust eventually erodes professional relationships and public confidence, remedial steps can be taken to build trust. In that endeavor, we also can learn lessons that facilitate our personal interactions in many other contexts and show us how to transform organizations so that they merit trust and commitment.

When asked how it feels to work in a high-trust environment, people respond with words like "fun," "supportive," "motivating," "productive," and "comfortable."[176] They describe the culture of high-trust organizations as being "mutually cooperative" and "win-win."[177] The words that people associate with a low-trust environment are quite different: "stressful," "threatening," "divisive," "unproductive," and "tense."[178] The culture in low-trust environments is depicted as "adversarial," "competitive," and "win-lose."[179]

To achieve the productivity, cooperation, and enjoyment associated with high-trust environments, our attention should be focused on the six components of trust summarized below.[180] These components of trust apply to personal relationships as well as organizational behavior:

---

[175] Ibid.
[176] Hurley, Robert (2006, September). The decision to trust. *Harvard Business Review*, p. 55.
[177] Hurley, Robert. (2012). *The decision to trust* (p. 75). San Francisco: Jossey-Bass.
[178] Hurley (2006), *supra* note 176 at 55.   [179] Hurley (2012), *supra* note 177 at 75.
[180] The six components of trust are derived from concepts in the following sources: Hurley (2012), *supra* note 177. Maule, A. John. *Risk communication in organizations*. (2008). In Hodgkinson, Gerard, & Starbuck, William (Eds.). *The Oxford handbook of organizational decision making* (pp. 517–533). New York: Oxford University Press. Frewer, L. J. (2003). Trust, transparency, and social context: Implications for social amplification of risk. In Pidgeon, N., Kasperson, R.E., & Slovic, P. (Eds.) *The social amplification of risk* (pp. 123–137). Cambridge: Cambridge University Press. Renn, O., & Levine, D. (1991). Credibility and trust in risk communication. In Kasperson, R.E., & Stallen, P.J.M. (Eds.). *Communicating risks to the public* (pp. 175–214). Dordrecht, The Netherlands: Kluwer Academic Publishers. Hurley (2006), *supra* note 176. Brockner, Joel. (2006, March). Why it's so hard to be fair. *Harvard Business Review*, pp. 122–129. DeSteno, David. (2014, March). Who can you trust? *Harvard Business Review*, pp. 112–115. Kim, W. Chan, & Mauborgne, Renee. (2003, January). Fair process. *Harvard Business Review*.

- *Affinity*. Affinity promotes trust and is composed of likeability, attractiveness, empathy, and similarity of background, appearances, values, personalities, education, status, and interests.[181] "We instinctively make assessments about which partners are worth the risk of trusting using a very simple shortcut: similarity," states psychology professor David DeSteno.[182] Even the simplest attempts to create similarity – like requiring strangers in a meeting to wear the same color wristbands – result in greater compassion and altruistic behavior.[183] To enhance affinity, start using the word "we" more and the word "I" less and emphasize common values, aspirations, and goals.[184] When you highlight what you have in common with someone else they "see you as someone with whom it's possible to build a lasting and beneficial relationship."[185]

- *Goodwill*. Goodwill connotes benevolence, good faith, kindness, sincerity, and the absence of deception, hidden agendas, and untoward motives.[186] It means, fundamentally, that you are putting the interests of other people ahead of your own interests and that the goals you express and achieve serve a common interest.[187] To convince people that you are acting in their interests, you have to walk the walk – bear a loss that results in an advantage for other people.[188] As attorney Kurt Schlichter notes, "you need to demonstrate that you put the welfare of your subordinates first, and the only way to demonstrate it is by doing it."[189]

- *Fairness*. To be considered fair in evaluating other people, a person or organization must meet three standards: engagement ("involving individuals in the decisions that affect them by asking for their input and allowing them to refute the merits of one another's ideas and assumptions"); explanation ("everyone involved and affected should understand why final decisions are made as they are"); and expectation clarity (people should "know up front by what standards they will be judged and the penalties for failure").[190] People place as much value on the process of evaluation as they place on the outcomes of evaluation.[191]

---

[181] Renn & Levine, *supra* note 180 at 185.   [182] DeSteno, *supra* note 180 at 115.   [183] Ibid.
[184] Hurley (2006), *supra* note 176 at 62.   [185] DeSteno, *supra* note 180 at 115.
[186] Renn & Levine, *supra* note 180 at 185.
[187] Hurley (2012), *supra* note 177 at 79. Renn & Levine, *supra* note 180 at 187. Hurley (2006), *supra* note 176 at 58.
[188] Hurley (2012), *supra* note 177 at 111.
[189] Schlichter, Kurt Andrew. (2009, March 30). Firm heads often confuse leadership with management. *San Francisco Daily Journal*, p. 5.
[190] Kim & Mauborgne, *supra* note 180. See Brockner, *supra* note 180.
[191] See Tyler, Tom. (2006). *Why people obey the law*. Princeton, New Jersey: Princeton University Press.

For that reason, "most people will accept outcomes that are not wholly in their favor" if the process is perceived to be fair.[192]

- *Competence.* Competence, as shown by expertise, reputation, and past success, is an essential element of trust. But unless competence is accompanied by honesty, it has a negligible effect on trust.[193] Public perceptions, as discussed earlier, place attorneys in the competence without honesty category – "respected but not trusted."[194] To preserve the perception of competence, attorneys must maintain a consistent record of good judgment, expert knowledge, and superb performance. And they need to start making progress on the honesty front. The first step toward honesty is to listen to yourself and make a note of every half-truth, white lie, evasive remark, unreliable assertion, insincere comment, and inauthentic reaction you express in a day. For many people, "lying is a commonplace strategy for managing impressions and social interactions."[195] Discovering whether deception has become embedded in your everyday interactions is the beginning of self-correction and genuine communication.
- *Communication.* To establish and maintain trust, communication must be clear, credible, honest, accurate, unbiased, open, candid, and devoid of artifice and ulterior motives.[196] The process of communicating also must be timely, informing people of conditions as they change and updating them promptly and fully. Effective communication further requires people to admit mistakes and be forthright about uncertainty and setbacks.[197] To improve communication, people and organizations should increase the frequency and expand the scope of communication, provide formal and informal methods of obtaining information, and probe to determine the effectiveness of communication and how it can be enhanced.[198]
- *Integrity.* Integrity is considerably more than legal compliance. It encompasses reliability, predictability, and consistency; it means that people can predict your future behavior by previous experiences with you and your communication.[199] To build trust, attorneys need to track how well their promises and predictions match reality and start adjusting what they say they will deliver to clients and colleagues to correspond with what they actually deliver. Explicitly stating the values

[192] Kim & Mauborgne, *supra* note 180.   [193] Frewer, *supra* note 180 at 126.
[194] Fiske, *supra* note 171.
[195] DePaulo, Bella, Kashy, Deborah, Kirkendol, Susan, & Epstein, Jennifer. (1996). Lying in everyday life. *Journal of Personality and Social Psychology*, 70(5), 980.
[196] Renn & Levine, *supra* note 180 at 182, 185.   [197] Ibid. at 182.
[198] See Hurley (2012), *supra* note 177 at 111.
[199] Renn & Levine, *supra* note 180 at 180. See Hurley (2006), *supra* note 176 at 59.

that underpin your decisions is also helpful in conveying integrity and ensuring that you comply with your own stated standards. Another critical step is to "adopt a rigorous daily process of self-examination of conscience," reviewing your conduct and comparing it with your values and ethics.[200]

Trust ultimately is a profoundly personal judgment. It is "a measure of the quality of a relationship – between two people, between groups of people, or between a person and an organization."[201] Trust reflects our hope and our conviction that we have intelligently judged and relied on someone else.

TEAMS

Working with people on a team presents an acute dilemma: we benefit from their ideas, skills, and output, yet differences of opinion inevitably arise and devolve into personal conflicts.[202] These conflicts, in turn, often lead to mistakes, inefficiencies, stress, and delays that make us wonder whether we should have made decisions unilaterally and performed the tasks by ourselves. This section examines these conflicts and identifies behaviors and attitudes that degrade and enhance group performance. We first look at the reasons groups fail to deliver expected results and then study the characteristics of high-performance teams.

Why Groups Fail

Groups fall victim to two fundamental problems: incompetent managers and leaders and poor group dynamics. Although we tend to believe that people in management and leadership positions have earned the right to manage and lead, the reality is that at least 50 percent of managers and leaders do not have the skills required for their positions and will fail. Twelve studies of managers show that the rate of managerial failure ranges from 30 to 67 percent; the average failure rate for managers is 50 percent.[203]

Based on the managerial failure data and employee surveys, researchers conclude "that two-thirds of existing managers are insufferable and that half

---

[200] Hurley (2012), *supra* note 177 at 111.   [201] Hurley (2006), *supra* note 176 at 62.

[202] See Simons, T. L., & Peterson, R. S. (2000). Task conflict and relationship conflict in top management teams: The pivotal role of intragroup trust. *Journal of Applied Psychology*, 85, 102–111.

[203] Hogan, Joyce, Hogan, Robert, & Kaiser, Robert B. (2011). Management derailment: Personality assessment and mitigation. In Zedeck, Sheldon (Ed.). *APA handbook of industrial and organizational psychology* (Vol. III) (table 1). Washington, DC: American Psychological Association.

will eventually fail."[204] Common characteristics of failing managers include arrogance, poor judgment, perfectionism, insensitivity, inability to deal with conflict, procrastination, low self-awareness, lack of strategic thinking and planning, blaming, and micromanagement. The dispositive factor in the studies of managerial failure is "overriding personality defects" that prevent people from building the constructive interpersonal relationships that teams require.[205]

Apart from managerial failures, groups stumble and often collapse for the reasons identified by Patrick Lencioni in *Five Dysfunctions of a Team*:

- *Absence of trust* – concealment of individual weaknesses and mistakes, excessive time spent on image management, and reluctance to seek help or ask questions because it might reveal personal shortcomings.
- *Fear of conflict* – resistance to openly expressing reservations and disagreements; disregard of critical, controversial issues because they generate unease; and resort to personal attacks and criticism in *ad hoc* networks.
- *Failure to make commitments* – inability to establish clear priorities, directions, and goals; delays caused by lack of decisiveness; and frustration resulting from lack of consensus or certainty about objectives.
- *Avoidance of accountability* – failure to impose uniform standards for personal performance and group performance; reluctance to enforce standards; tolerance of individual deviation from group goals; and lack of consistency in treatment of non-conforming performance.
- *Inattention to results* – self-interest and individual careers allowed to take priority over group goals; failure to keep a "visible scoreboard" showing progress toward goals or requirements and remaining time to achieve them; and laxity in obtaining individual commitments to group goals.

Deficiencies identified by other researchers include: too many people on the team; insufficient attention to details and implementation; escalation of commitment to bad projects; failure to share information and expand the scope of information being considered; team member compensation based on individual rather than team performance; no sense of urgency; lack of training in group communication and leadership skills; and using teams for work best done by individuals.[206]

---

[204] Ibid.   [205] Ibid.

[206] See Royer, Isabelle. (2003, February). Why bad projects are so hard to kill. *Harvard Business Review*, pp. 48–56. Harvard management update. (2008, February 28). Why some teams succeed (and so many don't). *Harvard Business Review*. Hackman, J. Richard. (1998). Why teams don't work. In Tindale, R. Scott, *et al.* (Eds.). *Theory and research on small groups* (pp. 245–267). New York: Springer-Verlag. Katzenbach, Jon, & Smith, Douglas. (2005,

Why Groups Succeed

When we turn our attention to successful teams, we find that some of our assumptions about effective teams are erroneous. We also learn that the way in which team members relate to each other may be more important than the complexity of their tasks and the tangible resources available to accomplish them. Specifically, studies show that individual intelligence is not a reliable predictor of the collective intelligence of a group, and the quality of group performance is determined by "soft" factors like equality in conversation time, accuracy in perceiving others' emotions, openness in expressing dissident opinions, and a sense of acceptance by group members.

A common assumption is that selecting the "best and the brightest" people for a team harnesses their individual expertise and produces an extraordinary, collective expertise.[207] In reality, individual intelligence and expertise do not contribute to group performance unless the group members understand and are proficient in group processes and interactions. Even smart people who know how to manage themselves may not know how to lead meetings, orient team members to their roles and tasks, facilitate reviews of team performance, and generally foster better teamwork.[208] In many circumstances, the best and the brightest are the worst and the dimmest when placed on teams, as demonstrated in a study of 120 simulated management teams:

> Some of the teams were composed entirely of people who were highly intelligent. But despite this obvious advantage, the high-IQ teams performed worse than the other teams whose members were not all so brilliant. And observation of the teams in action tells why: High-IQ members spent too much of their time in competitive debate, and the debating became an unending session of academic showmanship. Another weakness of the high-IQ teams was that all

July–August). The discipline of teams. *Harvard Business Review*. Cross, Rob, Rebele, Reb, & Grant, Adam. (2016, January–February). Collaborative overload. *Harvard Business Review*. Patel, Saurin, & Sarkissian, Sergei. (2016). To group or not to group? Evidence from mutual funds. (2016, March). *Journal of Financial and Quantitative Analysis* (forthcoming). Halvorson, Heidi. (2014, May). Get your team to do what it says it's going to do. *Harvard Business Review*. Lublin, Joann. (2014, August 26). Small boards get bigger returns. *The Wall Street Journal*. George, Elizabeth, & Chattopadhyay, Prithviraj. (2008). Group composition and decision making. In Hodgkinson, Gerard, & Starbuck, William (Eds.). *The Oxford handbook of organizational decision making* (pp. 361–379). New York: Oxford University Press.

[207] See Engel, David, Woolley, Anita, Jing, Lisa, Chabris, Christopher, & Malone, Thomas. (2014, December 16). Reading the mind in the eyes of reading between the lines? Theory of mind predicts collective intelligence equally well online and face-to-face. *PLoS One*, 9(12), e115212.

[208] Coutu, Diane. (2009, May). Why teams don't work: An interview with J. Richard Hackman. *Harvard Business Review*.

the members opted for the same kind of task: applying their critical abilities to the intellectually intriguing parts of the job at hand, engaging in analysis and counter analysis. No one got around to other necessary parts of the job: planning, collecting and exchanging practical information, keeping track of what had been learned, coordinating a plan of action. Everyone was so busy trying to be the intellectual star that the team flopped.[209]

Similar results occurred in a study of 700 people working in groups of two to five individuals.[210] Although individual intelligence was a significant predictor of performance when the individuals were working alone, "the average individual intelligence of the group members was not a significant predictor of group performance."[211]

Given the complexity of contemporary legal problems and the international context in which problems arise, attorneys are risking career failure by emphasizing how smart they are while ignoring basic group interaction skills. They appear to be especially resistant to the idea that high intelligence is not an omnibus skill that compensates for the absence of interpersonal skills. Attorneys' reliance on IQ and their defensiveness about learning how to work on teams are epitomized by one partner's comments:

> I've always won on my own: My college grades and LSAT scores got me into law school, my law school grades got me hired here, my associate review score got me to partner. I haven't played on a team since high school lacrosse. Why would I be a team player now?[212]

The short answer to the partner's rhetorical question is that attorneys are fungible until they learn how to work on cross-practice teams. As a Fortune 100 general counsel remarked, "Despite what they think, most individual lawyers are actually quite replaceable. I mean, I could find a decent tax lawyer in most firms. But when that lawyer teamed up with colleagues from IP, regulatory and ultimately litigation, I couldn't find a whole-team substitute in another firm."[213]

The essential group interaction skills are remarkably simple. In the study of 700 people mentioned above, in which the volunteers were tested on

[209] Goleman, *supra* note 26 at 204.
[210] See Wladawsky-Berger, Irving. (2016, April 29). Why some work groups thrive while others falter. *The Wall Street Journal*.
[211] Woolley, Anita, Chabris, Christopher, Pentland, Alex, Hashmi, Nada, & Malone, Thomas. (2010, October 29). Evidence for a collective intelligence factor in the performance of human groups. *Science, 330*, 688.
[212] Gardner, Heidi. (2015, March 9). Why it pays to collaborate with your colleagues. *The American Lawyer*.
[213] Ibid.

"real-world" skills like problem solving, negotiation, brainstorming, and making judgments, three factors proved to be determinative of group performance:

- *Equal contributions in conversations.* The number of speaking turns by group members is highly predictive of group performance. "Groups where a few people dominated the conversation were less collectively intelligent than those with a more equal distribution of conversational turn-taking."[214] And "groups that had smart people dominating the conversation were not very intelligent groups."[215]
- *High social sensitivity.* The ability to accurately determine the emotional states of other people, after seeing facial images showing only their eyes, was correlated with superior group performance.
- *More women.* The proportion of women on a team was predictive of group performance. In this study, "it was not 'diversity' (having equal numbers of men and women) that mattered for a team's intelligence, but simply having more women."[216] This result, however, "appears to be largely mediated by social sensitivity" because women scored higher on social sensitivity than men.[217]

These study results have been replicated in online experiments where the group members communicated only by text messages and could not see each other; "just like in the earlier studies, the best performing teams were better at communicating with each other, participating equally in the process and exhibiting higher emotion-reading skills."[218]

Major insights into group behavior also are emerging from Google's "Project Aristotle." After analyzing 180 teams at Google over five years, the project researchers found that clear goals and a culture of dependability are important to groups; but the most critical factor in group performance is "psychological safety." Amy Edmondson a professor at the Harvard Business School, defines psychological safety as "a climate in which people feel free to express relevant thoughts and feelings."[219] In a psychologically safe environment, people trust

---

[214] Wooley (2010), *supra* note 211.
[215] Woolley, Anita, & Malone, Thomas. (2011, June). Defend your research: What makes a team smarter? More women. *Harvard Business Review.*
[216] Wooley, Anita, Malone, Thomas, & Chabris, Christopher. (2015, January 16). Why some teams are smarter than others. *The New York Times.*
[217] Wooley (2010), *supra* note 211. The researchers also found that other factors they might have expected to be important to group performance – group cohesion, motivation, and satisfaction – did not have a significant effect on performance.
[218] Wladawsky-Berger, *supra* note 210.
[219] Edmondson, Amy C. (2012). *Teaming* (p. 118). San Francisco: Jossey-Bass.

and respect each other and "believe that if they make a mistake others will not penalize or think less of them for it. They also believe that others will not resent or humiliate them when they ask for help or information."[220]

Although Google did not invent the concept of "psychological safety," its research confirms that communication and empathy among team members are "the building blocks of forging real connections." Charles Duhigg, author of *Smarter Faster Better*, describes the impact of Project Aristotle and its emphasis on psychological safety:

> What Project Aristotle has taught people within Google is that no one wants to put on a "work face" when they get to the office. No one wants to leave part of their personality and inner life at home. But to be fully present at work, to feel "psychologically safe," we must know that we can be free enough, sometimes, to share the things that scare us without fear of recriminations. We must be able to talk about what is messy or sad, to have hard conversations with colleagues who are driving us crazy. We can't be focused just on efficiency. . . . We want to know that work is more than just labor.[221]

The Project Aristotle data makes it easier for individuals and organizations to recognize and discuss the effects of trust, respect, openness, support, and acceptance on group performance. "Just having data that proves to people that these things are worth paying attention to sometimes is the most important step in getting them to actually pay attention," states Julia Rozovsky, a lead researcher on Project Aristotle. "Don't underestimate the power of giving people a common platform and operating language."[222]

CULTURAL COMPETENCE

Ethnic minority groups comprise 30 percent of the U.S. population. But only 6 percent of practicing physicians and 9 percent of practicing attorneys are members of an underrepresented minority group.[223] In response to increasing national diversity and perceived cultural insensitivity, the Liaison Committee on Medical Education (LCME) and the Accreditation Council on Graduate Medical Education (ACGME), the governing bodies

---

[220] Ibid. at 118–119.
[221] Duhigg, Charles. (2016, February 25). What Google learned from its quest to build the perfect team. *The New York Times*.
[222] Ibid.
[223] American Bar Association. *Lawyer demographics year 2015.* Kripalani, Sunil, Bussey-Jones, Jada, Katz, Marra, & Genao, Inginia. (2006). A prescription for cultural competence in medical education. *Journal of General Internal Medicine*, 21(10), 1116–1120.

for medical schools, adopted cultural competency requirements in
2002.[224] These requirements include the ability to "communicate effectively
with patients, families, and the public, as appropriate, across a broad range of
socioeconomic and cultural backgrounds" and "sensitivity and responsiveness to a diverse patient population, including but not limited to diversity in
gender, age, culture, race, religion, disabilities, and sexual orientation."[225]
Some states require medical schools to teach cultural competence, and
many states mandate cultural competency training in physicians' continuing
education requirements.[226]

  Although the legal profession's cultural insensitivity and lack of diversity are
legend and at least as severe as the medical profession's,[227] neither law schools
nor state bar associations have followed the medical profession in correcting
bias and insensitivity with mandatory cultural competency programs and
periodic evaluation of those programs.[228] The American Bar Association's
adoption in 2008 of Goal III ("Eliminate bias in the legal profession and the
justice system"), without implementation requirements, is a faint effort relative to the medical profession's initiatives to increase diversity and cultural
competence. Indicative of the organized bar's tepid approach to bias is the
ABA Center for Professional Responsibility's responses to the annual Goal III
report:

  How much did your entity spend during FY 2014–2015 on efforts to support,
  promote or advance racial and ethnic diversity in the legal profession and
  what percentage of your overall budget for FY 2014–2015 does this represent?

[224] See Ambrose, Adrian Jacques H., Lin, Susan Y., & Chun, Maria B. J. (2013, *June*) Cultural
       competency training requirements in graduate medical education. *Journal of Graduate
       Medical Education,* 5(2), 227–231. Expert Panel on Cultural Competence Education for
       Students in Medicine and Public Health. (2012). *Cultural competence education for students
       in medicine and public health: Report of an expert panel.* Washington, DC: Association of
       American Medical Colleges and Association of Schools of Public Health.
[225] Stanford Medicine. Core competencies. Retrieved from http://med.stanford.edu/gme/cur
       rent_residents/corecomp.html.
[226] See Wilson, M. Roy, & Gamble, Vanessa. (2009). The role of academic centers in the
       elimination of racial and ethnic health disparities. In Kosoko-Lasaki, Sade, Cook, Cynthia,
       & O'Brien, Richard (Eds.). *Cultural proficiency in addressing health disparities* (p. 80).
       Sudbury, Massachusetts: Jones and Bartlett Publishing.
[227] See Negowetti, Nicole. (2015). Implicit bias and the legal profession's "diversity crisis": A call
       for self-reflection. *Nevada Law Journal,* 15(2), 930–958.
[228] Some state bar continuing education programs have "bias" or "elimination of bias" require-
       ments, e.g., Minnesota, California, and West Virginia. Their course objectives and content
       vary considerably and few are subjected to effectiveness evaluations. In general, they are
       different from cultural competency courses. See Association of American Medical Colleges.
       (2005). *Cultural competence education.* Expert Panel on Cultural Competence Education for
       Students in Medicine and Public Health, *supra* note 224.

[Response] Approximately $1,000 to fund expenses of the 2015 Jeanne P. Gray Diversity Scholarship recipient (0.003%).[229]

The Center for Professional Responsibility asserts that it "has provided national leadership and vision" in professional regulation and professionalism.[230]

To explore the concept of cultural competence and demonstrate some methods of achieving it, this section defines cultural competency, identifies its essential components, and outlines attitudes and actions that facilitate cross-cultural interactions. "Culture" refers to "integrated patterns of human behavior that include the language, thoughts, actions, customs, beliefs, and institutions of racial, ethnic, social, or religious groups."[231] "Cultural competence" is the combination of knowledge, attitudes, and skills necessary to function effectively "within the context of the cultural beliefs, practices, and needs" presented by clients, colleagues, judges, and other people.[232] Sylvia Stevens, general counsel for the Oregon State Bar, defines cultural competency as "the ability to adapt, work and manage successfully in new and unfamiliar cultural settings. Culturally competent people can 'grasp, reason and behave effectively' when faced with culturally diverse situations, where assumptions, values and traditions differ from those to which they are accustomed."[233] This ability to practice law with cultural competence, states law professor Mary Lynch, "is a fundamental lawyering skill, as is the ability to critically evaluate laws, culture, and societal systems from a variety of perspectives or lenses. Respect for difference and other cultures and beliefs is also a fundamental lawyer value."[234]

---

[229] Commission on Racial and Ethic Diversity in the Profession. (2016). *Goal III Report: The state of racial and ethnic diversity in the American Bar Association* (appendix) (p. 50).

[230] American Bar Association Center for Professional Responsibility. About us. Retrieved from www.americanbar.org/groups/professional_responsibility/about_us.html.

[231] Cross, T. L., Bazron, B.J., Dennis, K.W., & Isaacs, M.R. (1989). *Towards a culturally competent system of care: A monograph on effective services for minority children who are severely emotionally disturbed*. Rockville, Maryland: National Institute of Justice.

[232] Ibid. See Seeleman, Conny, Hermans, Jessie, Lamkaddem, Majda, & Essink-Bot, Marie-Louise. (2014). A students' survey of cultural competence as a basis for identifying gaps in the medical curriculum. *BMC Medical Education, 14*(1), 216. Seeleman, C., Suurmond, J., & Stronks, K. (2009). Cultural competence: A conceptual framework for teaching and learning. *Medical Education, 43*(3), 229–237.

[233] Stevens, Sylvia. (2009, January). Cultural competency: Is there an ethical duty? *Oregon State Bar Bulletin*. See Patel, Serena. (2014). Cultural competency training: Preparing law students for practice in our multicultural world. *UCLA Law Review Discourse, 62*, 140–156.

[234] Lynch, Mary. (2012). Contemporary issues in outcomes-based education: An evaluation of ten concerns about using outcomes in legal education. *William Mitchell Law Review, 38*, 1005.

Understanding cultural competence and learning how to be culturally competent can be bewildering, frustrating, and, for some people, resented endeavors. This negativity stems, in part, from the poor methods, superficial research, and unnecessarily complicated concepts espoused in many diversity training programs. These programs present "facts" that must be learned before relating to different people, and, as a result, they can be counter-productive:

> Such curricula often include lists of preferred words, images, or approaches for treating minority groups, portraying each group as having particular values, beliefs, and behaviors based on culture. This oversimplified practice fails to acknowledge diversity within groups and emphasizes differences between groups, potentially reinforcing stereotyping behavior.[235]

These stereotypes lead to absurd results. An American meeting an MTV-Japan executive, for instance, bowed deeply and expressed traditional Japanese greetings. The executive replied, "What's up with *that*, my man?"[236]

Many diversity programs overlook the fact that "the core value at the heart of effective functioning across cultures and geographic space is that of universal human dignity: a basic, foundational appreciation for the common humanity of oneself with and among all others."[237] To be culturally competent, therefore, is to extend to someone else the respect, kindness, deference, attention, tolerance, and gratitude that characterize our most effective interactions – and modify our behavior to respect different values and mirror different ways of relating to people. Cultural competence ultimately is more a frame of mind than a bundle of facts. When we emphasize human dignity we recognize that sometimes the most effective element of cultural intelligence is simply "a propensity to suspend judgment – to think before acting."[238]

Once we have internalized the essential element of dignity, other guidelines and techniques that may be instructive in building cultural competency include:

- *Practice nonjudgment.* The risk of negatively judging people "increases when you work cross-culturally due to the confusion inherent in

[235] Kripalani, *supra* note 223 at 1117.
[236] Program on Negotiation at Harvard Law School. (2012). International Negotiations (Negotiation Special Report #5).
[237] Lynch, Mary, Boyle, Robin, Magee, Rhonda, & Lopez, Antoinette Sedillo. (2015). Intercultural effectiveness. In Maranville, Deborah, *et al.* (Eds.). *Building on best practices: Transforming legal education in a changing world* (p. 342). New Providence, New Jersey: LexisNexis.
[238] Earley, Christopher, & Mosakowski, Elaine. (2004, October). Cultural intelligence. *Harvard Business Review.*

working out of one's own cultural framework, the resultant anxiety, and the attendant loss of control and clarity the lawyer may feel."[239] Cultural competence requires us to mitigate this risk with "nonjudgment – a focus on fact, observation, detail detached from evaluation, criticism or generalization."[240] Takeaway: be aware of how unfamiliarity and loss of control affect you and respond with keen observation and interim detachment.

- *Know when to be expressive.* Being emotionally expressive may be seen as "a lack of maturity or professionalism in a business context."[241] Even in cultures that appear to be emotionally expressive, people may be especially sensitive to direct expressions of disagreement, negative comments, and physical displays of affinity. Takeaway: "recognize what emotional expressiveness signifies."[242]

- *Learn protocols.* Different cultures have different expectations and protocols regarding eye contact, touching, deportment, expression of emotions, silence, eating, and greetings.[243] These surface behaviors can have deep effects. Takeaway: sensitivity to basics "allows you to avoid giving offense, demonstrate respect, enhance camaraderie, and strengthen communications."[244]

- *Separate culture from stereotypes.* To determine whether you are being sensitive to cultural features or perpetuating stereotypes, ask yourself these questions: "Do the characteristics I ascribe to a group different from mine have a negative value?" "Is what I believe about a group based on fact?" "Am I assuming all people in a certain group have this attribute?" "Do I use these 'beliefs' to make decisions or alternatively just to guide my further inquiry or validation?"[245] Takeaway: Don't mix stereotypes with actual attributes, traditions, and values.

- *Listen and elicit.* To encourage cross-cultural communication in a meeting, take three steps: stop dominating the conversation;

[239] Bryant, Susan, & Peters, Jean. (2007). Six practices for connecting with clients across culture: Habit four, working with interpreters and other mindful approaches. In Silver, Marjorie. *The affective assistance of counsel* (p. 187). Durham, North Carolina: Carolina Academic Press.
[240] Silver, *supra* note 239 at 186. See Patel, *supra* note 233 at 154.
[241] Meyer, Erin. Getting to si, ja, oui, hai, and da. (2015, December). *Harvard Business Review*, p. 77.
[242] Ibid.
[243] Sebenius, James. (2002, March). The hidden challenge of cross-border negotiations. *Harvard Business Review*, p. 80.
[244] Ibid.
[245] Jaeger, Judy. (2008, Winter). Growing cultural competence. *LAWPRO Magazine*, 7(1), 14.

balance speaking and listening among all participants; and elicit opinions from other people, especially less fluent speakers.[246] Referring to conference calls with his American counterparts, a Thai manager in a financial firm said, "They invite us to the meeting, but they don't suggest with their actions that they care what we have to say."[247] Takeaway: "dial down dominance, dial up engagement."[248]

- *Avoid "yes" or "no" questions.* "Yes" and "no" have different meanings in different cultures. As an Indonesian manager explained, it is rude to say "no" to someone, so "we try to show 'no' with our body language or voice tone."[249] The manager might say, "We will try our best," as a way of communicating, "We would like to do what you want, but it is not possible."[250] Apart from the confusion they generate, questions with "yes" or "no" responses fail to elicit a sufficiently broad range of information. Takeaway: open-ended questions show genuine curiosity and provide two types of information, the information that you think is necessary and the information that you were not aware is necessary.

- *Listen through the speaker's mind.* We imbue words and phrases with connotations, implications, and inferences. None of the meanings we attach to words and phrases, however, may apply in cross-cultural communications, and an entirely different set of meanings may apply. The challenge in cross-cultural communications is to "attribute the same meaning to behavior and words that the person intended to convey. Cross-culturally competent lawyers seek to understand the actions and words that they witness from the perspective of the actor or speaker, rather than from the lawyer's life experience."[251] Takeaway: strip language of your associations to understand what people are saying.

- *Avoid ethical stereotypes.* Negotiators often rely on stereotypes about the unethical behavior of people of different nationalities. These stereotypes mislead negotiators because "more variance often exists within cultures than between them."[252] Takeaway: "don't jump to harsh conclusions about the other side's motives when more benevolent explanations for their behavior are possible."[253]

---

[246] Neeley, Tsedal. (2015, October). Global teams that work. *Harvard Business Review*, p. 79.
[247] Meyer, Erin. (2015, October). When culture doesn't translate. *Harvard Business Review*.
[248] Neeley, *supra* note 246 at 79. [249] Meyer, *supra* note 241 at 79. [250] Ibid.
[251] Bryant & Peters, *supra* note 239.
[252] Program on Negotiation at Harvard Law School, *supra* note 236. [253] Ibid.

- *Don't assume.* In her study of American and Japanese negotiators, psychologist Wendi Adair found that they both relied excessively on stereotypes of each other's culture and assumed that those stereotypes would dictate negotiation behavior even when people were acting outside their culture. But each negotiator had already changed strategy to reflect "their counterpart's cultural assumptions about negotiating," resulting in clashes and confusion between the negotiators.[254] The negotiators, in effect, were negotiating with each other's cultural shadows rather than the people themselves. Takeaway: when people game each other, they become frustrated and confused dealing with their predicted behavior instead of their actual behavior.[255]

Perhaps the biggest challenge to lawyers in cross-cultural communication is to refrain from the assertive, dominating behavior that has been successful in many aspects of their lives and spend time, at least preliminarily, observing, learning, listening, adapting, and reevaluating.

CHAPTER CAPSULE

Nearly all work within organizations is now completed by collaborative teams rather than individual efforts. Although attorneys appear to perform legal services as independent professionals, these services invariably are rendered in a context that requires sound relationships with colleagues, adversaries, parties, witnesses, experts, judges, mediators, and other professionals. Despite the importance of interpersonal skills in attorneys' careers, many attorneys are neither outgoing nor attentive. Studies of attorneys' personalities indicate that they place an exceptionally high priority on autonomy and an unusually low priority on sociability and interpersonal sensitivity. This paradox leads to client dissatisfaction, conflicts with colleagues, and unsatisfactory interactions with other people whose assistance and cooperation are needed to achieve our clients' objectives.

Although attorneys may regard their personalities as immutable and their insensitivity as being the price clients must pay for their singular expertise, clients expect attorneys to function with a full set of skills – technical

---

[254] Adair, W. L, Taylor, M. S., & Tinsley, C. H. (2008). Starting out on the right foot: Negotiation schemas when cultures collide. *Negotiation and Conflict Management Research* 2(2), 138–163. See Luomala, Harri. (2015, May). When an intercultural business negotiation fails: Comparing the emotions and behavioural tendencies of individualist and collectivistic negotiators. *Group Decision and Negotiation*, 24(3), 537–561.

[255] Adair, Taylor, & Tinsley, *supra* note 254.

competence and social proficiency. To meet these client expectations, attorneys must master the essential components of social proficiency: under-standing others' perceptions, perspectives, and beliefs; knowing how to communicate, persuade, listen, share stories, empathize, build trust, apol-ogize, and work within teams; and developing and displaying cultural com-petence. Each of these components has been amplified and discussed in this chapter, and reliable methods of developing, evaluating, and enhancing our social proficiency have been presented for attorneys' consideration and implementation.

A threshold obstacle to acquiring and deploying essential skills is our misplaced confidence in our ability to accurately perceive what other people are feeling and thinking. Since many of us are persistently unaware of how we affect other people and what is really on their minds, we should devote more effort to "perspective getting" than "perspective taking." This may require a higher level of vulnerability than we normally tolerate, as we must learn to inquire sincerely and directly and relinquish our efforts to control other people's responses. But the advantages obtained by eliciting candid informa-tion from other people instead of making assumptions about them suggests vulnerability is a risk we must take to achieve understanding.

6

Wisdom

When asked to identify the purpose of law school teaching, the most common response by law professors is "to think like a lawyer."[1] Law students, too, report that the "ability to think like a lawyer" is the most important knowledge conveyed by law schools.[2] Although teaching law students how to think like lawyers might be an admirable ambition in theory, it is impracticable, counterproductive, and pedagogically backward for at least three reasons.

First, we know very little about how lawyers actually think. Absent scientific studies regarding lawyers' thought processes – and considering that 46 percent of entry-level professors hired by Tier One law schools have no prior practical legal experience working with lawyers – it is difficult to understand how law schools can teach students to think like practicing lawyers.[3] Studying judicial opinions in case books, the primary teaching method in law schools, does not reveal much about how attorneys think but instead tells students how the judges who wrote those opinions think. Just as Olympic athletes would question a training program based on video clips of referees, officials, and umpires, students may question how they will learn to think like lawyers, in the practice of law and the service of clients, by reading judges' opinions.

Second, even if we knew how attorneys think, it is not clear that existing methods and processes merit replication. Rampant client dissatisfaction with

[1] Rapoport, Nancy (2002). Is "thinking like a lawyer" really what we want to teach? *Journal of the Association of Legal Writing Directors*, 1, 91. Uphoff, Rodney, Clark, James, & Monahan, Edward. (1997, Winter). Preparing the new law graduate to practice law: A view from the trenches. *University of Cincinnati Law Review*, 65, 381.

[2] See Gee, E.G., & Jackson, Donald. (1982). Current studies of legal education: Findings and recommendations. *Journal of Legal Education*, 32, 471, 481. Mertz, Elizabeth. (2007). *The language of law schools*. New York: Oxford University Press.

[3] Newton, Brent. (2010). Preaching what they don't practice: Why law faculties' preoccupation with impractical scholarship and devaluation of practical competencies obstruct reform in the legal academy. *South Carolina Law Review*, 62, 105, 130.

legal services, disturbing levels of mental impairment among attorneys, public disdain for attorneys, and extraordinary costs limiting access to legal services suggest that we should pause before law schools spawn another 1.3 million attorneys whose thought processes are molded to replicate those of the current practitioners.[4]

Third, if we remain determined to train law students to think like lawyers, why not teach them, first, to be wise and then, second, to think like lawyers? Skipping the wise phase and moving directly to the partisan phase robs clients of the objective evaluation, sound advice, and thoughtful strategies they deservedly expect from their attorneys.[5] As legal scholar Karl Llewellyn observed in 1930, "a mere legal machine is a social danger. Indeed, a mere legal machine is not even a good lawyer. It lacks insight and judgment."[6] Since law schools neither teach nor stress insight and judgment, the crises currently enveloping the legal profession might be the social danger Llewellyn envisioned.

The partisan emphasis on advantage and expedience to the exclusion of wisdom has contributed to the excesses of adversarial legalism, the uniquely American legal system characterized by

> (1) more complex and detailed bodies of rules; (2) more frequent recourse to formal legal methods of implementing policy and resolving disputes; (3) more adversarial and expensive forms of legal contestation; (4) more punitive legal sanctions (including larger civil damage awards); (5) more frequent judicial review, revision, and delay of administrative decision making; and (6) more legal uncertainty, malleability, and, unpredictability.[7]

---

[4] For a depiction of the maladies currently affecting the legal profession, see Rhode, Deborah. (2015). *The trouble with lawyers*. New York: Oxford University Press. Barton, Benjamin. (2015). *Glass half full*. New York: Oxford University Press. Harper, Steven. (2013). *The lawyer bubble*. New York: Basic Books. Trotter, Michael. (2012). *Declining prospects*. North Charleston, South Carolina: CreateSpace.

[5] As a practical matter, we have little to lose and much to gain by starting with wisdom and, if necessary, reverting to partisan representation. Those attorneys experienced in client counseling will acknowledge that it is much easier to start with big picture wisdom and then descend to small picture partisanship than to start with partisanship and then, months later in the representation, attempt to elevate the client's perspective to reflect wisdom. See Sarat, Austin, & Felstiner, William L.F. (1988). Law and social relations: Vocabularies of motive in lawyer/client interaction. *Law and Society Review*, 22(4), 740. Felstiner, William L.F., Abel, Richard L., & Sarat, Austin. (1980–1981). The emergence and transformation of disputes: Naming, blaming, claiming. *Law and Society Review*, 15(3–4), 631, 641.

[6] Llewellyn, Karl. (1996). *The bramble bush* (p. 116). New York: Oceana Publications.

[7] Kagan, Robert A. How much do national styles of law matter? In Kagan, Robert A., & Axelrad, Lee (Eds.). (2000). *Regulatory encounters: Multinational corporations and American adversarial legalism* (p. 8–9). Berkeley, California: University of California Press.

By making wisdom an explicit priority in the education of lawyers and the practice of law – and relegating partisan representation to a secondary though episodically legitimate role – we not only mitigate some of the excesses of adversarial legalism but also start to restore public confidence in lawyers. Learning how to be wise enables attorneys to fulfill former Yale Law School Dean Anthony Kronman's "lawyer-statesman" ideal.[8] For Dean Kronman, a lawyer's objective and ambition should be "the attainment of wisdom that lies beyond technique – a wisdom about human beings and their tangled affairs that anyone who wishes to provide real deliberative counsel must possess."[9]

The critical importance of wisdom is again highlighted by Richard Posner, a judge on the United States Court of Appeals for the Seventh Circuit. Judge Posner recently asked Robert Hochman, a partner at Sidley Austin LLP, how he would advise a prospective client inquiring, "What are my chances of prevailing in this lawsuit that I am asking you to represent me in?" Mr. Hochman, a former law clerk to Judge Posner and United States Supreme Court Justice Stephen Breyer, said he would counsel the client with this advice:

> The way to approach the question is to set aside all the legal technicalities and ask: if this were a dispute submitted for resolution to a wise man who was not law-trained, but who simply applied his moral intuitions, would he resolve the dispute in your favor or your opponent's? His suggested resolution might be blocked by some legal technicality – statutory language, precedents, what have you – but in all likelihood we would be able to get around such obstacles.[10]

Judge Posner concurs in this advice, stating, "I think this is the right approach. Most judges evaluate cases in a holistic, intuitive manner, reaching a tentative conclusion that they then subject to technical legal analysis."

If Dean Kronman, Judge Posner, and Mr. Hochman are correct in asserting that lawyers should counsel clients from a wise person's perspective, we must ask ourselves, "Do we have – right now – the maturity, knowledge, objectivity, and discernment necessary to be considered wise?" In the absence of a serious effort by law schools or law firms to understand the nature of wisdom and to develop wisdom as an integral part of professional judgment, very few of us are equipped to answer that question affirmatively. To overcome that shortcoming, this chapter provides some insights to answer two critical questions: What

---

[8] Kronman, Anthony. (1993). *The lost lawyer.* Cambridge, Massachusetts: Belknap Press.
[9] Ibid. at 2.
[10] Posner, Richard. (2016). *Divergent paths* (p. 1). Cambridge Massachusetts: *Harvard University Press.*

is wisdom, and how does one acquire it? We tackle those enormous questions by studying the nature of wisdom and then examining seven aspects of wisdom: perceptiveness, foresight, creativity, fairness, judgment, self-renewal, and courage.

NATURE OF WISDOM

We avoid developing wisdom because it is difficult to define and even more difficult to learn. We struggle to identify what constitutes wisdom in the abstract, but somehow we can quickly determine who is not wise and who has not acted wisely. Wisdom seems to be an ambiguous concept in guiding our future behavior but is a tangible precept when evaluating another person's behavior. This suggests we know what characteristics constitute wisdom but have not spent enough time consciously extracting its elements. For that reason, it is worthwhile in this section to examine wisdom closely and identify its components.

There is no uniform definition of wisdom.[11] Because wisdom is an immensely complex trait, any definition of wisdom is necessarily incomplete and subject to criticism. As psychologist Robert Sternberg notes, "To understand wisdom fully and correctly probably requires more wisdom than any of us have. Thus, we cannot quite comprehend the nature of wisdom because of our own lack of it."[12] Despite these challenges, we must strive to be wise because that is precisely the trait that clients seek from attorneys to overcome clients' difficulties in resolving conflicts, protecting rights, complying with legal requirements, and anticipating future problems in the interpretation and enforcement of legal documents.

To fulfill our obligation to be wise, we can start by identifying key elements of wisdom, modifying them for the nuances of law practice, and integrating them into our client service. A synthesis of research regarding wisdom, modified to apply to law practices, yields seven elements of wisdom:

- *Perceptiveness* (seeing, linking, and reflecting on features, factors, dimensions, anomalies, inconsistencies, and repercussions that others might overlook).
- *Foresight* (imagining, modeling, visualizing, and predicting future behavior and events).

[11] Sternberg, Robert, & Jordan, Jennifer. (2005). *A handbook of wisdom* (p. xii). New York: Oxford University Press.
[12] Sternberg, Robert J. (Ed.). (1990). *Wisdom: Its nature, origins, and development* (p. 3). New York: Cambridge University Press.

- *Creativity* (making associations among seemingly unrelated ideas, products, events, entities, and individuals and solving problems with new associations).
- *Fairness* (forgoing personal gain to meet ethical standards of equality and equity and leading other people to follow standards that fulfill expectations of fairness and justice).
- *Judgment* (exhibiting knowledge, objectivity, proportion, sensitivity, and humaneness in making complex evaluations and decisions).
- *Self-renewal* (knowing when our knowledge and mental models have become invalid and learning how to renew our minds and bodies to foster wisdom).
- *Courage* (risking physical or emotional harm by compelling yourself to act for the benefit of others or to comply with your highest expectations of yourself).

Although wisdom may require additional qualities, these traits establish a sound foundation for providing sage advice, making effective decisions, and enacting ethical leadership. They can and should be augmented as your own experience illuminates other essential features of wisdom.

In addition to identifying the elements of wisdom, we should clarify what wisdom does *not* comprise. The traits that could, but do not reliably, contribute to wisdom include age, knowledge, high intelligence, and academic achievement.[13] For attorneys attempting to understand wisdom, the difference between knowledge and wisdom merits special attention:

> The essence of wisdom ... lies not in what is known but rather in the manner in which that knowledge is held and in how that knowledge is put to use. To be wise is not to know particular facts but to know without excessive confidence or excessive cautiousness. Wisdom is thus not a belief, a value, a set of facts, a corpus of knowledge or information in some specialized area, or a set of special abilities or skills. Wisdom is an attitude taken by persons toward the beliefs, values, knowledge, information, abilities, and skills that are held, a tendency to doubt that these are necessarily true or valid and to doubt that they are an exhaustive set of those things that could be known.[14]

People who are wise continually test the sources and ascertain the limits of their knowledge. They see knowledge as dynamic – continually challenged, frequently revised, and never complete. They are wary of expertise based on

---

[13] Sternberg & Jordan (2005), *supra* note 11 at xiv, 15, 16, 122, and 141.
[14] Sternberg (1990), *supra* note 12 at 187.

subject matter knowledge, recognizing that it often engenders conceit and overconfidence and induces complacency at least as often as it provokes growth.

While knowledge constitutes expertise in many law firms, the coin of the realm for clients is wisdom. Howard Siegel, a former partner in Pryor Cashman's Media & Entertainment Group who has represented recording artists like the E Street Band, Paula Abdul, Carly Simon, and the Rolling Stones' Bill Wyman, explains what the difference between knowledge and wisdom means in law practice:

> In the course of 43 years of practice, perhaps the single most useful lesson I've learned is the distinction between knowledge and wisdom. The truly successful attorneys are those who are able to relate to their clients on a personal level as well as on a professional level. Put another way, and I emphasize this in all of my classes, the best among us are able not only to explain the meaning and nuances of clause 7(a)(ii)(D), but also to closely identify with the client's personal goals. The client and, indeed, the law itself are best served by the attorney who can respond to the client's legal needs as well as to the client's personal concerns. The former talent requires knowledge; the latter wisdom. The distinction between the two is perhaps best stated in this way: knowledge will help you make a living, but wisdom will help you make a life.[15]

Apart from understanding the difference between knowledge and wisdom, wise attorneys recognize that knowing and doubting are not polar opposites but rather act synchronously. The course of wisdom, Sternberg counsels, is to achieve a balance between knowing and doubting – "adding to the knowledge that one does hold while simultaneously recognizing that there is much that one does not know."[16] When we recognize that wisdom entails both knowledge and doubt, we can more accurately determine where our knowledge fits into these four dimensions of knowing: knowing what we know, knowing what we do not know, knowing what can be known, and knowing what currently cannot be known.[17] Confucius captured this concept in his insight, "To know what you know and know what you don't know is the characteristic of one who knows."[18]

---

[15] Hamilton, Daniel. (2016, January 28). *Boyd Briefs*.
[16] Sternberg (1990), *supra* note 12 at 185.
[17] Sternberg, Robert. (2007). *Wisdom, intelligence and creativity synthesized* (p. 153). New York: Cambridge University Press.
[18] Birren, James, & Svensson, Cheryl. Wisdom in history. In Sternberg & Jordan (2005), *supra* note 11 at 9.

PERCEPTIVENESS

The importance of perceptiveness is vastly underestimated in law schools and law practice. This occurs because the importance of facts is similarly underestimated. Perceptiveness has nominal value when the facts that could be discerned play a minor role in legal analysis.

The reason law schools devalue facts and perceptiveness is that very few facts are disclosed in judicial opinions and, to the extent disclosed, they are "reduced," "ready-made," and "thoroughly hedged."[19] Consequently, the facts presented in judicial opinions are pedestrian, lacking the intellectual stimulation and thwarting the limitless discourse generated by legal theories, policies, rules, and principles. Facts also evade traditional teaching methods: how do students and lawyers shift from being preoccupied, inattentive bystanders to keen observers, astute investigators, and sage evaluators of facts? These skills can be taught, but they necessitate a different skill set from that developed by conventional law professors. One of the innovations at the University of California, Irvine School of Law was the appointment of Henry Weinstein, a former *Los Angeles Times* reporter, to teach factual investigation.[20] Commenting on this new course, ethics expert John Steele said, "based on my experience, digging out the facts and sorting them remains the top task for litigators. I never heard about that in my law school classes."[21]

In law practices, many attorneys deemphasize perceptiveness and facts because they were trained to do that in law schools, and more time can be spent on research and arguments about the law than the pertinent facts. Facts tend to be restrictive, sometimes immutable, while the law is infinitely flexible and expansive. Unlike facts, legal rules are "up for grabs in every case."[22] The plasticity of legal rules is illustrated in Karl Llewellyn's observation, "There is no precedent that the judge may not at his need either file down to razor thinness or expand into a bludgeon."[23]

Despite the tendency to diminish the role of facts, they are largely determinative of legal outcomes. Sven Erik Holmes, a former U.S. district court judge

---

[19] Noonan, John T. (2002). *Persons and masks of the law* (p. 141). Berkeley: University of California Press. Mertz, *supra* note 2 at 67.

[20] DeBenedictis, Don J. (2008, July 11). New law school at UC Irvine announces diversified faculty. *San Francisco Daily Journal*, p. 2.

[21] 2008, July 2. UCI to offer course on fact investigation. Legal Ethics Forum. Retrieved from www.legalethicsforum.com/blog/2008/07/uci-to-offer-co.html.

[22] Graham, Duffy. (2005). *The consciousness of the litigator* (pp. 50, 90, 112). Ann Arbor, Michigan: University of Michigan Press.

[23] Krieger, Stefan H., & Neumann, Jr., Richard K. (2007). *Essential lawyering skills* (p. 242). New York: Aspen Publishers.

for the Northern District of Oklahoma and the current Chief Legal Officer for the accounting firm KPMG LLP, confirms that facts trump law:

> Outcomes are based on the facts. Law schools are good at teaching students about the law but do little to impart the importance of the facts. Make no mistake: Legal decisions, like most decisions, are based on the facts. An analysis of the facts is more than simply ascertaining what happened; it is the process of determining which facts are relevant and assigning the proper weight to each fact. This, in turn, dictates how the law should be applied and which side of the argument should prevail. The process of decision-making, in law and elsewhere, is based on meticulous, factual inquiry. No matter the profession, knowing, understanding and evaluating details will bring greater success than locating and citing arcane precedent.[24]

Judge Holmes' veneration of facts is echoed by law professor Stefan Krieger: "Law school can mislead you. You are spending so much time learning law and how to analyze law that you might get the impression that factual issues are easy. They are not easy, and they are not marginal, either."[25]

Attorneys' disinclination to seek, perceive, evaluate, and respect facts is not restricted to the United States and might be an unfortunate common law phenomenon. In an interview with *Counsel*, a publication of the Bar of England and Wales, the United Kingdom's Supreme Court Justice Lord Sumption expressed his concern about barristers' and solicitors' inability to recognize and analyze facts:[26]

- the most difficult aspect of practicing law is "not the law but the facts."
- "Most arguments which pretend to be about law are actually arguments about the correct analysis and categorization of the facts. Once you've understood them it's usually obvious what the answer is. The difficulty then becomes to reason your way in a respectable way towards it."
- "the study of something involving the analysis of evidence, like history or classics, or the study of a subject which comes close to pure logic, like mathematics, is at least as valuable a preparation for legal practice as the study of law."
- "Appreciating how to fit legal principles to particular facts is a real skill. Understanding the social or business background to legal problems is essential. I'm not sure current law degrees train you for that, nor really are they designed to."

[24] Holmes, Sven Erik. (2015, September 28). Before going to law school, live your life. *The National Law Journal.*
[25] Krieger, *supra* note 23 at 11.
[26] (2012, July 8). The best lawyers are not law graduates, claims judge. *The Telegraph.*

Reversing law schools' emphasis on law over facts, Lord Sumption believes that identifying and analyzing facts are imperative skills, but legal knowledge can be acquired over time: "If you don't have them you are going to find it difficult to practise. If you don't know any law that is not a problem; you can find out."[27]

If a legal education does indeed sharpen the mind by narrowing it, as the adage holds,[28] then we need to counteract its influence by broadening our perception. We need to become, in novelist Saul Bellow's term, "first class noticers."[29] Perceptiveness is crucial because it separates novice decision makers from expert decision makers, as NASA psychologist Judith Orasanu and management professor Terry Connolly declare: "experts are distinguished from novices mainly by their situation assessment abilities, not their general reasoning skills."[30] This awareness enables them to see and recall relevant information, discern the most critical features of a situation, timely integrate the information into their decision making, and assess alternative solutions.[31] Consistent with their focus on context, expert decision makers "spend more time evaluating the situation while novice decision makers spend more time generating and evaluating courses of action."[32]

Concrete steps we can take to improve our perceptiveness and ability to identify and analyze critical facts include:

- *Avoid multitasking.* Multitasking degrades performance in general and is particularly harmful when it involves two visual tasks.[33] People think of visual tasks as being relatively effortless, and they underestimate the difficulty of processing multiple information streams. "Many people have this overconfidence in how well they can multitask," states communications professor Zheng Wang, and "this particularly is the case

---

[27] Ibid.   [28] Moll, Richard. (1990). *The lure of the law* (p. 27). New York: Penguin Group.
[29] Bellow, Saul. (1997). *The actual.* New York: Viking Press.
[30] Orasanu, J., & Connolly, T. (1993). The reinvention of decision making. In Klein, G., Orasanu, J., Calderwood, R., & Zsambok, C.E. (Eds.). *Decision making in action* (p. 20). Norwood, Connecticut: Ablex.
[31] Rosen, Michael, Salas, Eduardo, Lyons, Rebecca, & Fiore, Stephen. (2008). Expertise and naturalistic decision making in organizations: Mechanisms of effective decision making. In Hodgkinson, Gerard, & Starbuck, William (Eds.). *The Oxford handbook of organizational decision making* (pp. 218–219). New York: Oxford University Press.
[32] Ibid. at 219.
[33] Wang, Zheng, *et al.* (2012). Behavioral performance and visual attention in communication multitasking: A comparison between instant messaging and online voice chat. *Computers in Human Behavior,* 28(3), 968. Wang, Zheng, & Tchernev, John. (2012). The "myth" of media multitasking: Reciprocal dynamics of media multitasking, personal needs, and gratifications. *Journal of Communication,* 62(3), 493–513.

when they combine two visual tasks. People's perception about how well they're doing doesn't match up with how they actually perform."[34]

- *Mitigate biases.* Our biases prevent us from seeing. As Edgar Schein points out, "We block out a great deal of information that is potentially available if it does not fit our needs, expectations, preconceptions, and prejudgments."[35] As a consequence, "we do not think and talk about what we see; we see what we are able to think and talk about."[36] Being mindful of our biases and the resultant distortions helps to correct our perceptions and avoid motivated blindness.

- *See the context.* After looking at a tank of fish in one experiment, American participants recalled the largest and most colorful fish, while Japanese participants were more likely to remember background features like the rocks and plants.[37] In another experiment, American and Chinese students viewed images of a plane in flight, a tiger in the country, and a car on a road. Eye movement trackers showed that the American students fixated on the focal objects, but the Chinese students took more time to focus on the objects and then alternated their glances between the objects and the background (sunlight, mountains, clouds, and leaves).[38] The lesson here is to be aware of your tendencies and make a deliberate effort to ensure that you are observing the entire context. As Noreena Hertz, author of *Eyes Wide Open*, cautions, "the information we're most prone to focus on may only give us a very partial story, a fragment of the truth, and therefore risks misleading us. Being aware of this, and adjusting accordingly, will make a profound difference to the decisions you make."[39]

- *Take the outside view.* To avoid the biases of familiarity, routine, and incrementalism, look at situations through an outsider's eyes. Ask, "how would this appear to someone who was seeing it for the first time?" If an outsider would perceive a situation to be problematic, chances are that it is or will become problematic. As Max Bazerman, author of *The Power of Noticing*, explains, "Outsiders are better than insiders at noticing vulnerabilities and suggesting solutions to address them."[40]

[34] Wang (2012), *et al., supra* note 33.
[35] Schein, Edgar. (2013). *Humble inquiry* (pp. 90–91). San Francisco: Berrett-Koehler Publishers.
[36] Ibid.   [37] Brooks, David. (2011). *The social animal* (p. 141) New York: Random House.
[38] Hertz, Noreena. (2013). *Eyes wide open* (pp. 21–22). New York: HarperCollins. Chua, Hannah, Boland, Julie, & Nisbett, Richard. (2005). Cultural variation in eye movements during scene perception. *Proceedings of the National Academy of Sciences* 102(35), 12,629–12,633.
[39] Ibid. at 22.
[40] Bazerman, Max. (2014, July–August). Becoming a first-class noticer. *Harvard Business Review*. See Kahneman, Daniel. (2011). *Thinking, fast and slow* (pp. 247–249). New York: Farrar, Straus and Giroux.

- *Direct your attention.* Perceptiveness is considerably more than seeing; it also requires us to direct our attention to likely problems. Expert drivers, for instance, continually direct their attention to places where problems are likely to occur. Novice drivers, in contrast, look straight ahead. As a consequence, expert drivers detect 66 percent of the risks, while novice drivers detect only 36 percent of the risks.[41]
- *Be self-critical.* When we discover that we have failed to see or anticipate problems, our tendency is to think of all the reasons that justify our oversights, e.g., "no one could have predicted that." When we look for excuses, we prevent ourselves from identifying errors and developing more accurate perceptions. "First class noticers," Bazerman asserts, "always consider internal causes as well, which allows them to better learn from experience."[42]

FORESIGHT

"Talent hits a target that no one else can hit," said the nineteenth-century philosopher Arthur Schopenhauer. "Genius hits a target that no one else can see."[43] That capacity to see what "no one else can see" is foresight. Because a large part of wisdom consists of seeing beyond current conditions and moving beyond conventional knowledge, foresight is an essential element of wisdom.[44] At its core, this trait enables us to escape the constraints of our education and training and view the future without the biases of past experiences and current expectations. As Nassim Nicholas Taleb, the author of *The Bed of Procrustes*, observes, "A prophet is not someone with special visions, just someone blind to most of what others see."[45]

To accelerate the development of foresight, this section identifies the personal traits associated with accurate prediction and then summarizes methods of improving our prediction skills. As a preliminary matter, we should recognize that foresight and prediction are central to attorneys' work. Oliver Wendell Holmes, Jr., a justice of the U.S. Supreme Court between 1902 and 1932, regarded prediction as the principal feature and purpose of the law: "prophecies of what the courts will do in fact, and nothing more pretentious, are what I mean

---

[41] Klein, Gary. (2009). *Streetlights and shadows* (pp. 159–160). Cambridge, Massachusetts: MIT Press.
[42] Ibid.
[43] Page, Scott. (2008). *The difference* (p. 132). Princeton, New Jersey: Princeton University Press.
[44] See Sternberg & Jordan (2005), *supra* note 11 at xv.
[45] Taleb, Nassim. (2010). *The bed of Procrustes*. New York: Random House.

by the law."[46] He expressed concern that legal theory obscured the importance of prediction and "is apt to get the cart before the horse" when it separates a right or duty from the consequences of its breach. Clients do not care "two straws" about legal axioms, Holmes declared, but they do want to know what the "courts are likely to do in fact."[47] For that reason, Holmes argues, prediction is integral to the law and overrides reductionist legal theory:

> The primary rights and duties with which jurisprudence busies itself again are nothing but prophecies ... A legal duty so called is nothing but a prediction that if a man does or omits certain things he will be made to suffer in this or that way by judgment of the court; and so of a legal right.

"The object of our study," Holmes concludes, "is prediction, the prediction of the incidence of the public force through the instrumentality of the courts."

If prediction is both an element of wisdom and an essential skill for attorneys, how does one become an accurate predictor? The good news is that nearly everyone can become an accurate predictor by adopting certain attitudes and practices. The bad news is that developing this expertise may require many of us to change how we think not only about other people and events but about ourselves as well. Introspection is an essential component of prediction skills, asserts Phillip Tetlock, author of *Superforecasters*, because the "strongest predictor of rising into the ranks of superforecasters is perpetual beta, the degree to which one is committed to belief updating and self-improvement. It is roughly three times as powerful a predictor as its closest rival, intelligence."[48] High IQ cannot compensate for a lack of commitment to the arduous task of personal development – comparing your predictions with actual events over an extended period and "always more trying, more failing, more analyzing, more adjusting, and trying again."[49] Prediction skills, ultimately, are determined more by our capacity for introspection and self-improvement and our responsiveness to feedback than intelligence and innate ability.

Specific traits that are correlated with accurate prediction include open-mindedness, humility, numeracy, curiosity, tolerance of ambiguity, tenacity, pragmatism, and self-reflection.[50] The most accurate predictors also work on

[46] Holmes, Oliver Wendell, Jr. (1897). The path of the law. *Harvard Law Review*, 10, 457.
[47] Ibid.
[48] Tetlock, Philip, & Gardner, Dan. (2015). *Superforecasting* (p. 192). New York: Crown.
[49] Ibid. at 190.
[50] Tetlock & Gardner, *supra* note 48 at 191. Tetlock, Philip. (2005). *Expert political judgment*. Princeton, New Jersey: Princeton University Press. Schoemaker, Paul, & Tetlock. Philip. (2016, May). Superforecasting: How to upgrade your company's judgment. *Harvard Business Review*, p. 77.

teams. Factors that are *not* correlated with prediction accuracy include self-confidence, fame, education, occupation, political affiliation, and access to classified data.[51]

Extensive statistical studies of accurate and inaccurate predictors indicate that accurate predictors employ specific methods to improve their performance. As Tetlock explains, foresight "is the product of particular ways of thinking, of gathering information, of updating beliefs. These habits of thought can be learned and cultivated by any intelligent, thoughtful, determined person."[52] Specific methods of improving prediction skills, based on Tetlock's study of 25,000 forecasters, include:

- *Synthesizing multiple viewpoints.* Expert forecasters seek, aggregate, and synthesize multiple viewpoints. They know that valuable information is dispersed widely and sometimes emerges from unlikely sources.[53] Their practice of aggregating information is unusual, as Tetlock explains: "aggregation doesn't come to us naturally. The tip-of-your-nose perspective insists that it sees reality objectively and correctly, so there is no need to consult other perspectives."[54] Expert forecasters overcome this insularity by seeking and inviting alternative views.

- *Debiasing.* One hour of training in reasoning and debiasing improved forecasting accuracy by 14 percent.[55] The debiasing training alerted forecasters to cognitive biases in making predictions and showed them how to overcome those biases.

- *Building teams.* Predictions generated by teams were 23 percent more accurate than those produced by individuals.[56] When an individual forecaster qualified to become a superforecaster and was placed on a team, that person's predictions were 50 percent more accurate after joining the team.[57] Notably, the teams were organized to ensure intellectual diversity and included at least one person with subject matter expertise as well as non-experts.

- *Updating beliefs.* Good predictors "know how to jump, to move their probability estimates fast in response to diagnostic signals."[58] Knowing when and how to update your beliefs can be more difficult than formulating the initial forecast; prediction risks are heightened by underreactions and overreactions to new information.[59]

---

[51] Ibid. Ignatius, David. (2013, November 1). More chatter than needed. *Washington Post.*
[52] Tetlock & Gardner, *supra* note 48 at 18.   [53] Ibid. at 73.   [54] Ibid. at 77–78.
[55] Schoemaker & Tetlock, *supra* note 50 at 75.   [56] Tetlock & Gardner, *supra* note 48 at 201.
[57] Ibid. at 205.   [58] Ibid. at 281.   [59] Ibid. at 158.

- *Tracking performance.* To improve forecasting performance, we have to track prediction outcomes and evaluate the processes used to generate those predictions. Tetlock calls this, "Forecast, measure, revise: it is the surest path to seeing better."[60]

Additional methods of improving forecasting performance, derived from research undertaken by Paul Saffo[61] and J. Scott Armstrong,[62] include: (1) search for anomalies and facts that don't fit into familiar boxes and labels; (2) seek disconfirming evidence to challenge your ideas; (3) mitigate the recency bias by looking back in history "twice as far as you look forward;" (4) consider alternative explanations, especially in new situations; (5) list reasons why your forecast might be wrong; (6) hold strong opinions lightly so they can be adequately presented but quickly relinquished if untenable; and (7) use a devil's advocate to test your ideas.

CREATIVITY

Since wisdom requires us to see what others have overlooked and to formulate solutions that others have not imagined, creativity assumes a large role in wisdom. Despite the importance of creativity, few of us can pinpoint what it means, who has it, when it makes a difference, and how it can be enhanced. We overcome these problems in this section by defining creativity, identifying traits associated with creativity, explaining its importance, and showing methods of enhancing it.

Defining Creativity

Creativity is "figuring out how to use what you already know in order to go beyond what you currently think."[63] Looking at creativity through a legal lens, law professors Stefan Krieger and Richard Neumann assure us that "creativity is not an innate and mysterious personality trait possessed only by artists and others like them. Creativity is the process of solving problems through insights that you arrive at on your own."[64]

[60] Ibid. at 252.
[61] Saffo, Paul. (2007, July–August). Six rules for effective forecasting. *Harvard Business Review.*
[62] Armstrong, J. Scott. (2001). *Principles of forecasting.* Boston, Massachusetts: Kluwer Academic Publishers.
[63] Bruner, Jerome. (1983). *In search of mind* (p. 183). New York: Harper.
[64] Krieger, & Neumann, *supra* note 23 at 31.

Because creativity evokes novel ideas from existing knowledge, it is, in essence, an associative skill. It requires us to link seemingly disparate events, objects, ideas, and people to each other and then distill new interpretations, solutions, and strategies from those fresh associations. This associative skill can be learned and enhanced:

> Associating is like a mental muscle that can grow stronger by using the other discovery skills [questioning, observing, networking, and experimenting]. As innovators engage in those behaviors, they build their ability to generate ideas that can be recombined in new ways. The more frequently people in our study attempted to understand, categorize, and store new knowledge, the more easily their brains could naturally and consistently make, store, and recombine associations.[65]

Despite its apparent simplicity, the skill of associating is very difficult to develop because it conflicts with our conventional mental processes. We tend to think incrementally, moving in a familiar direction and changing, if at all, in small steps. Because we prefer the status quo and favor "mastery over originality," we feel more comfortable viewing and dealing with the world through conventional models.[66] Our preference for familiarity and predictability ultimately prevents us from making new associations and, as a consequence, we miss those opportunities where creativity and innovation could fundamentally change the way we see and function.

Traits of Creative People

We have stereotypes of creative people that diminish our motivation to become more creative.[67] Research indicates that these stereotypes are inaccurate, incomplete, and misleading because they portray creative people as being outlandish or impractical and perpetuate the misconception that creativity is a stable individual trait when, in fact, it is malleable.[68] Our level of creativity

---

[65] Dyer, Jeffrey H., Gregersen, Hal, & Christensen, Clayton M. (2009, December). The innovator's DNA. *Harvard Business Review*, p. 63.

[66] Martin, Roger. (2007). *Opposable minds* (p. 186). Cambridge, Massachusetts: Harvard Business School Press.

[67] Dumas, Denis, & Dunbar, Kevin. (2016). The creative stereotype effect. *PLoS One*, 11(2), e0142567. See Goncalo, Jack. (2012, January). The bias against creativity: Why people desire but reject creative ideas. *Psychological Science*, 23(1), 13–17.

[68] Sternberg, Robert, & Kaufman, James. (2010). Constraints on creativity: Obvious and not so obvious. In Kaufman, J. C., & Sternberg, R. J. (Eds.). *The Cambridge handbook of creativity* (pp. 467–482). New York: Cambridge University Press. Simonton, Dean. (2012). Genius. In Holyoak, Keith, & Morrison, Robert (Eds.). *The Oxford handbook of thinking and reasoning* (pp. 492–509). New York: Oxford University Press.

can be altered, for instance, by role-playing, music, mood, diet, cannabis, meditation, walking, travel, and multicultural experiences.[69]

When we study the personalities of creative people, we also learn that they exhibit a broad range of characteristics and are distinguished more by their breadth of emotion than any particular type of emotion. Based on interviews with 91 creative scientists, artists, politicians, and business leaders, psychologist Mihaly Csikszentmihalyi found that the creative personality consists of ten paradoxical traits: (1) high levels of physical energy, but often quiet and at rest; (2) smart, yet naïve; (3) disciplined, yet playful; (4) realistic, yet imaginative; (5) extroverted and introverted; (6) humble, yet proud; (7) aggressive, yet sensitive; (8) conservative, yet rebellious; (9) objective, yet passionate; and (10) high sensitivity to both pain and enjoyment.

Another study, based on tests of 481 actors, musicians, marketing students, lecturers, and managers, found that creative people exhibit higher levels of motivation, ambition, flexibility, rebelliousness, and associative orientation, and lower levels of emotional stability and sociability.[70] Of those traits, the two traits with the highest correlation with creativity are associative orientation (large volume of ideas, playfulness, imagination, commitment, and "sliding transitions between fact and fiction") and flexibility (ability to perceive multiple aspects of issues and develop superior solutions). "Associative orientation is linked to ingenuity," says Øyvind Martinsen, the study author. "Flexibility is linked to insight."[71]

Importance of Creativity

Lawyers' initial response when they hear the word "creativity" is that it probably has little effect on lawyering skills. In a profession centered on precedent, creativity seems irrelevant if not suspect. But corporate counsel, who determine which attorneys are retained to represent their corporations, know that creativity is a distinct, rare, and highly valuable skill. When asked what qualities they seek in attorneys, corporate counsel say that creativity is paramount:

- "We like lawyers to be creative: Creative with their legal arguments, creative with the solutions they help craft, creative when working with

---

[69]   Dumas & Dunbar, *supra* note 67.
[70]   Martinsen, Øyvind L. (2011). The creative personality: A synthesis and development of the creative person profile. *Creativity Research Journal, 23*(3), 185.
[71]   BI Norwegian Business School. (2013, April 2). The hunt for the creative individual. *ScienceDaily.*

us and having an appreciation for the creative business we're in."[72] (Alyson G. Barker, General Counsel, Lucky Brand, Inc.)

- "Lawyers need to be able to overcome obstacles and find creative ways to 'get to yes' within the bounds of the law. To do this, we need to be adept not only at identifying potential problems, but also at coming up with creative and workable solutions, as well as metrics for judging our solutions' value."[73] (Janice Block, Chief Legal Officer, Kaplan, Inc.)
- "Creative problem solving. This is really the highest function we have as lawyers. I want lawyers who are going to work to get to 'yes.' What I mean by that is a lot of lawyers have a knee-jerk reaction. When they hear something that's out of the box they want to say 'no,' because it's unfamiliar or it's risky. This involves digging in and really understanding what are the business objectives and what are the legal obstacles that might be standing in the way."[74] (Melinda Mehringer, Associate General Counsel, Mattel, Inc.)

Although clients seek attorneys who can present creative solutions and implement creative strategies, lawyers themselves "do not find it easy to innovate, especially in the way in which they deliver their services."[75]

Enhancing Creativity

Recognizing the importance of creativity to clients, attorneys might consider monitoring and evaluating their progress in becoming creative problem solvers. To accelerate that process, these techniques and methods may be helpful:

- *Ask the right questions.*[76] Among the five "discovery skills" that distinguish creative executives – associating, questioning, observing, experimenting, and networking – the most important skill is questioning because it engages and promotes the other skills. Effective questions alternately impose and remove constraints so that problems are viewed from different perspectives and invalid assumptions are exposed. Consider spending ten minutes each day formulating ten questions that challenge the status quo – that question how you and your organization currently

[72] Brisbon, Melanie. (2015, October 27). Beyond denim. *San Francisco Daily Journal*, p. 5.
[73] Block, Janice. (2011, August 1). Problem-solving activities strengthen legal departments. *Inside Counsel*.
[74] Sebold, Joshua. (2015, April 12). Toys 2.0. *San Francisco Daily Journal*, p. 4.
[75] Susskind, Richard. (2009). *The end of lawyers?* (p. 280). New York: Oxford University Press.
[76] The ideas in this paragraph are derived from Dyer, Gregersen & Christensen, *supra* note 65.

operate. "Question the unquestionable," urges Tata Group chairman Ratan Tata.[77]

- *Create psychological distance.* We can view problems more abstractly and creatively when we create psychological distance from them. In one experiment, for example, people who were told that a problem originated 2,000 miles away generated better insights and more creative solutions than people who were told the problem originated only two miles away.[78] Since immediacy and urgency hinder creative problem solving, imagining that the problem is occurring elsewhere, involves different people, or will happen at a different time changes our perspective and sparks creativity.

- *Change environments.* People who have lived in foreign countries demonstrate an exceptionally high level of creativity.[79] Just thinking about living in a foreign country heightens the creativity of people who previously lived abroad.[80] When our environment changes we are compelled to look "outside the realm of normality" and "see the world in multiple ways."[81] For that reason, even small changes in our environment and habits – lighting, ambient noise, walks, workspaces, rooms, and short trips – have a positive effect on creativity.[82]

- *Set ambitious standards.* "Always take a chance on better, even if it seems like a potential threat," asserts Ed Catmull, president of Pixar Animation Studios and one of the creative geniuses behind *Toy Story 3*, *Finding Dory*, *Inside Out*, and *Finding Nemo.*[83] When we take a chance on better, we reset our ambitions, force ourselves to develop broader

[77] Dyer, Gregersen & Christensen, *supra* note 65.
[78] Jia, Lile, Hirt, Edward, & Karpen, Samuel. (2009, September) Lessons from a faraway land: The effect of spatial distance on creative cognition. *Journal of Experimental Social Psychology*, 45(5), 1127–1131.
[79] Maddux, William, & Galinsky, Adam, (2009). Cultural borders and mental barriers: The relationship between living abroad and creativity. *Journal of Personality and Social Psychology*, 95(5), 1047–1061.
[80] Ibid. [81] Holmes, Jamie. (2015). *Nonsense* (p. 207). New York: Crown Publishers.
[82] See Schomaker, Judith, Van Bronkhorst, Marthe, & Meeter, Martjin. (2014, August 20). Exploring a novel environment improves motivation and promotes recall of words. *Frontiers in Psychology*, 5, Article 918. Steidle, Anna, & Werth, Lioba. Freedom from constraints: Darkness and dim illumination promote creativity. *Journal of Environmental Psychology*, 35, 67–80. Oppezzo, Marily, & Schwartz, Daniel. (2014). Give your ideas some legs: The positive effect of walking on creative thinking. *Journal of Experimental Psychology: Learning, Memory, and Cognition*, 40(4), 1142–1152. University of Minnesota. (2007, April 25). Ceiling height can affect how a person thinks, feels and acts. *ScienceDaily*. Mehta, Ravi, Rui, Zhu, & Cheema, Amar. (2012). Is noise always bad? Exploring the effects of ambient noise on creative cognition. *Journal of Consumer Research*, 39(4), 784–799.
[83] Catmull, Ed. (2014). *Creativity, Inc.* (p. 316). New York: Random House.

skills, and incorporate more ideas from sources and people previously neglected. As Catmull explains, "engaging with exceptionally hard problems forces us to think differently."[84]

- *Expand perspectives.* Catmull also warns us that "we distort our own view of the world, largely because we think we see more than we actually do."[85] Our self-confidence in our perspectives is even more dangerous when we have been successful because success fosters a belief that we are seeing *and* doing things correctly. And "there is nothing quite as effective, when it comes to shutting down alternative viewpoints, as being convinced you are right."[86] Alternative viewpoints, Catmull believes, are essential to creative problem solving; since we cannot comprehend or foresee all facets of a problem, we have to elicit and combine multiple perspectives. As Catmull notes, "different viewpoints are additive rather than competitive."[87]
- *Seek complexity.* Creative people have complex personalities. They are both differentiated (many distinctive parts) and integrated (several parts working together).[88] Their personalities blend traits that most people regard as contradictory and opposing. This complexity necessitates and generates a higher order of thinking that is simultaneously adaptable and critical. "Evolution," Csikszentmihalyi writes, "appears to favor organisms that are complex, that is, differentiated and integrated at the same time."[89]
- *Produce lots of ideas.* Many people seem to believe that creative geniuses produce one brilliant idea after another. In reality, creative people are distinguished by the sheer volume of their work: "the more total products, the more successful products – and the more unsuccessful products."[90] Pablo Picasso sketched, painted, and sculpted more than 20,000 works; Albert Einstein wrote 240 publications; Thomas Edison owned 1,093 patents; and Johann Sebastian Bach composed 20 pages per day.[91] The link between quantity and quality in creativity is called the "equal-odds rule," which states that "the relationship between the number of hits (i.e., creative successes) and the total number of works

[84] Ibid. at 318. [85] Ibid. at 172. [86] Ibid. at 173. [87] Ibid. at 174.
[88] Csikszentmihalyi, Mihaly. (1996). *Creativity* (p. 362). New York: HarperCollins. [89] Ibid.
[90] Simonton, Dean. (1997). Creative productivity: A predictive and explanatory model of career trajectories and landmarks. *Psychological Review*, 104, 66–89.
[91] Paik, S.J. (2013). Nurturing talent, creativity and productive giftedness: A new mastery model. In Kim, Kyung Hee, Kaufman, James, Baer, John, & Sriraman, Bharath. (Eds.). *Creatively gifted students are not like other gifted students* (p. 101). Rotterdam, The Netherlands: Sense Publishers. Robinson, Andrew. (2010). *Sudden genius* (p. 317). New York: Oxford University Press.

produced in a given time period is positive, linear, stochastic, and stable."[92] In other words, start generating ideas and don't wait for the Muse to arrive or for perfection to suffuse your thoughts.

FAIRNESS

Our expectation of fairness is timeless and universal. When we recall people who serve as icons of wisdom throughout history, a personal sense of fairness and a desire to ensure fairness for others are often distinguishing characteristics. To be wise, therefore, is to honor, practice, and inspire fairness.

The sense of fairness appears to be innate, hardwired into our brains.[93] After viewing fMRI scans showing areas of the brain activated when making ethical decisions, California Institute of Technology professor Steven Quartz concludes, "The fact that the brain has such a robust response to unfairness suggests that sensing unfairness is a basic evolved capacity."[94] Quartz adds, "Our basic impulse to be fair isn't a complicated thing that we learn."[95] Human reaction to unfairness thus is more visceral than deliberative and has evolved to protect individuals and advance society.[96]

Our visceral, innate rejection of unfairness is evident throughout the world. People consistently get angry when they perceive violations of fairness norms. In the "ultimatum game," for instance, two individuals have to agree on the allocation of a fixed sum of money, and they forfeit the entire sum if they cannot reach an agreement. Although any allocation is objectively better than forfeiting the entire sum, people are offended if they are offered less than one-half of the money available for distribution.[97] Consistent with fairness principles, the most common offer in the ultimatum game is $5 when $10 is

---

[92] Jung, Rex, Wertz, Christopher, Meadows, Christine, Ryman, Sephira, Vakhtin, Andrei, & Flores, Ranee. (2015, June 25). Quantity yields quality when it comes to creativity: A brain and behavioral test of the equal-odds rule. *Frontiers in Psychology*, 6, Article 864.

[93] See Hsu, M., Anen, C., & Quartz, S.R. (2008, May 23). The right and the good: Distributive justice and neural encoding of equity and efficiency. *Science*, 320(5879), 1092. Tabibnia, Golnaz, Satpute, Ajay B., & Lieberman, Matthew D. (2008). The sunny side of fairness: Preference for fairness activates reward circuitry (and disregarding unfairness activates self-control circuitry). *Psychological Science*, 19(4), 339.

[94] Nadin, Elisabeth. (2008, May 8). How fairness is wired in the brain. *Caltech*. [95] Ibid.

[96] See Zak, Paul. (2008). *Moral markets*. Princeton, New Jersey: Princeton University Press. Henrich, Joseph, *et al.* (2010, March 18). Markets, religion, community size, and the evolution of fairness and punishment. *Science*, 327(5972), 1480–1484.

[97] See Bazerman, Max. (2002). *Judgment in managerial decision making* (pp. 86–95). Hoboken, New Jersey: John P. Wiley & Sons. Kahneman, Daniel. (2011). *Thinking, fast and slow* (pp. 304–309). New York: Farrar, Straus and Giroux.

available. Offers below $2 are consistently rejected, even though both parties forfeit the entire $10 when they cannot agree on an allocation.[98] The rejection of unfair offers in the ultimatum game has been replicated around the world, and the results are insensitive to regional economic disparities. In Indonesia, for example, people reject unfair offers although the total sum available for distribution is equivalent to three days' work.[99]

Even capuchin monkeys refuse to cooperate when they see another monkey receiving preferential treatment. In one experiment, where two monkeys had received cucumber slices in exchange for pebbles and then one monkey was given a grape instead of a cucumber slice, the other monkey stopped trading and refused to eat the cucumber slice.[100] The monkey's remonstrations intensified when one monkey received a grape without having to provide a pebble in return. "In that case the other monkey often tossed away her pebble and trades took place only 20 percent of the time. In other words, the capuchins were willing to give up cheap food – after all, a cucumber for a pebble seems like a good deal – simply to express their displeasure at their comrades' unearned riches."[101]

In our efforts to be fair, we need to be mindful that fairness is expected in at least three dimensions: intent, process, and outcome. We may be perceived as acting unfairly if we violate fairness norms in any one of those dimensions. If we intend unfairness and somehow the outcomes are fair, we are nevertheless perceived to be unfair. Conversely, if unfairness is generated randomly, as in natural disasters, people are more willing to accept unfairness; they tolerate random inequality but not deliberate inequality.[102] If the process is unfair, but the outcome is fair, we may still be seen as being unfair or being indifferent to fairness.[103] And if the outcome is deliberately unfair, we certainly will be seen as acting unfairly. As indicated by the fact that at least three dimensions of fairness are critical to the perception of fairness, we have to be careful about emphasizing results ("all's well that ends well") and neglecting intentions and processes.

[98] Surowiecki, James. (2004). *The wisdom of crowds* (pp. 112–113). New York: Doubleday.
[99] Ibid. at 113.   [100] Ibid. at 113–114.   [101] Ibid.
[102] Huang, Peter. (2000). Reasons within passions: Emotions and intentions in property rights bargaining. *Oregon Law Review*, 79, 435. ("In other words, the same outcome can generate different levels of anger, depending on beliefs about the intentions of the other party.")
[103] See Tyler, Tom. (1990). *Why people obey the law*. New Haven, Connecticut: Yale University Press. Tyler, Tom. (2003). Procedural justice, legitimacy, and the effective rule of law. *Crime and Justice*, 30, 283. Robbennolt, Jennifer, & Sternlight, Jean. (2012). *Psychology for lawyers* (pp. 172–185). Chicago: American Bar Association. Brafman, Ori, & Brafman, Rom. (2008). *Sway* (pp. 115–123). New York: Doubleday. MacCoun, Robert. (2005). Voice, control and belonging. *Annual Review of Law and Social Science 2005*, 1, 171–201.

The imperative of fairness might seem incongruous in law practice because attorneys are charged with the duty of zealous advocacy on behalf of clients.[104] But the best attorneys recognize that advocacy without a sense of fairness is like a trial without admissible evidence; it's a nonstarter and makes the attorney look foolish and inexperienced. The best attorneys focus on fairness and build their cases from that foundation, as stellar trial attorneys attest:

- "Over the years I think I've placed more of an emphasis on the funda- mental fairness of a potential result. When you're a newer lawyer, you tend to be kind of clinical – adding up the evidence on each side and trying to make a precise determination. Whether it's a bench trial or a jury trial, the fairness is the most important issue."[105]
- "I spend time thinking about the simplest and clearest way to present my client's position in a manner that focuses on the fundamental fairness of what we are seeking."[106]
- "One thing I would say to myself is, 'How will I feel about this case on Sunday evening [before the case is called for trial on Monday morn- ing]? Is my position fair, just and reasonable? Do I feel good about my evaluation or do I have anxiety?' I know what anxiety is. When I had my first trials, I was assigned the worst cases – that's what happens when you start off – and I would look at them and say, 'This isn't right.' If I can say Sunday night in my heart of hearts, 'I can argue this to a jury, it's fair, just and reasonable,' and truly believe it, then I'm satisfied."[107]

Even if some attorneys are not enamored with the concept of fairness, they have to acknowledge that jurors and judges will base their decisions on the fundamental fairness of their clients' positions. As a noted litigation attorney explained, "Jurors see unfairness. If jurors perceive injustice, they don't always follow the law – they try to fix it."[108] Judges, for their part, also strive to be fair. "I think it's one of the few jobs where your mandate is to try to do the right thing," states Brian Hoffstadt, an Associate Justice of the California Court of Appeal.[109]

[104]   ABA Model Rules of Prof'l Conduct R. 1.3.
[105]   Kiser, Randall. (2011). *How leading lawyers think* (p. 45). Berlin, New York: Springer.
[106]   (2010, May 12). The List. *San Francisco Daily Journal*. (The quotation is from litigation attorney Laura W. Brill's description of her pretrial ritual).
[107]   Kiser, *supra* note 105 at 45.   [108]   Kiser, *supra* note 105 at 24.
[109]   Ortiz, Brandon. (2011, July 18). Student and teacher of the law. *San Francisco Daily Journal*, p. 2.

An expectation of fairness permeates transactional work as well.[110] The "code of fair behavior" in negotiations has three norms: (1) "you should always be trustworthy and reliable yourself;" (2) "you should be fair to those who are fair to you;" and (3) "you should let others know about it when you think they have treated you unfairly."[111] As negotiation expert Richard Shell states, "Unfair treatment, left unnoticed or unrequited, breeds exploitation – followed by resentment and the ultimate collapse of the relationship."[112]

JUDGMENT

It is axiomatic that sound judgment is an element of wisdom. Less clear is what sound judgment consists of and how it is acquired and enhanced. Although attorneys have reached a consensus that sound judgment is one of the most important skills – indeed, the most important skill by some accounts – no consensus exists about how attorneys define, develop, display, and measure sound judgment.[113]

Lawyers' judgment appears to be uniquely serendipitous in origin and operation. It is somehow acquired in law school without related courses and training and then expands spontaneously upon an attorney's passage of the bar examination. This phenomenon is especially perplexing because, as the Carnegie Foundation for the Advancement of Teaching notes, "a number of studies have shown that students' moral reasoning does not appear to develop to any significant degree during law school."[114] Law firm websites assert that their attorneys all have sound judgment, but they do not explain how it is formed, verified, and monitored after being launched from such an inauspicious base. Perhaps that is because studies indicate that practicing

[110] See Bazerman, Max, & Neale, Margaret. (1995). The role of fairness considerations and relationships in a judgmental perspective of negotiation. In Arrow, Kenneth, Mnookin, Robert, Ross, Lee, Tversky, Amos, & Wilson, Robert. (Eds.). *Barriers to conflict resolution* (pp. 87–106). New York: W.W. Norton & Company.
[111] Shell, G. Richard. (2006). *Bargaining for advantage* (p. 61). New York: Penguin Books.
[112] Ibid.
[113] See Dubey, Prashant, & Kripalani, Eva. (2013). *The generalist counsel* (p. 57). New York: Oxford University Press. Gerkman, Alli, & Cornett, Logan. (2016, July). *Foundations for practice: The whole lawyer and the character quotient* (p. 15). Denver, Colorado: Institute for the Advancement of the American Legal System. Farber, Daniel, & Sherry, Suzanna. (2010). Building a better judiciary. In Klein, David, & Mitchell, Gregory. (Eds.). *The psychology of judicial decision making* (p. 290). New York: Oxford University Press.
[114] Sullivan, William M., Colby, Anne, Wegner, Judith Welch, Bond, Lloyd, & Shulman, Lee S. (2007). *Educating lawyers: Preparation for the profession of law* (p. 133). San Francisco, California: Jossey-Bass.

attorneys' moral reasoning is "comparable to those of entering law students."[115]

If lawyers were receptive to evaluating their judgment, they would learn that there is ample room for improving judgment in litigation and transactional practices. As discussed below, attorneys' judgment suffers from overconfidence, intransigence, lack of strategy, reductionism, and motivated reasoning. Debiasing methods can correct some of these deficiencies, but many are embedded in legal reasoning and advocacy and thus are highly resistant to change.

Overconfidence. Judgment in litigation matters is persistently deficient, as demonstrated by the fact that most plaintiffs obtain a worse financial result at trial than they could have obtained by accepting the defendant's pre-trial settlement offer.[116] Defendants appear to be better calibrated than plaintiffs; one in four defendants obtains a worse financial result at trial. For those overconfident litigants who mistakenly surmised that they would do better at trial, the financial fallout is significant. The average loss for overconfident plaintiffs, as measured by the difference between what they would have obtained by accepting the pre-trial settlement offer and what they actually obtained at trial, is $73,400. For the errant defendants, the average loss is $1,403,654, as measured by the difference between the amount they could have paid in settlement and the actual amount they were ordered to pay in the verdict.[117] Plaintiffs, in sum, make errors of judgment more frequently than defendants, but defendants' errors are of greater magnitude than plaintiffs' errors.

Intransigence. On the transactional side, it is more difficult to measure the frequency and cost of poor judgment because we do not have the financial yardsticks of settlement proposals and verdicts. But the legal malpractice claims data shows that transactional practices experience a claims rate similar to litigation practices, indicating that errors in judgment are distributed equally among litigation and transactional attorneys.[118]

---

[115]   Ibid.
[116]   Kiser, Randall. (2010). *Beyond right and wrong: The power of effective decision making for attorneys and clients* (p. 85). Berlin, New York: Springer. Kiser, Randall, Asher, Martin, & McShane, Blakeley. (2008, September). Let's not make a deal: An empirical study of decision making in unsuccessful settlement negotiations. *Journal of Empirical Legal Studies*, 5(3), 551–591.
[117]   All data cited in this paragraph is derived from Kiser, *Beyond Right and Wrong*, *supra* note 116 at 85–86.
[118]   American Bar Association Standing Committee on Lawyers' Professional Liability. (2012, September). *Profile of legal malpractice claims, 2008–2011*. Chicago: American Bar Association.

We also know that, even when laws change and judicial interpretations indicate that templates and models need to be updated, attorneys are remarkably obdurate. One study of transactional attorneys, for example, revealed that there was "very little change" in contract language after an unexpected judicial interpretation of a key provision.[119] As a prominent lawyer told the law professors conducting the study, "The only time these contract terms change is when one firm gets fired and the new lawyers bring in their own standard forms. Or maybe when a senior lawyer retires and a new partner comes in with his set of forms."[120] The law professors found that "inefficient and harmful contract provisions could persist for long periods of time, even in the most sophisticated of financial markets."[121] After conducting more than 200 attorney interviews, the professors concluded, "Almost all of the lawyers producing these contracts follow the herd – a safe choice, if not one that makes a lot of sense. Maybe no one has enough time to figure out whether it makes sense or not."[122]

Lack of strategy/reductionism. Both litigation and transactional attorneys fail to exercise strategic judgment because they focus on procedures instead of outcomes and facets instead of entireties. They allow their judgment to be eclipsed by their education and training, and as a consequence, they view problem-solving reductively rather than strategically. Although "issue spotting" is a skill exalted in law school, it can be seen as narrow-mindedness and outcome avoidance in practice. Corporate counsel and a bankruptcy court judge describe the problems generated by this type of thinking:

- "Lawyers are taught to be very powerful analytically, but they are not always taught to ask large questions and then to understand what tools are necessary to answer those questions."[123] (Ben Heineman, Jr., former General Counsel, General Electric Co.)
- "I think many times attorneys get focused on the trees and forget the forest. They get wrapped on what their dispute is with the other side, the particular point they're making, and forget [to ask]: How does this motion fit into the bigger context of the case? If you succeed on this particular motion, what does it mean for your client in the rest of the case, whether it be debtor or creditor?"[124] (M. Elaine Hammond, U.S. Bankruptcy Court Judge, Northern District of California)

[119] Gulati, Mitu, & Scott, Robert. (2013). *The 3 ½ minute transaction* (p. 69). Chicago: University of Chicago Press.

[120] Ibid. at 61. [121] Ibid. at 4. [122] Ibid. at 178.

[123] Cullen, Robert. (2010). *The leading lawyer* (p. 1). St. Paul, Minnesota: West Academic Publishing.

[124] Gautham, Thomas. (2015, October 19). The forest and the trees. *San Francisco Daily Journal*, p. 2.

- "I divide the world of lawyers into those who do legal advice and those who do both business, strategic and legal advice combined. I'm looking for the latter lawyer who can combine strategic advice with business advice with legal advice so that I know when I'm going forward and doing an M&A transaction or a very significant financing or even the acquisition of a motion picture library, that I'm getting the advice based on a lawyer who has a broad breadth across a spectrum of companies in the field that I'm interested in. I'm far less concerned with the escrow agreements and the indemnities and the pure legal terms. We'll figure those out as time goes on."[125] (Wayne Levin, General Counsel, Lions Gate Entertainment Inc.)

- "I also want to make sure there's a strategic view of cases. You can sometimes end up in a situation with litigation where litigators are very good at, 'I'm going to file the next motion' or 'Here's the next thing that's going to happen.' They're very good at the tactical steps. But you say, 'What's the arc of this case? Where is it going? When are there going to be points of inflection when it's going to make sense to settle it or it's going to be very clear what the risk profile is?' And some litigators are not as good at thinking about it strategically . . . The cases where I've actually removed counsel, I thought they were just viewing it as a series of sequential steps with no particular direction or outcome."[126] (Kenneth Siegel, General Counsel, Cyan, Inc.)

Motivated reasoning. Attorneys underestimate the effects of motivated reasoning – the biased process of seeking information, evaluating evidence, and making inferences based on the desired result or conclusion.[127] In motivated reasoning, "the goal is to marshal the best available evidence for the preferred conclusion."[128] Physicist and author Leonard Mlodinow explains the difference between attorneys' motivated reasoning and scientists' evidence-based reasoning:

---

[125]   Brisbon, Melanie. (2015, August 25). The closer. *San Francisco Daily Journal*, p. 4.

[126]   Frost, Alison. (2015, April 21). Staying flexible. *San Francisco Daily Journal*, p. 4.

[127]   See Haidt, Jonathan. (2013). The new science of morality. In Brockman, John. (Ed.). *Thinking* (p. 302). New York: Harper Collins. Haidt, Jonathan. *The righteous mind* (p. 94). New York: Random House. Baumeister, Roy F., & Newman, Leonard S. (1994). Self regulation of cognitive inference and decision processes. *Personality and Social Psychology Bulletin*, 20, 3. Westen, Drew, Blagov, Pavel, Harenski, Keith, Kilts, Clint, & Hamann, Stephan. (2006). Neural bases of motivated reasoning: An fMRI study of emotional constraints on partisan political judgment in the 2004 U.S. presidential election. *Journal of Cognitive Neuroscience*, 81(11), 1947.

[128]   Baumeister & Newman, *supra* note 127 at 5.

[T]here are two ways to get at the truth: the way of the scientist and the way of the lawyer. Scientists gather evidence, look for irregularities, form theories explaining their observations, and test them. Attorneys begin with a conclusion they want to convince others of and then seek evidence that supports it, while also attempting to discredit evidence that doesn't. The human mind is designed to be both a scientist and an attorney, both a conscious seeker of objective truth and an unconscious, impassioned advocate for what we want to believe. Together these approaches vie to create our worldview.[129]

Although motivated reasoning is so well integrated into law school education and lawyers' behavior that it operates automatically and as though no other system of thinking could be activated, it is a uniquely unscientific and peculiarly ineffective approach to problem-solving.

When legal reasoning is transformed into motivated reasoning, the intended outcome, rather than the facts, drives the research, analysis, and argument. Motivated reasoning impairs the objectivity and realism required for sound judgment and renders attorneys vulnerable to biases like overconfidence, confirmation bias, and selective perception.[130] The narrow perspectives that characterize motivated reasoning spawn a host of adverse consequences ranging from biased liability evaluations to unrealistic damages projections, from excessively aggressive acquisition negotiations to indefensibly optimistic compliance counseling. Motivated reasoning brings attorneys too close to philosopher John Locke's "definition of a madman: someone 'reasoning correctly from erroneous premises.'"[131]

Once we acknowledge that attorneys' judgment can be suboptimal and frequently is impaired by overconfidence, intransigence, lack of strategy, reductionism, and motivated reasoning, we can start to develop sound judgment at two levels. First, sound judgment incorporates objectivity, foresight, discernment, strategy, a sense of proportion, compassion, and realism. Second, it reflects an absence or mitigation of decision-making biases, heuristics, and illusions like overconfidence, egocentrism, selective perception, confirmation bias, anchoring, halo effects, sunk cost bias, and status quo bias. Attorneys tend to think they meet all of the first-level requirements, and they disregard the second-level requirements. Psychologists call this the

[129] Mlodinow, Leonard. (2012). *Subliminal* (p. 200). New York: Random House.
[130] See Domnarski, William. (1994–1995). The autobiographical lawyer. *The Journal of the Legal Profession*, 19, 170. ("The lawyer's view of the law invariably becomes the view that is most consistent with the advancement of the client's cause. How the lawyer would feel about the particular legal issues if he were on the other side of the case or, better yet, on the bench, is not considered. He becomes a propagandist believing in the propaganda.")
[131] Taleb, Nassim. (2007). *The black swan* (p. 283). New York: Random House.

bias blind spot, indicating that we are unaware of our own bias. And attorneys are as susceptible to biases as the general population.[132]

To fulfill their four roles as an advisor, advocate, negotiator, and evaluator, attorneys need to overcome or at least mitigate the specific biases of over-confidence and motivated reasoning.[133] Methods to improve judgment, with a specific emphasis on mitigating biases, include:

- *Detect bias.* To probe for biases affecting how we view a particular problem and the solutions to that problem, psychologist Scott Plous recommends that we ask four questions: Am I motivated to see things a certain way? What expectations did I bring into the situation? Would I see things differently without these expectations and motives? Have I consulted with others who don't share my expectations and motives?[134]
- *Consider the opposite.* Decision-making biases are reduced when we are required to list facts and reasons contradicting our preferred position.[135] "An effective partial remedy for overconfidence," states psychologist Baruch Fischhoff, "is to search for reasons why one might be wrong."[136] In seeking and evaluating disconfirming evidence, integrative thinkers "have the predisposition and the capacity to hold two diametrically opposing ideas in their heads. And then, without panicking or simply settling for one alternative or the other, they're able to produce a synthesis that is superior to either opposing idea."[137]
- *Insist on multiple supports for positions.* Attorneys frequently fixate on a specific fact and ignore evidence inconsistent with that fact. But even the strongest fact or most incriminating piece of evidence is rarely sufficient to support an entire case or transaction. Decision makers who rely on multiple facts tend to make more accurate predictions of outcomes and hence make better decisions than people who rely on

---

[132] See Haidt (2012), *supra* note 127 at 94.
[133] Center for Professional Responsibility. (2007). *Model rules of professional conduct* (p. 1). Chicago, Illinois: American Bar Association.
[134] Plous, Scott. (1993). *The psychology of judgment and decision making* (p. 21). New York: McGraw-Hill, Inc.
[135] See Lord, Charles, Lepper, Mark, & Preston, Elizabeth. (1984). Considering the opposite: A corrective strategy for social judgment. *Journal of Personality and Social Psychology.* 47(6), 1231.
[136] Lichtenstein, Sarah, Fischhoff, Baruch, & Phillips, Lawrence. (1982). Calibration of probabilities: The state of the art to 1980. In Kahneman, Daniel, Slovic, Paul, & Tversky, Amos (Eds.). *Judgment under uncertainty: Heuristics and biases* (p. 321). Cambridge University Press.
[137] Martin, Roger. (2007). *The opposable mind* (p. 6). Boston, Massachusetts: Harvard Business School Press.

a major concept or fact.[138] Effective decision makers, therefore, insist on multiple supports for any position they take.

- *Conduct a premortem.* Decision scientist Gary Klein describes a premortem as the "hypothetical opposite of a postmortem."[139] In a premortem, attorneys imagine that a few months have elapsed and a case or transaction has failed miserably. The attorneys working on that case or transaction are "asked to independently write down every reason they can think of for the failure – especially the kinds of things they ordinarily wouldn't mention as potential problems, for fear of being impolitic."[140] The attorneys discuss each possible reason for the failure and then modify their plans and strategies to anticipate and avoid possible setbacks and failures. The premortem, Klein explains, "doesn't just help teams to identify potential problems early on. It also reduces the kind of damn-the-torpedoes attitude often assumed by people who are overinvested in a project."[141]

- *Evaluate decisions.* To improve our judgment, we must engage in an ongoing process of making decisions, evaluating them, setting new goals for our decision-making performance, and implementing new decisions. At a minimum, attorneys should keep a decision diary that includes: (1) every major decision they make; (2) the minimum requirements for that decision; (3) the three most significant premises that underpin that decision; and (4) their level of confidence in that decision. At least once per month, attorneys should review their entries in the decision diary and compare them with the actual decision outcomes.[142] This process can be harsh and, when executed properly, pushes us beyond our comfort zones, as Daniel Coyle, author of *The Talent Code*, states: "Struggle is not optional – it's neurologically required: in order to get your skill circuit to fire optimally, you must by definition fire the circuit suboptimally; you must make mistakes and pay attention to those mistakes; you must slowly teach your circuit."[143]

SELF-RENEWAL

In the short story "Nothing Succeeds," author and attorney John William Corrington uses a central character, René Landry, to depict an attorney's

---

[138] See Tetlock, *supra* note 50.
[139] Klein, Gary. (2007, September). Performing a project premortem. *Harvard Business Review*.
[140] Ibid.   [141] Ibid.
[142] See Drucker, Peter. *The effective executive*. New York: HarperBusiness.
[143] Coyle, Daniel. (2009). *The talent code* (pp. 43–44). New York: Bantam Dell.

moral exhaustion. Mr. Landry, a senior attorney trying to settle the multi-million-dollar Boudreaux estate,[144] muses:

> One of the results of aging in the law is that you are not easily gotten to. By the time you have been at it thirty or forty years, you have done so many things no one should have to do that something has drained out of you, to be replaced with the law, like a creature trapped in the mud which is hard pressed for a long, long time, leaching away the soft parts, making everything over. In stone.[145]

The lawyers in Corrington's stories are both observers and actors, simultaneously witnessing and participating in their clients' crises.[146] They find that their personal lives are overtaken and transformed by their professional lives. To reclaim their lives, they have to "break through the limitations of their lawyering" and recognize that the law has engulfed their moral sensibilities.[147]

For Corrington's fictitious lawyers and many of this nation's real lawyers, law practice functions as a compress, flattening out the uprisings of sensibility and conscience that would otherwise disrupt their lives. These disruptions are acute and threaten attorneys' efficiency in the initial years of practice. But this unease usually subsides and cedes to a professional ethos that thrives on the client satisfaction derived from the cleverest – and frequently narrowest – interpretation of legal and ethical constraints. Over time, that leaves many attorneys as listless and fossilized as René Landry.

The disconnect between the authentic self and the professional self is revealed again in Benjamin Sells' book, *The Soul of the Law*. Sells, a psychotherapist and former attorney, recalls his early encounters with the impostor syndrome (discussed in Chapter 3) and the pressures to project confidence to clients. He remembers preparing for a document production when the client's general counsel asked him whether a specific document was covered by the attorney-client privilege. Although he was familiar with the privilege, he stopped and pondered:

> But that document? Was it covered by the privilege? Damned if I knew, and I was getting ready to tell the general counsel just that when the words of the partner running the case intoned through my memory. "Don't ask any stupid

[144]   Heilman, Robert. (1994). Scene, tradition, and the unresolved in Corrington's short stories. In Mills, William, (Ed.). *John William Corrington: Southern man of letters* (p. 89). Conway, Arkansas: UCA Press.

[145]   Corrington, John. (1982). *The Southern Reporter and other stories* (p. 69). Baton Rouge, Louisiana: Louisiana State University Press.

[146]   Domnarski, William. (1994). Corrington's lawyer as moralist. In Mills, *supra* note 144 at 149.

[147]   Ibid. at 149–150.

questions," he had instructed, "We don't want them to think that we aren't on top of things. We have to build their confidence in us."[148]

Sells read the document again and calmly told the general counsel it was protected by the attorney–client privilege. The general counsel nodded in agreement, and Sells "figured he hadn't wanted to produce the document in the first place or he wouldn't have asked."[149] In his own mind, Sells "was surprised at how easy it had been," and he told himself, "what the hell, if I was wrong we could always produce it later."[150]

These tensions between the moral self and the advocate self and between the genuine self and the projected self, depicted by Corrington and Sells, are enervating. They tend to diminish our self-esteem, blunt our sensitivities, and deplete our enthusiasm. Over many years, they produce complacency without composure and cynicism without insight. They fuel what John O'Neil, author of *The Paradox of Success* and *Leadership Aikido*, calls the five most dangerous internal enemies: failure to grow emotionally, failure to make creative connections, failure to manage ego, failure to empathize, and failure to overcome alienation and boredom.[151]

Recognizing and overcoming the physical, intellectual, and moral fatigue that often attends law practice is part of being wise. That recognition requires self-reflection, self-knowledge, self-monitoring, self-regulation – and a conviction that self-renewal is a professional responsibility. When we neglect self-renewal, we downgrade the quality of service provided to clients because we lack energy, creativity, flexibility, perception, imagination, and empathy. We cannot meet clients' expectation of fidelity and competence when we are exhausted in every dimension of our personal and professional lives and can access only a small fraction of our capabilities.

Self-renewal is the antidote to torpor, and it starts with introspection and self-respect. It requires divestment of habits, beliefs, assumptions, and frames of mind that have outlived their usefulness. In developing the art of continual divestment and abandonment, Peter Drucker, the distinguished management theorist, urges us to identify our "posteriorities – the things that should no longer be done."[152] He implores, "Don't tell me what you're doing, tell me what you stopped doing."[153] That abandonment is part of wisdom was recognized by Chinese philosopher Lao Tzu nearly 2,600 years ago in his

[148] Sells, Benjamin. (1994). *The soul of the law* (p. 131). Rockport, Massachusetts: Element.
[149] Ibid. at 131.   [150] Ibid.
[151] O'Neil, John. (1997). *Leadership aikido* (pp. 64–65). New York: Harmony Books.
[152] Krames, Jeffrey. (2008). *Inside Drucker's brain* (p. 158). New York: Portfolio.
[153] Ibid. at 159.

observation, "In pursuit of knowledge, every day something is acquired. In pursuit of wisdom, every day something is dropped."[154]

In addition to identifying posteriorities and adopting the practice of continual divestment and abandonment, attorneys may benefit from considering and implementing recognized methods of self-renewal. These methods include:

- *Perspective.* Taking time off to reflect – whether two days or two months – is imperative for self-renewal. Ask yourself the basic question, "If my life continues as it is now for another ten years, what will I think about myself and how will I feel?" Questions that highlight values and facilitate career insights are: What are my core values for career, family, relationships, emotional well-being, and physical health? Am I living those values or do I just talk about them? Have any of my values changed? Do any of my values no longer fit with what I'm doing in my professional life?[155]

- *Meaning.* Aristotle said that man is a "goal seeking animal." He was only partly correct; we now recognize that "we are the meaning-seeking animal."[156] Over the long term, we need to know that our lives have positively affected the world in at least a small way. Trial attorney Richard Bridgford describes this search for meaning: "Money's always a challenge, hard work is always a challenge, but to me the biggest challenge as you grow older is you want your life to have meaning. And I feel that what we do is very important and it does have meaning and we've made the world a better place and we've forced changes that are positive."[157] Attorneys who cannot derive a sense of meaning in their current practices might consider other types of practices or become more involved in pro bono representation, nonprofit organizations, bar association programs, and civic leadership.

- *Career constraints.* Attorneys tend to limit their career options and narrowly define what it means to be successful in terms of compensation, practice areas, and law firms. As employment lawyer David Sanford observes, "Most people in law are like lemmings. They go to good schools, go for the prized big firm jobs and think – in a profoundly

[154] Muller, W. (1999). *Sabbath: Restoring the sacred rhythm of rest* (p. 134). New York: Bantam.
[155] The questions in this sentence are derived from Boyatzis, Richard, McKee, Annie, & Goleman, Daniel. (2002, April). Reawakening your passion for work. *Harvard Business Review*.
[156] Sacks, Jonathan (2011). *The great partnership: Science, religion, and the search for meaning* (p. 37). New York: Schoken Books.
[157] Newman, Deirdre. (2015, August 21). Underdog mentality. *San Francisco Daily Journal*, p. 4.

wrong way – that it's the only context to be a lawyer. The typical story in this situation is that a person takes a courageous stand and discovers there's another world. People write me that they're much happier out of big law firms. The reality is that it's a big world."[158]

- *Integration vs. reinvention.* When the practice of law has become acutely distressing, many attorneys think they need an altogether different career. They may be right, but they should consider applying their legal skills in a different context. Many successful second careers are forged from the strong analytical and problem-solving skills developed by attorneys in their initial, conventional law practices. As Marc Freedman, author of *The Big Shift: Finding Work That Matters in the Second Half of Life*, relates, "After years studying social innovators in the second half of life – individuals who have done their greatest work after 50 – I'm convinced the most powerful pattern that emerges from their stories can be described as reintegration, not reinvention. These successful late-blooming entrepreneurs weave together accumulated knowledge with creativity, while balancing continuity with change, in crafting a new idea that's almost always deeply rooted in earlier chapters and activities."[159]

- *Core habits.* The core habits – eating, exercising, and sleeping – exert an enormous effect on self-renewal and professional performance. But attorneys "sacrifice sleep and healthy habits to meet unrealistic expectations. They skip meals, eat out, skip exercising."[160] To get back on track, try eating smaller meals of lean proteins and complex carbohydrates five or six times per day. Smaller, more frequent meals modulate glucose production and increase energy.[161] Aerobic exercise also increases energy, reduces stress, and appears to retard mental deterioration. Sleep research, moreover, indicates that expert performers sleep more hours than ordinary performers, and sleep deprivation impairs memory and perception.[162]

[158] Chen, Vivia. (2016, September 13). Should Big Law be afraid of David Sanford? *The American Lawyer.*

[159] Freedman, Marc. (2014, January 1). The dangerous myth of reinvention. *Harvard Business Review.*

[160] Gordon, Leslie. (2015, July 1). How lawyers can avoid burnout and debilitating anxiety. *ABA Journal.*

[161] Schwartz, Tony. (2011, September). The skill that matters most. *Harvard Business Review.*

[162] Van der Helm, Els, Gujar, Ninad, & Walker, Matthew. (2010, March). Sleep deprivation impairs the accurate recognition of human emotions. *Sleep,* 33(3), 335–342. Havekes, Robert, et al. (2016). Sleep deprivation causes memory deficits by negatively impacting neuronal connectivity in hippocampal area CA1. *eLife,* 5, e13424. See Mah, Cheri, Mah, Kenneth,

At the center of most attorneys' unease and disenchantment is a gnawing sense that their work does not epitomize their personal values and aspirations.[163] "When people tell me that they feel stale and need some sort of renewal," John O'Neil explains, "they almost always include the need to discover a larger meaning and purpose in what they do."[164] Many attorneys satisfy this need for meaning and purpose by making changes in their personal lives and professional careers. These changes are initially difficult but ultimately enriching. But many if not most attorneys override their need for meaning by foreclosing alternatives and focusing on monetary constraints and family obligations. "What's notable about lawyers' unhappiness," states Jeena Cho, author of *The Anxious Lawyer*, "is that there's a sense of acceptance rather than outrage. Why do we accept this as the norm?"[165]

COURAGE

The novelist C. S. Lewis recognized that courage is the fulcrum of wisdom. "Courage is not simply one of the virtues," he states, "but the form of every virtue at the testing point, which means, at the point of highest reality."[166] Each constituent of wisdom – perceptiveness, foresight, fairness, creativity, judgment, and renewal – collapses if we lack the courage to act on our insights, values, and convictions. Absent courage, we voice but do not embody our values; we amplify but do not exemplify our beliefs. To better understand the requirements and risks of courage, this section discusses four distinct features of courage and then shows how it is demonstrated in two cases.

The threshold act of courage is assuming responsibility for an outcome that could be ignored, avoided, hidden, or foisted on someone else. For that reason, volition is a primary characteristic of courage. Courageous acts are intentional, voluntary, and unilateral; acts that are automatic, required, or

Kezirian, Eric, & Dement, William. (2011). The effects of sleep extension on the athletic performance of collegiate basketball players. *Sleep*, 34(7), 943.

[163] See Rhode, Deborah. (2000). *Ethics in practice* (p. 5). New York: Oxford University Press. ("Indeed, the greatest source of disappointment among surveyed lawyers is the sense that they are not 'contributing to the social good.'") Linder, Douglas, & Levit, Nancy. (2014). *The good lawyer* (p. 219). New York: Oxford University Press. ("Only 16% of lawyers surveyed indicated that their 'ability to contribute to the social good' matched their expectations when they began practicing law. A full quarter of lawyers reported, on this measure, that their expectations were 'not at all' met in their jobs.")

[164] O'Neil, John. (1993). *The paradox of success* (p. 162). New York: G.P. Putnam's Sons.

[165] Gordon, *supra* note 160.

[166] Meilaender, Gilbert. (1978). *The taste for the other: The social and ethical thought of C.S. Lewis* (p. 217). Vancouver, British Columbia: Regent College Publishing. (The Screwtape Letters, Letter XXIX).

reciprocal usually do not merit the insignia of courage. Because courage is volitional, people who are waiting for the "right opportunity" to be courageous will not find it. You must seize the opportunity to be courageous; it will not seize you. Many opportunities to be courageous may have passed by you already, treated as distractions if you were waiting for an event rather than your conscience to ignite courage.

A second quality of courage is that we are honored when we elect to be courageous but not dishonored when we decline to be courageous. Courage is admired when displayed but neither expected nor missed when suppressed. We can choose to be courageous in rescuing a drowning child in a river, for instance, but we are not blamed for deciding to stay on the riverbank in justifiable fear of the foaming waters.[167] Rational self-interest and detachment are the default mode in American society, so we are not risking financial loss, legal sanctions, or moral opprobrium if we choose to conduct our entire lives without courage. The practical consequence of our axiological ambivalence about courage is that its absence will have no discernible effect on our professional careers. If it did, you would see vastly more attorneys acting courageously.

A third feature of courage is risk – presented as a danger to our physical well-being, reputation, and financial security; a threat to our freedom, autonomy, and discretion; or an imminent loss of property, family, and friends. This is the risk that confronts and defines courageous leaders and archetypal heroes. And it is an unusual kind of risk, typified by its transparency and irreversibility. Courageous people seem to be aware of the risks they are taking before they decide to be courageous and, consequently, do not seem to be terribly surprised by the harsh consequences of their decisions. Once that courageous decision is made, moreover, it sets in motion a predictable and oftentimes irreversible chain of dangers, threats, and losses. Courage, once displayed, cannot be fully reversed, as it frequently exposes and challenges existing practices and the beneficiaries of those practices. For attorneys contemplating courage, it is important to recognize that the risks are large, palpable, and frequently irreversible. Although courageous acts may be honored in the long term, they can be immensely damaging in the short term.

---

[167] Curiously, there is no prefix or commonly used antonym for "courage." Many words have the opposite meaning when the prefixes "un," "dis," "in," or "im" are used, e.g., friendly or unfriendly and precise or imprecise, but no prefix can form an antonym of courage. It is not clear what the opposite of being courageous is since the word applies to acts of commission and lacks an antonym for acts of omission. "Cowardice," for instance, may be shameful, but the absence of courage is not necessarily cowardice.

The fourth characteristic of courage is that it is purposeful. Courage is different from raw aggression, self-sacrifice, and boldness because it is consciously directed toward the accomplishment of a socially desirable goal or a personally meaningful objective. The connection between courage and the intended result may become attenuated, but it must always be tangible. Courage without purpose is like dedication without accomplishment – admirable in the abstract but lacking the transformative quality that makes it worthwhile.

Two actual experiences serve to illustrate courage in accepting professional responsibility, eschewing conventionality, taking risks, and trying to achieve goals. The first incident, described by Michael Tigar, the renowned trial attorney and law professor, occurred after a former law review editor-in-chief had joined a major law firm and accepted a court appointment as counsel for a criminal defendant:

> He rose to cross-examine the prosecution's leading witness, and realized that he did not know how to get the impeaching document into evidence before the jury. The jury found his client guilty. He then moved for a new trial, confessing his difficulty, on the basis that the client had received ineffective assistance of counsel. The trial court granted the motion. The law firm was not pleased, but they got over it.[168]

This attorney could have walked away from that trial and never filed the motion. Only the trial judge, opposing counsel, and perhaps the client recognized his mistake. But, as Tigar notes, this attorney "understood a basic principle about advocacy – accepting responsibility." He knew that, once he filed the motion for new trial based on his own ineffectiveness, he had irreversibly set in motion a process that would tarnish his reputation but achieve the ethically appropriate outcome.

The second experience is outside the field of law but again demonstrates the risks of being courageous. William LeMessurier had served as the structural engineering consultant for the construction of the Citicorp Center in New York City, a 59-story building. After construction was completed and the building was occupied, he was reviewing the as-built plans. He discovered that the structural steel did not comply with his plans; the joints had been bolted instead of welded.[169] He later learned that "the diagonal braces had not been treated as columns as he believed they should have been, but were,

[168] Tigar, Michael. (2009). *Nine principles of life and litigation* (p. 4). Chicago: American Bar Association.
[169] Chiles, James. (2001). *Inviting disaster* (p. 197). New York: Harper Business.

instead, treated as trusses."[170] This meant that each connection had only half the number of required bolts. After spending a weekend studying the structure and making notes and calculations, LeMessurier realized that 70-mile-per-hour winds would topple the building.[171] At that point, LeMessurier recalls, he decided that he had three options: "stay silent; commit suicide; or tell others of the problem."[172] He also considered destroying his notes.[173]

Instead of staying quiet, killing himself, or throwing his notes away, "LeMessurier blew the whistle on the whole thing."[174] He met with Citicorp's chairman and executive vice-president, explained the entire predicament and submitted a repair proposal. Citicorp representatives, in turn, met with the American Red Cross and the city's Office of Emergency Management to develop an evacuation plan for the building in case of severe winds. After the repairs were completed, LeMessurier and Citicorp executives, without attorneys, worked out a $2 million settlement. Looking back on the crisis, LeMessurier offers insights as applicable to the legal profession as they are to the engineering profession: "You have a social obligation. In return for getting a license and being regarded with respect, you're supposed to be self-sacrificing and look beyond the interests of yourself and your client to society as a whole. And the most wonderful part of my story is that when I did it, nothing bad happened."[175]

CHAPTER CAPSULE

Despite law schools' insistence on teaching students to "think like lawyers," attorneys would be more effective if they first learned to think like wise people and then learned to think like lawyers. Clients expect attorneys to be wise and assume that their legal advice reflects more sagacity than casuistry; and judges resolve disputes by relying more on their wisdom than technical legal grounds. If wisdom is the paramount quality in counseling clients and resolving conflicts, as more experienced attorneys and judges contend, attorneys should focus first on becoming wise and then, if necessary, resort to the partisan advocacy and sophistry that all too often characterize the American legal system.

Since wisdom has been neglected in attorneys' education and training, it may be difficult for attorneys to discern its constituents and learn how to apply

---

[170] Vardaro, Michael. *LeMessurier stands tall: A case study in professional ethics* (p. 5). Washington, DC: AIA Trust.

[171] Ibid. at 6.   [172] Ibid. at 7.   [173] Chiles, *supra* note 169 at 197.   [174] Ibid.

[175] Vardaro, *supra* note 170 at 17.

them in serving their clients and improving the legal profession. We can start by reflecting on the importance of seven elements of wisdom and incorporating them into our law practices: perceptiveness, foresight, creativity, fairness, judgment, self-renewal, and courage. Although attorneys may believe that other elements are equally important in developing wisdom, each of the seven elements can make an independent contribution to attorneys' performance and should be considered an integral part of professional development. If attorneys intend to merit clients' confidence in their problem-solving abilities and restore the public's confidence in their integrity, they will recognize that wisdom is more constructive than argument, more durable than opportunism, and more insightful than advocacy.

7

Leadership

Although lawyers occupy many of the most important leadership positions in the United States, they do not place a high priority on developing leadership skills and are ill-prepared for leadership positions. As law professor Deborah Rhode notes, there is a "disconnect between qualities that enable lawyers to achieve a leadership position and qualities that are necessary once they get there."[1] This disconnect is described succinctly by John Dean, the former White House Counsel for President Richard Nixon whose career was scarred by the Watergate scandal: "Lawyers are often drawn to leadership positions, but they are not very good at leading."[2]

Surveys of attorneys indicate that leadership skills are secondary to revenue-generating skills, and public opinion surveys show that attorneys are perceived to be untrustworthy in leadership positions. In the IAALS survey of 24,137 lawyers, discussed in Chapter 2, only 19 percent of attorneys thought that "demonstrate leadership" was a necessary trait for a new lawyer in the short term, and 57 percent believed that it was not necessary in the short term but must be acquired over time.[3] Nearly one in four lawyers regarded leadership as "not necessary at any point but advantageous to the lawyer's success."[4] Traits ranked higher than leadership include "adhere to proper timekeeping and/or billing practices," "learn and use relevant technologies effectively," and "delegate to and manage support staff appropriately."[5] Reflecting the relative unimportance of leadership skills, a survey of managing law firm partners

[1] Rhode, Deborah. (2011). What lawyers lack: Leadership. *University of St. Thomas Law Journal*, 9(2), 476.
[2] Dean, John. (2013, November 1). Teaching lawyers, and others, to be leaders. *Verdict*.
[3] Gerkman, Alli, & Cornett, Logan. (2016, July). *Foundations for practice: The whole lawyer and the character quotient* (p. 20). Denver, Colorado: Institute for the Advancement of the American Legal System.
[4] Ibid.   [5] Ibid. at 15, 18, 20, 21.

shows that only 30 percent of law firms provide leadership training for current and future leaders.[6] When asked, "Which resources or tools aid in the development of your strategic plan?" managing partners rank "financial analysis and reports" at the top and "firm leadership" at the bottom.[7]

The public also perceives lawyers as lacking in leadership skills and disinterested in public service. An American Bar Association (ABA) survey of public attitudes indicates that only 34 percent of citizens see lawyers as providing "leadership in the community."[8] In another ABA survey, only 39 percent of respondents agreed with the statement, "Most attorneys try to serve the public interest well."[9] The ABA pollster reported, "Americans are also uncomfortable with the connections that lawyers have with politics, the judiciary, government, big business, and law enforcement."[10] That power, the public believes, "enables them not only to play the system, but also to shape that very system."[11]

Attorneys' attitudes toward leadership are shortsighted, destructive of the public trust, and broadly irresponsible. Leadership merits a higher level of attention and respect from attorneys because attorneys are, and will remain, leaders by virtue of the power, prestige, and responsibility that accompany the license to practice law – whether they see themselves as leaders or not. The exclusive privilege to represent clients in matters that could result in their execution, loss of the right to see their own children, forfeiture of every asset they own, and expulsion from a business or organization to which they have devoted their lives makes every attorney a leader in the eyes of jurors, judges, colleagues, friends, family members, and ordinary citizens. The decision for attorneys, therefore, is not choosing or declining the mantle of leadership but determining how effectively they will discharge that duty throughout their careers.

To assist attorneys' efforts to effectively discharge the duty of leadership that attends their professional status, this chapter presents an overview of leadership concepts; identifies essential leadership traits; analyzes leadership styles; discusses the appropriate role of followers; and shows how leadership skills can be applied to the specific responsibilities of planning, leading teams, managing cases and projects, promoting moral leadership, and handling crises. Its

[6] The Remsen Group. (2013, May 9). _MPF managing partner survey results_. Atlanta, Georgia: The Remsen Group.

[7] ALM Legal Intelligence. (2012, October). Thinking like your client: Law firm strategic planning (p. 20).

[8] Hengstler, G. A. (1993). Vox populi: The public perception of lawyers: ABA poll. _American Bar Association Journal, 79_, 60.

[9] Section of Litigation, American Bar Association. (2002). _Public perceptions of lawyers: Consumer research findings_ (p. 7). Chicago: American Bar Association.

[10] Ibid. at 4.   [11] Ibid. at 4.

emphasis is on leadership in law firms, law departments, bar associations, and other legal organizations. Due to space limitations, it does not extend to lawyers' leadership in political parties, electoral campaigns, and ballot initiatives.

LEADERSHIP CONCEPTS

We tend to think of leadership in a large political or military context and overlook the fact that most of us act as leaders every day in a less public context. When we respond to a client's email, talk with a colleague about a transaction or case, or converse with a family member, we often are acting as leaders, in addition to any other roles we assume. A leadership dimension exists in many if not most of our interactions because leadership is fundamentally an effort to influence someone else – to affect their feelings, beliefs, and behavior at least in a small way. We are invariably leading people to a way of thinking or a conclusion that is either consistent with our own values or desires or compatible with our expectations of people.

To encourage a broader concept of leadership and show how leadership permeates human interactions, this section presents alternative definitions for, and describes different types of, leadership. These definitions may alert attorneys to the leadership positions they occupy but do not necessarily fulfill and the leadership types they perceive and exhibit but do not necessarily comprehend. This emphasis on leadership fundamentals is warranted because, unlike business school, law schools generally do not provide leadership training. As law professor Scott Westfahl explains, "Lawyers begin their professional careers at a significant disadvantage and it is hard to catch up, especially when you do not know what you do not know."[12]

Definitions

Because leadership occurs in multiple contexts, there is no single, generally accepted definition of leadership. Leading experts on leadership proffer a variety of leadership definitions:

- "Leadership is not magnetic personality – that can just as well be a glib tongue. It is not 'making friends and influencing people' – that is flattery. Leadership is lifting a person's vision to higher sights, the raising

[12] Westfahl, Scott. (2015). Learning to lead: Perspective on bridging the lawyer leadership gap. In Normand-Hochman, Rebecca (Ed.). *Leadership for lawyers* (p. 80). Surrey, England: Globe Law and Business Ltd.

of a person's performance to a higher standard, the building of a personality beyond its normal limitations."[13] (Peter Drucker, *Management:
Tasks, Responsibilities, Practices*)

- "Leadership is the art of mobilizing others to want to struggle for shared
aspirations."[14] (James Kouzes and Barry Posner, *The Leadership Challenge*)
- "Leadership defines what the future should look like, aligns people with
that vision, and inspires them to make it happen despite the obstacles."[15]
(John Kotter, *Leading Change*)
- "I define leadership as leaders inducing followers to act for certain
goals that represent the values and the motivations – the wants and
needs, the aspirations and expectations – of both leaders and followers.
And the genius of leadership lies in the manner in which leaders see and
act on their own and their followers' values and motivations."[16] (James
MacGregor Burns, *Leadership*)

These definitions suggest that leadership has inspirational, educational, inno-
vational, motivational, and organizational dimensions but does not require
that all dimensions be evident at the same time. Considering the broad range
of conduct that qualifies as leadership, we may find psychologist Howard
Gardner's definition of a leader to be useful: "A leader is an individual (or,
rarely, a set of individuals) who significantly affects the thoughts, feelings, and/
or behaviors of a significant number of individuals."[17] And that is exactly what
nearly all attorneys do over the course of their careers.

Types

Leadership scholars recognize two basic categories of leadership: transactional/
transformative and direct/indirect.[18] The difference between transactional
and transformative leaders is critical and provides a useful framework for
understanding our expectations of leaders:

---

[13] Drucker, Peter. (1974). *Management: Tasks, responsibilities, practices.* (pp. 370–371). London: Routledge.
[14] Kouzes, James, & Posner, Barry. (1995). *The leadership challenge* (p. 30). San Francisco: Jossey-Bass.
[15] Kotter, John. (1996). *Leading change* (p. 25). Brighton, Massachusetts: Harvard Business Press.
[16] Burns, James MacGregor. (1978). *Leadership* (p. 19). New York: Harper Torchbooks.
[17] Gardner, Howard. (1995). *Leading minds* (p. ix). New York: Basic Books.
[18] For applications of leadership concepts and research to attorneys, see Polden, Donald. (2012). Leadership matters: Lawyers' leadership skills and competencies. *Santa Clara Law Review*, 52, 899. Apistola, Martin, & Gottschalk, Petter. (2012). *Essential knowledge and management issues in law firms* (pp. 164–167). Boca Raton, Florida: Universal-Publishers. Besmer, Matthew. (2015, March 13). Your brain on leadership. *Law Practice Today*.

The relations of most leaders and followers are *transactional* – leaders approach followers with an eye to exchanging one thing for another: jobs for votes, or subsidies for campaign contributions. Such transactions comprise the bulk of the relationships among leaders and followers, especially in groups, legislatures, and parties. *Transforming* leadership, while more complex, is more potent. The transforming leader recognizes and exploits an existing need or demand of a potential follower. But, beyond that, the transforming leader looks for potential motives in followers, seeks to satisfy higher needs, and engages the full person of the follower. The result of transforming leadership is a relationship of mutual stimulation and elevation that converts followers into leaders and may convert leaders into moral agents.[19]

Leadership in law firms usually fits into the transactional model, which is characterized by three norms: (1) contingent rewards (money is exchanged for effort and good performance); (2) management by exception (action is taken only when rules or standards are violated); and (3) passivity (decisions are avoided).[20] People working with transactional leaders tend to be less motivated, and organizations led by transactional leaders "are less effective than those whose leaders are transformational."[21]

In addition to making a distinction between transactional and transformative leadership, scholars distinguish between direct and indirect leadership. Direct leaders are purposeful and frequently forceful in attempting to affect others' behavior. Indirect leaders do not necessarily intend to influence other people but ultimately change their behavior through their ideas and personal lives. Gardner uses Winston Churchill and Albert Einstein as examples of these two types of leadership:

> Churchill exerted his influence in a direct way, through the stories he communicated to various audiences; hence, I term him a *direct* leader. Einstein exerted his influence in an indirect way, through the ideas he developed and the ways that those ideas were captured in some kind of a theory or treatise; hence, he qualifies as an *indirect* leader.[22]

"Direct leadership," Gardner points out, "is more tumultuous and risky, but in the short run, it can be more efficient and more effective."[23] Indirect leaders, in contrast, do not have the sense of immediacy that frequently drives direct

---

[19] Burns, *supra* note 16 at 4. For additional information regarding transformative leadership, see Bass, Bernard M. (1990). From transactional to transformational leadership: Learning to share the vision. *Organizational Dynamics*, 18(3), 19–31. Simola, S., Barling, J., & Turner, N. (2012). Transformational leadership and leaders' mode of care reasoning. *Journal of Business Ethics*, 108(2), 229–237.

[20] Bass, *supra* note 19 at 22.   [21] Ibid.   [22] Gardner, *supra* note 17 at 6.   [23] Ibid. at 294.

leaders, and they can afford to be more reflective and less efficient. Assessing the impact of indirect leaders, Gardner finds that "often their impact proves more enduring, if slower to emerge."[24] Gardner also notes that leaders may change their style over their lifetimes; some leaders transition from being indirect to direct leaders as their influence grows, but it is rare for someone to shift from being a direct leader to an indirect leader.

LEADERSHIP TRAITS

When attorneys think of leadership, they often visualize a stereotypical, charismatic person leading a cadre of followers. This is a very narrow view of leadership and leads to negative perceptions of leadership and permanent self-perceptions as either a follower or a leader. Leadership, in fact, is a highly nuanced skill that is displayed in a vast range of personalities and has little to do with charisma. As Peter Drucker, whose consulting clients included General Electric, Coca-Cola, and Toyota, explains:

> Among the most effective leaders I have encountered and worked with in a half century, some locked themselves into their office and others were ultra gregarious ... Some were quick and impulsive; others studied and studied again and then took forever to come to a decision. Some were warm and instantly "simpatico;" others remained aloof even after years of working closely with others, not only with outsiders like me but with the people within their own organization ... Some were as austere in their private lives as a hermit in the desert; others were ostentatious and pleasure-loving and whooped it up at every opportunity. Some were good listeners, but among the most effective leaders I have worked with were also a few loners who listened only to their own inner voice. The one and only personality trait the effective ones I have encountered did have in common was something they did not have: they had little or no "charisma" and little use either for the term or for what it signifies.[25]

Although charisma "has fertilized the study of leadership," its meaning evades consistent application; and even when charisma appears to promote leadership effectiveness, we cannot discern whether it is an independent personality characteristic or a quality created and superimposed by followers. Consequently, as Burns declares, "it is impossible to restore the word to analytic duty."[26]

---

[24] Ibid.
[25] Hesselbein, Frances, Goldsmith, Marshall, & Beckhard, Richard (Eds.). (1997). *The leader of the future* (p. xii). San Francisco: Jossey-Bass.
[26] Burns, *supra* note 16 at 244.

In attempting to identify the traits of successful leaders, researchers have produced a litany of studies with seemingly inconsistent results.[27] This inconsistency may reflect the fact that leadership skills are context-dependent and are not amenable to identification and ranking in the abstract. Despite the limitations of the leadership research, we can discern some traits that come close to being uniformly defined and displayed. Reviewing the research regarding leadership skills, Rhode finds that they "cluster in five categories:

- values (such as integrity, honesty, trust, and an ethic of service);
- personal skills (such as self-awareness, self-control, and self-direction);
- interpersonal skills (such as social awareness, empathy, persuasion, and conflict management);
- vision (such as forward-looking and inspirational);
- technical competence (such as knowledge, preparation, and judgment)."[28]

"Not only are these qualities neglected in legal education, many of them are not characteristic of individuals who choose law as a career," asserts Rhode. "Several decades of research find that attorneys' distinctive personality traits can pose challenges for lawyers as leaders, particularly when they are leading other lawyers."[29]

Research regarding leadership traits is not so much conflicting as it is diffuse. Researchers may be describing similar traits, but they lack a common vocabulary and consistent methodology to identify essential leadership traits. To provide a balanced perspective on leadership traits, it is instructive to review and compare the results of leadership research conducted by Warren Bennis, Joan Goldsmith, James Kouzes, Barry Posner, and the consulting firm Accenture. Bennis and Goldsmith find that leaders share six competencies: (1) mastering the context (seeing and understanding how external events will affect their decisions); (2) knowing themselves (acquiring self-knowledge

---

[27] Rhode, Deborah. (2013). *Lawyers as leaders* (p. 8). New York: Oxford University Press. For leadership traits, see Goleman, Daniel. (2004, January). What makes a leader? *Harvard Business Review*. Avolio, Bruce, & Hannah, Sean. (2008). Developmental readiness: Accelerating leader development. *Consulting Psychology Journal*, 60(4), 331–347. Kirkpatrick, Shelley, & Locke, Edwin. (1991). Leadership: Do traits matter? *Academy of Management Executive*, 5(2), 48. Judge, Timothy, Bono, Joyce, Ilies, Remus, & Gerhardt, Megan. (2002). Personality and leadership: A qualitative and quantitative review. *Journal of Applied Psychology*, 87(4), 765. McClelland, David. (1998). Identifying competencies with behavioral event interviews. *Psychological Science*, 9(5), 331.

[28] Rhode (2013), *supra* note 27 at 4.

[29] Rhode, Deborah. (2015). Teaching leadership. In Maranville, Deborah, Bliss, Lisa Radtke, Kaas, Carolyn Wilkes, & Lopez, Antoinette Sedillo. (Eds.). *Building on best practices: Transforming legal education in a changing world* (p. 315). New Providence, New Jersey: LexisNexis.

through introspection and feedback); (3) creating a vision (forming and living a compelling vision to direct their plans and motivate others to make changes); (4) communicating with meaning (shaping communication to incorporate followers' concerns and intentions); (5) building trust through integrity (demonstrating values through consistent and reliable actions); and (6) realizing intentions through actions (producing concrete results that embody visions and values).[30] Although leaders "come in every race, ethnicity, age, sexual orientation, role, and circumstance imaginable," Bennis and Goldsmith assert, they all share these "six clear and powerful competencies."[31]

Kouzes and Posner make a valuable contribution to our understanding of leadership by identifying and comparing the traits we expect from leaders and colleagues. Based on their surveys of more than 15,000 managers and their reviews of 400 case studies, Kouzes and Posner rank the ten most desirable characteristics of leaders as follows: honest, forward-looking, inspiring, competent, fair-minded, supportive, broad-minded, intelligent, straightforward, and courageous.[32] The ten most desirable characteristics of colleagues, they report, are: honest, cooperative, dependable, competent, intelligent, supportive, straightforward, broad-minded, imaginative, and inspiring.[33] The traits considered to be critical for leaders, but not for colleagues, are forward-looking, fair-minded, and courageous. Conversely, the traits considered to be important for colleagues, but not for leaders, are cooperative, dependable, and imaginative. Although honesty and competence are highly ranked traits for both leaders and colleagues, leaders are separated from colleagues by a future orientation (vision and courage); and colleagues are separated from leaders by a collaborative orientation (cooperation and reliability).

The Accenture global survey of 3,600 business professionals presents additional perspectives on leadership traits. The five most important leadership traits that emerge from that survey are "effective communications skills; ability to manage change; ability to inspire and bring new ideas; understanding roles, responsibilities and expectations of each team member; and willingness to make difficult decisions."[34] This survey also identifies five traits most likely to cause leadership failures: "poor interpersonal skills and inaccessibility with peers and supervisors; ineffective communications skills; lack of clarity to roles, responsibilities and expectations of each team member; lack of inspiration and new ideas; and lack of proficiency with tools and technologies."[35]

---

[30] Bennis, Warren, & Goldsmith, Joan. (2010). *Learning to lead* (pp. xxi–xxii). New York: Basic Books.

[31] Ibid. at xxi.

[32] Kouzes, James, & Posner, Barry (1993). *Credibility* (p. 255). San Francisco: Jossey-Bass.

[33] Ibid.   [34] Accenture. (2015). *#ListenLearnLead Global Research* (p. 37).   [35] Ibid. at 36.

These leadership failure traits mirror deficiencies and errors detected in other studies. The major factors in leadership failures, according to those studies, are "incompetence, rigidity, arrogance, callousness, dishonesty, indecision, and intemperance. Inability to establish a clear mission, learn from mistakes, model integrity and respond to the needs of others are among the fatal flaws that can derail an otherwise promising career."[36]

This survey of leadership traits reveals that leadership skills are always within our grasp. We can discern the qualities that enable us to function as effective leaders, yet we sometimes lack the focus and motivation necessary to merit respect and inspire achievement. This survey of traits also assists us in demolishing the "five myths" of leadership: leadership is a rare and unusual talent; leaders are born, not developed; leaders are always charismatic; leadership exists only at the top of an organization; and leaders control and direct others.[37] As Rhode observes, "most leadership skills are acquired, not genetically based, and decades of experience with leadership development indicate that its major capabilities can be learned."[38]

LEADERSHIP STYLES

In addition to identifying leadership traits, researchers have defined and categorized leadership styles. These styles generally fall into six categories. Although you might not have considered what your leadership style is, these categories provide a framework for understanding the strengths and weaknesses of your individual approach to leading people:

- *Directive/coercive.* This is a "command and control" approach used by high achievers trying to lead under stress.[39] The directive/coercive style might be appropriate in crises, but it tends to quash creativity and individual initiative.
- *Visionary/authoritative.* Authoritative leaders "mobilize people toward a vision."[40] They articulate a strategy and inspire people to adopt and implement that strategy.[41]
- *Affiliative/supportive.* Affiliative leaders emphasize the employees' emotional needs and tend to be conflict avoidant. They are supportive,

[36] Rhode (2013), *supra* note 27 at 9.   [37] Bennis & Goldsmith, *supra* note 30 at 22–25.
[38] Rhode (2013), *supra* note 27 at 24.
[39] Spreier, Scott, Fontaine, Mary, & Malloy, Ruth. (2006, June). Leadership run amok. *Harvard Business Review.*
[40] Rhode (2013), *supra* note 27 at 12.
[41] Richard, Larry, & Sirkin, Mark. (2008, December). Six styles of leadership: How will you handle your firm's reins? *Law Practice Magazine.*

empathetic, and positive and devote little time to changing others' performance.

- *Participative/democratic leaders.* Participative leaders are consensus builders. They elicit others' opinions and try to engage all affected parties in the decision-making process.
- *Pacesetting/heroic.* Pacesetters lead "by example and personal heroics."[42] They set high standards and are easily frustrated when other people are not committed to meeting those standards. As a consequence, they find it difficult to delegate work and will take work back when necessary to "get it right." The pacesetting style eventually demoralizes people.
- *Coaching/mentoring.* A coaching leader "works closely with individuals and strives to bring out the best in people by building relationships."[43] He/she takes a long-term perspective on developing people and sees their investment in people "as a means of developing the firm for the future."[44]

These leadership styles have dramatically different effects on followers' motivation and performance. When these styles are ranked by their effectiveness in motivating and engaging employees, the most effective style is visionary/ authoritative, followed in descending order by affiliative/supportive, participative/democratic, coaching/mentoring, pacesetting/heroic and directive/coercive.[45] The most common leadership styles for attorneys are pacesetting/heroic and directive/coercive – the two least effective styles.[46]

PLANNING AND STRATEGY

Leaders convey a vision, and perhaps more importantly, they develop plans for implementing that vision. They "convert purpose and vision into actions that will produce results," state Bennis and Goldsmith.[47] Planning skills, therefore, are central to a leader's success, and although many people can articulate

[42] Spreier, Fontaine, & Malloy, *supra* note 39.   [43] Richard & Sirkin, *supra* note 41.
[44] Ibid.
[45] Spreier, Fontaine, & Malloy, *supra* note 39. Polden, *supra* note 18 at 909. See Goleman, Daniel. (2000, March–April). Leadership that gets results. *Harvard Business Review.* Brown, Archie. (2014). *The myth of the strong leader: Political leadership in the modern age.* New York: Basic Books.
[46] Wanser, Donna. (2012, February). *The emotional intelligence of general counsels in relation to lawyer leadership* (pp. 4, 31). Unpublished doctoral dissertation, Pepperdine University Graduate School of Education and Psychology. See Richard & Sirkin, *supra* note 41. Goleman, Daniel. (2013). *Focus* (pp. 227–230). New York: HarperCollins.
[47] Bennis & Goldsmith *supra* note 30 at xxi.

a vision, few can implement it. Perhaps the primary reason that many vision-aries do not become leaders is their inability to develop and implement feasible plans to execute an otherwise compelling vision.

Vision can be so captivating and inspiring that we overlook the importance of plans and strategy and confuse the power of an idea with the effectuation of that idea. Some ideas appear to be so fundamentally correct and persuasive that they must be self-executing, but history informs us that concepts without sound plans are stimulating but unavailing; they make for great reading and lousy logistics. We frequently look at ideas that failed and conclude that they were "ahead of their time," but it would be more accurate to conclude that they were ahead of their strategies and plans.

Would-be leaders flounder when they fail to understand that "a strategy is *not* a vision, which is an inspiring portrait of what it will look and feel like to pursue and achieve the organization's mission and goals."[48] Strategy, unlike vision, requires explicit decisions about how and when resources will be allocated to actualize a vision and about who can be entrusted with that responsibility. When people disregard planning and blithely say, "I'm a big picture person," they are signaling that they may not become leaders; a person who can envision but not implement has limited value and may not pass the leadership threshold. They overlook the fact that "most leaders are pragmatic dreamers *and* practical idealists who create solutions to seemingly overwhelm-ing problems."[49]

When leaders turn their focus to plans and strategies, they must be alert to three basic problems: (1) optimistic overconfidence; (2) unrealistic time estimates; and (3) reluctance to abandon ideas that are not working. Each of these problems is rooted in hubris, the egocentric force that enables us to believe we will achieve results that are denied to mere mortals. When we are enveloped by this cognitive conceit, we ignore discrepancies between our constructed image and our actual performance; and even when our plans and strategies are undermined by reality, we decide that we just need to be patient or change the metrics. The concept of hubris is captured in the biblical paraphrase, "pride cometh before a fall."[50] But as management consultant Steven Berglas points out, in actuality "pride did not just goeth before the fall; it actually *caused* the fall."[51]

---

[48] Watkins, Michael. (2007, September 10). Demystifying strategy: The what, who, how, and why. *Harvard Business Review*.

[49] Bennis & Goldsmith, *supra* note 30 at xxi. Emphasis provided.

[50] "Pride goeth before destruction, and an haughty spirit before a fall." Proverbs 16:18. (King James Version).

[51] Berglas, Steven. (2014, April 14). Rooting out hubris, before a fall. *Harvard Business Review*.

To mitigate optimistic overconfidence, especially in the early phases of a project, leaders benefit from challenging the information that underpins proposals and developing more expansive "worst-case scenarios." Leaders should probe to determine whether proponents are affected by self-interest that leads to motivated reasoning and then causes motivated errors. "A proposal from a set of individuals who stand to gain more than usual from the outcome – either in financial terms or, more frequently, in terms of organizational power, reputation or career options – needs especially careful quality control," states psychologist Daniel Kahneman.[52] To counter biases arising from self-interest, leaders can ask about other alternatives that were considered and dissenting viewpoints that may have been minimized or disregarded.

An additional method of testing biases is challenging the worst-case and best-case scenarios envisioned by plan proponents. When developing worst-case scenarios, people remain guardedly optimistic about plans they support, and that optimism suffuses their worst-case scenarios. As Kahneman explains, our worst-case scenarios are fairly rosy relative to the actual risks:

> Many companies, when making important decisions, ask strategy teams to propose a range of scenarios, or at least a best and a worst case. Unfortunately, the worst case is rarely bad enough. A decision maker should ask: Where did the worst case come from? How sensitive is it to our competitors' responses? What could happen that we have not thought of?[53]

Conversely, decision makers need to question whether the best-case scenario is excessively cautious. When demand for the Subaru Forester automobile exceeded expectations, for example, Subaru of America Chairman Takeshi Tachimori realized that his company had planned adequately for worst-case scenarios but inadequately for best-case scenarios: "We know how to study worst-case scenarios, but we've never examined a best-case scenario. It will be more problematic if we miss out on an important opportunity so we should examine these kinds of best-case scenarios as well."[54] As Kahneman and Tachimori's comments indicate, the quality of our plans and strategies is dependent on our imagination, and our imagination is curiously limited in bracketing worst-case and best-case scenarios.

Once plans have been probed for decision-making biases, effective leaders question the time and scheduling estimates to determine whether they are

[52] Kahneman, Daniel, Lovallo, Dan, & Sibony, Olivier. (2011, June). The big idea: Before you make that big decision. *Harvard Business Review*.

[53] Ibid.

[54] Takahashi, Yoshio & Koh, Yoree. (2013, August 19). Subaru's got a big problem: It's selling too many cars. *The Wall Street Journal*.

realistic. These estimates tend to be dangerously positive because people succumb to the "planning fallacy" – our inclination to "habitually under-estimate how long it will take to get tasks done."[55] We are chronically opti-mistic about how soon we can complete projects and chronically tardy in actually completing them. In one study, for example, students were asked to estimate how long it would take to complete their honors thesis under three scenarios: a best-case scenario, a realistic scenario, and a worst-case scenario. The student predictions were 27 days (best-case scenario), 34 days (realistic scenario), and 49 days (worst-case scenario). In fact, the students' average time for completion of their thesis was 55 days, and most of the students did not complete their thesis within the time projected for the worst-case scenario ("if everything went as poorly as it possibly could").[56] These results have been replicated in numerous contexts, and although most study participants did not meet their projected deadline, "they were quite confident that they would meet their predictions."[57] Even when requested to "make a highly conserva-tive forecast, a prediction that they felt virtually certain that they would fulfill, students' confidence in their time estimates far exceeded their accomplishments."[58]

Our persistent inability to meet projected deadlines is aggravated by our inability to focus on the tasks we consider to be most important. So even if our actual time estimates for a project are accurate, the estimates become irrele-vant because we end up spending our time on different tasks. When managers were asked in one study to list the most important problems facing their organizations and then were asked a week later how they actually spent their time, "no manager reported any activity which could be directly associated with the problems he had described."[59] When law firm managing partners are asked, "What do you believe to be your most important contributions in your role as managing partner?" the contribution they rank highest is "Initiating changes necessary to ensure long-term success." But when asked, "Where do you spend most of your time?" the partners' most common response is "managing day-to-day administrative affairs of the firm." The two tasks they ranked lowest in actual time spent are "initiating changes necessary to ensure long-term success" and "defining and implementing long-term strategic

---

[55] Epley, Nicholas. (2014). *Mindwise* (p. 18). New York: Alfred A. Knopf. [56] Ibid.

[57] Buehler, Roger, Griffin, Dale, & Ross, Michael. (2002). Inside the planning fallacy: The cause and consequences of optimistic time predictions. In Gilovich, Thomas, Griffin, Dale, & Kahneman, Daniel (Eds.). *Heuristics and biases* (p. 252). New York: Cambridge University Press.

[58] Ibid.

[59] Heath, Chip, & Heath, Dan. (2013). *Decisive* (p. 187). New York: Crown Business.

objectives."[60] One of the most challenging responsibilities for leaders, therefore, is devoting time to the most consequential tasks instead of the most immediate tasks and determining whether time estimates are not only feasible but also practical.

In addition to mitigating overconfidence and assessing time estimates in plans and strategies, effective leaders strive for flexibility and are receptive to modifying and abandoning plans.[61] They recognize the limitations of planning and avoid the mistake described in the military as "mistaking a map for the terrain." They constantly monitor and evaluate the implementation of plans, knowing that their purpose is adaptation rather than vindication. Even plans that, in retrospect, seem brilliant in concept and execution were continually tested and modified and would have failed absent leaders' flexibility and adaptability. The Marshall Plan for the reconstruction of Europe after World War II, for example, is considered a masterpiece of vision and planning. But it was subjected to numerous, ongoing changes: "The Marshall Plan was less a plan than a long series of planning activities – a set of well-reasoned beliefs – each of which had to take into account new variables, new limits, and practical choices among equally desirable (or noxious) alternatives, all the while holding firm to a few key principles."[62] Although planning is essential to effective leadership, it serves to guide, not control, organizations; and it can be most effective when it exposes disparities between the problems we identified and the problems that emerged.

TEAM LEADERSHIP

For most attorneys, the crucible of leadership will be teams. Attorneys may lead teams of professionals on client cases and transactions, and they may be asked to join committees, task forces, boards of directors, and advisory councils in a community service capacity or as members of the organizations in which they practice law. Although attorneys may perceive these responsibilities to be practicing law or collaborating with similarly dedicated people, they are fundamentally leadership positions and require leadership skills. When we regard leadership positions as just an extension of practices and habits we have adopted for our own work, we are disappointing the people who look to us for leadership and missing an opportunity for personal growth.

---

[60]   The Remsen Group, *supra* note 6.
[61]   See Royer, Isabelle. (2003, February). Why bad projects are so hard to kill. *Harvard Business Review.*
[62]   O'Neill, John. (1997). *Leadership aikido* (p. 139). New York: Harmony Books.

Psychologists have studied expert "dream teams" extensively. They find that highly effective expert teams display nine distinct characteristics:[63]

Beliefs

1. *Explicit purpose and vision.* Expert teams share and articulate common missions, values, purposes, visions, and goals.

Relationships

2. *Clear roles and accountability.* Each team member has clearly defined, but flexible, responsibilities and understands the roles, skills, and responsibilities of other members.

3. *Mental models.* Team members have shared mental models of the team objectives, what members can expect from each other, and how they can anticipate each member's requirements and actions. Because they have a shared understanding of the team's processes and objectives, they anticipate needs without the necessity of explicit communication.

4. *Confidence and trust.* Expert team members trust each other's intentions, play down status and power differences, and are highly confident about the group's abilities. They can confront each other with relative ease and resolve conflicts promptly.

5. *Strong leadership skills.* Leaders of expert teams "are not just technically competent; they possess quality leadership skills."[64] They know how to motivate, organize, and lead groups; and they merit team members' trust and respect by consistently exhibiting domain expertise and exceptional leadership skills. In working with people, they convey a genuine interest in and concern about them, and they motivate them through clear tasks, cooperation, coordination, and regular updates. Leaders of expert teams are highly motivated themselves; they monitor their own leadership skills and "self-correct" when necessary.

Operations

6. *Organization and coordination.* Expert teams assign work thoughtfully to optimize individual expertise while balancing out the workload; they

---

[63] The nine characteristics summarized in this section are based on Salas, Edward, Rosen, Michael, Burke, C. Shawn, Goodwin, Gerald, & Fiore, Stephen. (2006). The making of a dream team: When expert teams do best. In Ericsson, K. Anders, Charness, Neil, Feltovich, Paul, & Hoffman, Robert. (Eds.). *The Cambridge handbook of expertise and expert performance* (pp. 446–449). New York: Cambridge University Press. The description of these characteristics includes concepts and excerpts from Kiser, Randall. (2010). *Beyond right and wrong: The power of effective decision making for attorneys and clients* (p. 384). Berlin, New York: Springer.

[64] Salas, *supra* note 63 at 448.

exhibit a keen ability to assess the task requirements and match those requirements with team members' expertise and availability. They also change work environments (e.g., proximity of physical space and technical support) to facilitate communication and coordination.

7. *Self-correction and adaptation.* Expert teams are flexible and adaptable; they reassign functions and form new routines as necessary to adjust to different challenges.

8. *Prebriefing and debriefing.* Members of expert teams regularly self-assess their effectiveness with prebrief/perform/observe/assess/debrief protocols to provide feedback, anticipate problems, and confirm priorities.[65] Evaluation is both an informal, ongoing process and a formal, periodic procedure. It includes objective factors like results and efficiency and subjective factors like morale and motivation.

Results

9. *Managed outcomes.* Expert teams make better-quality decisions and are less likely to commit errors than ordinary teams. Their optimal decision-making performance is attributable, in part, to a highly efficient system of disseminating information critical to task accomplishment. Each individual understands not only what information she needs to perform effectively but anticipates and comprehends what information another team member will require to achieve the team's objectives.

As shown by these nine characteristics of expert teams, the leader's unique duties include: ensuring that the mission and vision are clearly understood by team members; confirming that each team member's expertise, role, and responsibilities are acknowledged by the entire team and consistent with the individual team member's understanding; promoting formal and informal communication among team members to enable them to anticipate problems and needs without explicit communication; creating a culture of candor, trust, and openness to foster prompt identification, discussion, and resolution of problems; and conveying genuine empathy, care, and support for team members. The leader also is responsible for engaging team members with regular updates and ongoing coordination; deferring to team members' preferences and optimizing their expertise in assigning projects; monitoring and adjusting assignments to reflect evolving expertise and capabilities and to respond to different challenges; showing a commitment to individual development, team achievement, and team members'

---

[65] Ibid. at 447–448. See Ericsson, K. Anders (Ed.). (2009). *Development of professional expertise.* New York: Cambridge University Press.

well-being through regular evaluation and feedback; and providing information that team members will need to fulfill both their current and anticipated responsibilities.

The soft skills necessary to fulfill these responsibilities – empathy, openness, trust, candor, listening, motivation, fairness, foresight, feedback, goal setting, communication, and vision – have been defined, analyzed, and synthesized throughout this book. Each of these skills, traits, and qualities is difficult to develop and master over a lifetime and exceedingly difficult to acquire and execute while we are leading other people. To bring these leadership challenges down to a manageable level in the short-term, we can start by focusing on how we communicate. Experts who have worked with leaders throughout the world suggest that exceptional communication skills underpin effective leadership:

- "Too often, in planning our communications, we focus on what we *want* to say rather than on the person to *whom* the communication is directed. When communicating, leaders keep in mind the interests, needs, concerns and priorities of their listeners, so that the content of their intended message is received."[66] (Warren Bennis and Joan Goldsmith, *Learning to Lead*)

- "Even people who understand the importance of relationship responsibility often do not tell their associates and do not ask them [what they are trying to do, why they are trying to do it, how they are going to do it, and what results to expect]. Whenever anyone goes to his or her associates and says: 'This is what I am good at. This is how I work. These are my values. This is the contribution I plan to concentrate on and the results I should be expected to deliver,' the response is always, 'This is most helpful. But why haven't you told me earlier?' And one gets the same reaction – without a single exception in my experience – if one then asks: 'And what do I need to know about your strengths, how you perform, your values, and your proposed contribution?'"[67] (Peter Drucker, *Management Challenges for the 21st Century*)

- "U.S. culture's emphasis on task performance, interpersonal competitiveness, and telling rather than asking makes it more difficult to be humbly inquiring because that may show weakness and in fact, makes one vulnerable. But, paradoxically, only by learning to be more humbly inquiring can we build up the mutual trust needed to work together

---

[66] Bennis & Goldsmith, *supra* note 30 at 129.
[67] Drucker, Peter. (1999). *Management challenges for the 21st century* (pp. 186–187). New York: HarperBusiness.

effectively and open up the communication channels. Such opening can occur around the task itself by becoming more personal."[68] (Edgar Schein, *Humble Inquiry*)

These expert insights tell us that effective leadership requires a higher degree of self-disclosure, reciprocity, and responsibility than we may have been willing to risk. They present a fundamental challenge to attorneys' preference for autonomy and their tendency to be skeptical, distrustful, and self-protective. If attorneys are determined to remain autonomous, skeptical, distrustful, and self-protective, how can they fulfill the leadership responsibilities that are commensurate with their intellect but currently incompatible with their personalities?

FOLLOWERS' ROLES AND RESPONSIBILITIES

Frequently overlooked in the extensive literature on leadership is the appropriate role of followers. Although our attention over centuries has gravitated toward leaders, we should acknowledge that followers play a critical role in shaping, modifying, and implementing leaders' ideas and decisions. Followers ultimately determine leaders' effectiveness, and without consideration of followers' roles, duties, and responsibilities we are analyzing and evaluating leaders unrealistically – as though the best leaders can act unilaterally and erase the timeless tension between leaders and followers.

The conventional role of followers, as defined by leaders, is epitomized in the remarks of Robert Gates, the former U.S. Secretary of Defense. Speaking to an assembly of information technology leaders, Gates declared,

> The responsibility of the follower is to be willing to speak up and say "we can do this better, there is a better way to do this," and then hopefully if it is a good idea it will get incorporated. And then whatever decision the leader then makes, it is incumbent on the follower to salute and help implement the decision the leader makes.[69]

Unfortunately, this traditional concept of a follower's role – speak up initially but then comply – has led historically to a host of bad outcomes and reflects an arrogance that undermines sound organizational decision making.

---

[68] Edgar, Schein. (2013). *Humble inquiry* (pp. 81–82). San Francisco, California: Berrett-Koehler Publishers.

[69] Loftus, Tom. (2016, October 19). Former U.S. Secretary of Defense makes case for leading through transparency. *The Wall Street Journal*.

The obeisant follower model causes serious problems for at least four reasons. First, poor-quality decisions do not get any better when followers quietly implement defective decisions. Silence and conformity have never transformed a bad decision into a good one. Second, this concept assumes that decisions, once made, are static and should not be challenged by followers. This attitude curtails criticism and dissent when the conditions underpinning a decision have changed and no longer support the original decision. Third, it ignores the fact that even good decisions may be implemented ineptly. When dissent about decisions is stifled, followers will not take the risk of reporting that the implementation of an otherwise good decision is causing negative results. Fourth, if the followers' opinions were important enough to elicit before making a decision, why would they be any less important after the decision was made? The quality of followers' inputs does not diminish simply because leaders seek closure and become impatient with dissonant information. Followers have critical insights, and both leaders and organizations benefit from them at every stage of decision making – including implementation, evaluation, and reappraisal.

Effective leaders and healthy organizations provide followers with "psychological safety," as discussed in Chapter 5, and they encourage followers to voice dissident opinions by promoting a "duty to dissent."[70] Unhealthy organizations, in contrast, attempt to quash dissident and disconfirming viewpoints. A critical factor in the emissions testing scandal that engulfed Volkswagen in 2015 was a culture that apparently placed a higher priority on conformity and compliance than candor and integrity. Although Volkswagen initially depicted the decision to install a "defeat device" as being made by a small group of engineers, within a few weeks after the scandal erupted "50 potential whistle-blowers had come forward, hinting at wider knowledge of the cheating."[71] Emanuela Montefrancesco, a Volkswagen engineer, describes the company's culture as "hard charging." She reflects, "Here at Volkswagen in the last few years, we have forgotten to say, 'I won't do this. I cannot. I am sorry.'"[72] A former Volkswagen management trainee observes, "VW had this special culture. It was like North Korea without the labor camps.

---

[70] See Harford, Tim. (2011). *Why success always starts with failure* (p. 78). New York: Farrar, Straus and Giroux. Davenport, Thomas, & Manville, Brook. (2012). *Judgment calls* (pp. 10–11). Boston, Massachusetts: Harvard Business Review Press. Gerstein, Marc. (2008). *Flirting with disaster* (p. 273). New York: Union Square Press. Hertz, Noreena. (2013). *Eyes wide open* (p. 265). New York: HarperCollins.

[71] Ewing, Jack, & Bowley, Graham. (2015, December 13). The engineering of Volkswagen's aggressive ambition. *The New York Times*.

[72] Ibid.

You have to obey."[73] Responding to the scandal, Bernd Osterloh, head of the Volkswagen works council, asserts, "We need in future a climate in which problems aren't hidden but can be openly communicated to superiors. We need a culture in which it's possible and permissible to argue with your superior about the best way to go."[74]

In considering the appropriate role of followers, we also are refining the responsibilities of leaders. Followers are duty-bound to express their opinions and objections to leaders, especially when leaders expect them to collaborate in making and implementing unethical and otherwise improper decisions. Leaders concurrently are duty-bound to establish a context and culture in which followers are free from inappropriate pressures and convinced they can communicate their insights and concerns candidly and continually.

LEGAL PROJECT MANAGEMENT

Legal project management (LPM) is a systematic effort to change the legal services industry from a collection of highly variable attorneys and law firms to a uniformly reliable group of service providers specifically trained to deliver value as determined by clients. It presents major leadership challenges to attorneys as they attempt to reconcile client and law firm objectives and inspire other attorneys to change work habits and upgrade their client service and accountability. A minority of law firms currently implement LPM practices, but those practices are becoming compulsory in very large matters as clients fight the "rule of mega-projects:" over budget, over time, over and over again.[75]

LPM has been defined loosely as a method that "adapts proven management techniques to the legal profession to help lawyers achieve their business goals, including increasing client value and protecting profitability."[76] A more precise definition is "the discipline of planning, organizing, securing, and managing resources to achieve specific goals relating to the control and management of legal cases and matters."[77] Regardless of definitions,

---

[73] Ibid.

[74] Cremer, Andreas, & Bergin, Tom. (2015, October 10). Fear and respect: VW's culture under Winterkorn. *Reuters*.

[75] Flyvbjerg, Bent. (2014). What you should know about megaprojects and why: An overview. *Project Management Journal*, 45(2), 6. For information regarding the extent of LPM programs and software in law firms, see Extero. 2016 *law firm benchmarking report* (pp. 14–15).

[76] Hassett, Jim. (2013). *Legal project management, pricing and alternative fee agreements*. Boston, Massachusetts: LegalBizDev.

[77] Ibid.

LPM's overall purpose is to manage legal matters more efficiently.[78] LPM practices, consequently, are forcing many law firms to replace scorched earth strategies and open-ended due diligence activities with spreadsheets and dashboards.

Although LPM is promoted as a method for attorneys to increase their competitiveness, it reflects a fundamental shift in the economic power exercised by clients and attorneys. In the new LPM regime, clients define, evaluate, and determine value, and attorneys who cannot lead teams in compliance with LPM standards are not retained for future engagements. LPM is revolutionary only to the extent it imposes upon attorneys the same market demands that have governed business/customer relationships for centuries – responsiveness, timeliness, reliability, quality, and cost.

Clients and attorneys working under LPM principles attempt to achieve six principal objectives: economic value to the client; efficiency in staffing and managing to budget; predictability of costs and outcomes; communication of accurate and complete information in a timely and concise manner; mutual understanding of client's business, priorities, and interests; and alignment of client's objectives with the law firm's conduct.[79] These objectives are to be effectuated during each of these phases of legal projects:[80]

- *Initiate* – determine expectations, objectives, scope, costs, constraints, phases, deliverables, responsible parties, and time requirements.
- *Plan* – prepare budget, tasks, phases, schedules, responsibilities, assignments, communication protocols, and time estimates.
- *Execute* – implement plan, perform legal work, manage team, comply with schedule and budget, communicate, evaluate quality, and provide feedback.
- *Monitor* – monitor and measure progress, assess risk to budget and schedule, and make adjustments in scope, schedule, assignments, or budget for unanticipated events.
- *Review* – discuss outcomes with clients, review budget-to-actual, assess performance, identify lessons learned, and ensure that performance data is accessible for future projects.

---

[78] Filisko, G. M. (2011, May 1). The lowdown on LPM: System stirs buzz, but does it have bite? *ABA Journal*.

[79] Woldow, Pamela, & Richardson, Douglas. (2013). *Legal project management* (p. ix). Chicago, Illinois: American Bar Association.

[80] These phases are described in Association of Corporate Counsel. (2011). *Guide to ACC Value Challenge–Guide to project management*. Hassett, Jim. (2016). *Legal project management* (4th Ed.). Boston, Massachusetts: LegalBizDev. Woldow & Richardson, *supra* note 79.

For clients, attorneys' LPM skills have become as important as their legal knowledge. The ability to lead a project team, prepare a project budget, manage resources to comply with the budget, and deliver results consistent with projections is now a paramount skill. Attorneys who deliver great results at great expense are losing their value as clients increasingly emphasize economy, efficiency, and predictability. Clients' insistence on LPM skills presents a leadership opportunity for motivated attorneys and a career restriction for recalcitrant attorneys, especially in complex litigation and transactions.

Relatively simple on their face, LPM objectives present unique leadership challenges because they often clash with law firms' business models. The emphasis on efficiency and budgets can conflict with attorneys' desire for autonomy and their need to meet billable hour targets. As one disparaging attorney said to Grant Collingsworth, an LPM proponent and partner at Morris, Manning & Martin, "All you've managed to do is turn a $200,000 project into a $100,000 project."[81] For their part, clients have lost their patience with attorneys' disinclination to manage costs, as an in-house lawyer relates:

> You order a tree house, and they give you the Hoover Dam. In-house counsel want, and ask for, lean staffing, quick resolutions and a low price. Law firms need to keep associates employed, want to cover every base and work under what clients often see as outmoded billing models.[82]

Another in-house lawyer describes his frustration in attempting to monitor and control costs: "A lot of big firms, when they get a bit of an open door, they overstaff the matter and milk it."[83] This is precisely the type of inefficiency and billing abuse that provoked and motivates an increasing number of clients to impose LPM cost, quality, reporting, and time requirements.

Although clients attribute attorneys' inefficiency to their economic incentives, the underlying problems are more serious than avarice. Attorneys urging their law firms to adopt LPM practices and attorneys leading LPM teams should be aware of four chronic problems that have undermined previous efforts to align attorney–client interests:

- miscommunication between attorneys and clients;
- divergent definitions of success;
- attorneys' failure to understand how legal expenditures fit into clients' overall objectives; and
- attorneys' persistently inaccurate fee estimates.

---

[81] Filisko, *supra* note 78.
[82] Paonita, Anthony. (2014, October). Failure to communicate. *The American Lawyer*, p. 55.
[83] Ibid.

Absent an understanding of these problems, attorneys in leadership positions will find that LPM initiatives fail despite their best efforts and apparent support within the law firm.

The first problem – miscommunication – occurs because clients do not convey and attorneys do not elicit basic information regarding objectives and anticipated costs. As Jeff Carr, former General Counsel for FMC Technologies, Inc., states, "We often don't tell outside counsel what we want and how they're doing. We often don't insist on a budget, and then we complain about outside counsel not meeting our expectations."[84] John DeGroote, former Chief Legal Officer of BearingPoint, Inc., has attempted to understand how often attorneys ask their clients, "What is an acceptable outcome in this matter?" In discussions with law firm attorneys and in-house counsel, he has heard two responses: "Outside counsel tell me 'I always ask that question,' and their clients tell me '[m]y lawyers rarely ask that question.'"[85] As DeGroote observes, "Like it or not, there's a disconnect here."[86] Clients seem to assume that attorneys understand their objectives, and attorneys assume that clients understand and will pay the cost of achieving their imputed objectives.

This lack of direct communication is compounded by different definitions of success. Attorneys measure outcomes as they did in law school, analyzing the range of remedies, the type and amount of recoverable damages, and all of the possible actions that can be contemplated and documented. Attorneys define success as achieving an optimal result under their theories, interpretations, and scenarios. Although the client's objectives may coincide with the attorney's objectives on occasion, most of the time clients have different interests and goals; they place a higher value on resolution, ongoing relationships, reputation, costs, probabilities, risk management, and the organization's ability to concentrate resources on its core enterprises.

Attorneys also view cases and transactions as stand-alone projects and do not inquire about how they fit into a client's overall plans, goals, and financial condition. Attorneys see a project as a challenging endeavor to which they dedicate their knowledge and talents in service of the client. The client, however, sees the project as an endeavor that places at risk resources best spent on its major functions. Victoria Stratman, General Counsel for the California Institute of Technology and its Jet Propulsion Laboratory, describes this conflict:

[84] Ibid. at 56.
[85] DeGroote, John. (2010, March 11). Toward better client service: A few questions for outside counsel. Retrieved from http://settlementperspectives.com/2010/03/toward-better-client-service-a-few-questions-for-outside-counsel/.
[86] Ibid.

We're looking for lawyers who know how to assemble a team, because most matters require a team but a team of appropriate size and a team of appropriate skills. How well that team is managed is important to us. There are some things that you may end up spending a ton of time on, but if you take a step back and look at what the value is to the client, it is not worth the hours and you have to be able to recognize that and bill accordingly. It's important for me to see a firm that is proactively doing that as opposed to waiting for me to call and say is this really what you're charging me? Every dollar spent on an outside law firm is a dollar less that can be spent on research. We take that very, very seriously.[87]

For the attorney, every charge above a threshold amount increases the likelihood of a sound outcome, but for the client each additional increment of expense raises the risk of waste. The client, explains Sara Lee Keller, General Counsel of Clear Channel Outdoor Holdings, Inc., emphasizes "the economic return on spending these dollars because, as with any company, dollars are fungible. If you can take dollars away from spending on litigation and turn it into dollars you can spend on growth, it's a much better spend."[88]

A final impediment to aligning the interests of attorneys and clients is attorneys' difficulties in providing accurate cost projections. Attorneys traditionally have lacked motivation and training in preparing budgets, and many attorneys still regard budgets as a necessary evil to placate overanxious clients, not as a planning tool for both clients and attorneys. Consistent with attorneys' aversion to budgets, a 2013 survey of corporate counsel reported that attorneys submitted litigation bills "with the average disparity between budget and the final bill being nearly 40 percent."[89] The disparities were even greater in litigation cases reviewed by former U.S. Magistrate Judge John Leo Wagner. He compared the attorneys' fee estimates provided by attorneys at the inception of cases with the actual fees through trial – and discovered that "the actual costs to litigate ended up being three to five times more than what attorneys originally estimated their costs to be."[90] It is unclear whether these chronic

[87] Brisbon, Melanie. (2015, April 14). Reaching for the stars. *San Francisco Daily Journal*, p. 5. See Grubbs, Shelby. (2005, January/February). It's not just the money: How do you define a successful settlement? *Business Law Today*, 14(3). ("Trained from law school to seek the best *legal* outcome in litigation, outside counsel serving a business client can be puzzled by a 'win' or a favorable settlement that leaves the client cold. Yet an outcome at the wrong cost, or that otherwise fails to address a client's needs is, at best, a tie.")

[88] Gilfillan, Christopher. (2014, March 10). Sign language. *San Francisco Daily Journal* (p. 3).

[89] Ames, Jonathan. (2013, December 2). Clients rail against botched litigation budgets. *The Lawyer*.

[90] Wai, Melissa. (2015). Techniques in mediation: A closer look at decision analysis. *American Journal of Mediation*, 8, 58.

underestimates stem from inattention, optimism, or guile. But absent penalties for inaccurate projections and incentives for data-driven fee estimates, attorneys will continue to formulate fee estimates with the rosiest of colored glasses.

MORAL LEADERSHIP

Although LPM provides practical standards, tools, and directions for leaders in law firms and the legal profession, moral leadership operates at an idealistic, seemingly impractical level. Moral leadership, explains historian James MacGregor Burns, differs from other types of leadership in "its capacity to transcend the claims of the multiplicity of everyday wants and needs and expectations, to respond to the higher levels of moral development, and to relate leadership behavior – its roles, choices, style, commitments – to a set of reasoned, relatively explicit conscious values." Because moral leadership necessarily implicates our ethics, morals, values, and priorities, it is fundamentally personal and frequently controversial. It has a singular ability to instill in attorneys a deep, permanent sense of meaning and in their adversaries a profound, abiding sense of anger – all depending on how one feels about the ends sought in moral leadership.

Moral leadership embodies convictions, aspirations, and duties that may disrupt orthodox career progression. The principles underpinning moral leadership sometimes conflict with the amoral convention of representing clients that occasionally seek the protection of laws to evade responsibility for socially harmful behavior. For some attorneys dedicated to moral leadership, lawyers' routine disregard of their personal beliefs while representing all clients willing to pay – "a crude instrumentalism in which lawyers sell their services without regard to the ends to which those services are put"[91] – is not only personally repugnant but also universally reprehensible. But for those attorneys accustomed to providing legal representation to all paying parties, an attorney's refusal to represent a client for personal reasons may be regarded as unethical and antithetical to a duty to honor, assert, and protect constitutional guarantees and other legal rights.

Attorneys considering the extent and depth of their commitment to moral leadership may find it useful to evaluate their moral leadership in three dimensions: personal, professional, and societal. We may not fulfill our

[91] Sarat, Austin, & Scheingold, Stuart. Cause lawyering and the reproduction of professional authority: An introduction. In Sarat, Austin, & Scheingold, Stuart. (1998). *Cause lawyering* (p. 3). New York: Oxford University Press.

expectations of moral leadership in each of these dimensions, but we can become more purposeful leaders by explicitly acknowledging the dimensions in which we choose to exercise and expand moral leadership. As Howard Gardner points out in *Leading Minds*, "enhanced knowledge about leadership may go hand-in-hand with more morally desirable forms of leadership."[92]

The first dimension of moral leadership is our own conduct. Lawyers may regard their personal conduct as an entirely private matter; but the reality is that other people look to lawyers for models of personal behavior, and lawyers' moral reasoning about their own behavior affects how they define, identify, and react to moral dilemmas in the profession and society. The role of personal moral leadership in our overall leadership development has been neglected, as John O'Neil, author of *Leadership Aikido*, explains:

> Many writers on leadership skate past the issue of character development. In my experience, however, one of the biggest obstacles to enduring success is a leader's moral lapses. A fully developed moral sense is a mark of adulthood, and the lack of one is a sign of lingering immaturity. Without a well-tempered moral sense leaders are easy prey for the temptations that arise from success. Their achievements may make them feel exempt from inconvenient bourgeois notions of fair play, honesty, and moral consistency ... Leaders with lax or nonexistent morals almost always self-destruct and lose their effectiveness – not to mention their friends, families, and allies – sooner or later.[93]

Our personal moral development, as O'Neil states, has an enormous effect on the quality and duration of our leadership. It also directly affects the moral development of the people around us. From the age of three years old, people derive rules and norms by watching the behavior of other people; they "go from observed actions to prescribed actions and do not perceive them simply as guidelines for their own behavior but rather as objective normative rules applying to everyone equally."[94] Personal moral leadership requires us to accept responsibility for the rules and models that we inculcate in others and acknowledge that our personal behavior serves as templates for our future actions as well as others' future conduct.

The second dimension in which we assert moral leadership is professional. "Our profession's need for leaders with inspiring visions and values has never been greater," asserts law professor Deborah Rhode. "Yet our

---

[92]   Gardner, *supra* note 17 at 297–298.   [93]   O'Neil, *supra* note 62 at 69.
[94]   Schmidt, Marco, Butler, Lucas, Heinz, Julia, & Tomasello, Michael. (2016, September). Young children see a single action and infer a social norm: Promiscuous normativity in 3-year-olds. *Psychological Science*, 27(10), 1360.

current educational system does little to produce them."[95] Worse yet, attorneys do not perceive either the lack of leaders or the lack of leadership training to be a problem.[96] Although the legal profession faces a public that is distrustful, clients that are dissatisfied, and new attorneys who cannot find jobs, the profession has failed to produce leaders and moral leadership to match its challenges. And the profession has been woefully ineffective in leading private law firms to acknowledge and correct gender and racial disparities in compensation, evaluation, client marketing opportunities, and partnership admission. It is both ironic and disturbing that a profession that promotes the rule of law and the importance of ethics in social regulation lacks the moral leadership necessary to remedy its own shortcomings in public trust, client service, job creation, employment conditions, and racial and gender bias.

Society is the third dimension in which attorneys assert moral leadership. For many attorneys, the vehicle for moral leadership in society is "cause lawyering." Professors Austin Sarat and Stuart Scheingold, authors of *Cause Lawyering*, define it as

> any activity that seeks to use law-related means or seeks to change laws or regulations to achieve greater social justice – both for particular individuals (drawing on individualistic "helping" orientations) and for disadvantaged groups. Whether the means and strategies used are legally based "rights" strategies or more broadly based "needs" strategies, the goals and purposes of the legal actor are to do good – to seek a more just world – to do "lawyering for the good."[97]

Over many decades, cause lawyering has been called "public interest" lawyering, "activist" lawyering, and "lawyering for social change;" and legal representation in cause lawyering has encompassed multiple law practice areas including civil rights, poverty, disability, labor, and consumer.[98]

Although cause lawyers do not exhibit consistent backgrounds and interests, they share the common objective of seeking "to work within the system, to use the law, either to change it or to hold it to its promises."[99] For many cause lawyers, who forgo market-rate compensation and job security, the legal work enables them to "reconnect law and morality and make tangible the idea that lawyering is a 'public profession.'"[100] The moral dimension is not an incidental facet of cause lawyering; it is the core purpose, motivation, and benefit of

---

[95] Rhode, Deborah. (2010). Lawyers and leadership. *The Professional Lawyer*, 20(3), 1.
[96] Ibid. [97] Sarat & Scheingold, *supra* note 91 at 37. [98] Ibid. at 33. [99] Ibid. at 47.
[100] Krishnan, Jayanth. (2006). Lawyering for a cause and experiences from abroad. *California Law Review*, 94, 577.

cause lawyering. As law professor Jayanth Krishnan notes, cause lawyers "view their lawyering as the representation or manifestation of their own personal, moral, political and professional values."[101]

Both lawyers and the public can argue in good faith about the positions advocated by cause lawyers. But those arguments obscure the disturbing facts that less than 1 percent of all attorneys are sufficiently committed to indigent legal services to practice in legal aid and public defender offices; and prestige within the legal profession is negatively correlated with "public service" and "service to persons of low social status."[102] The profession has come a long and decidedly materialistic way from the values of legal legends like Clarence Darrow, who explained why he continued to represent the hopeless and indigent: "Well, what can a fellow do when some poor devil comes to him, without a cent or a friend in the world, trembling in his shoes and begging for a chance before the law?"[103]

CRISIS MANAGEMENT

Don Norman, director of the Design Lab at the University of California, San Diego, tells us, "We know two things about unexpected events: first, they always occur; and second, when they do occur, they are always unexpected."[104] Because unexpected events always occur and we are continually surprised by their force and unpredictability, leaders are responsible for learning crisis management skills. That crisis management skills are an essential skill for attorneys is demonstrated by the IAALS survey in which 97 percent of attorneys reported that the following three abilities were either necessary in the short term or must be acquired over time: (1) "react calmly and steadily in challenging or critical situations;" (2) "exhibit flexibility and adaptability regarding unforeseen, ambiguous, or changing circumstances;" and (3) "make decisions and deliver results under pressure."[105]

It is virtually certain that a leader will confront a crisis – personal or professional – while leading a team of attorneys or law firm. Since the only issue is when, not whether, a crisis will occur, sound practices dictate that we

---

[101]   Ibid. at 584.
[102]   American Bar Association (2016). *Lawyer demographics year 2016.* Heinz, John, Nelson, Robert, Sandefur, Rebecca, & Laumann, Edward. (2005). *Urban lawyers* (pp. 86–92). Chicago, Illinois: The University of Chicago Press. ("The more a field [of law] is oriented toward public service, rather than profit, the lower its prestige, again net of other factors.")
[103]   Farrell, John. (2011). *Clarence Darrow: Attorney for the damned* (p. 12). New York: Vintage Books.
[104]   Norman, Donald. (2007). *The design of future things* (p. 13). New York: Basic Books.
[105]   Gerkman & Cornett, *supra* note 3 at 17.

start expanding our leadership repertoires to deal with crises. Some crises that you will face in the future may be in the gestation phase at this time, and you may benefit from conducting a quick, private inquiry to determine how well prepared you are to handle a major disruption in your personal or professional life. If you are like most people, your strategy for crisis management rests more on the improbability of a crisis than the preparation for it.

We tend to assume that crises will not affect us, especially if we have avoided them so far. But crises are remarkably common. "Roughly 15 percent of Americans," states author Jamie Holmes, "will experience a natural or human-made disaster in their lifetimes. If you include personal traumas like the untimely death of a loved one or a serious car crash, the figure rises to over two-thirds."[106] Other studies indicate that about 90 percent of Americans will experience at least one large-scale, traumatic event during their lifetime.[107] Many Americans already have experienced traumas that generally are considered to be rare events; 22 percent recall sexual abuse during childhood, 21 percent report physical abuse, and 14 percent say they have seen their mother being beaten.[108] Consistent with this data regarding trauma, another study found that about 8 percent of Americans experience Post Traumatic Stress Disorder at some point in their lives.[109]

Our preparation for crises must necessarily begin long before their inception. The personality that will emerge during a crisis is not a newfound amalgam of courage, insight, fortitude, and judgment but rather a highly stressed version of the person you are today. If you currently are experiencing difficulties coping with the challenges of your personal and professional lives, a crisis will rapidly dissolve the thin veneer of habit that gives you and others the impression that you are organized and stable. Laurence Gonzales, author of *Deep Survival*, explains how a crisis tests your existing skills:

A survival situation brings out the true, underlying personality. Our survival kit is inside us. But unless it's there before the accident, it is not going to appear magically at the moment it's needed. When you consolidate your personality as a survivor, what you get is the essence of what you always had. A survival situation simply concentrates who you are. It drives the natural system you've developed over a lifetime, and it drives it harder. Whether or

[106] Holmes, Jaime. (2015). *Nonsense* (p. 68). New York: Crown.
[107] Southwick, Steven, & Charney, Dennis. (2012). *Resilience* (p. 1). New York: Cambridge University Press.
[108] Barondes, Samuel. (2012). *Making sense of people* (p. 87). Upper Saddle River, New Jersey: FT Press.
[109] Southwick & Charney, *supra* note 107 at 217.

not it becomes chaotic at the boundaries depends on what you've put into it over a lifetime. Your experiences, education, family, and way of viewing the world all shape what you would be as a survivor.[110]

Crises do not bring out the worst or the best in people; they simply incite and subject to extreme stress the qualities you already possess and exhibit. As Patrick Lagadec, author of *Preventing Chaos in a Crisis*, observes, "The ability to deal with a crisis situation is largely dependent on the structures that have been developed before chaos arrives. The event can in some ways be considered as an abrupt and brutal audit: at a moment's notice, everything that was left unprepared becomes a complex problem, and every weakness comes rushing to the forefront."[111] People who imagine that they will "rise to the occasion," but have taken no concrete efforts to build and test their independence, flexibility, resilience, and stamina, fare poorly in crises. Rigid people, gung-ho types, and rule-followers who have lived in structured environments also are among the first to collapse in crises.[112]

To prevent adverse reactions to crises, many organizations provide training programs that simulate crises. These simulations enable participants to experience and learn from crises in a safe environment:

> Prior research indicates that exposing people to simulated crises and then having follow-up debriefing sessions during which they talk about their personal experiences as participants can function as stress inoculation: Being exposed to preparatory information and related training experiences make people aware, at the visceral as well as cognitive level, of what anticipated crises will actually be like. It stimulates them to develop personal coping devices. As a result, they are able to control their emotions and perform much more effectively if and when actual crises subsequently materialize.[113]

Within law firms, simulations can include the death of a managing partner, sudden departures of rainmaker partners, defection of an entire department, computer security failures, illnesses of lead trial and deal attorneys, physical destruction of offices, loss of major clients generating most of a firm's revenue, and adverse publicity resulting from a large malpractice judgment against the

[110] Gonzales, Laurence. (2003). *Deep survival: Who lives, who dies and why* (p. 223). New York: W.W. Norton and Company.
[111] Lagadec, Patrick. (1993). *Preventing chaos in a crisis: Strategies for prevention, control and damage limitation* (p. 54). London: McGraw-Hill International.
[112] See Siebert, Al. (1996). *The survivor personality.* New York: Penguin Group. Ripley, Amanda (2008). *The unthinkable: Who survives when disaster strikes.* New York: Three Rivers Press. Gonzales, *supra* note 110.
[113] Janis, Irving. (1989). *Crucial decisions* (p. 252). New York: The Free Press.

firm. Although law firm leaders can dispute the likelihood that one of these events will occur, they cannot seriously contend that none of them will occur.[114] Nevertheless, law firm leaders are reluctant to prepare for crises. Like clients who delay preparation of their wills, they seem to harbor a subliminal belief that anticipating negative events will somehow accelerate their occurrence.

When crises actually hit organizations, they present unique opportunities to abandon faulty ideas, systems, and operations. Because crises eclipse the acrimonious, seemingly endless debates that otherwise stymie change in law firms, leaders are temporarily empowered to make dramatic changes. As Rahm Emanuel said shortly after his appointment as chief of staff to President Barack Obama in November 2008, "You never want a serious crisis to go to waste."[115]

Commenting on the General Motors legal department and its ignition switch debacle, attorney Thomas Campbell, who leads the crisis management practice at Pillsbury Winthrop Shaw Pittman LLP, declares, "The very best time to overhaul a system that has historical problems is immediately in the aftermath of the crisis. Bureaucracies like GM become very rigid, and during a crisis the basic structures of the company are shaken."[116] The temporary instability and loss of confidence that follow crises, Campbell asserts, make people more "willing to change in a way they never would have been able to."[117] Campbell also discerns a change in the "predictable cycle of crises," noting that crises previously hit companies every 20–30 years but now occur about every five years. Consequently, crisis management has become an integral part of corporate counsel's job, and 20 percent of their success or failure, Campbell opines, is dependent on their ability to manage crises.[118]

Apart from seizing the opportunity to change an organization following a crisis, leaders must develop and exhibit a sense of compassion toward the people who are deeply affected by a crisis. "Unleashing compassion in the workplace not only lessens the immediate suffering of those directly affected by trauma, it enables them to recover from future setbacks more quickly and effectively, and it increases their attachment to their colleagues and hence to

---

[114] See March, James. *A primer on decision making* (p. 48). New York: The Free Press. ("Predicting precisely which extremely unlikely event with important consequences will occur is impossible but some such event will almost certainly occur. Yet plans tend to ignore all such events. As a result, plans are developed for a future that is known (with near certainty) to be inaccurate.")

[115] Seib, Gerald. (2008, November 21). In crisis, opportunity for Obama. *The Wall Street Journal*.

[116] Maleske, Melissa. (2015, February 20). Challenging road awaits GM's new top lawyer. *Law360*.

[117] Ibid.   [118] Ibid.

the company itself," explains business professor Jane Dutton. "For those who witness or participate in acts of compassion, the effect is just as great; people's caring gestures contribute to their own resilience and attachment to the organization."[119]

In their efforts to be compassionate during and after a crisis, leaders must ensure that their organizations act compassionately in four ways:

- *Scope* – the range of assistance, including financial support, flexible hours, child care, and service providers.
- *Scale* – the extent of assistance, including money, equipment, technology, and temporary living or work spaces.
- *Speed* – the timing of responses, including speed of decision making and turnaround time for providing resources.
- *Specialization* – customization of responses, including type of communication and resources provided and sensitivity of reaction and recovery methods.[120]

Projecting warmth and strength in a crisis also is crucial, as demonstrated by online retailer Zappos' handling of a cyber attack that breached 24 million customer accounts. In communicating with employees, CEO Tony Hsieh projected warmth and strength by validating how employees were feeling, releasing timely and complete information, demonstrating thorough knowledge of the problem, voicing determination to resolve the problem, and identifying the concrete steps he was taking to fix it and prevent a reoccurrence. In the Zappos crisis, as in most crises, "projecting strength and warmth is always paramount. The people affected need to know that the responsible organization is doing everything possible to protect them, and that it is working in good faith toward a shared goal of getting things back on track."[121]

Crises bind and test many of the soft skills discussed throughout this book. They simultaneously challenge our ability to understand and develop ourselves while requiring deep knowledge of other people and their need for assurance, security, cooperation, empathy, trust, and leadership. Crises, in many respects, are the ultimate test of our soft skills. They are merciless in exposing soft skills deficiencies and unrestrained in illuminating soft skills proficiencies. By anticipating and preparing for crises, we perforce assess our soft skills and can use that

---

[119] Dutton, Jane, Frost, Peter, Worline, Monica, Lilius, Jacoba, & Kanov, Jason. (2002, January). Leading in times of trauma. *Harvard Business Review*, p. 59.

[120] Ibid. at 61.

[121] Neffinger, John, & Kohut, Matthew. (2014). *Compelling people* (p. 205). New York: Plume. See Cuddy, Amy J.C., Kohut, Matthew, & Neffinger, John. (2013, July–August). Connect, then lead. *Harvard Business Review*, p. 55.

opportunity to determine which skills are underdeveloped and merit more attention. That self-assessment and self-development should be comprehensive and rigorous because leadership in a crisis demands the fullest set of soft skills, not just the skills at which we are proficient today.

LEADERSHIP QUICK START

During the next ten years, younger attorneys will be catapulted into law firm leadership positions at an unprecedented rate. The demand for new law firm leaders will be driven by partnership demographics – the current class of law firm leaders is remarkably old and will be aging out of law firm leadership roles rapidly if not willingly. In addition, many other partners will be retiring or forced out of their law firms, ensuring that the newly vacated leadership positions will be occupied by a different generation of attorneys.

Law firm leadership currently is controlled by a venerable group of senior partners. They are considerably older than their client representatives. Twelve percent of the attorneys leading Am Law 100 firms are in the Silent Generation (born between 1925 and 1945), but only 2 percent of the general counsel of Fortune 100 companies and 1 percent of the general counsel of Nasdaq 100 companies are in that generation.[122] Baby boomers (born between 1946 and 1964) comprise 85 percent of Am Law 100 leaders, but they represent only 73 percent of Fortune 100 general counsel and 50 percent of Nasdaq 100 general counsel.[123]

Law firm partners, in general, are old, and nearly one-half of them will have retired from their firms when today's law students become partners. The average age of partners in the 20 largest law firms in the United States is 50.76, and in some prominent law firms like Schiff Hardin, Proskauer, and Steptoe the partners' average age is 57.[124] Attorneys in the Silent and Boomer generations comprise about half of all law firm partners.[125] By 2021, about

---

[122] McQueen, M. P. (2015, September 5). Study: Big Law leaders are much older than clients. *The American Lawyer*. Olson, Elizabeth. (2015, November 4). Graying firms wrestle with making room for young lawyers. *The New York Times*.

[123] Ibid.

[124] McQueen, M. P. (2016, February 29). Hold old is your firm? *The American Lawyer*. In contrast, "just four percent of partners at the U.K.'s 14 largest law firms by revenue are over the age of 60." Johnson, Chris. (2016, August 29). Brexit: In Britain, many lawyers retire by age 55. *The American Lawyer*. The average age at which partners in the accounting firm Deloitte LLP retire is 58. Cohn, Michael. (2014, September 19). Mandatory retirement becomes an issue at firms. *Accounting Today*.

[125] Triedman, Julie. (2016, August 29). Retiring partners pose big challenges for firms. *The American Lawyer*. See McQueen, M.P. (2015, July 30). A lateral boom of older lawyers.

16 percent of all existing partners will have retired, and by 2026 two out of every five current partners will have retired.[126] These retirements will clear the generational obstructions "clogging the arterial pathway to leadership and business for younger attorneys"[127] and will impose immediate leadership responsibilities on Gen X and Millennial attorneys. Those responsibilities will include dealing with the aftermath of questionable decisions driven by the short-term objectives of Silent and Boomer generation leaders. As law professor William Henderson observes, "Some law firms could crumble after this generation because they don't have a lot to sell to the next generation."[128]

Because new leaders will assume enormous responsibilities at unpredictable moments, it is imperative for them to understand five basic leadership concepts right now. Those concepts are presented here as a quick start guide to leadership: self-awareness, motivation, priorities, delegation, and perspective.

- *Self-awareness.* "Authentic leadership begins with self-awareness, or knowing yourself deeply," states William George, former CEO of the medical technology company Medtronic.[129] He believes that self-awareness is "a capacity you develop throughout your lifetime;" and he defines it as "your understanding of your strengths and weaknesses, your purpose in life, your values and motivations, and how and why you respond to situations in a particular way."[130]

  Jeff Jordan, a partner at venture capital firm Andreessen Horowitz, also believes that leadership "demands tremendous self-awareness."[131] He rounds out George's view of self-awareness by noting that it requires "an understanding of how others experience you, perceive you, and respond to you."[132]

  Self-awareness, in sum, enables us to lead through a profound knowledge of ourselves and our impact on others rather than a rigid reliance on titles, positions, and rules.

- *Motivation.* Genuine leaders are motivated to achieve for reasons independent of money and status. They seek leadership roles not for the

The American Lawyer. Weiss, Debra Cassens. (2014, October 22). As fewer law grads become lawyers the profession shows its age. *ABA Journal.*
[126] Triedman, *supra* note 125.
[127] Fitzgarrald, Jonathan. (2015, May 4). How law firms can navigate the generational divide. *Bloomberg Law.*
[128] Olson, *supra* note 122.
[129] William, George. (2004, January). Find your voice. *Harvard Business Review*, p. 35.
[130] Ibid.
[131] Jordan, Jeff. (2014, May). Leaving it all on the field. *Harvard Business Review*, p. 40.
[132] Ibid.

tangible benefits they confer but rather for the sheer enjoyment of setting new goals and achieving difficult objectives. Their motivation has five distinguishing characteristics: a strong interest in learning and achieving; a habit of increasing expectations and being dissatisfied with the status quo; a system of measuring progress by results; a pattern of remaining optimistic in the face of failure; and a persistent commitment to their organization.[133] Genuine leaders also recognize that they can learn the soft skills essential to effective leadership; they candidly acknowledge that, when they fall short on soft skills, the "central issue isn't a lack of ability to change; it's the lack of motivation to change."[134]

- *Priorities.* Leaders are easily overwhelmed by their responsibilities and the sense that they can never master all of the skills required of leaders. They wonder whether they should focus their efforts on "role modeling, making decisions quickly, defining visions," or "should they stress the virtues of enthusiastic communication?"[135] To determine how leaders should prioritize their skills, McKinsey & Company identified 20 key leadership traits[136] and then surveyed 189,000 people in 81 organizations throughout the world. After analyzing the survey results and leadership performance in those organizations, McKinsey discovered that four skills "explained 89 percent of the variance between strong and weak organizations in terms of leadership effectiveness."[137] Those four skills are: be supportive, seek different perspectives, operate with strong results orientation, and solve problems effectively.

Although different organizations will require different leadership skills, this large-scale study suggests that leaders will obtain the greatest return from initially developing these four skills and building the other 16 skills later. We inevitably have to prioritize leadership skills development, and the McKinsey findings provide an empirical basis for making our selections.

---

[133] Goleman, *supra* note 27 at 82. Avolio & Hannah, *supra* note 27 at 331.
[134] Boyatzis, Richard. (2004, January). Get motivated. *Harvard Business Review*, p. 30.
[135] Feser, Claudio, Mayol, Fernanda, & Srinivasan, Ramesh. (2015, January). Decoding leadership: What really matters. *McKinsey Quarterly*.
[136] The 20 leadership traits are: be supportive; champion desired change; clarify objectives, rewards, and consequences; communicate prolifically and enthusiastically; develop others; develop and share a collective mission; differentiate among followers; facilitate group collaboration; foster mutual respect; give praise; keep group organized and on task; make quality decisions; motivate and bring out the best in others; offer a critical perspective; operate with strong results orientation; recover positively from failures; remain composed and confident in uncertainty; role model organizational values; seek different perspectives; and solve problems effectively.
[137] Feser, Mayol & Srinivasan, *supra* note 135.

- *Delegation*. New leaders are reluctant to delegate responsibilities. They default to performing the tasks themselves, thinking that their "just do it" attitude is "what got them promoted in the first place." They also are anxious about losing control over the direction or quality of a project, fear losing stature and credit for accomplishments, and feel uncomfortable assigning work to former peers, believing they may be resented.[138]

  Thomas Grella, a law firm managing partner and author of *Lessons in Leadership: Essential Skills for Lawyers*, urges leaders to give up power and delegate responsibilities to other attorneys so that they, too, can develop leadership skills. "Delegation is easier," he says, "when you see it as a critical part of your duty as a leader to raise up other leaders."[139] To encourage leaders to create new leaders, he suggests they ask themselves, "Is this really something that only I can do?" and "Is this a task that can be given to someone else as a means of development of that other person as a leader?"[140] Law firm leaders, Grella asserts, build trust and earn the right to influence others through selflessness, generosity, and patience – and by demonstrating that they are "a leader who creates leaders."[141]

- *Perspective*. Rookie leaders, states leadership consultant Carol Walker, "have a real knack for allowing immediate tasks to overshadow overarching initiatives."[142] They spend their time on activities rather than strategies because they feel more comfortable engaged in familiar tasks; they find that activities are easier to control and bring to fruition than strategies; and they do not understand what leaders are expected to accomplish.[143] When leaders cannot transition from line responsibilities to strategic planning and execution of a vision they fail as leaders, substituting activity for perspicacity and tactical interventions for strategic thinking.

  The essence of leadership is "taking folks from the present into the future."[144] That endeavor requires leaders to imagine, conceptualize, formulate, articulate, and execute that future. Leaders must develop and maintain a long-term, strategic perspective and avoid the instant gratification derived from short-term, familiar tasks. For lawyers in leadership positions, this means that they must forgo the predictable satisfaction derived from client service and routine management and assume responsibility for directing the firm into a future that is neither predictable nor benign.

---

[138] Walker, Carol. (2002, April). Saving your rookie managers from themselves. *Harvard Business Review*, p. 97.

[139] (2013, November). Strategies to succeed at law firm leadership. *YourABA*.   [140] Ibid.

[141] Ibid. See Bennis & Goldsmith, *supra* note 30 at xx–xxi.

[142] Walker, *supra* note 138 at 100.   [143] Ibid. at 101.   [144] *YourABA, supra* note 139.

CHAPTER CAPSULE

Lawyers are in the anomalous position of serving as leaders but generally lacking leadership training and skills. Competency in lawyering skills often functions as a proxy for leadership skills, despite the evidence that leadership skills are distinct and may take years to develop. Our neglect of leadership skills is reaching crisis proportions because nearly half of all current law firm partners will retire within the next ten years, creating an urgent need for new leaders whose skills are presently undeveloped and untested.

To accelerate our leadership development, we need to identify the styles and traits associated with effective leaders. The most effective leadership styles are visionary/authoritative, participative/democratic, coaching/mentoring, and affiliative/supportive; but the leadership styles most commonly exhibited by attorneys are pacesetting/heroic and directive/coercive. The two leadership styles favored by attorneys are the only styles considered to be *in*effective among six different styles. Many key leadership traits also reflect qualities that are neither cultivated nor compensated in law firms: trust, empathy, vision, self-awareness, introspection, broad-mindedness, and innovativeness. Any attorney touting these qualities in seeking a law firm leadership position might be asked to show proof of his/her bar membership.

When attorneys occupy organizational leadership positions their efforts may be undermined by a lack of vision, deficient strategies, poor planning, optimistic overconfidence, unrealistic time estimates, and a reluctance to abandon ideas that should have worked but are not working. If the leadership challenges prove to be daunting or unrewarding, attorneys' general lack of resilience may lead them to retreat from leadership responsibilities and assume more familiar roles in which the problems are predictable and their success is virtually assured. Attorneys' leadership also may be impaired by colleagues who tend to tell them what they would like to hear rather than what they need to hear. As law firm consultant David Maister notes, law firm leaders are achievement-driven, and it is "the natural thing" for them "to look for confirmation that what they are doing is all right."[145]

Apart from their responsibilities for organizational leadership, attorneys serve as team leaders in public interest law firms, corporate legal departments, governmental law departments, and private law firms. In the private law firm context, clients increasingly expect a high level of legal project management skills to meet their demands for efficiency, predictability, communication,

[145] Maister, David, Green, Charles, & Galford, Robert. (2000). *The trusted advisor* (pp. 53–54). New York: Free Press.

and explicit, shared objectives. Whether practicing in a public interest, corporate, governmental, or private law firm context, attorneys will inevitably encounter a crisis and should start developing crisis management skills long before a crisis threatens to overwhelm them. Simulating crises is an especially valuable technique, and attorneys also will benefit from enhancing the skills, qualities, and characteristics discussed in previous chapters: resilience, flexibility, foresight, willpower, goal setting, communication, compassion, empathy, trust, and teamwork.

8

Professionalism

The first question members of any profession must ask themselves is, "For what and to whom are we responsible and accountable?" Unfortunately, the legal profession has not addressed that question directly and instead has channeled the issue of professionalism into two narrow straits: discipline for professional ethics violations and tort liability for legal malpractice.[1] Apart from the constraints of disciplinary action and tort liability, attorneys do not share a common set of values and convictions about their professional responsibilities. Like the law itself, legal professionalism acts proscriptively and provides scant guidance for socially beneficial behavior.

As a consequence of the legal profession's reluctance to confront fundamental issues of responsibility and accountability, the legal system in the United States, like its health-care system, is distinguished by crippling costs, limited access, and poor outcomes. When professionalism is delimited to ethical rules and malpractice standards, lawyers become complacent about a legal system that is superficially just in its reliance on rules and procedures but practically ineffectual for ordinary citizens. Although John Adams declared in 1780 that the United States would be a nation "of laws, not men,"[2] he probably did not envision a legal system that would evolve under attorneys' leadership to enshrine legalism and disenfranchise most of its constituents.[3]

---

[1] See Bernstein, Anita. (2003). What clients want, what lawyers need. *Emory Law Journal*, 52, 1053.

[2] Samuelson, Richard. (2003). John Adams and the republic of law. In Frost, Bryan-Paul, & Sikkenga, Jeffrey. (Eds.). *History of American political thought* (p. 114). Lanham, Maryland: Lexington Books.

[3] See ABA Commission on the Future of Legal Services. (2016, August). Report on the future of legal services in the United States. Chicago, Illinois: American Bar Association. Hadfield, Gillian. (2009). Higher demand, lower supply? A comparative assessment of the legal resource landscape for ordinary Americans. *Fordham Urban Law Journal*, 37, 129. Steinberg, Jessica. (2015). Demand side reform in the poor people's court. *Connecticut Law Review*, 47(3), 741.

This chapter analyzes the concept of professionalism and asserts that its central tenets must be responsibility and accountability. The chapter begins with an overview of the U.S. legal system, the degree of control exercised by attorneys over that system, and the consequences of a legal system that grants a franchise to attorneys but imposes minimal levels of responsibility and professionalism in exchange for that franchise. The chapter then discusses professionalism in the context of these duties: (1) duties to self; (2) duties to clients; (3) duties to other attorneys and judges; (4) duties to the legal profession; and (5) duties to society.

If law students and attorneys are uncomfortable with the concept that professionalism is a series of duties, that unease may be due to the over-promotion of law as a prestigious, financially rewarding, and intellectually engaging endeavor. The top reasons for applying to law school – intellectual stimulation, an interest in the subject matter, and a desire for professional training – suggest that the service component of law practice has been obscured.[4] Consequently, only a small percentage of students cite altruistic motivations as their reason for applying to law school; more commonly cited reasons include financial security, wealth, and prestige.[5] Although financial and status considerations are legitimate factors in choosing an occupation, they can be seriously misleading when a typical workday is spent in the service of demanding clients rather than the enjoyment of expected rewards. And even the intellectual stimulation of law practice may be overrated. As U.S. District Court Judge Patrick Schiltz cautions law students interviewing at law firms, "When a lawyer tells you that he gets a lot of interesting assignments, ask for examples. You may be surprised at what passes for 'interesting' at the firm."[6]

OVERVIEW

Among wealthy countries, the U.S. legal system is exceptional in four critical respects: (1) it is ranked among the lowest in providing its citizens with access

Leo J. Shapiro & Associates. (2002, April). *Public perceptions of lawyers: Consumer research findings* (p. 26). Chicago, Illinois: Section of Litigation, American Bar Association. Seidenberg, Steven. (2012, June 1). Unequal justice: U.S. trails high-income nations in serving civil legal needs. ABA Journal. Bergmark, Martha. (2015, June 2). We don't need fewer lawyers. We need cheaper ones. *The Washington Post.* Hubbard, William. (2015, August). A year of progress. ABA Journal, 8. ("Lack of access to justice is a flaw in our nation's fabric.")
4   Daicoff, Susan. (2004). *Lawyer, know thyself* (pp. 55–56). Washington, DC: American Psychological Association. Moll, Richard. (1990). *The lure of the law* (p. 25). New York: Penguin Books.
5   Ibid.   6   Heath, Chip, & Heath, Dan. (2013). *Decisive* (p. 103). New York: Crown Business.

to justice and protecting fundamental rights;[7] (2) its citizens express extremely low levels of confidence in its courts;[8] (3) it has the highest rates of incarceration and an unprecedented level of life sentences;[9] and (4) its jails and prisons function as the primary treatment centers for the mentally ill.[10] These abysmal results demonstrate that, for many attorneys, professionalism does not extend to the laws, procedures, systems, and institutions that ensure a relatively high standard of living for attorneys but yield deplorable results for ordinary citizens. Niall Ferguson, historian and author of *The Great Degeneration*, depicts the chasm between attorneys' perceptions and the public's experiences: "Rich countries can get poorer if their institutions deteriorate, particularly the rule of law. Today only lawyers think the United States has the world's best legal system."[11]

The responsibility for these disturbing deficiencies in the legal system rests squarely on attorneys, judges, law professors, and bar associations. They have

---

[7] World Justice Project. (2015). *Rule of law index 2015*. Washington, DC: World Justice Project. The World Justice Project's Rule of Law Index is available at http://worldjusticeproject.org /rule-of-law-index. See (2014, October). Need to know: Americans don't see their issues as legal matters, study says. *ABA Journal* (p. 63). Hubbard, *supra* note 3.

[8] *World Values Survey Wave 6: 2010–2014*. Online data analysis is available at www .worldvaluessurvey.org/WVSOnline.jsp. The United States' civil justice system is ranked #21 among 31 high-income countries; its criminal justice system is ranked #23; and its ability to protect fundamental rights, e.g., due process and equal treatment, is ranked #25. See GBA Strategies. (2015, November 17). *Analysis of national survey of registered voters* Report to National Center for State Courts. Saad, Lydia. (2011, July 11). *Americans express mixed confidence in criminal justice system*. Washington, DC: Gallup. Faucheux, Ron. (2012, July 6). By the numbers: Americans lack confidence in the legal system. *The Atlantic.*

[9] Collier, Lorna. (2014, October). Incarceration nation. *Monitor on psychology*, 45(9), 56. Office of the President of the United States, Council of Economic Advisers. (2016, April). *Economic perspectives on incarceration and the criminal justice system* (pp. 3–4). Washington, DC: U.S. Executive Office of the President. Williams, Timothy. (2016, August 17). Number of women in jail has grown far faster than that of men, study says. *The New York Times*. Furman, Jason, & Holtz-Eakin, Douglas. (2016, April 21). Why mass incarceration doesn't pay. *The New York Times*. Nellis, Ashley. (2013). *Life goes on: The historic rise in life sentences in America*. Washington, DC: The Sentencing Project.

[10] James, Doris, & Glaze, Lauren. (2006, December 14). *Mental health problems of prison and jail inmates*. U.S. Department of Justice Bureau of Justice Statistics Special Report. Washington, DC: Bureau of Justice Statistics. Kim, KiDeuk, Becker-Cohen, Miriam, & Serakos, Maria. (2015, March). *The processing and treatment of mentally ill persons in the criminal justice system*. Washington, DC: The Urban Institute. Torrey, E.F., Zdanowicz, M.T., Kennard, A.D., Lamb, H. R., Eslinger, D.F., Biasotti, M.D., & Fuller, D.A. (2014, April 8). *The treatment of persons with mental illness in prisons and jails: A state survey* [A Joint Report of the Treatment Advocacy Center and the National Sheriffs' Association]. Daniel, Anasseril E. (2007). Care of the mentally ill in prisons: Challenges and solutions. *The Journal of the American Academy of Psychiatry and the Law*, 35, 406.

[11] Ferguson, Niall. (2013, June). Is the business of America still business? *Harvard Business Review*.

sought and been accorded an exclusive right to enforce the nation's statutes, regulations, rules, and ordinances; establish attorneys' standards of ethical conduct; impose discipline on wayward attorneys; determine who can be admitted to the practice of law; accredit law schools and thereby control the number of attorneys; establish criteria for admission to law school; and dictate the content and methods of law school education.[12] They have achieved vertical integration of legal services. Their authority and control range from the initial selection of law school applicants to hearings on attorneys' fitness to practice law and from the imposition of a law school curriculum that ensures that students will be incapable of practicing law upon graduation to the leadership of a criminal justice system that incarcerates one out of every 111 American adults.[13]

Historically, the combination of power, revenue, and privilege without public accountability has proven to be socially harmful, politically volatile, and ethically indefensible. The legal profession is unlikely to defy this time-honored sequence of harm, discontent, volatility, and dénouement. If the 1.3 million attorneys in the United States are not accountable for its legal system, having wrested control of its law schools, bar admissions, disciplinary functions, and courts, the public can legitimately question why attorneys are permitted to extract the financial benefits of a franchise while disclaiming responsibility for its practical consequences. The public is increasingly aware of the social costs of attorneys controlling the U.S. legal system without an operative definition of professionalism. These social costs have been persistently high and decidedly unnecessary in a profession that attracts many of the nation's best minds but does not seem to bring out their best intentions.

RESPONSIBILITY AND ACCOUNTABILITY

To be a professional is to accept responsibility and promote accountability. The practice of law is fundamentally a responsibility to provide ethical and competent legal services to others, whether rendered in a private, governmental, or nonprofit context. Legal professionalism, consequently, does not exist separate from the ethical, moral, and mundane responsibilities owed to the

---

[12] Legislators, of course, also exercise control over the legal system. In state and federal legislatures, the percentage of legislators who are lawyers ranges from 14 percent to 37 percent. See Fifield, Jen. (2015, December 10). State legislatures have fewer farmers, lawyers; But higher education level. *Stateline*. Rampell, Catherine. (2012, February 23). First thing we do, let's elect all the lawyers. *The New York Times*.

[13] Gelb, Adam, & Gramlich, John. (2016, January 25). Share of U.S. adults under correctional control down 13 percent since 2007. The Pew Charitable Trusts.

people, organizations, and social systems served by attorneys. Just as physicians' professionalism is defined relative to patients, the medical profession, and the communities in which physicians serve, lawyers' professionalism must be defined relative to their clients, the legal profession, and their communities. For judges and law professors, who do not work with clients, the service ethos nevertheless applies although the constituency (citizens and law students) changes. Once we accept the concept of responsibility and accountability to clients, law students, and citizens, the policy debates regarding the legal system and law schools are more easily resolved in favor of the constituencies rather than the service providers.

The disconnect between the legal profession and its constituencies is reflected in the "Oath of Professionalism" taken by law students. Although students state that they commit themselves to "service without prejudice" and "will act with courtesy and cooperation toward others," the word "client" is conspicuously absent from the oath, as is any responsibility for improving the legal system.[14] The law students' oath is vacuous relative to a medical student's oath, which specifically addresses patients and the duty to improve medical care. The Student Oath administered at the Washington University School of Medicine in St. Louis, for example, includes specific commitments of service and accountability:

> I will faithfully serve the well-being of my patients and strive to prevent, treat, and cure disease. I will endeavor to be worthy of their trust through honest and sensitive communication. I will treat my patients with dignity, respect their individuality, safeguard their confidence, and serve as their advocate. I will educate and empower them as guardians of their own health.
>
> As a representative of the medical profession I will hold myself accountable to the public for the trust placed in me. I will strive to improve the quality of health care for all.
>
> In the pursuit of excellence I dedicate myself to a lifetime of learning, teaching, and advancing the art and science of medicine.[15]

[14] For examples of the Oath of Professionalism, see University of San Diego School of Law. (2013, August 22). USD School of Law's entering class takes oath of professionalism. Retrieved from www.sandiego.edu/law/school/news/detail.php?_focus=45632. Heneghan, Meghan. (2012, August 23). Legal career begins for Class of 2015. Retrieved from http://we blaw.usc.edu/press/article.cfm?newsid=3901. University of Dayton School of Law Oath of Professionalism. Retrieved from www.udayton.edu/law/students/professionalism_oath.php. University of Illinois College of Law Pledge of Professionalism. Retrieved from www.law .illinois.edu/content/Pledge.pdf.

[15] Washington University School of Medicine in St. Louis. 2012 White Coat Ceremony. Retrieved from: https://medicine.wustl.edu/education/traditions/white-coat-ceremony/wcc-2012/

The law students' oath is inward-looking, focusing on the student and the legal profession ("I hereby accept my new status as a professional" and will "conduct myself with the dignity befitting an advocate and counselor in a learned profession"). The medical student's oath, in contrast, is outward-looking, emphasizing duties owed to patients and the health-care system. The vision of professionalism imparted by the law students' oath is a mildly altruistic blend of self-absorption and self-satisfaction, while the medical students' oath imposes concrete obligations in caring for and relating to patients, improving health-care quality, and advancing the science of medicine. Although both the legal and medical professions are confronted with affordability, efficiency, quality, and access problems, the medical profession is far ahead of the legal profession in explicitly taking responsibility and endorsing accountability for solving those problems.

DUTIES TO SELF

Our fundamental professional duty is competence – the ability to render legal services that are knowledgeable, skillful, and thorough.[16] To discharge that duty, we must continually engage in self-evaluation, assessing our subject-matter expertise, skills, habits, emotional well-being, and physical condition.[17] We also are required to improve our skills and update and expand our knowledge.[18] When we fulfill the duties of competence, self-evaluation, and self-development, we recognize that our professional performance is constantly evolving and, ideally, never reaches the stage of mastery. The most dedicated attorneys, therefore, must learn to live with the somewhat dissonant idea that tomorrow they will be a better attorney than they are today.

Although it seems that law students and attorneys would accept if not embrace the responsibility of self-development, this responsibility turns out to be objectionable to many professionals. Most first-year law students, as indicated by their self-reports, are not committed to professional self-development, although they express a generalized interest in it.[19] A significant segment of attorneys also minimizes the importance of professional self-development. In the IAALS survey, 12 percent of attorneys consider "an

[16] ABA Model Rules of Prof'l Conduct R. 1.1.

[17] ABA Model Rules of Prof'l Conduct R. 1.16.

[18] American Bar Association, Section of Legal Education and Admissions to the Bar. (1992, July). *Legal education and professional development – an educational continuum* (p. 141). Chicago: American Bar Association.

[19] Hamilton, Neil. (2016, January). Half of 1L students are still at early stages of taking ownership over their professional development. *NALP Bulletin*.

internalized commitment to developing toward excellence" to be a trait that is either not necessary or not relevant to an attorney's success.[20] Similarly, 18 percent consider the ability to "develop expertise in a particular area" to be unnecessary or irrelevant; and 11 percent regard the ability to "seek out work or training that will expand skills, knowledge or responsibilities" as unnecessary or irrelevant.[21] Although these percentages may seem small relative to the entire attorney population, the consequences for the individual client represented by an attorney with little or no interest in self-development may be devastating. And if the survey results are representative of all attorneys, then roughly 140,000–230,000 attorneys tossed their self-development anchors into the mud shortly after law school graduation and have no intention of lifting them for the balance of their careers.

Attorneys committed to self-development readily acknowledge that it requires a frank evaluation of their skills so that they can strategically direct their study and training. Many of the most valuable evaluations occur when we think we are performing competently and then are shocked to discover that other people do not share our high opinion of ourselves. These are the most painful yet most informative lessons, if we can internalize them and avoid the tendency to deflect the message and discredit its source.

For inspiration in accepting and learning from tough criticism, we can find no better example than U.S. Supreme Court Justice Sonia Sotomayor's description of the brief she prepared while a summer associate at Paul, Weiss and her subsequent reaction upon learning that the firm would not extend a job offer to her:

> I finally handed in my effort to a young associate one notch up the totem pole. Only when I saw what he eventually wrote himself and passed up to the next level did I fully realize how poor a job I had done. I obviously wasn't thinking like a lawyer yet. If this was what it means to work in a prestigious law firm, I clearly was not ready.
>
> The sense of failure was confirmed when I concluded my stint as a summer associate without receiving a job offer ... [I]n my own eyes I had officially blown it. I had worked hard – I always had and still do – but somehow that wasn't enough. And it was difficult not to conclude that I simply was not in the same league as my classmates who were pulling in job offers from firms just like this one. There were some around me encouraging me to view the rejection as an expression of bias or personal animus, but I had seen no

[20]   Gerkman, Alli, & Cornett, Logan. (2016, July). *Foundations for practice: The whole lawyer and the character quotient* (p. 14). Denver, Colorado: Institute for the Advancement of the American Legal System.
[21]   Ibid.

evidence of that, while my sense of having underperformed seemed to me well enough substantiated. For this pain of failure – the first real failure since having enrolled in law school – I had only myself to blame, and knowing that, I was profoundly shaken.

The way forward was daunting if obvious. I needed to figure out what I was doing wrong and fix it.[22]

Justice Sotomayor recognized that she was deficient in writing a brief, and she was determined to overcome that deficiency. She applied her remedial efforts as she had always done: "break the challenge down into smaller challenges, which I could get on with in my methodical fashion."[23] Her approach to criticism, implemented throughout her life, is to treat criticism as a professional learning opportunity.

In our self-development efforts, we tend to concentrate on professional skills and overlook our ethical development. This oversight occurs because we think that skills can be developed, but ethical judgment is static. We imagine that people are either ethical or unethical and that once ethical rules are inculcated people either resist or succumb to temptations as a result of their ethical dispositions. This "moral compass" approach to ethics – based on the idea that people either possess or have lost their moral compass – is appealingly simple but neurologically groundless. As we discussed in Chapter 3, our minds do not have moral compasses, moral centers, moral cores, or moral headquarters despite the attention given to these pre-scientific concepts.[24] Instead, our minds selectively respond to stimuli and process multiple, competing impulses, drives, and sensations while determining and executing a preference. Under some circumstances, even people who self-define as highly ethical will act unethically because the circumstances – not rules, temperaments, or dispositions – generally determine our behavior.[25] For that reason, researchers find that

[22] Sotomayor, Sonia. (2013). *My beloved world* (p. 233). New York: Vintage Books.
[23] Ibid. at 234.
[24] See Zimbardo, Philip. (2007). *The Lucifer effect* (p. 211). New York: Random House. ("Good people can be induced, seduced, and initiated into behaving in evil ways. They can also be led to act in irrational, stupid, self-destructive, antisocial, and mindless ways when they are immersed in 'total situations' that impact human nature in ways that challenge our sense of the stability and consistency of individual personality, of character, and of morality.")
[25] See Sommers, Sam. *Situations matter*. (2011). New York: Riverhead Books. O'Grady, Catherine Gage. (2015). Behavioral legal ethics, decision making, and the new attorney's unique professional perspective. *Nevada Law Journal*, 15(2), 671. Smith, N. Craig, Simpson, Sally, & Huang, Chun-Yao. (2007). Why managers fail to do the right thing: An empirical study of unethical and illegal conduct. *Business Ethics Quarterly*, 17(4), 633. Sternlight, Jean R., & Robbennolt, Jennifer K. (2013). Behavioral legal ethics. *Arizona State Law Journal*, 45, 1107.

"90% of people – most of whom identify themselves as morally upstanding – will act dishonestly to benefit themselves if they believe they won't get caught."[26] Yet more surprising is the fact that people who act unethically do not see their conduct as unethical; "they rationalize their behavior even while condemning the same in others."[27]

Because circumstances exert a powerful influence over our ethical decisions, it is helpful to anticipate and contemplate the ethical dilemmas that could arise from current client cases and firm controversies. This practice enables us to identify upcoming problems and simulate our responses without the sense of urgency and the pressure to conform that frequently attend poor-quality ethical decisions. Philip Zimbardo, the social psychologist popularly identified with the Stanford Prison Experiment,[28] urges people to see themselves as "Heroes in Waiting." His premise is that nearly all of us will be confronted with a serious dilemma requiring heroic action, and unless we are prepared before the opportunity is presented, we probably will regret the choice we make at the moment heroic action is required. "By getting everyone to think of themselves as heroes in waiting," Zimbardo states, "I think that will make it more likely when the opportunity comes that they'll take action."[29] Our duties to ourselves, therefore, include contemplating and preparing for ethical decisions that require heroism but will evoke acquiescence if we are not prepared for the challenge.

In anticipating ethical dilemmas and considering how we might respond to them, we start to redefine what it means to be an ethical person and build a more durable model of ethical behavior. Instead of perceiving ethics as a dilemma of detection – and melding into the 90 percent of people who will act unethically when the chance of being caught is low – we can conceptualize ethics as behavior that meets our own expectations of ourselves. Our ethical affirmation is then derived from the consonance between our behavior and our own expectations rather than the reactions of other people. This fundamental difference in defining what it means to be ethical is described by philosopher Kwame Anthony Appiah:

It's important to understand that while honor is an entitlement to respect – and shame comes when you lose that title – a person of honor cares first of all not about being respected but about being worthy of respect. Someone who

---

[26] DeSteno, David. (2014, March). Who can you trust? *Harvard Business Review.*   [27] Ibid.
[28] For a description of the Stanford Prison Experiment, see Konnikova, Maria. (2015, June 12). The real lesson of the Stanford prison experiment. *The New Yorker.*
[29] Carmichael, Mary. (2009, December 28). Northwest Flight 253: The psychology of heroism. *Newsweek.* See Zimbardo, *supra* note 24.

just wants to be respected won't care whether he is really living up to the code; he will just want to be thought to be living up to it. He will be managing his reputation, not maintaining his honor. To be honorable you have both to understand the honor code and to be attached to it ... For the honorable person, honor itself is the thing that matters, not honor's rewards. You feel shame when you have not met the standards of the honor code; and you feel it ... whether or not anyone else knows you have failed.[30]

When you think about the people throughout history who have acted courageously and ethically, it is clear that their purpose was to be worthy of respect, not to seek affirmation from other people whose ethical concepts may be transient, expedient, or simply wrong. For attorneys, the practice of anticipating ethical dilemmas and contemplating what type of behavior would meet their personal honor code is more likely to yield a sound result than complying with the urgent needs of clients and colleagues. All too often, the extemporaneous pressures exerted by clients and colleagues are biased by their determination to achieve a particular outcome and their preference that someone else be identified with the decision if it turns out to be ill-advised.

DUTIES TO CLIENTS

Lawyers practice law in two different worlds of client service. In the first world of client service, the clients' needs are paramount, and the opportunity to serve clients is considered to be a privilege. In the second world of client service, attorneys are deeply unhappy about their career choices and are so distressed by student loan debt or overwhelmed by despair and indifference that clients are little more than entries on a loathsome timesheet.

The first world is epitomized by Justice Sotomayor's belief that "being a lawyer is one of the best jobs in the whole wide world, because every lawyer, no matter whom they represent, is trying to help someone."[31] For Justice Sotomayor, "lawyering is the height of service – and being involved in this profession is a gift. Any lawyer who is unhappy should go back to square one and start again."[32] This commitment to client service is echoed by the eminent trial attorney James Brosnahan:

---

[30]　Appiah, Kwame Anthony. (2010). *The honor code* (p. 16). New York: W.W. Norton & Company.

[31]　Campos, Paul. (2013, January 28). Sonia Sotomayor debate: Should unhappy lawyers blame themselves? *Time.* See Weiss, Debra Cassen. (2013, January 23). Sotomayor: Lawyering is a gift, and unhappy lawyers should "go back to square one." *ABA Journal.*

[32]　Ibid.

It's very simple for me, the practice of law. The client always comes first, OK? Your self-interest and your personal comfort is not first ... You get better as the years go by in putting the flak to one side and saying, okay, what's the best thing for this client? You aren't always right, but you try.[33]

Attorneys in this first world believe that the practice of law "exists only for the sake of clients and our basic obligation is to provide services to those clients," according to former California State Bar president Howard Miller.[34]

The second world of client service consists of attorneys who are dissatisfied with their career choices, preoccupied with high levels of student debt, see themselves as autonomous actors with fungible clients, or continue employment with high-paying firms whose clients they detest. Emblematic of this second world is this letter sent to law professor Paul Campos by an attorney who graduated from law school six years ago with a student loan indebtedness of $150,000:

Over the last six years, I have discovered that I hate our system of justice, our courts, our law and everyone remotely connected to them. I hate the actual work of being a lawyer and having to deal with other lawyers. Being chained to this computer and phone every day feels like torture. It has affected my physical and mental health negatively. I don't want to talk or interact with people, and the anger and rage I feel every day has swallowed up my sense of humor.

Luckily in our small office I can close the door and sob hysterically without anyone much noticing. I feel terrible taking up a scarce job that someone else may be able to love and run with and really work the hell out of, while I hang on and avoid work as much as possible ... But I don't feel like I have any choice but to keep going on due to the debt and lack of other employment options ... The amount of contempt I feel for myself for getting in this situation is killing me.[35]

Campos says, "I receive letters like this one regularly."[36]

In criminal law practices, many defense attorneys enter this second world of client service when they allow a growing sense of disillusionment, futility, and cynicism to eclipse their duties to clients. As a public defender remarks,

I don't know how it works in other public defender's offices, but you won't find people here running out to jail to calm a guy down because he might

---

[33] Randazzo, Sara. (2009, June 25). After 50 successful years, Brosnahan fights on. *San Francisco Daily Journal*, p. 1.

[34] McCarthy, Nancy. (2009, July). Law, academia and public service will guide Howard Miller's presidential path. *California Bar Journal*.

[35] Campos, *supra* note 31.   [36] Campos, *supra* note 31.

have a question. More times than not you'll just say, "Ah, shit, let him stew." The only time that you see your client is either at arraignment or just before trial.[37]

This attitude of indifference and detachment from clients pervades many criminal defense practices and can impair the client's right to adequate representation. In one nationwide study, for example, one half of the criminal defense attorneys "did not conduct a thorough investigation, do legal research, or develop a theory of defense before plea negotiations."[38] Failing to undertake any serious preparation for plea negotiations violates the most basic standard of care in criminal defense matters and is a grievous disservice to criminal defendants. Those clients legitimately expect their attorneys to provide a professional level of service and probably will never know that their cases were resolved through inadequate representation.

Recognizing that attorneys function in two very different worlds of client service, attorneys need to explicitly ask themselves, "In which world of client service will I choose to practice law – the first world in which clients' needs are more important than attorneys' feelings, problems, and preferences, or the second world in which attorneys' feelings, problems, and preferences are more important than clients' needs?" This question is not argumentative but simply reflects the fact that the law imposes upon attorneys a fiduciary duty – the highest duty recognized by law – to act in the clients' best interests and to place those interests above their own at all times. If you have doubts about which world you will choose, assume that you are in the second world because it is unfair to clients and a breach of fiduciary duties to have this question resolved in favor of the attorney's gratification during a client's representation.

Although it may be difficult to acknowledge that your personality, lifestyle, or priorities place you in the second world of client service, there actually is nothing wrong or immoral about that choice. The only wrong or immoral choices are (1) continuing to represent clients in a fiduciary capacity when you do not intend to function as a fiduciary; (2) practicing law when psychological impairment, personal problems, alienation from clients, and lack of motivation prevent you from fulfilling your duty of competence; and (3) persuading yourself that you are committed to the first world of client service when your prior behavior and current priorities inform you that the second world is more

[37] Flemming, Roy. (1986, Spring). Client games: Defense attorney perspectives on their relations with criminal clients. *American Bar Foundation Research Journal*, 1(2), 261.

[38] Doyel, R. (1986). National College-Mercer criminal defense survey: Some preliminary observations about interviewing, counseling and plea negotiations. *Mercer Law Review*, 37(3), 1026.

compatible with your life. Once you have decided that the fiduciary life is not for you, it is important to transition promptly into another position or occupation that has conventional duties to clients and customers. Continuing in a fiduciary capacity while resisting fiduciary responsibilities violates duties to clients, increases malpractice and disciplinary action risks, degrades the legal profession, and blocks the career progression of numerous unemployed attorneys and new law school graduates who are genuinely committed to client service.

DUTIES TO OTHER ATTORNEYS AND JUDGES

During the last three decades, the legal profession has suffered from an epidemic of incivility among attorneys and a contagion of disrespect toward judges. Both conditions violate attorneys' ethical duties, display a lack of professionalism, and contribute to the public's low opinion of attorneys.[39] They reflect a behavioral race to the bottom that many attorneys have confused with zealous advocacy and loyalty to clients. As former U.S. Supreme Court Justice Sandra Day O'Connor observes, "the legal profession has narrowed its focus to the bottom line, to winning cases at all costs, and to making larger amounts of money."[40] To better understand how attorneys undermine professionalism in their relationships with other attorneys and judges, this section explores the content, frequency, and consequences of attorneys' incivility and disrespect toward their peers and judges.

Incivility Among Attorneys

Attorneys' unprofessional conduct includes hitting another attorney at a deposition;[41] referring to opposing counsel as a "Nazi" and "red neck pepperwood" in voice mail messages;[42] ordering opposing counsel at a deposition to "shut the f___ up;"[43] telling a female opposing counsel that it "wasn't 'becoming of a woman or an attorney' to raise her voice during a deposition;"[44]

---

[39]   See ABA Model Rules of Prof'l Conduct R. 3.1, 3.2, 3.3, 3.4, 4.1, 8.2 and 8.4.
[40]   O'Connor, Sandra Day. (1998, January). Professionalism. *Washington University Law Review*. 76, 6.
[41]   Filisko, G.M. (2013, January 1). You're out of order! Dealing with the costs of incivility in the legal profession. *ABA Journal*.
[42]   *Board of Professional Responsibility of the Supreme Court of Tennessee v. Edward A. Slavin, Jr.*, 145 S.W.3d 538 (Tennessee, August 27, 2004).
[43]   *GMAC Bank v. HTFC Corp.*, 248 F.R.D. 182, 196 (E.D. Pa. 2008).
[44]   Weiss, Debra Cassens. (2016, January 14). Lawyer sanctioned for telling opposing counsel it's "not becoming of a woman" to raise her voice. *ABA Journal*.

and asking "a court-appointed parenting consultant in a deposition about past allegations of sex with minors, without any good faith basis to make the accusation."[45]

Not all of attorneys' misbehavior occurs verbally or extemporaneously, as evidenced by an attorney's letter to opposing counsel, an assistant attorney general representing a public entity:

> I don't know if because you feed off the public trough, you have your head so far up your anus you think it's a rose garden, but I don't appreciate the unnecessary commentary included in the aforesaid pleading filed with the Illinois Human Rights Commission . . . If you want to be an idiot, be an idiot on your own time, punk, because I do not suffer idiots or punks kindly.[46]

After disciplinary charges were filed against the attorney who wrote the letter, he retained an expert witness. The expert testified that his letters "followed the structure of a persuasive or complaint letter" and included "imagistic language" for the purpose of "escalating the discourse between the parties to a higher level."[47] This argument appears not to have been entirely persuasive, as the Supreme Court of Illinois denied the attorney's petition for leave to file exceptions to a Review Board report recommending a 30-day suspension.

Incivility in the legal profession is pervasive and increasing.[48] In a 2015 survey of 4,450 attorneys sponsored by the Illinois Supreme Court Commission of Professionalism, for example, "more than 85 percent of respondents reported experiencing at least one instance of uncivil or unprofessional behavior within the past *six* months, with sarcastic or condescending attitudes, misrepresenting or stretching the facts, or negotiating in bad faith as the most reported unprofessional behavior."[49] Seven years earlier, responding to a similar survey by the same commission, a smaller percentage of attorneys (81 percent) reported that they had experienced unprofessional behavior during the prior 12 months.[50]

---

[45] Weiss, Debra Cassens. (2015, December 1). Lawyer's deposition question was "serious misconduct," top state court says in suspension order. *ABA Journal.*

[46] *In re Marvin Ira Gerstein*, M.R. 18377, 99 SH 1 (2002).

[47] Grogan, James M. (2010, November). *Not only sleepless in Seattle. (Labor and employment law ethics issues that might give you insomnia) – A regulatory perspective.* Case summary presented at the American Bar Association's 4th Annual Section of Labor & Employment Law Conference.

[48] Mashburn, Amy R. (2011). Making civility democratic. *Houston Law Review, 47,* 1162.

[49] 2Civility. (2015, May 28). *Results of 2014 survey on professionalism released.* Illinois Supreme Court Commission on Professionalism. Retrieved from www.2civility.org/results-of-2014-survey-on-professionalism/.

[50] Leo J. Shapiro & Associates. (2007, December). *A survey on professionalism: A study of Illinois attorneys* (p. 21). See Reardon, Jayne. (2014, September). Civility as the core of professionalism. *Business Law Today.*

About 90 percent of the surveyed attorneys believe that uncivil and unprofessional behavior (1) results in decreased public/client confidence in the judicial system; (2) makes the practice of law less satisfying; (3) increases the difficulty of resolving matters; and (4) raises litigation and transaction costs.[51] Incivility also transforms customary courtesies like extensions of time and rescheduling hearings and depositions into time-consuming, unnecessary skirmishes. As former trial attorney Janet Kole notes, "it will inevitably come to pass that you will need your opponent to be courteous to you, and if you have trampled on his or her feelings, or willingness to be cooperative, you can find yourself in a terrible predicament."[52]

Disrespect Toward Judges

Most attorneys probably expect their peers to be more respectful in dealing with judges than other attorneys. A survey of disciplinary actions against attorneys indicates, however, that attorneys are increasingly democratic in their rudeness, letting judges have it almost as often as attorneys. The targets of attorneys' incivilities, in descending order, are: opposing counsel (58.7 percent), judges (52.2 percent), opposing parties (27.4 percent), witnesses (11.9 percent), judicial employees (7.0 percent), and attorneys' own clients (3.5 percent).[53] When the unprofessional behavior is categorized as speech or behavior, the most popular forms of uncivil acts appear to be rudeness, defiance, and accusations of bias:

> The majority of the impolite speech was rude (67.7%) and defiant (59.7%). The next largest category of speech (22.9%) that prompted condemnation was speech that accused judges or other members of the legal system of general bias against the lawyer or his/her client. Speech that accused judges of incompetence was present in 15.9% of the cases, followed by vulgar speech at 13.9%. Another 10.0% of the incidents involved threatening speech, while 7.5% consisted of accusations that a judge was racist. ... In the behavior category, defiant behavior represented the majority of uncivil acts at 57.2%. The filing of actions with no evidentiary support or repetitive motions occurred in 13.4% of the cases. Inappropriate gestures (8.0%), sexual misconduct (3.5%), and violent or aggressive acts (2.5%) comprised the remainder of uncivil behavior.[54]

---

[51] National Center for Professional and Research Ethics, University of Illinois Urbana-Champaign. (2014). *Survey on Professionalism: A Study of Illinois Lawyers 2014* (p. 15).
[52] Kole, Janet. (2015, June). The golden rule. *ABA Journal*, p. 26.
[53] Mashburn, *supra* note 48 at 1162.   [54] Ibid. at 1163.

In another study, most judges reported receiving threatening messages and "nearly half of the judges indicated a fear that violence could affect a judge's decision."[55]

A disciplinary case that illustrates the antagonism directed against judges is *Grievance Administrator v. Fieger.*[56] Attorney Geoffrey Fieger had represented a client, Salvatore Badalamenti, in a medical malpractice case. The jury's $15 million verdict was vacated, due to insufficiency of evidence, by Michigan Court of Appeals judges Jane Markey, Richard Bandstra, and Michael Talbot. Following the appellate court's decision, Fieger appeared on his radio program and declared:

> Hey Michael Talbot, and Bandstra, and Markey, I declare war on you. You declare it on me, I declare it on you. Kiss my ass, too. . . . [Badalamenti] lost both his hands and both his legs, but according to the Court of Appeals, he lost a finger. Well, the finger he should keep is the one where he should shove it up their asses.[57]

A few days later he called the judges "three jackass Court of Appeals judges" and remarked, "They say under their name, 'Court of Appeals Judge,' so anybody that votes for them, they've changed their name from, you know, Adolf Hitler and Goebbels, and I think – what was Hitler's – Eva Braun, I think it was, is now Judge Markey, she's on the Court of Appeals."[58]

In trial courts, many attorneys are routinely disrespectful toward judges. As a consequence, trial court judges identify "poorly prepared or disrespectful counsel" as one of the most stressful aspects of their work.[59] "Sometimes when you're making rulings," states California Superior Court Judge Jesse Rodriguez, "they show their displeasure by sarcastic remarks, or sarcastically laughing or smiling or gestures with their hands or rolling their eyes. I think sometimes lawyers want to bait you into flaring up."[60]

When attorneys attack judges, both in the courtroom and in public forums, they risk bringing the judicial system into disrepute, violating the prohibition against false statements concerning a judge's qualifications or integrity, and

[55] Chamberlain, Jared, & Miller, Monica. (2009). Evidence of secondary traumatic stress, safety concerns, and burnout among a homogeneous group of judges in a single jurisdiction. *The Journal of the American Academy of Psychiatry and the Law,* 37, 214–224.
[56] 476 Mich. 231, 719 N.W.2d 123 (Mich.2006).   [57] Ibid.
[58] Ibid. See Mashburn, *supra* note 48 at 1167.
[59] Eells, T.D., & Showalter, C.R. (1994). Work-related stress in American trial judges. *The Bulletin of the American Academy of Psychiatry and the Law,* 22, 70–83.
[60] Keys, Laurinda. (2015, February 24). People person. *San Francisco Daily Journal,* p. 2.

jeopardizing their client's representation.[61] Even when criticisms seem to be justified, attorneys need to be aware of the practical consequences of criticizing a judge in open court instead of following the procedures for judicial misconduct complaints. As trial attorney John Tucker explains in his book *Trial and Error*, "judges have enormous influence with jurors and large areas of discretion in their rulings. They are human beings in robes, and hard as they may try to avoid it, if they dislike or distrust a lawyer, it is likely to have an effect on their rulings."[62]

DUTIES TO LEGAL PROFESSION

In addition to their duties to themselves, clients, other attorneys, and judges, attorneys must assume responsibilities for the legal profession itself. Under the Fundamental Values of the Profession, attorneys are expected to participate in activities to improve the profession; assist in training and preparing new lawyers; and eliminate bias based on race, religion, ethnic origin, gender, sexual orientation, or disability.[63] They also are required to "rectify the effects of those biases."[64] The Preamble to the Model Rules of Professional Conduct, moreover, imposes upon attorneys duties to "seek improvement of the law;" enhance the "quality of service rendered by the legal profession;" employ knowledge of the law "in reform of the law;" and "work to strengthen legal education."[65] Collectively, these duties transform attorneys from being members of a profession to being responsible for it.

To aid attorneys' efforts to fulfill these duties, this section explores four responsibilities grounded in the Fundamental Values and the Preamble: (1) improving the quality and delivery of legal services; (2) promoting diversity in law practices; (3) reporting other attorneys' unethical behavior; and (4) mentoring attorneys. These responsibilities, once undertaken, serve to implement the ideals and standards set forth in the Fundamental Values and

---

[61] See ABA Model Rules of Prof'l Conduct R. 8.2. Attorneys also are required to report judicial misconduct. ABA Model Rules of Prof'l Conduct R. 8.3(b) states: "A lawyer who knows that a judge has committed a violation of applicable rules of judicial conduct that raises a substantial question as to the judge's fitness for office shall inform the appropriate authority."

[62] Tucker, John. (2003). *Trial and error* (p. 210). New York: Carroll & Graf Publishers. See Berg, David. *The trial lawyer* (p. 260). Chicago: American Bar Association. ("In every case I've been in, when the judge has gotten mad at the other side, they never recovered.")

[63] American Bar Association Section of Legal Education and Admissions to the Bar. *supra* note 18 at 216.

[64] Ibid.

[65] Center for Professional Responsibility. (2007). *Model rules of professional conduct* (p. 1). Chicago, Illinois: American Bar Association.

the Preamble. As law professors Larry Gantt and Benjamin Madison assert, "All lawyers are responsible not only for their clients' interests, but also for the legal system as a whole."[66]

Improving Legal Services

The initial duty to improve legal services encounters resistance because it runs contrary to the backward orientation of the law and its emphasis on precedent and the status quo. Although adherence to precedent and maintenance of the status quo contribute to stability in the law, they also retard its improvement. As Judge Benjamin Cardozo noted, "to determine to be loyal to precedents and to the principles back of precedents, does not carry us far upon the road."[67]

Improving the legal profession is hindered not only by the retrospective nature of the law but also by attorneys' self-interest and complacency. Attorneys Katherine A. Helm and Joel Cohen describe a legal system sustained by self-centeredness and petrified by obeisance:

> [L]awyers are narrowly concerned with self-interest. We worry about or confine ourselves to what impacts us directly. We concern ourselves with keeping our jobs in the midst of epochal change that is restructuring the business of law. We say we want a revolution, but well, you know, we really just want things to stay comfortably secure. And so we stay within the box of the protocols and customs that the law and profession have created for us and never wonder why things are the way they are. We don't ask why, indeed, lawyers need to succumb to client demands for "killer" lawyers; why procedural maneuvering has become a time-honored substitute for substantive resolutions; why lawyers don't discourage clients hell bent on vendettas.[68]

This peculiar passivity in accepting the prevailing norms and attitudes in the legal profession – many of which are antithetical to a fair, efficient, and respected legal system – suggests that attorneys are more interested in preserving a flawed system than reforming it. Not surprisingly, studies of law

[66] Gantt, Larry, & Madison, Benjamin. Teaching knowledge, skills, and values of professional identity formation. In Maranville, Deborah, Bliss, Lisa Radtke, Kaas, Carolyn Wilkes, & Lopez, Antoinette Sedillo (Eds.). (2015). *Building on best practices: Transforming legal education in a changing world* (p. 258). New Providence, New Jersey: LexisNexis.

[67] Noonan, John. (1976). *Persons and masks of the law* (p. 123). Berkeley, California: University of California Press.

[68] Helm, Katherine A., & Cohen, Joel. (2009, May 1). Particularly in tough times, civility among lawyers can go a long way. *San Francisco Daily Journal*, p. 6.

students' development during law school show that they become more cynical about the legal profession "but also more protective of it."[69]

Eliminating Bias

Lawyers also disappoint the public and belie their stated respect for the rule of law when they discriminate against female and ethnic minority attorneys. Although the Fundamental Values of the Profession identify the elimination of bias and the correction of "the effects of those biases" as one of the three most critical steps in improving the profession, the profession's actual progress has been glacial in speed and largely imaginary in effect. Females have comprised more than 40 percent of law school graduating classes since the mid-1980s, but "they account for only 18 percent of equity partners in the Am Law 200 and earn 80 percent of what their male counterparts do for comparable work, hours and revenue generation."[70] Minority men constitute 4.97 percent of law firm partners, and minority women constitute 2.55 percent of equity and non-equity partners; African-American women "were just 0.64 percent of all law firm partners, and Hispanic women were 0.63 percent."[71] Worse yet, "women of color continue to leave firms faster than any other group."[72]

The failure to recruit, retain, and equitably compensate female and ethnic minority attorneys is reprehensible in a profession that espouses the rule of law. It is particularly disturbing to see that law firms lag behind other professions in achieving diversity, as Danielle Holley-Walker, dean of Howard University School of Law, states: "We're still a profession less diverse than doctors or engineers and that is 88 percent white. We've been at this for 40-plus years – firms have been recruiting lawyers of color since the late '60s. There should be no mystery about how you create a diverse workforce. It's just a commitment."[73]

Reporting Misconduct

Attorneys also thwart improvements to the profession when they decline to report another attorney's unethical and incompetent behavior to their state bar

---

[69] Daicoff, Susan. (2015). Lawyer, form thyself: Professional identity formation strategies in legal education through "soft skills" training, ethics, and experiential courses. *Regent University Law Review*, 27(2), 206.

[70] Jackson, Liane. (2016, March 1). Minority women are disappearing from BigLaw – and here's why. *ABA Journal*.

[71] McQueen, M.P. (2016, August 1). Minority women: Still left out. *The American Lawyer*.

[72] Ibid.   [73] Jackson, *supra* note 70.

disciplinary organizations. Model Rule 8.3 specifically requires attorneys to
report to their disciplinary authorities conduct that "raises a substantial question as to that lawyer's honesty, trustworthiness or fitness as a lawyer in other
respects."[74] Although no one wants to be a snitch, the consequences of not
reporting unethical conduct in the legal profession can be very different from
the consequences of passivity in other circumstances for at least four reasons:
(1) it may be unethical and a violation of professional rules not to report ethical
violations; (2) your license to practice law could be suspended or revoked for
declining to report ethical violations; (3) other attorneys' clients will continue
to be harmed if you choose to overlook their attorneys' unethical behavior; and
(4) you may become implicated and complicit in unethical behavior that you
decide not to report.[75]

No matter how many ethics courses they take during and after law school,
attorneys still seem to be surprised to learn that the reporting rules apply to
attorneys with whom they work, not just bad actors in other law firms. Law
firm partners often act as though their earnestness in helping an errant
colleague supersedes the organized bar's interest in protecting clients from
and compensating them for that colleague's misconduct. In their strenuous
efforts to preserve collegiality and promote a firm's image, law firm partners
and associates sometimes overlook basic disclosure and reporting rules
regarding their own colleagues, e.g., attorneys may be required to report
unethical behavior by another attorney in their own law firm; an associate
attorney may have to inform the court when a partner is misrepresenting facts
to a judge; and a partner may have to report an associate attorney's unethical
conduct.[76]

The infrequency of attorney-initiated complaints to state bar disciplinary
commissions indicates that very few attorneys understand and perform their
reporting obligations. In Wisconsin, for example, attorneys initiate only

[74] ABA Model Rules of Prof'l Conduct R. 8.3
[75] Ibid. See *In re Rivers*, 331 S.E.2d 332 (S.C. 1984). *In re Himmel*, 533 N.E.2d 790 (Ill. 1998). ABA
      Formal Opinion 03–431. ("A lawyer who believes that another lawyer's mental condition
      materially impairs her ability to represent clients, and who knows that that lawyer continues to
      do so, must report that lawyer's consequent violation of Rule 1.16(a)(2), which requires that
      she withdraw from the representation of clients.") ABA Formal Opinion 03–429. ("When the
      impaired lawyer is unable or unwilling to deal with the consequences of his impairment, the
      firm's partners and the impaired lawyer's supervisors have an obligation to take steps to assure
      the impaired lawyer's compliance with the [ABA] Model Rules. ... The firm's paramount
      obligation is to take steps to protect the interests of its clients.")
[76] See *Skolnick v. Altheimer & Gray*, 730 N.E. 2d 4 (Ill. 2000). *In Re Rivers, supra* note 75.
      Daniels v. Alander, 818 A.2d 106 (Conn. 2003). Conn. Informal Ethics Op. 89–21 (1989).
      Gendry, Cynthia. (1994, Spring). An attorney's duty to report the professional misconduct of
      co-workers. *Southern Illinois University Law Journal*, 18, 603.

3 percent of the disciplinary complaints; in Washington State, only 4 percent of the disciplinary grievances are filed by attorneys; and in Utah, attorneys are the source of only 8 percent of complaints.[77] This low reporting rate is suspect because, as Mary Robinson, former administrator of the Attorney Registration and Disciplinary Commission of the Supreme Court of Illinois, states, "lawyers are in positions to know things about other lawyers that might not be known to others and to understand the significance of matters that might be lost on others. Yet very few lawyers want to make reports, and many would talk themselves out of it if they felt free to ignore Rule 8.3."[78]

Instead of reporting misconduct, many attorneys operate on the rule of convenience: the duty to disclose and report is directly proportionate to the convenience of disclosure and reporting. If disclosure and reporting would disrupt an important relationship, then they are unlikely to occur. Stated differently by the legal theorist Karl Llewellyn in 1930, "All that is needed, to assure you of success (once you acquire *any* clients) is for you to choose the convenient ethic at the convenient time."[79] For attorneys who adopt this approach, Llewellyn states, "the spine is absent, but the beak is strong."[80]

Mentoring Other Attorneys

Much of the mystery of complying with ethical requirements and practicing law in general could be solved by providing more mentoring programs to attorneys. In addition to providing practical advice to new attorneys, mentoring programs fulfill experienced attorneys' ethical duty to train and prepare new lawyers. As 3M General Counsel Marschall Smith explains, "The absolute requirement of lawyers as professionals is that we transmit and educate our colleagues and the next generation as it comes along. That sort of broad educational function probably is the defining aspect of what we do for a living. And on a day-to-day basis, the way that's done in the real world is mentoring."[81]

---

[77] Office of Lawyer Regulation and Board of Administrative Oversight. (2016). *Annual report fiscal year 2015–2016* (Appendix 8C, p. 47). Washington State Bar Association. *Discipline system 2015 annual report* (p. 9). Utah State Bar Office of Professional Conduct. *Annual Report, August 2015* (p. 23).

[78] Robinson, Mary T. (2007). A lawyer's duty to report another lawyer's misconduct: The Illinois experience. *The Professional Lawyer* (Symposium Issue), 47.

[79] Llewellyn, Karl. (1930). *The bramble bush: On our law and its study*. Dobbs Ferry, New York: Oceana Publications.

[80] Ibid.

[81] Vorro, Alex. (2012, March 27). Mentoring helps attorneys at all levels advance their careers: Programs allow seasoned lawyers to impart wisdom to the next generation. *Inside Counsel.*

Mentoring programs are remarkably successful. Most attorneys surveyed by the California State Bar, for example, report that mentoring "was crucial to my success."[82] In a survey of attorneys participating in the Illinois State Bar mentoring program, 99 percent of participants said they would "recommend the mentoring program to a fellow attorney," and 98 percent "plan to maintain a relationship with their mentoring partner."[83] An attorney participant described her mentor as "truly inspirational in her conversations about why she loves being an attorney" and says she "cannot wait to sign up as a mentor in the future."[84]

DUTIES TO SOCIETY

About one hundred years ago, the Carnegie Foundation sponsored a study of the administration of justice in the United States. Reginald Heber Smith, the then managing partner of Hale & Dorr (later WilmerHale) and counsel to the Boston Legal Aid Society, published the study results in his 308-page tract, *Justice and the Poor: A Study of Present Day Denial of Justice to the Poor*.[85] He found that delays, high court costs, and prohibitively expensive attorneys fees beset the legal system. As a consequence, Smith wrote, the legal system effectively "has operated to close the doors of the courts to the poor and has caused a gross denial of justice in all parts of the country to millions of persons."[86]

Elihu Root, a well-respected attorney and recipient of the Nobel Peace Prize, wrote the foreword to Smith's book in 1919. In that foreword he describes the circumstances that caused the poor to lose access to the courts:

> I do not think that we should be over-harsh in judging ourselves, however, for the shortcomings have been the result of changing conditions which the great body of our people have not fully appreciated . . . But the rapid growth of great cities, the enormous masses of immigrants (many of them ignorant of our language), and the greatly increased complications of life have created conditions under which the provisions for obtaining justice which were formerly sufficient are sufficient no longer. I think the true criticism which we should

[82] The State Bar of California Mentoring Task Force. (2015, July 1). *Preliminary report and recommendations* (p. 7).
[83] 2Civility. (2015). *2015 Annual Report: Illinois Supreme Court Commission on Professionalism* (p. 9). Retrieved from www.2civility.org/wp-content/uploads/Annual-Report-2015.pdf.
[84] Ibid. at 10.
[85] Smith, Reginald Heber. (1919). *Justice and the poor: A study of present day denial of justice to the poor*. Boston: D.B. Updike–The Merrymount Press.
[86] Ibid. at 8.

make upon our own conduct is that we have been so busy about our individual affairs that we have been slow to appreciate the changes of conditions which to so great an extent have put justice beyond the reach of the poor. But we cannot confine ourselves to that criticism much longer; it is time to set our own house in order.[87]

One hundred years after Root urged us to "set our own house in order," the conditions that impede access to the courts, as he described, have persisted if not worsened. Lamenting these conditions, former American Bar Association President William Hubbard notes that "eighty percent of low-income Americans do not have access to civil justice," and the United States is ranked "65th of 99 countries in accessibility and affordability of civil justice."[88] Contemporary efforts to improve access still meet the same type of criticisms leveled at Smith in 1919; his book was attacked as being based on "a few striking though hardly typical instances of delay and expense" and as being "used by radicals to aid them in their attacks upon our institutions."[89]

Under Rule 6.1 of the ABA Model Rules of Professional Conduct, "a lawyer should aspire to render at least (50) hours of pro bono publico legal services per year," and "a substantial majority of the 50 hours" should be provided without fee or expectation of fee to "persons of limited means" or organizations that "address the needs of persons of limited means."[90] But only one-third of attorneys meet this requirement by providing legal representation without compensation.[91] One in five attorneys do not contribute a single hour to pro bono legal representation.[92] Although Rule 6.1 requires "*at least* 50 hours of pro bono legal services," most law firms impose a 50-hour cap on the total pro bono hours that may be counted toward an attorney's billable hours requirement, ensuring that billable hours will not be sacrificed once the minimum requirement under Rule 6.1 is met.[93] Rule 6.1 further provides, "In addition, a lawyer should voluntarily contribute financial support to organizations that provide legal services to persons of limited means."[94] The most recent survey of the nation's largest and

---

[87] Ibid. at ix–x.   [88] Hubbard, *supra* note 3 at 8.   [89] Noonan, *supra* note 67 at 145.
[90] ABA Model Rules of Prof'l Conduct R. 6.1.
[91] American Bar Association Standing Committee on Pro Bono and Public Service. (2013, March). *Supporting justice III: A report on the pro bono work of America's lawyers* (p. vii). Chicago, Illinois: American Bar Association.
[92] Ibid. at vi.
[93] (2010, April). A look at associate hours and law firm pro bono programs (Table 6). *NALP Bulletin*.
[94] ABA Model Rules of Prof'l Conduct R. 6.1.

TABLE 8.1. *Comparative importance of pro bono services and other attorney activities*

Quality/skill	Necessary immediately (%)	Necessary over time (%)	Necessary immediately or over time (%)
Adapt work habits to meet demands and expectations	70.8	26.9	97.7
Adhere to proper timekeeping and/or billing practices	74.5	11.5	86
Have a personality that fits the firm or organization	53.0	20.8	73.8
Be visible in the office	47.4	14.7	62.1
Have a passion for public service	24.8	14.2	39
Engage in pro bono work	10.2	17.1	27.3
Volunteer or take on influential positions in the community	4.5	19.9	24.4
Be involved in a bar association	11.0	12.8	23.8

Source: IAALS, Foundations for Practice (2016)

wealthiest law firms, however, shows that they donate only 0.1 percent of their revenue to legal aid.[95]

Attorneys report that the five most significant factors that discourage them from providing pro bono services are (1) lack of time, (2) commitment to family obligations, (3) lack of skills or experience in the practice areas needed, (4) billable hour expectations and policies, and (5) cost and burden to law practice.[96] But the IAALS survey suggests that attorneys do not provide pro bono services because they are immaterial to an attorney's success. Seventy-three percent of attorneys in the IAALS survey reported that engaging in pro bono legal work is either "not relevant" or "advantageous but not necessary" to an attorney's success.[97] As shown in Table 8.1, the surveyed attorneys report that it is far more important for an attorney to "have a personality that fits the firm or organization" than to provide pro bono services to the indigent or to participate in community service.

[95] Beck, Susan. (2015, June 29). The justice gap: How Big Law is failing legal aid. *The American Lawyer*.

[96] American Bar Association Standing Committee on Pro Bono and Public Service. *supra* note 91 at 30.

[97] Gerkman & Cornett, *supra* note 20 at 10.

Discussing the organized bar's chronic difficulties in providing access to justice, former ABA President Robert Raven depicts the problem as a constitutional issue of critical importance to every attorney:

> You know, a lot of attorneys worry about the image of the profession. They should worry because the system just isn't working and the image is painfully close to the truth ... Correcting the system is not a "liberal" notion. Access to justice is not a political cause. The preamble of the Constitution says, "to establish justice." That doesn't mean pursue justice, it means establish justice. That's what we all should worry about – in our professional associations, in our firms, and in our lives ... We don't need more people in the law who look at their profession primarily as a business. Lawyers have a social obligation. People who don't understand the burden of that should look elsewhere for work.[98]

Raven's remarks crystallize the concept of professionalism: taking responsibility for a legal system that should not merely pursue justice but embody justice; earning public trust and esteem by ensuring that the legal system is accessible to all citizens; acknowledging and assuming a responsibility to serve society; and recognizing that attorneys who cannot fulfill both their private and public responsibilities should yield their positions to other attorneys who embrace both responsibilities. Raven's concept of professionalism also is consonant with the Preamble to the Model Rules of Professional Conduct, stating, "A lawyer, as a member of the legal profession, is a representative of clients, an officer of the legal system and a public citizen having special responsibility for the quality of justice." It is imperative for attorneys to accept that responsibility for the administration and quality of justice so that attorneys will not read Raven's comments 100 years from now and wonder, just as we wonder when reading Root and Smith's statements from 1919, why attorneys' commitment to social justice was inexcusably faint and stunningly ineffective.

CHAPTER CAPSULE

For lawyers, professionalism frequently is defined as an internal set of principles, ethics, values, and aspirations – commonly subsumed under the category "character." Although character is indeed important, the emphasis on character misdirects our attention when we attempt to define professionalism and delineate professional conduct. Character necessarily turns our focus inward,

[98] Moll, *supra* note 4 at 139–140.

resulting in an egocentric perspective on professionalism that obscures our responsibilities and duties to others.

If a medical school student graduated but never treated a patient or otherwise advanced patient welfare through research or teaching, we might hesitate to consider him a professional or a person whose conduct is circumscribed by professionalism. But attorneys appear to have little difficulty viewing professionalism and referring to their professional identity as an attribute detached from their duties to and effects on clients, other attorneys, judges, the legal profession, and society in general. This difference between physicians and lawyers may have its genesis in the first year of professional education when medical students realize they soon will be diagnosing and treating patients, while law students realize they can and usually will graduate without seeing a single client. Sir William Osler, regarded as the "father of modern medicine," captured this difference between the professions in 1901 when he remarked, "To study the phenomenon of disease without books is to sail an uncharted sea, while to study books without patients is not to go to sea at all."[99] Employing a different metaphor, legal historian Lawrence Friedman characterizes law school pedagogy as "a geology without rocks, an astronomy without stars."[100]

This detachment from clients and practical outcomes continues as attorneys transition from law school to law practice. It fosters professionalism without responsibility and accountability to the people, organizations, systems, and institutions directly affected by attorneys. It has led to a legal system that is inaccessible to most Americans and inferior in critical respects to those of other industrialized countries.

In attempting to understand and exhibit professionalism, we may benefit from a more comprehensive concept centered on attorneys' duties to themselves, clients, other attorneys, judges, the legal profession, and society. As former U.S. district court judge Sven Erik Holmes asserts, attorneys must "understand that being a lawyer means taking on a special role in your community and that you must never lose sight of your responsibility to the law and to the society it serves."[101]

[99] Calabrese, Leonard. (2005, May). Sir William Osler then and now: Thoughts for the osteopathic profession. *The Journal of the American Osteopathic Association, 105,* 245–249.

[100] Friedman, Lawrence. (1985). *A history of American law* (2nd ed.). (p. 617). New York: Touchstone.

[101] Holmes, Sven Erik. (2015, September 28). Before going to law school, live your life. *The National Law Journal.*

9

Conclusion

Sea squirts are small, colorful marine animals with a transparent covering that ranges in texture from tough to gelatinous. Their name is derived from their impulse to squirt water when disturbed. Some live alone, others live in colonies; they all have well-developed cardiovascular systems and spinal cords. Sea squirts feed by filtering plankton from the surrounding water and then excrete waste by positioning themselves in the current so that their intake siphons are always upstream, free from their own contaminants.

When young, sea squirts look like tadpoles and are quite mobile. But as they mature, they quickly and permanently affix themselves to a hard surface, like shells or rocks, developing a barrel-shaped body and leading a sluggish existence. Once affixed, sea squirts ingest their cerebral ganglion, their counterpart to the human brain. Because the sea squirt will remain inert for the rest of its life, the ganglion is no longer necessary for exploration, navigation, and movement.

Sea squirts are "distant cousins of humans."[1] Like sea squirts, many attorneys find a comfortable, secure niche early in their careers and start to disconnect their nerves and dull their senses. They reduce their involvement with the world outside their law firms and departments, avoid circumstances where they would meet dissimilar people, and devote their efforts to familiar tasks and routines. Their interactions with the world, like those of sea squirts, become largely passive and reactive, dependent on external conditions over which they relinquished control. Because they have immobilized themselves and disconnected the more advanced sources of sensation and cognition, they feel neither dissonance nor fulfillment, neither lassitude nor challenge.

For many attorneys, this process of disassociation begins in law school. As law professor Susan Daicoff notes, students become

---

[1] Coates, John. (2012). *The hour between dog and wolf* (p. 40). New York: Penguin Press.

less philosophical, less introspective, and less interested in abstractions, ideas, and the scientific method; and less focused on intrinsic satisfactions, while more motivated by external rewards. They become less interested in helping their communities and more interested in image and attractiveness, a shift that is linked to a decline in well being. Law students' moral and ethical decision-making also changes in law school; they tend to shift away from relational, contextual decision-making and an ethic of care towards more rational, logical, rule-oriented approaches.[2]

Law students, state law professors Larry Gantt and Benjamin Madison, also become "more self-centered and less service-oriented."[3]

Once in law practice, many attorneys lose their natural inquisitiveness, disengage from their work, and retreat from any effort to influence their colleagues or improve their work product. As one associate describes the impact of templates and forms on her transactional work:

> If an associate tried to change the language – especially with an important term – she will be asked, "Why are you doing this?" Or, "Why didn't you bring this up last time [on the last deal]?" That will be followed by, "If it was going to be brought up, it would have been brought up twenty years ago, when we put this in." The risk of doing things differently makes everyone nervous, very nervous – especially when you don't know what the clause means in the first place.
>
> The firm told us when we got here that we were not to circulate anything that we didn't understand. Talk about a contradiction. Most of what we mark up and send around, we don't understand at all.[4]

Another associate explained that his passivity resulted from a combination of inexperience and isolation: "The lawyers who wrote the earlier contract we were using as a template were meant to be learned from, not challenged. Plus, I did not feel like my intellect was respected or valued on the deal team."[5]

Over time, many attorneys develop a chronic sense of disassociation, boredom, alienation, and powerlessness. They lose their enthusiasm, resiliency,

---

[2] Daicoff, Susan. (2015). Lawyer, form thyself: Professional identity formation strategies in legal education through "soft skills" training, ethics, and experiential courses. *Regent University Law Review*, 27(2), 206.

[3] Gantt, Larry O. Natt, & Madison, Benjamin V. (2015). Teaching knowledge, skills, and values of professional identity formation. In Maranville, Deborah, Bliss, Lisa Radtke, Kaas, Carolyn Wilkes, & Lopez, Antoinette Sedillo (Eds.). *Building on best practices: Transforming legal education in a changing world* (p. 259). New Providence, New Jersey: LexisNexis.

[4] Gulati, Mitu, & Scott, Robert. *The 3 ½ minute transaction* (pp. 93–94). Chicago: The University of Chicago Press.

[5] Ibid. at 94.

and commitment to the values that initially attracted them to law practice – yet they make very few efforts to find a more satisfying job. Although more than one-third of attorneys say that they intend to leave their job within a year, only 3–5 percent actually do that.[6] Money plays an outsized role in attorneys' assessments of their career satisfaction, acting as a salve over an underlying dissatisfaction. When asked "Overall, how satisfied are you with your life as an attorney when you factor your compensation into the equation?" only 10 percent of equity partners report they are slightly, moderately, or very dissatisfied.[7] But when equity partners are asked "Overall, how satisfied are you with your life as an attorney when you DO NOT factor your compensation into the equation?" the level of dissatisfaction is nearly doubled, 19 percent of equity partners reporting they are slightly, moderately, or very dissatisfied.[8]

This book serves as an invitation to attorneys to recognize that, when they separate themselves from the self-awareness, emotions, perceptions, and sensibilities that underpin soft skills and then accept the ensuing alienation and disenchantment, they ignore their most valuable resources and sever their most important attributes. In their quest for professional success, they emphasize technical competencies to the exclusion of soft skills, unaware that their soft skills are more determinative of career success and personal fulfillment than technical competencies. They not only narrow themselves but also diminish their prospects for achieving their own career and personal goals.

Soft skills, fortunately, can be recovered and enhanced, as demonstrated by the hundreds of studies cited in this book. If we are resistant to discovering and developing our soft skills, the source of that resistance lies within each individual and is not supported by empirical research. The toughest obstacle, then, might be convincing ourselves that we succeed when we acknowledge the primacy of soft skills. As U.S. Supreme Court Justice Sonia Sotomayor notes, recalling her experience as an assistant district attorney, "Granting myself permission to use my innate skills of the heart, accepting that emotion was perfectly valid in the art of persuasion, amounted to nothing less than a breakthrough."[9] It was the "single most powerful lesson I would learn," she states. "It changed my entire approach to jurors, from the voir dire to the structure of my summations, and the results spoke for themselves: I never lost a case again."[10]

[6] Neil, Martha. (2008, June 23). Why don't unhappy lawyers leave? *ABA Journal Law News Now*.

[7] Lowe, Jeffrey A. (2016). *2016 Partner compensation survey* (p. 62). Washington, DC: Major, Lindsey & Africa.

[8] Ibid. at 65.

[9] Sotomayor, Sonia. (2013). *My beloved world* (p. 268). New York: Vintage Books.   [10] Ibid.

APPENDIX

Summary of Less Recent Lawyering Skills Studies

As explained in Chapter 2, the less recent studies of essential lawyering skills are summarized in this Appendix.

CLIENT-BASED STUDY

Male inmates/Boccaccini and Brodsky (2001).[1] The researchers asked 250 male inmates, who had been incarcerated for an average of 3.21 years and had an average of 7.25 years left to serve on their sentences, to answer this question: "I want you to pretend that you have a new attorney, and he/she is exactly the kind of attorney you want. Please describe what he/she would be like by writing some sentences in the space below."

Their responses were coded independently by two evaluators, yielding this list of "ideal attorney characteristics" in descending order: advocates for client's interests; effective lawyering skills; works hard on client's case; keeps client informed about their case; cares about the client; honest; gets client a favorable outcome; would not do whatever prosecution says; listens to what the client says; and spends time with the client before court date.[2] "Although it seems that clients facing incarceration would be most concerned about their attorneys' lawyering abilities," the researchers explain, "the findings of this study suggest that criminal defendants are equally as concerned with their attorneys' client relations skills. Half of the ideal attorney characteristics identified by participants were client relations skills."[3]

---

[1] Boccaccini, Marcus, & Brodsky, Stanley. (2001, Spring). Characteristics of the ideal criminal defense attorney from the client's perspective: Empirical findings and implications for legal practice. *Law and Psychology Review*, 25, 81.

[2] Ibid. at 116.   [3] Ibid. at 99–100.

ATTORNEY-BASED STUDIES

Female Super Lawyers/Snyder (2012).[4] Female attorneys selected for inclusion in
the *Super Lawyers* directory agreed to take the Brief Strengths Test (BST) and to
participate in a telephone interview. Eighty-one percent were partners in law
firms; 19 percent were solo practitioners. The attorneys' BST results showed "top
strengths" in gratitude, kindness, social intelligence, zest, bravery, forgiveness,
hope, love, prudence, and self-control.[5] Most of the attorneys "reported that they
used their top strengths daily."[6] Although all attorneys "had a mixture of
head and heart strengths," the heart strengths were the most commonly
occurring top strengths. In the interviews, the attorneys identified these
strengths as being "most responsible for their professional success:" positive
relationships with others, hard work, persistence, legal skills, meaning, luck,
intelligence, and risk-taking.[7]

Am Law 100 law firm associates/Berman and Bock (2012).[8] In this study
of associates in a large law firm, Lori Berman and Heather Bock, professional
development officers at Hogan Lovells US LLP, analyzed the comparative
effects of four technical competencies (legal research and knowledge of
law; written advocacy; oral advocacy, trial, and negotiation skills; and
factual development, investigation, and discovery) and four behavioral
competencies (drive for excellence; teamwork; leadership and case
management; and client service and communication). Regression analyses
"revealed that three behavioral competencies and one technical competence
seemed especially critical in predicting performance."[9] The three critical
behavioral competencies were drive for excellence, leadership and case
management, and teamwork; the critical technical competence was written
advocacy.[10]

High performers, the study finds, differ from other associate attorneys in
three respects: (1) their mindset and philosophy; (2) managing the work

[4] Snyder, Patricia. (2012, August 1). *Super women lawyers: A study of character strengths.*
     Unpublished masters thesis. Retrieved from http://repository.upenn.edu/mapp_capstone/38/.
[5] Ibid. at 70, appendix C.   [6] Ibid. at 24   [7] Ibid. at 23.
[8] Berman, Lori, & Bock, Heather. (2012). Developing attorneys for the future: What can we
     learn from the fast trackers? *Santa Clara Law Review,* 52(3), 875.
[9] Ibid. at 888.
[10] Ibid. at 888–889. The researchers also sought to determine whether four behavioral
     competencies – locus of control (a belief that we can influence our own environment); self-
     efficacy (a belief that we can succeed in multiple contexts); learning orientation (a belief
     that challenges provide opportunities for personal growth and development); and achieve-
     ment orientation (an intent to meet a high standard of accomplishment) – were related to
     associate performance in a large law firm. They found that these factors "did not predict
     either competencies or performance" (at 891).

environment and results; and (3) working hard and collaborating with others. In mindset and philosophy, high performers exhibit equanimity, action-oriented mental strength, intrinsic and extrinsic needs for achievement, and a strong sense of self. In managing the work environment and results, high achievers show exceptional flexibility in handling unforeseen or ambiguous situations; demonstrate openness in considering multiple solutions to problems and seeking external advice; and display effort, persistence, and ownership in handling new challenges. Lastly, in working and collaborating with others, high-performing associates develop and use professional relationships to meet personal and team goals; seek to influence and have an impact on others; and maintain emotional independence by setting boundaries with colleagues' "feelings and intimate emotions."[11]

General Counsel/Wanser (2012).[12] Donna Wanser, Vice President of Legal at Panda Restaurant Group, Inc., assessed the emotional intelligence levels of general counsel in California. She found that "their mean total EQ [emotional quotient] was virtually the same as that of the normative sample representing the general population."[13] Their specific scores on flexibility and self-awareness matched those of the normative sample. On the surface, these scores suggest that general counsel are average; but as Wanser points out, this finding is anomalous because, unlike the general counsel sample, only 9 percent of the normative sample held advanced degrees. The general counsel "scored significantly higher in independence, assertiveness, stress tolerance, and positive impression." The high score on positive impression, Wanser explains, "can indicate self deception, lack of self-awareness, or problematic self-esteem" and is consistent with research indicating that "lawyers tend to be narcissistic."[14]

U.S. trial attorneys/Kiser (2011).[15] Analyst Randall Kiser interviewed 78 trial attorneys in California and New York who had been selected as exceptionally accurate case evaluators from a dataset of 8,114 attorneys. He found that their mental frameworks – the perception, conception, construction, and presentation of a client's case – had seven major features. First, they employ a technique known as "backward mapping," starting at the end of a case and working backward to realize that end. Second, they form a composite view of the case, taking a global outlook on the evidence and eschewing a narrow,

[11] Ibid. at 896–897.
[12] Wanser, Donna. (2012, February). *The emotional intelligence of general counsels in relation to lawyer leadership.* Unpublished doctoral dissertation, Pepperdine University Graduate School of Education and Psychology.
[13] Ibid. at 51 [14] Ibid. at 52.
[15] Kiser, Randall. (2011). *How leading lawyers think* (p. 42). Heidelberg, New York: Springer.

deconstructionist approach. Third, they create overarching themes to link facts and hook into jurors' values and sense of morality. Fourth, they recognize that jurors process information visually, and they are visual thinkers themselves or have learned how to convey vivid pictures of critical case facts and events. Fifth, they have the capacity to see the case through multiple lenses, assuming the roles of jurors, judges, mediators, insurers, and opposing counsel to develop a persuasive argument and presentation. Sixth, they integrate both explicit knowledge and tacit knowledge into their legal representation, enabling the client to obtain the benefit of their technical legal knowledge and their personal judgments about people. Seventh, they have peripheral vision, a habit and skill of scoping, scanning, interpreting, and probing beyond the immediate field to anticipate problems and avoid mishaps.[16]

Arizona lawyers/Gerst and Hess (2009).[17] Law professors Stephen Gerst and Gerry Hess asked Arizona State Bar Association members to rank 44 professional skills and values. The ten skills and values most frequently rated as "essential" or "very important" were: legal analysis and reasoning; act honestly and with integrity; show reliability and willingness to accept responsibility; strive to provide competent, high-quality legal work for each client; written communication; treat clients, lawyers, judges, staff with respect; legal research; drafting legal documents; listening; and oral communication.[18] Although these skills and values are evenly balanced between technical competencies and behavioral competencies, the behavioral competencies had a higher average ranking.

California lawyers/Shultz and Zedeck (2009).[19] To determine lawyer effectiveness factors, law professor Marjorie Shultz and psychology professor Sheldon Zedeck conducted interviews with lawyers, law professors, law students, judges, and clients, asking questions like, "If you were looking for a lawyer for an important matter for yourself, what qualities would you most

---

[16] Ibid. at 42. (This paragraph is a modified version of the original description of these frameworks.) The interviews also indicated that the attorneys relied on five traits and attitudes that facilitated continual learning: "(1) reliance on 'developed' talents instead of 'innate' abilities; (2) openness to improvement and change; (3) humility, modesty and caution; (4) a belief that performance can be improved through effort and self-evaluation; and (5) active solicitation of feedback and criticism" (p. 88.).

[17] Gerst, Stephen & Hess, Gerald. (2009). Professional skills and values in legal education: The GPS model. *Valparaiso University Law Review*, 43(2), 513.

[18] Ibid. at 524–525.

[19] Shultz, Marjorie M., & Zedeck, Sheldon. (2009, January 30). Final report: Identification, development, and validation of predictors for successful lawyering. Retrieved from http://papers.ssrn.com/sol3/papers.cfm?abstract_id=1353554.

look for?" and "What kind of lawyer do you want to teach or be?"[20] Based on these interviews, they identified 26 "effectiveness factors," listed below. Overall, 20 of the 26 factors are soft skills.

The soft skills competencies of "networking, building relationships, practical judgment, ability to see the world through the eyes of others, and commitment to community service" were negatively correlated with high academic performance. In fact, very few of the effectiveness factors had any relation to academic performance, as law professor William Henderson points out: "Remarkably, LSAT scores, undergraduate GPA, and first year law school grades were correlated at statistically significant levels with between zero and six of the 26 success factors, depending upon the subgroup."[21] In other words, less than 25 percent of the success factors had an arguably significant relation to LSAT scores, undergraduate GPAs, and 1L grades.

Shultz and Zedeck Lawyer Effectiveness Factors

1. Intellectual and cognitive
   - Analysis and reasoning
   - Creativity/innovation
   - Problem solving
   - Practical judgment
2. Research and information gathering
   - Researching the law
   - Fact-finding
   - Questioning and interviewing
3. Communications
   - Influencing and advocating
   - Writing
   - Speaking
   - Listening
4. Planning and organizing
   - Strategic planning
   - Organizing and managing one's own work
   - Organizing and managing others (staff/colleagues)
5. Conflict resolution
   - Negotiation skills
   - Able to see the world through the eyes of others

[20]   Ibid. at 25.
[21]   Henderson, William D. (2009). The bursting of the pedigree bubble. Articles by Maurer Faculty. Paper 119. Retrieved from www.repository.law.indiana.edu/facpub/119.

6. Client and business relations – entrepreneurship
   - Networking and business development
   - Providing advice and counsel and building relationships with clients
7. Working with others
   - Developing relationships within the legal profession
   - Evaluation, development, and mentoring
8. Character
   - Passion and engagement
   - Diligence
   - Integrity/honesty
   - Stress management
   - Community involvement and service
   - Self-development

Criminal defense lawyers Boccaccini, Boothby, and Brodsky (2002).[22] Surveys were completed by 252 criminal defense attorneys. The attorneys rated these skills as being the five most important, in descending order: standing up for clients' rights, listening skills, comprehensive knowledge of criminal law, courtroom speaking skills, and caring about what happens to clients.[23] Psychology professors Marcus Boccaccini, Jennifer Boothby, and Stanley Brodsky found that both the attorneys and inmates surveyed in this study "viewed many client-relations skills as being as or more important than legal skills." Attorneys and inmates ranked "caring about what happens to clients" and "involving clients in decision making" as more important than "legal skills such as being a good deal maker and establishing relationships with prosecutors and judges."[24]

Canadian lawyers/Taylor (2001–2004).[25] In this extensive study of Canadian attorneys, consultant Irene Taylor analyzed leading attorneys in four categories: corporate transactional attorneys,[26] corporate litigation attorneys,[27] female attorneys,[28] and attorneys 40 years of age and younger.[29] Taylor's assessments

---

[22] Boccaccini, Marcus, Boothby, Jennifer, & Brodsky, Stanley. (2002, Spring). Client-relations skills in effective lawyering: Attitudes of criminal defense attorneys and experienced clients. *Law & Psychology Review, 26*, 97.

[23] Ibid. at 117–121. [24] Ibid. at 112–113

[25] Taylor, Irene E. (2002, November). Canada's Top 30 corporate dealmakers. *LEXPERT Magazine.* Taylor, Irene E. (2002, July). Canada's Top 25 corporate litigators. *LEXPERT Magazine.* Taylor, Irene E. (2004, November). Top 40 under 40, *LEXPERT Magazine.* Taylor, Irene E. (2003, September). Carpe diem! Canada's Top 25 women lawyers. *LEXPERT Magazine.* Taylor, Irene E. (2001, February 1). How smart are you really? *LEXPERT Magazine.*

[26] Taylor (2002, November), *supra* note 25. [27] Taylor (2002, July), *supra* note 25.

[28] Taylor (2003, September), *supra* note 25. [29] Taylor (2004, November), *supra* note 25.

of emotional intelligence for the general population of Canadian attorneys indicate that, although they have higher IQ levels than the average person, they do not score higher on emotional intelligence than the average person. (But attorneys generally score higher on emotional intelligence than the physicians tested by Taylor.)[30]

Taylor found that attorneys who are "star" performers, based on peer recognition, score considerably higher on emotional competencies than the average Canadian attorney. Specifically, star performers displayed high levels of empathy, stress management, optimism, social responsibility, and self-actualization.[31] (The traits specific to the four categories of attorneys are shown below.) Reflecting on the study results, Dale Lastman, one of the star performers, said, "The difference between successful people and others is a matter of caring about what you do, and that is emotional. These are the things that separate you from a commoditized world and I have to believe that a big reason people retain me is because I care."[32]

Star Corporate Litigator Traits

- Independent self-starters, sensitive, introverted, creative/abstract thinkers, moderately trusting optimists
- Primarily motivated by self-actualization, mastery, peer recognition, and altruism rather than money or power
- Strong work ethic with conscious long-term career commitments
- Highly and selectively competitive – winning the "right cases and tough cases" is more important than simply winning
- Thinking style is "abstract creative" – "conceptualize patterns and are future, end-game focused"
- "Closet introverts," deriving energy and ideas from their inner world and requiring time alone for problem solving; may have problems with team collaboration "even when they value it"
- High capabilities in empathy, reading other people's emotions, and factoring emotional considerations into decisions; enjoy aesthetic interests
- Above-average emotional intelligence and personal strengths in independence, self-direction, optimism, reality testing, and stress endurance
- Likely to be "high-maintenance" people, requiring strong support system, and having high expectations of people

[30] Taylor (2001, February), *supra* note 25. [31] Ibid. [32] Ibid.

Star Corporate Transactional Attorney Traits

- Extroverted and team-oriented, creative and inventive in a practical sense, and attach a premium to self-control
- Self-directed but, unlike litigators and attorneys under 40, the self-selection into corporate law "was not a calling"
- Tend to need constant and immediate gratification, like "action hero" quest for intellectual adventure, and seek self-actualization through accomplishment or closure
- Display high levels of self-awareness, raw intelligence, and a drive to succeed
- Exercise superb judgment in risk analysis, strategy, and problem solving and knowing how to instill trust and demonstrate commitment
- Are independent, stress tolerant, optimistic, and pragmatic and show positive self-regard
- Talents tend to be more focused and in a narrower range than litigation attorneys – "renaissance people they are not"
- Seek variety, change, intellectual challenge, and pragmatic action and thrive on stress
- Represent a "meritocracy" of first-generation lawyers – parents unlikely to be lawyers

Star Female Attorney Traits

- High emotional intelligence scores in independence, stress tolerance, assertiveness, and optimism
- Higher scores on empathy than other lawyers but lower than general population
- Lower scores on interpersonal relationships than other attorneys and general population[33]
- Strong skills in "reframing" problems, seeing adversity as a challenge, and redefining priorities to reflect actual urgency and consequence
- Most "made a point of seeking out a mentor," identifying "someone in their field for whom they had a great deal of respect and would use that person as a sounding board and adviser"[34]
- Well-honed time management techniques

[33] See Snyder, *supra* note 4.
[34] Stein, Steven, Book, Howard, & Kanoy, Korrel. (2013). *The student EQ edge*. San Francisco: Jossey-Bass.

Star Attorney 40 and Younger Traits

- Emotional intelligence strengths in independence, stress tolerance, assertiveness, and optimism
- Relative emotional intelligence weaknesses in flexibility, interpersonal relationships, self-awareness, and happiness
- Strong leadership abilities with above-average need for control, "particularly hands-on control," which can "negatively impact on effective delegation, mentoring, and ultimately, assumption of leadership roles"
- Notable capabilities in "big picture" and "small picture" thinking; highly effective at detail orientation *and* broad strategic thinking
- High motivation scores in engagement, persistence, dominance, and confidence in success
- Exceptional concentration abilities, awareness, and comprehension; low internal and external distractibility
- High levels of self-confidence and strategic and conceptual problem solving; rapid speed in decision making
- Adversity in formative years for two-thirds of study attorneys, e.g., death or serious illness of parent and financial hardship and language difficulties experienced with parents who immigrated to Canada, imposing "responsibility where younger siblings and others relied upon them"

Minnesota lawyers/Sonsteng (2000).[35] Minnesota lawyers ranked these legal skills as being the ten most important skills in descending order: ability to diagnose and plan solutions for legal problems; ability in legal analysis and legal reasoning; written communication; oral communication; instilling others' confidence in you; negotiation; sensitivity to professional and ethical concerns; fact gathering; drafting legal documents; and organization and management of legal work.[36] "Knowledge of procedural law" and "knowledge of the substantive law" did not appear among the ten most important skills.[37] Comparing the Minnesota results with earlier studies, the researchers found that the skills showing the largest increases in importance were computer legal research, the ability to obtain and keep clients, counseling, sensitivity to professional and ethical concerns, and fact gathering. The skill "knowledge of the substantive law" decreased in importance over a 24-year period.[38]

---

[35] Sonsteng, John & Camarotto, David. (2000). Minnesota lawyers evaluate law schools, training and legal education. *William Mitchell Law Review*, 26, 327.
[36] Ibid. at 337. [37] Ibid at 337. [38] Ibid. at 345.

Chicago lawyers/Garth and Martin (1993).[39] Although old, this study is informative because the researchers surveyed attorneys in a broad range of practice settings (corporate, government, and private practice), and its findings reveal major changes in legal practice since its publication. The surveyed attorneys were asked to "rank the 'importance' of seventeen legal skills and areas of knowledge."[40] The ten most highly rated legal skills, in descending order, are oral communication, written communication, ability in legal analysis and legal reasoning, instilling others' confidence in you, drafting legal documents, knowledge of substantive law, ability to diagnose and plan solutions for legal problems, organization and management of legal work, negotiation, and sensitivity to professional and ethical concerns. "Counseling" and "computer legal research" were among the lowest rated skills.[41]

Montana lawyers/Mudd and LaTrielle (1988).[42] All members of the Montana State Bar received a list of 149 abilities and were asked, "Based upon your experience, what level of competence should a lawyer have in order to perform in a professionally competent manner?" The skills rating the highest level of competence needed were: possesses the trait of honesty; possesses the trait of integrity; capacity to act ethically; possesses the trait of reliability; possesses the trait of judgment; capacity to analyze; capacity to communicate effectively in writing; possesses the trait of maturity; ability to make appropriate objections to evidence at trial; and understanding of the steps in a state civil action and organization of the courts, their jurisdiction, and venue.[43] Most of the highly ranked skills were, to use the researchers' term, in the "personal attribute category."

Criminal defense lawyers/Doyel (1986).[44] Fifty experienced criminal defense attorneys rated the importance of twenty abilities and traits in pretrial representation. Their highest ratings, in order of importance, were "knowledge of available sentencing alternatives to incarceration, the ability to negotiate with the prosecutor, the ability to establish a rapport with clients, knowledge of statutory minimum/maximum punishments, the ability to counsel clients, the ability to interview, and compassion."[45] The ability to establish a rapport with clients, compassion, and client relations skills "were

[39] Garth, Bryant G. & Martin, Joanne. (1993). Law schools and the construction of competence. *Journal of Legal Education, 43,* 469.

[40] Sonsteng & Camarotto, *supra* note 35 at 342.   [41] Garth & Martin, *supra* note 39 at 473.

[42] Mudd, John O., & LaTrielle, John W. (1988). Professional competence: A study of new lawyers. *Montana Law Review, 49,* 11.

[43] Ibid. at 17–18.

[44] Doyel, R. (1986). National College-Mercer criminal defense survey: Some preliminary observations about interviewing, counseling and plea negotiations. *Mercer Law Review,* 37(3), 1019.

[45] Boccaccini, Boothby, & Brodsky, *supra* note 22 at 106.

rated higher than other traditional legal skills such as the ability to get along with judges and to predict trial outcomes."[46]

Chicago attorneys/Zemans and Rosenblum (1981).[47] In a study sponsored by the American Bar Foundation, researchers surveyed a random sample of 828 practitioners in Chicago. About 550 practitioners responded to the survey, identifying the skills most important to law practice. Law professor Cynthia Kelly summarizes the results:

> Among the skills considered to be most important by practicing lawyers are the ability to gather facts and apply them to relevant concepts, to instill in others a belief in the lawyer's competency, and to use oral communication skills effectively. Accounting skills, knowledge of the social sciences, or the ability to write briefs or opinions were viewed as being the least important skills.[48]

The ranking of the skills varied with the surveyed attorneys' practice areas. Kelly notes: "In general the greater the prestige attributed to a specialty, the more important was the ability to understand and interpret opinions, regulations and statutes, draft legal documents, opinions and letters, and possess accounting skills and financial sense. The lower the specialty prestige, the more important was effective oral communication, knowledge of procedural law and interviewing skills."[49]

[46] Ibid. at 107.
[47] Zemans, Frances Kahn, & Rosenblum, Victor G. (1981). *The making of a public profession.* Chicago: American Bar Foundation.
[48] Kelly, Cynthia. (1982). The making of a public profession. *DePaul Law Review, 31,* 667. See Schultz, Franklin. (1995). Teaching "lawyering" to first year law students: An experiment in constructing legal competence. *Washington & Lee Law Review, 52,* 1655. (1982, January). The Bar: An inward look in the mirror. *ABA Journal,* p. 54.
[49] Kelly, *supra* note 48 at 667, 669.

Index

Francis, John, 150
Frantz, Cynthia, 167
Fredrickson, B. L., 105
Freedman, Marc, 219
Frensch, Peter A., 14
Freshman, Clark, 76
Frewer, L.J., 171, 173
Fried, Jesse M., 25
Friedman, Gabe, 26
Frost, Alison, 212
Frost, Bryan-Paul, 263
Fryer, Bronwyn, 57
Fundamental Values of the Profession, 42, 55,
    87, 279, 281
Furman, Jason, 265
Furnham, A., 10

Galinsky, Adam, 83, 86, 126–128, 167, 204
Gallman, J. Matthew, 125
Gallo, Carmine, 151
Gamble, Vanessa, 180
Gantt, Larry, 163, 280, 290
Garcia, Emma, 5
Gardner, Amy, 21
Gardner, Dan, 119, 198
Gardner, Heidi, 177
Gardner, Howard, 228, 250
Garner, Dwight, 163
Garth, Bryant G., 25, 301
Garvin, David, 109
Gates, Bill, 82
Gautham, Thomas, 211
Gazzaniga, Michael S., 53
Gazzola, Valeria, 162
Gee, E.G., 187
Gelb, Adam, 266
Gendry, Cynthia, 282
general-ability fallacy, 16
George, Elizabeth, 176
Gerdy, Kristin, 25, 27
Gerkman, Alli, 12, 25, 29, 30, 61, 269, 286
Gerst, Stephen, 295
Gerstein, Marc, 243
Gest, John Marshall, 35
Gibson, Steve, 15
Gigerenzer, Gerd, 119
Gilbert, Natasha, 138
Gilfillan, Christopher, 248
Gilkey, Roderick, 11, 47
Gilman, Gregory, 92
Gilovich, Thomas, 125, 142, 237

Gino, Francesca, 57, 86, 107, 145
Giridharadas, Anand, 83
Gladwell, Malcolm, 7, 9, 81, 88
Glaze, Lauren, 265
goal achievement, 121, 124, 125
Goldsmith, Joan, 231, 232, 241
Goldsmith, Marshall, 230
Goleman, Daniel, 7–9, 88, 141, 153, 161, 162, 218,
    231, 234
Golonka, Sabrina, 126
Goncalo, Jack, 201
Gonzales, Laurence, 253
Google, 178, 179
Gordon, Leslie, 219
Gorlitz, D., 120
Gottlieb, Anita, 25
Gottschalk, Petter, 228
Goulston, Mark, 153
Goyal, Madhav, 131
Graham, Duffy, 193
Gramlich, John, 266
Grant, Adam, 176
Greaves, Jean, 9, 105
Greene, Jenna, 158
Greever, Kathryn, 99
Gregersen, Hal, 201
Grewal, Daisy, 20, 83
Griffin, Dale, 44, 237
grit, 10, 135
Grogan, James M., 276
Gross, James, 47, 48
Grossman, P., 131
Grote, G., 94
Guenther, Elisabeth, 166
Guillen, L., 11
Gujar, Ninad, 219
Gulati, Mitu, 211, 290
Gully, Stanley, 101
Guthrie, Chris, 45, 117, 139

Hackman, J. Richard, 175, 176
Hagger, Martin S., 95
Haidt, Jonathan, 212
Hall, C.S., 78
Hall, Judith, 140
Halpert, Rita, 99
Halvorson, Heidi, 176
Hamilton, Daniel, 192
Hamilton, Neil, 11, 14, 25, 108, 152, 268
Hanna, Julia, 127
Hannah, Sean, 231